KEY
Germany and Occupied Territories
Countries in association with Germany
Allied Countries
Neutral Countries
SOVIET UNION
Leningrad
Moscow
Rzhev
Volga
Don
Minsk
Smolensk
Kursk
Voronezh
Stalingrad
Dnepr
Kiev
Rostov
Caspian Sea
CAUCASUS OIL FIELDS
Odessa
GARY
ROMANIA
Bucharest
Danube
Black Sea
BULGARIA
IRAN
TURKEY
GREECE
Athens
SYRIA
IRAQ
CYPRUS
CRETE
PALESTINE
TRANS-JORDAN
SAUDI-ARABIA
Gazala
Tobruk
Alexandria
Halfaya Pass
El Alamein
EGYPT
Alam el Halfa
El Agheila

Soviet KV-1 heavy tanks
IWM MSTT889

German Grenadiers and Panther tank

British column under attack
IWM B006017

US soldiers about to land in Normandy, D-Day 1944
US Signal Corps, NARA

FLAMES OF WAR®

THE WORLD WAR II MINIATURES GAME

All of us here at Battlefront are proud to bring you this, the third installment of the world's most popular World War II miniatures game. This is thanks in no small part to the support and feedback of yourself and the thousands of other Flames of War players all around the globe. This edition retains all the features that have already given us so many hours of enjoyable historical tactical challenges, while improving the speed of play and how the rules are presented.

From all of us here at Battlefront to all of you... happy gaming and may all your rolls be 's.

Phil Yates
Game Design

Casey Davies
Graphic Design

Peter Simunovich
Editor

John-Paul Brisigotti
Editor

CREDITS

Battlefront Design Studio:
Tim Adcock, Evan Allen, James Brown, Blake Coster, Sean Goodison, Mike Haught, Mike Haycock, Mark Hazell, Matt Parkes, Victor Pesch, Chris Townley, Wayne Turner.

With Support From:
Derek and Josh Forrester, Nick Garden, Marcelle Walden, and Battlefront Staff everywhere.

Internal Art: Vincent Wai.

Playtest Groups:
Arizona Desert Rats (Thomas Weller), Dad's Army (Andy Duncan), Dog Kompanie (Troy Fuller), Einherjar (Gísli Jökull Gíslason), First Born Gamers (Charles McCall), Golf Kompanie (Jason Rose), Oregon Flames of War (Michael McSwiney), Spritz of War (Nicolò Da Lio), La Brigada de Madrid (Jorge Sancho), The Rat's Patrol (Ed Leland), The Regiment (Simon McBeth), Sons of Liberty (Paul Kitchin).

Outstanding Playtesters:
Andy Blozinski, Russell Briant, John Goetzinger, Aaron Hanten, Brjánn Jónasson, Bryan Koches, Tom Leamy, Grant McCaw, Matthew McCarthy, Alex McEwen, Chris Maddox, Francesco Mioni, Jeff Plaine, James Pittman, Gavin van Rossum, Federico Sopracordevole, Tony Vodanovich, Eric Warren.

Proof Readers:
Russell Briant, Troy Fuller, Chris Maddox, Mark Scaletti, Gregg Siter, Neal Smith, Brian Wright.

Photographs:
National Library of New Zealand, Imperial War Museum, NARA, Deutsches Bundesarchiv.

ISBN 978-0-9864661-6-8

Product Code FW003R

Flames Of War website: http://www.FlamesOfWar.com

German Grenadier
IWM HU5144

TABLE OF CONTENTS

1939—THE WAR BEGINS

Adolf Hitler's Nazi Party took total control of Germany in early 1933. Three months later a new German Empire, the Third Reich, was declared. Under the Nazi regime, Germany began openly re-arming and unilaterally repudiated the Treaty of Versailles that ended the First World War. In 1935 the Germans regained control of the Saar industrial area from the French, and in 1936, sent the army into the demilitarised Rhineland on the French border.

Becoming bolder, Hitler demanded that Austria be annexed to Germany. The Austrian government responded by organising a referendum on the matter. On 12 March 1938, the day before the referendum was due, Germany invaded Austria. Unsurprisingly, when the Germans held its own referendum a month later, the result was a landslide in favour of unification with Germany.

Hitler's next target was Czechoslovakia. Citing the principle of national self-determination, he demanded that the Sudentenland with its largely German population be handed over to Germany. France and Britain had been re-arming since the reoccupation of the Rhineland, but were unready to confront Germany militarily. Instead, they accepted Hitler's argument and the great European powers, Britain, France, Italy, and Germany (but notably excluding the Soviet Union), signed the Munich Agreement on 30 September 1938 giving the Sudentenland to Germany —without the consent of Czechoslovakia. After further talks that followed in Vienna (again without the Czechoslovak government having a say), Poland occupied Teschen and Hungary annexed Subcarpathia on Czechoslovakia's southern border.

The British Prime Minister, Neville Chamberlain, famously stated after the talks 'I believe it is peace for our time'. He couldn't have been more wrong. Having got his own way so far, Hitler was not about to stop. On 15 March 1939, he invaded what was left of Czechoslovakia, creating the Slovak Republic from the remains. Having lost their border fortifications with the Sudentenland, there was little the Czech government could do to resist.

7 March 1936
Germany breaks the Treaty of Versailles, remilitarising the Rhineland

17 July, 1936
Spanish Civil War begins

12 March, 1938
Germany invades Austria

30 September, 1938
Munich Agreement—Germany occupies Sudentenland

15 March
Germany invades Czechoslovakia

1 April
Spanish Civil War ends

7 April
Italy invades Albania

11 May – 15 September
Battle of Khalkhin Gol
Soviet–Japanese border war

JANUARY	FEBRUARY	MARCH	APRIL	MAY	JUNE

Massed Polish cavalry

German Panzer I light tank

Germany's terror weapon, the Ju 87 Stuka dive-bomber

By now Hitler was convinced that Britain and France would not go to war to stop him, and planned the destruction of Poland. However, Britain and France were becoming increasingly concerned by Germany's aggression, and guaranteed Poland's security. They also sought an alliance with the Soviet Union against Germany, but Stalin, recognising that Russia would be likely to bear the brunt of such a war, declined. Instead, the Soviet Union signed a secret agreement with Germany guaranteeing peace between Germany and the Soviet Union (named the Molotov-Ribbentropp Pact after the Soviet and German foreign ministers).

Confident that Britain and France would back down, Hitler invaded Poland using a plan labelled Case White on 1 September 1939. Unlike Czechoslovakia though, Poland was big enough to fight back, and with Britain's and France's guarantee, it could hope to last long enough for its allies to intervene.

This hope was given substance on 3 September when France and Britain declared war on Germany. Unfortunately, neither country was prepared for war, and their limited attacks were largely ineffective.

Meanwhile, the German armoured forces had smashed through the Polish frontier defences, pushing nearly 200 miles (320km) into the heart of Poland to reach Warsaw on 8 September. With their capital surrounded and under aerial bombardment, the Polish army fought on as best it could.

The cessation of the French offensive on 16 September was followed by even worse news on 17 September when the Soviet Union invaded eastern Poland. The Molotov-Ribbentropp Pact had included a partition of Poland, and with the German success threatening an early end to hostilities, the Soviet Union crossed the almost undefended eastern border to secure its share of the spoils.

Fighting stubbornly, the Polish capital held out until 27 September, but by this time the end was in little doubt and most Polish forces were making for the borders with Hungary, Romania, and Lithuania, hoping to make their way to France to continue the fight. By 6 October, the fighting was over.

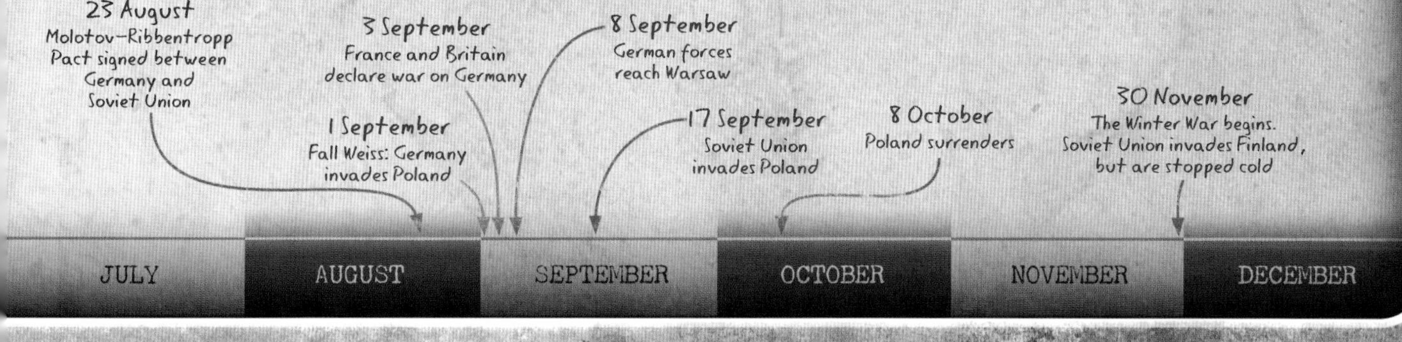

1940—THE BLITZKRIEG

The uneasy calm is shattered on 9 April when German forces invade Denmark and Norway. The invasion of Denmark is almost bloodless—their small army is no match for the mighty *Wehrmacht* (German Armed Forces) and the Danes quickly surrender. However, Norwegian resistance proves stronger and, aided by a hastily-landed force of British, French, and Polish troops, the Norwegian Army fights desperately to expel the invaders. But within two months brave Norway has fallen to the Germans, securing them vital air and sea bases for future offensives.

While the Allied nations are still reeling from this twin blow, Hitler launches *Fall Gelb* (Plan Yellow), the invasion of France and the Low Countries—Belgium and the Netherlands. Spearheaded with revolutionary airborne attacks by German paratroopers—the *Fallschirmjäger*—the seemingly unstoppable panzers roll into the Low Countries on 10 May.

As the British Expeditionary Force, sent to help defend France, rushes north to meet the invasion, a surprise German armoured thrust through the Ardennes forest strikes a lightly defended sector of the French line.

Breaking through, the panzers drive towards the Channel ports, splitting the Allied forces in two. The British and French armies fight desperately as the jaws of the German trap closes, buying valuable time to enable a mass evacuation from the beaches of Dunkirk.

Having missed their opportunity to destroy the British Army, the panzers turn south across the Somme River in *Fall Rot* (Plan Red). The French Army resists bravely, but proves unable to react effectively to the speed and intensity of the

September 1939 – May 1940
Phoney War.
The Allies and Germany prepare for war throughout the winter

13 March
Winter War ends
Finland cedes territory

9 April
Germany invades Denmark and Norway

17–19 April
British, French, and Polish troops land in Norway

10 May
Fall Gelb: Germany invades the Netherlands, Belgium and France

15 May
Netherlands surrenders

27 May – 3 June
British and French evacuate over 300,000 troops at Dunkirk

28 May
Belgium surrenders

5 June
Fall Rot: Germany crosses the Somme River into central France

10 June
Norway surrende
Italy declares war
France

JANUARY | FEBRUARY | MARCH | APRIL | MAY | JUNE

Destroyed French Char B-1 bis tank

British troops at Dunkirk

German attack. As the French Army crumbles, the Italian Army, Germany's ally in the Axis of Steel, invades France from the south. The Italian dictator, Mussolini, has thrown in his lot with the seemingly unbeatable Germans, eager to establish a modern-day Roman Empire. However the poorly-organised Italian Army, the *Regio Esercito*, is incapable of mounting an effective attack, and makes little headway before the surrender of France on 22 June.

Great Britain now stands alone against the might of Germany. The new British Prime Minister Winston Churchill faces his country's darkest days. Across the English Channel, Britain is a nation under siege as U-boats patrol the Atlantic in feared wolf packs, preying on the vulnerable merchant ships carrying vital supplies.

The German Air Force, the *Luftwaffe*, begins a massive bombing Blitz that turns the great industrial cities of Coventry, Manchester, Liverpool, and the capital London, into landscapes of rubble and twisted metal. All the while, *Wehrmacht* forces gather in France, preparing for Operation Sealion, the invasion of Britain.

The Battle of Britain unfolds in the skies above the English countryside. Although vastly outnumbered, the courageous fighter pilots of the RAF (Royal Air Force) strive to hold back the waves of German bombers. 'The Few' emerge victorious, inflicting a heavy loss upon the *Luftwaffe*. Operation Sealion is postponed and later cancelled.

In September, Germany, Italy, and Japan sign the Tripartite Pact, expanding the Axis across the globe. Through this alliance they aim to establish a new world order. Later in the year Hungary and Romania join the Axis powers.

The war bursts from the confines of Europe onto the blazing deserts of North Africa when the Italians invade Egypt from their Libyan colony on 13 September. The invaders advance only a few miles before setting up defensive positions. In October the Italian Ninth Army invades Greece, but is dealt a crippling blow and driven from the country.

This is not the only reverse suffered by the *Regio Esercito*. In December, the poorly-equipped and poorly-led Italians are thrown back across the Egyptian border by daring British attacks in Operation Compass. Initially intended as a four-day raid, the British attacks are an outstanding success leading to a major British offensive.

Despite the setbacks suffered by her Axis partner, and the stubborn defiance of Great Britain, the year has been a stunning success for Germany. Hitler's forces have demonstrated their mastery of mechanised warfare and stand poised to deliver yet another stunning blow, this time against an unsuspecting ally.

15–17 June
Soviets invade Lithuania, Latvia and Estonia

22 June
France surrenders

28 June
Soviet Union takes Bessarabia from Romania

10 July
The Battle of Britain begins

30 August
Hungary takes Transylvania from Romania

13 September
Italy invades Egypt

28 October
Italy invades Greece

31 October
The Battle of Britain ends

20 November
Hungary joins Axis

23 November
Romania joins Axis

9 December
Operation Compass: British push Italians back into Libya

JULY | AUGUST | SEPTEMBER | OCTOBER | NOVEMBER | DECEMBER

1941—THE WAR WIDENS

In North Africa the British maintain the initiative. The Western Desert Force under Lieutenant General Richard O'Connor drives deep into Libya capturing 90,000 Italian soldiers in the process. The key port of Tobruk falls to British and Australian forces on 22 January.

In March, Winston Churchill sends a British Expeditionary Force to Greece, to prevent the Italians renewing their attacks.

With Mussolini's troops struggling on both fronts, Hitler is compelled to support his Italian ally in North Africa, Greece and Yugoslavia. Control of the strategically important Mediterranean area is vital to his plans.

In February, General Erwin Rommel, a veteran of the conquest of France, arrives in North Africa with the vanguard of his *Deutsches Afrikakorps* (DAK) to bolster the hard-pressed Italians. Rommel immediately sets about altering the course of events.

On 6 April, German forces invade the Balkans. Yugoslavia cannot withstand the onslaught of the German panzers and quickly surrenders, while Greece follows soon after. Yet again the speed and ferocity of the German attack almost succeeds in trapping another British Expeditionary Force. But the British and Commonwealth soldiers narrowly escape and are evacuated to the island of Crete.

The Germans launch Operation Mercury on 20 May, aiming to seize Crete as an air base in the eastern Mediterranean. Instead of a seaborne attack the Germans plan an audacious airborne invasion on a scale hitherto unheard of. The German paratroopers meet unexpectedly fierce resistance from the battered Commonwealth defenders. Although ultimately triumphant, the Germans pay dearly for the victory with the blood of their elite *Fallschirmjäger* paratroopers.

22 January Australians take Tobruk

7 February Operation Compass ends with the destruction of the Italian Army at Beda Fomm

12 February Rommel arrives in Libya

4 March British & Commonwealth forces sent to Greece

24 March Rommel attacks in Libya

31 March Bulgaria joins Axis

6–30 April Axis invasion of Yugoslavia and Greece

30 April – 1 May Rommel assaults Tobruk

15 May Operation Brevity: British attempt to relieve Tobruk

20 May – 1 June Operation Mercury: German airborne assault on Crete

8 June British Invade French Syria

15–17 June Operation Battleaxe: British attempt to relieve Tobruk

JANUARY | FEBRUARY | MARCH | APRIL | MAY | JUNE

German soldiers inspect abandoned KV-1 and T-34 tanks

In the Atlantic, Admiral Donitz's U-boats continue to feast on prime merchant targets taking a heavy toll. To counter this threat, the British introduce convoys that use small warships to shepherd vulnerable cargo vessels across the Atlantic.

In North Africa the brilliant offensives of Rommel, reverse the gains made by the British. The campaign ebbs and flows across the barren desert. As the *Deutsches Afrikakorps* begin to gain the upper hand, their progress is hampered by the difficulties of supply across such a vast landscape. Newly-raised special forces, such as the famed SAS (Special Air Service) and LRDG (Long-range Desert Group), wreak havoc on the German supply lines—striking with the swiftness of the scorpion and then melting away into the desert.

Hitler, buoyed by the unprecedented speed and success of the Blitzkrieg in Western Europe, now makes a critical decision. On 22 June, without any declaration of war, the first waves of German armour cross the Soviet border. Operation Barbarossa, the German invasion of the Soviet Union, has begun.

The *RKKA*, or Red Army, is caught totally unprepared as the fast-moving Wehrmacht strike deep behind their defences. The Soviet dictator, Josef Stalin, throws wave after wave of untrained conscripts in the path of the panzers in a desperate but futile effort to slow the German advance. The casualties suffered by the Red Army are enormous. Whole armies are captured in huge encirclements like at Uman and Smolensk, as city after city falls to the German, Hungarian, and Romanian invaders.

The advancing army is split into three groups. Army Group North, commanded by Field Marshal von Leeb, rumbles northwards through the Baltic States of Latvia, Estonia, and Lithuania, securing vital ports along the Baltic coast. In conjunction with the army of their ally, Finland, the Germans lay siege to the Soviet Union's second largest city—Leningrad. Army Group Centre, commanded by Field Marshal von Bock, captures the cities of Minsk then Smolensk before driving on the capital of the Soviet Union—Moscow. Army Group South, commanded by Field Marshal von Rundstedt, captures the third largest city of Kiev, inflicting a severe defeat upon the Red Army—five hundred thousand Soviet troops are killed or taken prisoner. Rostov and Kharkov are next to fall as the Germans capture a further one hundred thousand troops.

Just as it seems as if nothing can stop the onslaught, the onset of the fiercest Russian winter in fifty years freezes the Germans in their tracks. The Red Army, so close to complete collapse, is able to cling on. In December desperate Soviets counterattack are partially successful in driving the German lines back.

Now united against a common enemy, Great Britain and the Soviet Union sign a mutual assistance agreement. The United States, outwardly neutral, has begun to become more involved in the conflict. Earlier in the year US President Roosevelt signed the important Lend Lease Act, which would ultimately see masses of American manufactured equipment shipped to their hard-pressed British and Soviet allies. Despite their President's foreign policy, the American people still see the conflict as a European one. This illusion is about to be shattered.

On 7 December 1941—'a date that will live in infamy'—bombers of the Japanese Imperial Navy attack the US Pacific Fleet in Pearl Harbor. The devastating attack, launched without a declaration of war, achieves almost total surprise. Several battleships are destroyed or disabled, crippling the US Navy. Belatedly, Japan declares war on the USA. Her Axis partners, Germany and Italy follow on 11 December.

In a well-planned offensive, the Japanese make excellent use of the shock and surprise caused by Pearl Harbour to sweep across the Pacific Ocean like an unstoppable wave. Within two weeks Japanese forces have invaded Guam, the Philippines, Burma, British Borneo, and Hong Kong.

As the year closes, the Axis powers have the upper hand on all fronts and appear to have ultimate victory within their grasp. Germany now dominates much of Europe. The entry of Japan and America has spread the clouds of war over the previously tranquil Pacific. World War II is now truly a global conflict.

22 June – eration Barbarossa: German invasion Soviet Union begins

10 July – 10 September – Battle of Smolensk: Three Soviet armies encircled

15 July – 8 August – Battle of Uman: Two Soviet armies encircled

23 August – 26 September – Battle of Kiev: Four Soviet armies encircled

8 September – Siege of Leningrad begins

24 October – Operation Typhoon: German drive on Moscow begins

19 November – 30 December – Operation Crusader: British push Germans and Italian back to El Agheila in Libya

22–27 November – British Tobruk breakout

5 December – Soviet Moscow counter offensive begins

7 December – Japanese bomb US Fleet in Pearl Harbor, Hawaii

JULY | AUGUST | SEPTEMBER | OCTOBER | NOVEMBER | DECEMBER

1942—THE HIGHWATER MARK

The Japanese continue to steamroll their way across the Pacific and South East Asia. On 15 February, Fortress Singapore—the bastion of the British Empire in the Far East—falls to a Japanese attack. At the same time their ground forces push their way into Burma. Using superior jungle fighting skills, they inflict defeat after defeat upon the British Indian forces. By 6 March the capital Rangoon has fallen, and by 30 April all of Central Burma is in Japanese hands. The British Indian troops suffer 10,000 casualties, while Japanese casualties are only half that.

While the cold, dark depths of the North Atlantic are the realm of the silent U-boats, in the blue Pacific it is the mighty aircraft carriers that will decide the outcome of the war. In May, Admiral Nimitz, the US Pacific commander, orders a naval task force to intercept a Japanese invasion force en route to Port Moresby. On 8 May, at the Battle of the Coral Sea, carrier-based US and Japanese aircraft strike at each other's fleets inflicting serious damage to both sides. The Japanese are forced to concede a tactical, if not a strategic, defeat.

Undeterred by this reversal, Admiral Yamamoto, commander of the Japanese Navy, orders an attack on the US Naval base on the island of Midway. On 6 June, at the Battle of Midway, US dive-bombers sink no less than four Japanese aircraft carriers. This decisive victory is a turning point in the Pacific War.

On 7 August the US forces in the Pacific take the offensive with the amphibious landings at Guadalcanal in the Solomon Islands. The campaign to take the islands lasts six months, with heavy losses to both sides in men and ships before the Americans are at last victorious.

8 January Battles for the Rzhev Salient begin, continuing until March 1943

21 January Rommel counter-attacks, advancing to Gazala

8 – 18 May Battle of Kerch: Three Soviet armies destroyed

12–30 May Second Battle of Kharkov: Two Soviet armies encircled and destroyed

26 May – 21 June Battle of Gazala: Germans capture Tobruk

2 June – 4 July Battle of Sevastopol: Germans capture Crimea

28 June – 24 July Battle of Voronezh: Operation Blue begins as the Germans smash the Soviets on the Don!

JANUARY | FEBRUARY | MARCH | APRIL | MAY | JUNE

British Grant tank passes a knocked out German Panzer I in the desert
IWM E12920

German soldier surrendering during the bloody street battles of Stalingrad
IWM HU3014

In North Africa the irrepressible Rommel renews his offensive. By June *DAK* and their Italian allies, organised together as the *Panzerarmee Afrika*, have finally recaptured the port of Tobruk. Besides securing a vital port they capture a large haul of British supplies and equipment. Pushing on, Rommel crosses the border into Egypt. The British people, still suffering under the morale sapping attentions of the *Luftwaffe*, and seemingly struggling for survival on all fronts, are desperate for a victory. Disgruntled with the perceived inability of his generals to deliver, Churchill appoints General Bernard Montgomery to the command of the Eighth Army in Egypt. It will prove an inspired choice.

Montgomery is a popular and decisive commander, willing and able to match wits with the Desert Fox. He wastes no time in stamping his mark on the struggle and within one short month of assuming command has succeeded in stalling Rommel's invasion of Egypt.

At last on 23 October, Monty—as Montgomery had become known—delivers the victory Britain seeks, smashing through the Axis lines at the Second Battle of El Alamein and ending Rommel's dream of conquering the ancient land of Egypt. *Panzerarmee Afrika* begins a long fighting withdrawal across nearly 2000 miles of desert to Tunisia. The Eighth Army follows, nipping at their heels like a tenacious terrier.

On the Eastern Front, the *Wehrmacht* attack once again with the end of winter. The German advance builds in momentum like the rivers running with the spring melts, threatening to carry away the Russian defences before them. The Germans drive into the Caucasus, intent on seizing valuable oilfields.

In September, on the flank of this advance, a battle unfolds for the city which carries the Soviet leader's name—Stalingrad. Despite fierce Soviet resistance the Sixth Army of General von Paulus stands on the brink of capturing the city, only to be cut off by a Soviet counterattack that encircles the besiegers. Months of bitter and bloody house-to-house fighting ensues that is devastating to both sides. The cost in human life is mind-boggling—the Soviets alone lose over half a million men in the battle for the city.

Meanwhile, the industrial might of the United States has been lifted to full war footing and a steady stream of arms and ammunition floods to the aid of her Soviet and British allies.

By the end of 1942, the US Army is ready for battle. On 7 November American forces join their seasoned British allies in North Africa with Operation Torch. Under overall command of General Dwight D Eisenhower, the Allies land on the beaches of Morocco and Algeria. After putting up a brief resistance, the Vichy French defenders surrender. The Allied force now turns east, intending to crush the remnants of Rommel's *Panzerarmee Afrika* retreating into Tunisia.

The overall Axis commander in the Mediterranean, Field Marshal Kesselring, rushes reinforcements into Tunis to meet the invaders. Although almost totally obsessed with the unfolding conflict on the Eastern Front, Hitler orders that North Africa must be held.

The Axis defenders, many of them elite *Fallschirmjäger*, throw up a hasty defensive perimeter around Tunis. They also seize key defensive positions in the south of the country to keep open an escape route for Rommel's forces back into Tunisia. The initial Allied advances are thrown back, before the heavy rains of winter force an end to all offensive operations.

For the Axis a year that started so promisingly ends in disappointment and disaster. The start of 1943 will bring no respite.

1-27 July First Battle of El Alamein: German advance stopped

9 July Germans thrust south towards Stalingrad and the Caucasus oil fields

19 August Dieppe Raid: Canadian infantry and tanks, and British Commandos raid French port

23 August Battle of Stalingrad: German troops reach the city

30 August–5 September Battle of Alam Halfa: German advance on Alexandria stopped

23 October–3 November Second Battle of El Alamein: Axis forces retreat from Egypt and Libya

7 November Allied Forces invade Morocco and Algeria

19 November Operation Uranus: Soviets encircle German forces in Stalingrad

12-29 December Operation Winter Storm: Germans fail to relieve Stalingrad

16 December Soviets begin clearing Caucasus of Axis troops

JULY | AUGUST | SEPTEMBER | OCTOBER | NOVEMBER | DECEMBER

1943—THE TIDE TURNS

The German Sixth Army begins the year still besieged within the bloody crucible of Stalingrad. The head of the Luftwaffe, Field Marshal Göring, assures Hitler that the trapped Germans can be supplied from the air, but his assurances prove to be empty bombast. On 31 January, with the remnants of his army frozen and starving, von Paulus has no alternative but to surrender. Of the 250,000 German troops that had entered Stalingrad, just 91,000 are taken into Russian captivity.

The Soviet army follows up its success with a punishing offensive, driving the *Wehrmacht* back and retaking lost territory. The cities of Kursk, Kharkov and Rostov are wrested from the invaders in February. Despite Manstein's 'backhand blow' retaking Kharkov, the tide has turned on the Eastern Front.

Once the winter mud dries out in North Africa, British and US forces resume their drive into Tunisia, closing in on the Axis forces who fight valiantly to stave off defeat. Raw US tank crews suffer a reversal in their first encounter with the veterans of the *Afrikakorps* at Kasserine Pass. Through this baptism of fire they learn quickly and develop into excellent soldiers. In May, the Allied forces break through the defensive perimeter guarding Tunis, capturing the last bastion of Axis power in North Africa on 12 May. The Allies take 252,000 German and Italian prisoners.

To restore the situation on the Eastern Front, the German High Command launches Operation Citadel on 5 July, a massive armoured counteroffensive in the area of Kursk. Anticipating just such an action, the Red Army has time to heavily fortify their positions. The German armoured thrust is blunted by these defences.

31 January German Sixth Army in Stalingrad surrenders, 90,000 Germans are captured

16 February – 15 March Third Battle of Kharkov: Soviets capture city, but are cut off losing four armies

19–25 February Battle of Kasserine Pass: First major US battle against the Germans

23 March – 7 April Battle of El Guettar: Patton's famed victory in Tunisia

22 March Germans evacuate Rzhev Salient

26 March Operation Supercharge II: British assault and outflank Mareth Line in Tunisia

6 April British forces breakthrough German defences at Wadi Akarit

7 May Allied forces capture Tunis

13 May Axis forces surrender in Tunisia, yielding over 252,000 prisoners. The war in Africa is over

5 July – 1 August Operation Citadel: the last great German offensive at Kursk is stalled by Soviets who then counterattack

JANUARY | FEBRUARY | MARCH | APRIL | MAY | JUNE

German infantry and assault guns in winter whitewash camouflage
IWM HU28325

Soviet ZIS-3 field gun
IWM MH9707

British Bren Carriers advance through a ruined North African town
IWM KID2492

On 12 July, in a titanic clash of armour, Soviet tank corps meet the elite panzer divisions head on near the town of Prokhorovka, bringing the German attack to a standstill. Although casualties are heavy on both sides, the Soviets have the manpower to replace them. Three years of heavy fighting is beginning to tell on the resources of the German nation. Once again, the Red Army follows up victory with a devastating counteroffensive, reclaiming yet more territory from the invaders, and crossing the Dnepr before the year is out.

With Africa now in their hands, the Allies go on the offensive in the Mediterranean once more, seeking an early end to the war that has ravaged Europe for three years. On 10 July, British and US Forces invade Sicily in Operation Husky. Spearheading the landing are British and American paratroopers but the airborne assaults prove a costly disaster. The amphibious assault proves more successful, with the two-pronged offensive that follows clearing the island of Axis forces within six weeks. The Allies have gained a toehold into Southern Europe. Growing weary of an unpopular war, the Italian people overthrow and arrest Mussolini.

The Allies push on to mainland Italy—supposedly 'the soft underbelly of Europe'—landing at Salerno on 9 September. The new Italian Government surrenders but the German forces occupy Italy and fight on against the invaders. The Allied troops make slow headway against such determined resistance. Their advance finally grinds to a halt before the formidable German defences of the Gustav Line, which stretches across the Italian Peninsula.

In the Pacific, the combined British and US fleets now dominate the ocean. The jungles and beaches of the Solomons and New Guinea are turned into battlefields as the Allies drive the Japanese back island by island. Emperor Hirohito of Japan describes his country's situation as truly grave.

By the end of 1943 the Axis alliance is crumbling. Italy has defected to the Allied cause and Japan and Germany are buckling under intensifying pressure. German morale remains high, however, with a strong belief in Hitler's propaganda that new 'secret weapons' will soon turn the tide of war in their favour once more.

7 August – 2 October
Second Battle of Smolensk: German threat to Moscow removed

9 July – 17 August
Operation Husky: Allied invasion of Sicily

13 August – 22 September
Dnepr Offensive: Soviets secure crossings over the Dnepr River

9 September
Operation Avalanche: Allied landing at Salerno. Italy surrenders

2 October – 22 December
Battle of Kiev
Soviets push Germans back across Dnepr River and take Kiev

12–13 October
Battle of Lenino
Polish troops attempt to pierce the Panther-Wotan Line

20–28 December
Battle of Ortona: Canadians take city with heavy losses

JULY | AUGUST | SEPTEMBER | OCTOBER | NOVEMBER | DECEMBER

1944—TO THE BORDERS OF GERMANY

17 January – 23 March
Allied forces repelled in three Battles of Monte Cassino

22 January
US and British forces land at Anzio, Italy

18 January
German siege of Leningrad broken after 900 days

24 January – 16 February
Battles for the Korsun Pocket: Soviets encircle and maul two German corps

2 February – 10 August
Battle of Narva: Soviet attempts to break into Estonia foiled

11 – 18 April
Fourth Battle of Monte Cassino: Allied forces outflank the Germans forcing them to withdraw

10 April – 12 May
Battle of Crimea: Soviet troops take Odessa & the Crimea

25 April – 4 June
US forces breakout of Anzio bridgehead and capture Rome

10 June – 9 August
Soviet Offensive against Finland

6 June
Operation Overlord: D-Day, Allied landings in Normandy, France

13 July – 29 Augu
Lvov–Sandomierz Offensive: Soviet offens into southern Polanc

22 June – 19 August
Operation Bagration: Soviet offensive captures Minsk and reaches Warsaw

JANUARY	FEBRUARY	MARCH	APRIL	MAY	JUNE

• 1944 •

The German High Command are still confident of their ability to ultimately prevail. They brace to hold back the encroaching Soviet tide in the East. In the West they prepare to deal a crippling blow to the expected Allied invasion of France, before then turning their full attentions to smashing Soviet resistance once and for all.

But the Soviet offensive rolls on. The siege of Leningrad is lifted after 900 days. Without pause the Red Army drives the Germans back everywhere, from the Baltic States in the North to the Crimea in the South.

In Italy, the elite *Fallschirmjäger*, mount an incredible defence of the town and ancient monastery at Cassino, repelling wave after wave of attacking Allied troops. Unable to break the defenders of the Gustav Line, the Allies decide to go around it.

On 22 January a combined US and British amphibious force lands at Anzio just south of Rome, catching the Germans off-guard. Field Marshal Kesselring rushes forces to the area in time to stop the ponderous Allied advance. The Germans counterattack, but with naval support the Allied troops are able to cling to their beachhead. Months of bitter fighting follow as the conflict descends to a stalemate. The Allies are unable to break out of Anzio until the Gustav Line falls in May, forcing the Germans to withdraw. Rome is captured by the Allies on 4 June, but this triumph will be quickly overshadowed by events in Western Europe.

Meanwhile, the Japanese forces in Burma invade India, but in April their offensive grinds to a halt at Kohima and Imphal. By October Allied counterattacks have killed half of the original 60,000 men of the attacking Japanese Fifteenth Army.

Back in Europe, after months of planning, on 6 June—D-Day—the Allies invade Normandy, France. Operation Overlord is the largest amphibious assault in history. US, British, Canadian, and French forces land from the storm-tossed English Channel onto five beaches, code named Utah, Omaha, Gold, Juno and Sword. Thanks to an ingenious deception plan the German defenders manning Hitler's 'Atlantic Wall' are taken by surprise. In bloody combat, particularly at Omaha, the invaders fight their way off the beaches, linking up with US and British paratroopers who had assaulted inland by air on the previous night.

As the buildup of men and materiel in the Allied beachhead continues apace, General Omar Bradley's US First Army captures the wrecked port of Cherbourg on 30 June. The Allies capture St. Lô and Caen in some of the hardest fighting of the war. Then, at the end of July, Bradley's men

18 July
Operation Goodwood: British capture Caen

25 July
Operation Cobra: US forces breakout from Normandy

8-24 August
Operations Totalize and Tractable: 50,000 German troops captured in the Falaise Pocket

1 August – 1 October
Warsaw Uprising: Poles rise up against Germans, but fail due to lack of Soviet support

20-29 August
Iassy–Kishinev Operation: Soviets destroy German forces in Romania. Romania switches sides

25 August
Allies liberate Paris

3 September
Allies liberate Brussels

4 September
Finland signs armistice with Soviet Union

17-24 September
Operation Market Garden: Failed attempt to cross the Rhine at Arnhem

9 October – 8 November
Canadians clear the Scheldt estuary of Germans and open port of Antwerp

10-29 October
Battle of Debrecen: Soviet attack in Hungary stopped by German armoured forces

23 December – 16 January
Battle of the Bulge: After being caught flat-footed by German surprise offensive, US forces defeat German attack through the Ardennes aimed at Antwerp

25 December
Siege of Budapest begins 100 days of intense fighting

JULY | AUGUST | SEPTEMBER | OCTOBER | NOVEMBER | DECEMBER

Allied forces swarm ashore after the D-Day landings
US Signal Corps, NARA

finally punch a hole in the German lines in Operation Cobra. 100,000 retreating Germans are now cut off in the Falaise pocket by the advancing Allies. Their capture delivers a massive blow to the rapidly-deteriorating German military. After two months of bitter fighting amongst the hedgerows of Normandy, the Allied armour finally rolls into open country.

On the Eastern Front, things fare little better for Germany. The Soviet command launches its summer offensive, Operation Bagration, on 22 June. Masterfully executed, the operation drives a wedge into the German Army Group Centre, leaving them in disarray. With the Germans are still reeling from the punch, the Soviets follow up with a flurry of blows, shattering the German centre, ripping a hole in the defensive line, and costing the German Army 350,000 men.

British and American forces pursues the retreating Germans towards the German border. The newly-promoted Field Marshal Montgomery launches the daring Operation Market Garden, a two-part plan to seize the bridges across the Lower Rhine River around Arnhem with a massive airborne landing, with an armoured strike force advancing 100 km (64 miles) to relieve them. Bloodied and dazed, the Germans are not yet finished. Through a miracle of reorganisation the shattered German armies are rebuilt and brace once more against the Allied onslaught, halting advances in both the East and West within sight of the German border.

In a last throw of the dice, the Germans launch a surprise armoured attack westward through the Ardennes forest. Begun in the depths of winter, the offensive seeks to emulate the success enjoyed in the same area four years previously.

The panzer spearhead initially catches the US Army flat-footed. Their initial advances promise the same spectacular success as their 1940 campaign. Yet on this occasion it is a vastly more experienced opponent the Germans face. US paratroopers hold firm at the pivotal town of Bastogne. In the face of increasing opposition and suffering a shortage of fuel for the powerful panzers, the German advance grinds to a halt.

In the Pacific, the US Marines continue to regain control of the Pacific islands one by one. Driven by desperation, the Japanese begin *Kamikaze* suicide attacks against the US Navy. In October, US forces under General MacArthur land in the Philippines. In a daringly-conceived attack the remnants of Japan's once mighty fleet strike at the American amphibious force on 24 October in the Battle of Leyte Gulf, the greatest naval battle in history. After three days of manoeuvring and fighting the Japanese are defeated, losing four carriers and three battleships, including the mighty *Musashi*. As the Americans draw ever nearer, the US Army Air Force steps up bombing operations against industrial targets on the mainland of Japan, further hampering Japanese military efforts.

The defeat of the Axis powers is now only a matter of time, but refusing to concede defeat they cling on into what will be the last year of the war.

1–17 January
Operation Konrad: Germans make three failed attempts to relieve Budapest

12 January – 2 February
Vistula–Oder Offensive: Red Army launches drive on Germany

14 January – 5 March
Battle of the Rhineland: Allies destroy German forces west of the Rhine

7–26 March
British and US forces cross the Rhine into Germany

6–17 March
Lake Balaton Offensive: Last German offensive, attempt to halt Red Army in western Hungary

1–21 April
British and US forces destroy German forces in the Ruhr Pocket.

2–13 April
Soviets capture Vienna

6 April – 2 May
Operation Grapeshot: Allies break the Gothic Line and take the Po Valley

16 April – 5 May
Oder–Berlin Offensive: Red Army strikes for Berlin

16–19 April
Battle of Seelow Heights: Germans attempt to stop frontal drive on Berlin

23 April – 2 May
Battle of Berlin: Soviets capture Berlin afte savage street fighting

30 April
Hitler commits suicide

7–8 May
German unconditional surrende

JANUARY | FEBRUARY | MARCH | APRIL | MAY | JUNE

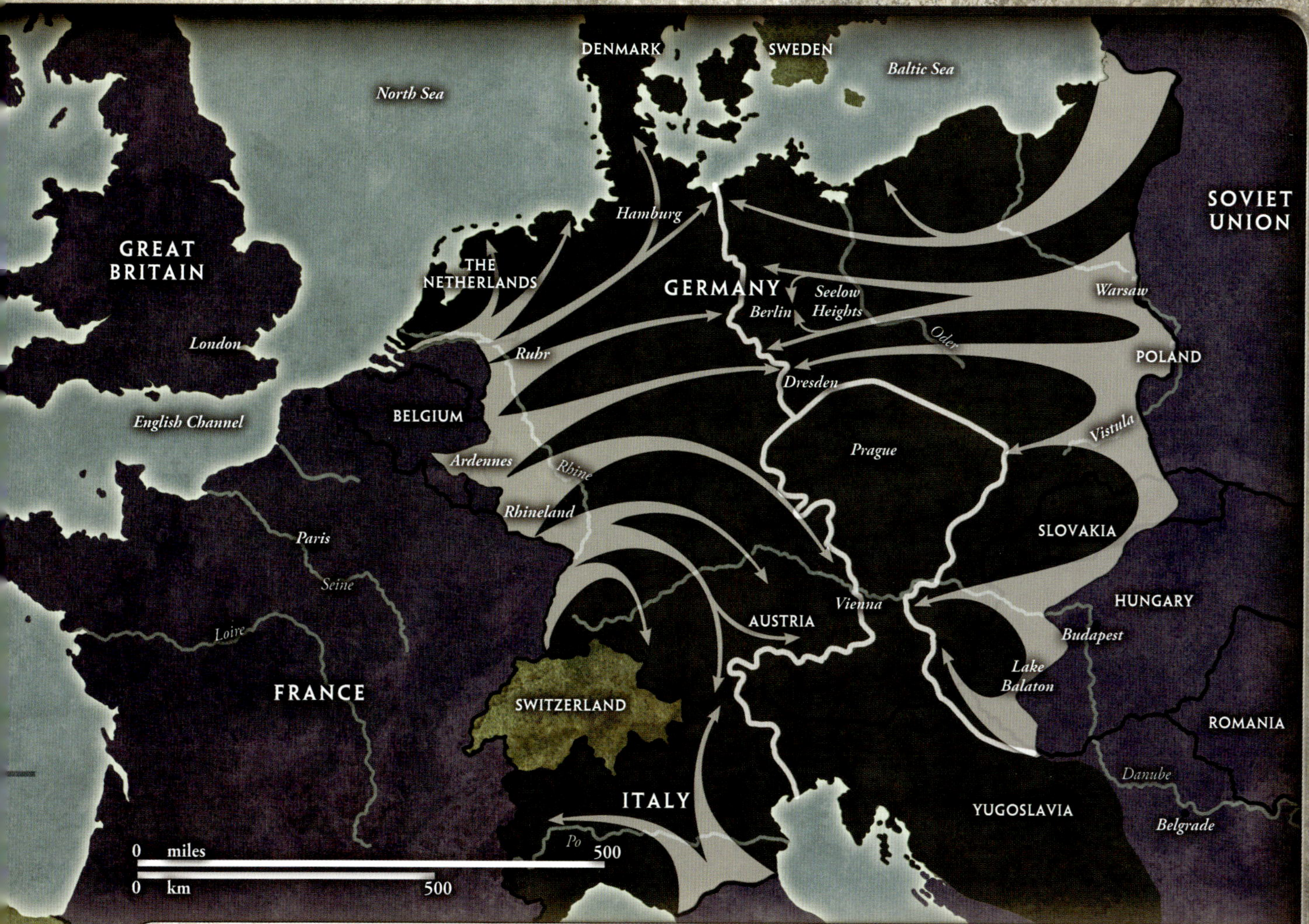

1945—THE END OF THE THIRD REICH

The Red Army battles its way across the German border. Seeking revenge for the suffering inflicted on the Soviet peoples at the hands of the German invaders, they inflict a harsh punishment upon the German populace. British and US forces advancing in from the West cross the Rhine river and enter Germany.

On 30 April, as the Allied noose closes from all sides on the capital of Berlin, Adolf Hitler takes his own life in his bunker. Within a week the German army has laid down its arms on all fronts, unconditionally surrendering and thus ending the war in Europe.

The Allied offensive in Burma picks up speed. More than 100,000 Japanese are killed in this final drive, which recaptures Rangoon on 2 May. Burma is now firmly back in Allied hands.

In the Pacific, the US Marines begin an amphibious assault on the island of Iwo Jima on 19 February. Their bloody victory gains an new, closer, air base from which to strike at Japan's cities.

The long island-hopping campaign of the US Marines comes to an end with the 1 April attack on Okinawa. While the Japanese defenders fight a ferocious land battle against the Marines, *Kamikaze* pilots attack the ships of the invasion fleet, sinking 36. Although ultimately victorious, the Marines suffer almost 40,000 casualties, the Japanese 107,000, making Okinawa the bloodiest battle of the Pacific War.

With the threat from the west neutralised, the Red Army turns its attention to the east and declares war on Japan.

As preparations are being made for Allied ground forces to invade the Japanese mainland, on 6 and 9 August the US Army Air Force drops the first ever atomic bombs on the Japanese cities of Hiroshima and Nagasaki. The incredible destruction caused shatters the will of the Japanese people to resist. On 15 August Japan surrenders. The war in the Pacific has ended.

After six long years of bitter struggle, the Second World War is finally over.

April – 21 June
Operation Iceberg: forces take Japanese island of Okinawa

2 May
British and Indian forces capture Rangoon, Burma after six-month offensive

6 and 9 August
US Atomic Bombs dropped on Japanese cities of Hiroshima and Nagasaki

15 August
Japanese Emperor announces Japan's unconditional surrender on the radio

9–23 August
Soviets invade Manchuria, defeat Japanese

JULY | AUGUST | SEPTEMBER

• 1945 •

WHAT IS FLAMES OF WAR?

A lone jeep drives slowly down a deserted road as the crew scan the village ahead for signs of life. Without warning the distinctive ripping canvas sound of a German machine-gun tears the silence, bullets whizzing past as the driver throws the jeep into reverse. Guns start barking as the watching armoured cars open fire covering the jeep's speedy retreat.

The captain watching the unfolding drama from the turret of his tank spoke into his throat mike. 'OK John, they're there. Clear 'em out. Over' The rearguard is no surprise. His company has dealt with a dozen just like it in the last week alone. Like a well-oiled machine his platoons swing into action. Tanks and armoured infantry advancing on the town as the artillery's first shells start falling amongst the defenders. A second group swings across country, flanking the position.

'Ambush! Tigers!' a strained voice bursts over the radio, punctuated by deeper cracks as the heavy tanks opened fire. 'Three Tigers in the north woods,' a calmer voice crackles in the headphones. 'I've lost two tanks. I need smoke. We'll back off and try to flank them, Over.'

The captain faces a dilemma. Should he call forward his reserve tank platoon against the Tiger tanks? Or should he send it around the other flank, seeking an easier route forward?

The captain is you. What will you do?

What you have just read is a description, not of an actual battle, but of a miniature wargame being played. All of the action takes place on a miniature battlefield, with model tanks and soldiers that represent the real-life troops that fought in the decisive battles of the Second World War. You and your opponent assume the roles of the commanders, pitting your wits and cunning against one another to attain victory and, more importantly, to have fun.

The Challenge of Command

Flames Of War allows you to re-fight the decisive battles of the Second World War. You take charge of Patton's spearhead or Monty's Desert Rats. Can you out-fox Rommel, the Desert Fox? Can you withstand Zhukov's hammer blows? *Flames Of War* lets you recreate history to find out.

This rulebook is your guide to fighting historical battles in miniature. With it you can take command of a company of soldiers and pit yourself against cunning opponents on the field of battle. You will see for yourself what made the Tiger tank so feared by every Allied soldier. You will find out if you have the guts to stop a massed infantry charge, or the cold-blooded ruthlessness to launch one!

Flames Of War combines the joys of painting and modelling your own miniature army with the challenge of facing off against your opponent across a gaming table in a social setting, and you'll get to recreate history—or change it!

Getting Started

Reality is immensely complex and rather messy. This has the advantage of giving players virtually unlimited opportunities to fight new battles and collect new armies. Unfortunately, it also requires a lot of rules to cover all of the many aspects of something as big as the Second World War, making this book rather long. The good news is that you don't need to know all of the rules to play the game. You can start with the basics and add things like aircraft, fortifications, and even armoured trains when you are ready.

The easiest way of learning the rules is to visit a store where the staff can run you through an introductory game and introduce you to other players. If you don't have a store near you, the Open Fire box and Boot Camp on the *Flames Of War* website provide a quick-start introduction to the core rules, allowing you to start playing immediately and learn the details of the rules later.

What's New

Players who are familiar with *Flames Of War* will find the core of the game much the same, with a number of exciting changes. The assault rules are cleaner and simpler, making getting you up close and personal easier than ever. Massed artillery delivers devastating bombardments, while anti-tank guns go to ground, safe until the time comes to strike. Aircraft and their arch-enemy, anti-aircraft guns, are easier to use and more deadly. Armoured cars and transports are faster and much more effective. Now, Soviet tankers can conduct sweeping manoeuvres across the Steppes, firing as they advance at speed. To top this off, thirteen new and revised missions provide a whole new set of challenges.

Website

The *Flames Of War* website (***www.FlamesOfWar.com***) has a lot of useful material for new and experienced gamers. It has information on various armies, downloadable play aids, as well as piles of other hobby material. The website also has the *Flames Of War* forum where players discuss tactics, meet new gamers, get feedback on the new army they are planning, ask for help with rules questions, or just chat about the hobby.

WHAT YOU NEED

An Opponent

Flames Of War is a social game played by two or more players, so grab a friend and get started.

Two Armies

The *Flames Of War* range of 15mm (1/100th) scale miniatures is specifically designed for the game and is available through all good hobby stores.

This Rulebook

This rulebook contains all the rules you need to play *Flames Of War*.

Templates

Artillery and aircraft are not precision weapons. Their shells and bombs blanket a wide area, possibly wiping out dozens of the enemy at a time. Templates make it easy to work out who is hit, and who isn't.

A Battlefield

Whether it's the kitchen table or a custom-built gaming table, you'll need a large flat surface to play the game. A 6' x 4' (180cm x 120cm) sheet of custom board covered with a green sheet or painted and flocked makes an ideal battlefield.

Terrain

You'll need a selection of terrain like hills, woods, hedges, buildings, and roads to create a realistic battlefield for your troops to fight over.

The pre-painted terrain in the Battlefield in a Box range makes setting up a battlefield easy.

Dice

Flames Of War uses ordinary six-sided dice. You can personalise your force with army-specific dice marked with your division's insignia.

Tokens

Even though they are toy soldiers, your troops react to heavy fire like real soldiers. Sometimes they get pinned down or bail out of their tanks. They get stuck in rough terrain and go to ground, hiding from the enemy. Tokens help you keep track of the state of your troops.

Tape Measure

You'll need a tape measure or ruler to measure movement and shooting ranges. You can use metric or Imperial measurements, whichever suits you best.

HOW DOES IT WORK?

In *Flames Of War* the two sides take turns to move and fight with troops. Each player's turn has four steps: the Starting, Movement, Shooting and Assault Steps.

Once one side has finished their turn, the other side takes a turn. The two sides keep alternating their turns until one side or the other wins by taking their objective.

Starting Step (see page 32)

At the start of each turn a player checks to see if they have won. If they haven't, they rally any of their troops that are pinned down by enemy fire, and drag bogged down tanks out of the mire. That done, they bring their reserves onto the battlefield.

Movement Step (see page 33)

Shooting Step (see page 71)

Assault Step (see page 141)

Morale Checks (see page 171)

No matter what the generals may want, soldiers don't usually fight to the death. When things look hopeless, they retreat to fight again another day. Soldiers in *Flames Of War* are the same. If they take heavy casualties, the player needs to roll better than their troops' motivation rating to stop them leaving the battlefield.

The Opponent's Turn

TEAMS

Though the heroic acts of a few individuals are always glorified by the media back home, in reality a soldier never does anything on their own. Soldiers are trained to operate as a team, and it is this teamwork that keeps them alive. In *Flames Of War* your miniature soldiers also operate in teams. There are four types of teams: Tank, Transport, Infantry, and Gun teams. Tank and Transport teams are described collectively as vehicles.

Every team has a set of characteristics describing it in the game. Here is a typical arsenal entry for an American M4A1 Sherman tank. Vehicles and their weapons are described together in Arsenals. The first line describes the vehicle. The second line in *italics* describes its main weapon. Tanks with more than one main weapon (or one that can fire as artillery) will have additional weapons lines. Standard vehicle machine-guns are shown on page 112. Every Intelligence Briefing has an arsenal that describes the teams found in it.

		Armour			
Name	**Mobility**	**Front**	**Side**	**Top**	**Equipment and Notes**
Weapon	***Range***	***ROF***	***Anti-tank***	***Firepower***	
M4A1 Sherman	Standard Tank	6	4	1	Co-ax MG, Hull MG, .50 cal AA MG.
M3 75mm gun	*32"/80cm*	*2*	*10*	*3+*	*Smoke, Stabiliser.*

TANK TEAMS

Tank teams are vehicles whose primary purpose is to shoot the enemy.

MOBILITY

One of the important characteristics of any team is how fast it moves. This is given by its mobility rating. The different Mobility ratings are described on page 36.

FULLY-TRACKED VEHICLES

Fully-tracked vehicles have tank tracks giving them good cross-country mobility at the cost of road speed. Four mobility ratings are classed as Fully-tracked: Standard Tank, Light Tank, Slow Tank, and Very Slow Tank.

FULLY-TRACKED VEHICLES IN OLD ARSENALS

In the past, *Flames Of War* showed the speed of Fully-tracked vehicles in the Equipment and Notes rather than in the Mobility column. Any vehicle with Fully-tracked in its Mobility column and no speed in the Equipment and Notes has a Mobility rating of Standard Tank.

ARMOUR

Tanks, half-tracks, and armoured cars are protected by armour plating. The degree of protection is measured by an armour rating ranging from values of 0 to 16 or more, the higher the number the thicker the armour.

A vehicle's protection is divided into three areas: the Front, Side, and Top armour ratings. The front armour of a tank is usually the strongest part as that's where the enemy should be. The side (and rear) armour of tanks is thinner than the front armour to save weight. The top armour of a tank protects against infantry assaults, artillery, and aircraft bombs.

ARMOURED VEHICLES

Armoured vehicles are any vehicles with armour ratings other than '-'. They are further subdivided into Fully-armoured vehicles and Open-topped vehicles.

FULLY-ARMOURED VEHICLES

Armoured vehicles with Top armour 1 or 2 are described as Fully-armoured vehicles. They have complete protection on the top of the vehicle.

OPEN-TOPPED ARMOURED VEHICLES

Armoured vehicles with Top armour 0 are described as Open-topped vehicles. They either have large openings in the top of the vehicle or rubber tyres making them vulnerable to grenades at short range.

UNARMOURED VEHICLES

Unarmoured vehicles have no armour protection, and are distinguished by having an armour rating of '-' instead of a number.

Weapons

No weapon is perfect and different weapons are better suited to different jobs. For example, a big, high-velocity anti-tank gun is very effective against tanks, but its low rate of fire makes it a poor choice for knocking down large numbers of infantry.

To help define those strengths and weaknesses, each weapon has four characteristics that describe how it operates in the game. These are its **Range**, **ROF** (Rate Of Fire), **Anti-tank**, and **Firepower** ratings.

M4A1 Sherman Weapons

Weapon	Range	ROF	AT	FP	Notes
M3 75mm gun	*32"/80cm*	*2*	*10*	*3+*	*Smoke, Stabiliser.*

Weapon	Range	ROF	AT	FP	Notes
.50 cal AA MG	*16"/40cm*	*3*	*4*	*5+*	*Self-defence Anti-aircraft.*
Vehicle MG	*16"/40cm*	*3*	*2*	*6*	

Range

The range of a weapon tells you the maximum distance over which the weapon can be fired effectively. This is given in both inches and centimetres.

ROF (Rate Of Fire)

A weapon's ROF (Rate Of Fire) reflects how quickly the weapon can deliver rounds on target. The number given is the maximum number of dice that the team rolls when shooting this type of weapon. This ranges from 1 for a slow-firing heavy artillery piece, to 6 for a rapid-firing belt-fed heavy machine-gun.

Anti-tank

A weapon's anti-tank rating tells you how good the gun is at punching holes in armoured vehicles. Effective weapons usually combine a good heavy shell and a long barrel to propel it at a high velocity.

Firepower

A weapon's firepower rating is basically a measure of how big the weapon's explosive charge is, and therefore how likely it is to destroy a protected target. The firepower rating shows the score you need to roll to destroy a protected target like a tank or troops hiding in trenches.

Firepower Tests

To make a Firepower Test, roll a die. If the score is at least equal to your weapon's Firepower rating, you have passed the Firepower Test. If the score is lower, you have failed the Firepower Test.

Firing Bombardments

Many weapons have the ability to fire artillery bombardments. These weapons will have an extra line of weapon characteristics for firing bombardments. This will not list a ROF rating as artillery bombardments plaster an area with shells rather than firing individual shots at specific targets.

Multiple Weapons

Some teams are equipped with a choice of weapons (such as submachine-guns and *Panzerfaust* anti-tank launchers), or distinctly different ammunition for the same weapon (like the German 3.7cm PaK36 which can fire normal ammunition or special muzzle-loaded anti-tank bombs). Teams with such choices have an extra line of weapon characteristics. Players can choose which they will use each time they shoot, but must fire all of their shots with the same weapon.

Special Attributes

Some vehicles and weapons have special attributes to reflect their specific advantages and disadvantages. These are listed after their normal characteristics. Any special rules that a vehicle has are shown in the notes at the end of the arsenal entry.

Armoured Tank Teams

Königstiger heavy tank

T-34/85 obr 1943 medium tank

StuG G assault gun

Staghound armoured car

Sexton self-propelled gun

Unarmoured Tank Teams

Unarmoured vehicles have no armour protection at all, leaving their crew exposed to enemy fire. They are distinguished by having an armour rating of '-' instead of a number.

Recce Jeep

6 pdr portee

Bofors self-propelled anti-aircraft gun

Vehicle Basing

Vehicles are not normally mounted on bases in *Flames Of War*, although some vehicles are cast with a base. You can base other vehicles too if you want, but bases on vehicles have no effect on the game.

Some self-propelled artillery pieces don't have room on the vehicle for the entire crew. You can either model these on a large base containing both the vehicle and crew, or model the loading crew on a separate base.

Wasp Carrier

BM-13 Katyusha rocket launcher with loading crew

M12 155mm GMC with crew

MOTORCYCLE RECONNAISSANCE TEAMS

Infantry mounted on fast-moving vehicles like motorcycles and jeeps are the ideal support for armoured cars. They have the speed to keep up, are usually well-armed to fight mounted, and can dismount when needed to clear stubborn enemy positions.

In *Flames Of War*, these Motorcycle Reconnaissance teams are a type of Tank team. Motorcycle Reconnaissance teams are unusual in that they are always based as shown below.

MOTORCYCLE COMMAND SMG TEAM | MOTORCYCLE LIGHT MORTAR TEAM | MOTORCYCLE MG TEAM

COMMAND SMG TEAM | LIGHT MORTAR TEAM | MG TEAM

SMALL MOTORCYCLE RECONNAISSANCE TEAMS

Motorcycle Reconnaissance teams with a single motorcycle and sidecar or jeep have a medium base and face the short edge. These teams dismount as Infantry teams of two or three miniatures.

LARGE MOTORCYCLE RECONNAISSANCE TEAMS

Motorcycle Reconnaissance teams with two motorcycles and sidecars or jeeps have a large base and face the short edge. These teams dismount as Infantry teams of four or five miniatures.

TRANSPORT TEAMS

Transport teams are vehicles whose main task is moving other teams around the battlefield, including armoured half-tracks, trucks, and jeeps. Supply, pioneer and demolition carriers, and recovery vehicles are also Transport teams.

They have the same characteristics as Tank teams, although few have much in the way of armament.

SD KFZ 9 RECOVERY VEHICLE

OPEL BLITZ TRUCK

M3 HALF-TRACK

ZIS-5 PIONEER SUPPLY TRUCK

Name	Mobility	Armour Front	Armour Side	Armour Top	Equipment and Notes
M3 half-track	Half-tracked	1	0	0	Passenger-fired .50 cal AA MG.

GUN TEAMS

Gun teams are weapons intended to fight the enemy at a distance, such as heavy machine-guns, mortars, anti-tank guns, anti-aircraft guns, rockets, and artillery.

Base Sizes

There are three standard base sizes:

- Small: 1¼"/32mm wide by 1"/25mm deep
- Medium: 2"/50mm wide by 1¼"/32mm deep
- Large: 2"/50mm by 2½"/65mm deep.

All *Flames Of War* miniatures are supplied with the appropriate bases.

Each Gun team is mounted on a base to keep the gun and crew together. The size of the base depends on the size of the weapon and its crew as shown in the Intelligence Briefing.

Teams That Don't Fit

If a team cannot easily fit on the normal base you might need to rotate the base so they face the short edge or use a larger base. Some gun teams have particularly large crews, making it easier to mount some of the crew on an additional medium base. Any extra bases like this are ignored during play.

Vickers HMG

ML 3" Mortar

ML 4.2" Mortar

Man-Packed Gun Teams

Man-packed Gun teams such as HMG and Mortar teams have a medium base and face the long edge.

Heavy Mortar Teams

Mortars that are not Man-Packed Guns have a large base and face the short edge.

Small Gun Teams

Other Gun teams with four crew have a medium base and face the short edge.

5cm PaK38 Anti-tank Gun

15cm sIG33 Heavy Infantry Gun

Large Gun Teams

All Gun teams with five or more crew have a large base and face the short edge.

8.8cm PaK43 Anti-tank Gun

15cm sFH18 Howitzer

Since Gun teams don't have armour their arsenal entries only have weapons lines with an extra column for their mobility, as shown in the following examples.

Weapon	Mobility	Range	ROF	Anti-tank	Firepower	Notes
5cm PaK38 gun	Medium	24"/60cm	3	9	4+	Gun shield.
15cm sFH18 howitzer	Immobile	24"/60cm	1	13	1+	Bunker buster, Smoke.
Firing bombardments		80"/200cm	-	5	2+	Smoke bombardment.

INFANTRY TEAMS

Infantry are expected to close with the enemy, either on foot or on horseback, and destroy them. The soldiers fight in small, mutually-supporting groups and fire teams.

In a *Flames Of War* battle, miniature soldiers operate in teams mounted together on a common base. The size of the base depends on the number and type of troops and weapons in the team.

Small Infantry Teams

Infantry teams of one to three miniatures have a small base and face the long edge.

Large Infantry Teams

Infantry teams of four or five miniatures have a medium base and face the long edge.

Command Rifle team

Bazooka team

Rifle/MG team

Small Cavalry Teams

Cavalry teams of one or two miniatures have a medium base and face the short edge. These teams dismount as Infantry teams of two or three miniatures.

Large Cavalry Teams

Cavalry teams with three or four miniatures have a large base and face the short edge. These teams dismount as Infantry teams of four or five miniatures.

Large Cavalry team

Arsenals only define the weaponry of Infantry teams, as their mobility is the same regardless of weaponry.

Team	Range	ROF	Anti-tank	Firepower	Notes
Rifle team	16"/40cm	1	2	6	
SMG team	4"/10cm	3	1	6	Full ROF when moving.

COMMAND AND WARRIOR TEAMS

Command Teams

In *Flames Of War*, leadership is provided by command teams made up of an officer, their assistant, and a messenger or signaller. In order of rank the four types of command teams are:

- Higher Command teams,
- Company Command teams,
- 2iC (Second-in-Command) Command teams, and
- Platoon Command teams.

Warrior Teams

Warriors are outstanding soldiers who perform amazing feats. Whether their actions are heroic fights against the odds or inspiring leadership in desperate situations, these warriors can change the outcome of battles by their strength of will and personal courage.

Warriors can be any type of team. While some warriors are infantrymen, others are tank commanders, and some are even generals travelling in their transport vehicle. Each Warrior team is unique. There can only be one of each particular Warrior in any force.

Independent Teams

Senior commanders and artillery observers follow the flow of the battle moving where they are needed most. These soldiers are known as Independent teams and are free to move about the battlefield at will.

INTELLIGENCE BRIEFINGS

The most important thing you need to play *Flames Of War* is a force to lead into battle. There are a wide variety of different forces to choose from as each army that fought in World War II had their own way of organising their troops and fighting battles. These evolved as the war continued in response to combat experience, combat losses, and the arrival of new weapons and equipment.

Flames Of War has an ever-increasing range of Intelligence Briefings covering most of the armies that fought in the Second World War. The core of every Intelligence Briefing is the organisational diagrams that show the composition of the different combat forces of the armies described. By following these diagrams you'll be able to create a force that is just like its real-life counterpart. Each handbook also contains an arsenal listing the game characteristics of every team, weapon, and vehicle used by the forces covered.

As well as game-based material, each Intelligence Briefing also contains a wealth of information on the organisation, weapons, and battlefield tactics they used, as well as battle histories, famous warriors, and lots more.

The armies of the Second World War were constantly developing new weapons and tactics. The heaviest tanks of 1940 would barely have rated as medium tanks by the end of the war, and even the lightest of battle tanks at the end of the war totally outclass anything in service even three years earlier. As a result *Flames Of War* divides the Second World War into three periods—Early War (1939-1941), Mid-War (1942-1943) and Late War (1944-1945). Every Intelligence Briefing is specific to one or another of these periods and should only be used with other Intelligence Briefings from the same period.

As well as publishing Intelligence Briefings in books like those shown below, there are a wide variety of Intelligence Briefings downloadable from the *Flames Of War* website (*www.FlamesOfWar.com*).

◀ GREY WOLF, A LATE-WAR GERMAN INTELLIGENCE HANDBOOK

Flames Of War is a military simulation, so it's helpful to know a little bit about military organisation. During World War II, every army used a similar structure to organise its troops as shown in this summary.

PLATOON **LIEUTENANT** *Commanding 25 to 50 Soldiers or 3 to 5 Tanks*	**COMPANY** **CAPTAIN OR MAJOR** *Commanding 100 to 200 Soldiers or 10 to 20 Tanks*	**BATTALION** **LIEUTENANT COLONEL** *Commanding 500 to 1,000 Soldiers or 30 to 90 Tanks*
A lieutenant ('loo-tenant' in the US Army and 'left-tenant' in the British Army!) commands a platoon of two to four sections or squads, and a few extra weapons like a light mortar or bazooka.	The normal force you will field in *Flames Of War* is a company of two to four platoons. Rifle companies often have an additional weapons platoon equipped with light machine-guns and mortars.	A battalion has three or four companies plus a heavy weapons company of heavy machine-guns, mortars, and light guns. It is the biggest force you will see on a *Flames Of War* battlefield.

PICKING A FORCE

Before fighting a battle, you need to choose your force. The most common form of force selection, and the best way of ensuring a fair fight and an interesting game, is to select your force based on the points given for each unit in the Intelligence Briefings. The points value is calculated based upon the size and fighting capability of each unit—the larger and more powerful a unit is the higher its points value.

Agree with your opponent on the maximum points value that you may both spend on your armies. 500, 750, or even 1000 points is a good place to start, while 1500 points is a good size for a two to three hour game. Later, as you become a more skilled and experienced commander you may want to build your army up to 2000-3000 points or even more!

SCHWERE PANZER PLATOON

GRENADIER PLATOON

SCHWERE PANZER PLATOON

MOTORISED ARTILLERY BATTERY

REGIMENT OR BRIGADE

BRIGADIER GENERAL

Commanding 2,000 to 3,000 Soldiers or 100 to 300 Tanks

A regiment groups together two to four battalions of the same type, along with supporting arms. A brigade is like a regiment, but usually combines a number of battalions of different types.

DIVISION

MAJOR GENERAL

Commanding 5,000 to 25,000 Soldiers and up to 100 to 300 Tanks

Divisions vary widely in strength, but all have a similar organisation with two to four regiments of infantry (or tanks in armoured divisions) and another of artillery, along with supporting battalions.

CORPS OR ARMY

GENERAL

Commanding 50,000 or more Soldiers and up to 2000 Tanks

A corps of two to four divisions is usually tasked with a major operation by the army commander. An army of up to four corps is the biggest formation in most battles.

PLATOONS

In *Flames Of War* your force is usually a company of three or more platoons, each of 30 to 60 men, or three to six tanks or guns, led by a lieutenant. In battle a platoon operates together as a unit, manoeuvring across the battlefield and engaging the same foes.

Every platoon in *Flames Of War* has two characteristics: Skill and Motivation. While planning and luck play a large part—it is the skill and bravery of the soldiers that wins battles. These two ratings reflect the training and determination of your force.

US Armored Rifle Platoon

Platoon

HQ Section with Light MG Squad, 60mm Mortar Squad, and:

2 Rifle Squads	225 points
1 Rifle Squad	180 points

Options

- Replace AA MG on any or all M3 half-tracks with .50 cal AA MG for +5 points per half-track.
- Replace Bazooka team in HQ Section with an M3 37mm gun at no cost.

RELUCTANT	CONSCRIPT
CONFIDENT	TRAINED
FEARLESS	VETERAN

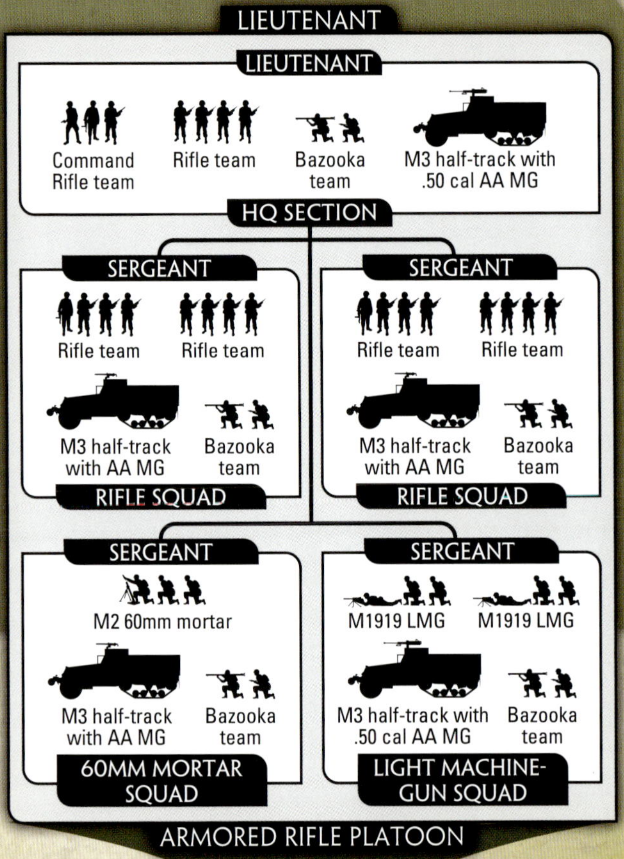

Each armoured rifle platoon is an army unto itself. Dismounting from their M3 half-track, the armoured infantry lay down a withering fire with their semi-automatic Garand rifles, and bazookas, supported by a 60mm mortar and two M1919 light machine-guns.

US Armored Rifle Platoon

Specialist Platoons

While most platoons are straight-forward combat troops, some units are specialists with specific roles and ways of fighting.

Multi-part Platoons

Some platoons, particularly reconnaissance platoons, operate as numerous detached patrols rather than as a single large entity. This allows them to spread out across the front probing for weaknesses.

A Multi-part Platoon is made up of several platoons, each with their own Platoon Command team. Each of the platoons is a separate platoon for all purposes, including deployment.

In missions with Ambushes or Reserves (see pages 266 to 269), each platoon in a Multi-part Platoon is counted as a separate platoon when working out how many platoons may be held in Ambush or Reserves.

Assault Groups

When faced with a difficult task and given time to carefully prepare an assault, a commander may organise a special task-oriented platoon with just the right equipment for the job. Perhaps the simplest example of this is the decision as to whether assault engineers should break out their flame-thrower equipment or not.

A platoon that is an Assault Group can change its composition from game to game. The Intelligence Briefing will describe the changes that the platoon can make in its equipment.

Reconnaissance Platoons

Reconnaissance platoons (recce platoons for short) are a commander's 'eyes and ears' on the battlefield. Composed of lightly-armoured vehicles or stealthy infantry, their task is to push out in front of an advancing army and ascertain the strength and disposition of the enemy. This information allows a commander to direct his attacks against points in the enemy line where the opposition is the weakest. In defence, recce platoons act as a screen, keeping the enemy from learning a force's dispositions while gathering information about when and from where any attack will come.

A Reconnaissance Platoon is any platoon noted as such in the Intelligence Handbooks. All teams in a Reconnaissance Platoon are Recce teams. Teams attached to a Reconnaissance Platoon are not Recce teams unless they are attached from another Reconnaissance Platoon. Recce teams use the special rules on pages 193 to 195.

Transport Platoons

Transport platoons are units of trucks. They have no combat capability whatsoever and spend most of their time carrying supplies to and fro in the rear areas. Sometimes commanders need to move infantry faster than they can march and order transport platoons forward to get the infantry where they are needed.

A Transport Platoon is any platoon noted as such in the Intelligence Handbooks.

A US Armored Rifle Platoon as part of a larger American force attacking an SS defensive position in the Normandy Bocage

SKILL

A soldier gains skill through a combination of basic training and battlefield experience. You need the basic training to survive your first few days of battle, but there are many important battlefield survival skills that can only be learnt on the front line. If a soldier survives the first couple of weeks of combat then his chances of survival get a lot higher. This is because he begins to learn the unwritten rules of combat that only his battle-hardened comrades can teach him.

A platoon's Skill rating is arguably the most important characteristic they possess. Not only are skilful troops better at moving across treacherous terrain, digging in, and finishing off the enemy in hand-to-hand combat, they also survive longer because they know how to take cover and avoid being seen and hit by enemy shooting.

Troops are classified according to their prior training and experience into three categories:

- Conscript
- Trained
- Veteran

German machine-gunner advancing

Conscript

Conscript platoons have been hustled into battle with little or no training and are ignorant of even the most basic battlefield techniques. They are only used as a last resort buying their successes with horrendous casualties.

Trained

Trained platoons are those who have at least received basic training and are ready for battle, but that haven't had many opportunities to test their skills in combat.

Veteran

Veteran platoons are battle-tested troops, hardened under fire, or highly trained professionals. They have learned all the tricks they need to keep alive on the battlefield and are exceptionally effective soldiers.

Skill Tests

The skill and training of soldiers can affect how well they do all kinds of jobs—from crossing a river, to directing artillery fire, to fighting in an assault.

When your troops attempt a task like this in *Flames Of War* you may have to make a Skill Test.

To make a Skill Test, roll a die and compare it to the platoon's Skill rating on the table below. If the score equals or exceeds the score needed, you have passed the Skill Test. If the score is lower, you have failed the Skill Test.

Team's Skill	Score Needed
Conscript	5+
Trained	4+
Veteran	3+

Shooting and Skill

One of the things that makes *Flames Of War* unique as a game is its use of the target's skill rating as the primary factor when working out the score needed to hit a target (most games use the skill rating of the shooting team).

The reason for this is simply that it is a better reflection of modern combat. While skilled troops certainly shoot more accurately than unskilled troops, this isn't the most important factor in hitting the enemy. The most important factor is seeing the enemy in the first place!

Modern weapons are so accurate and deadly that even a raw recruit can bring down any target they can see. Given a machine-gun, anyone can mow down hordes of conscripts charging across an open field—the casualties of the First World War attest to this. However, a unit of veteran commandos using every available bit of cover and fire and movement tactics will cross the same open field with few if any casualties.

MOTIVATION

It goes without saying that a battlefield is a terrifying place to be. One thing soldiers always say about a battlefield is that it is noisy—incredibly noisy. Imagine yourself in a muddy trench as high-explosive shells explode dangerously close, spraying mud and deadly metal fragments through the air, while machine-gun bullets whine overhead like angry wasps. The machine-gun next to you begins blasting back at the enemy, the staccato bark deafening as the weapon showers you with hot shell casings. You realise your Lieutenant is shouting something above the din, by his gestures you guess that he is saying that your platoon is about to attack.

It is no wonder that in an environment like this the motivation of your soldiers is a vitally important part of the battle. Sometimes they'll keep it together and do heroic things, and sometimes they'll crack under the pressure, just like real people might do.

In *Flames Of War*, the Motivation rating measures the courage and determination of your fighting soldiers. Troops are classified according to their motivation into three categories:

- Reluctant
- Confident
- Fearless

Reluctant

There are many reasons that troops can be reluctant. They may simply be unenthusiastic conscripts sent into battle against their will, or they might not care two cents about the cause they're fighting for. Maybe they're just good soldiers who have seen too much fighting, who have had their fill of battle and feel that it's about time someone else started taking the risks. Regardless, reluctant troops are likely to break under pressure.

Confident

Faith in both yourself and your leaders can be critical for an army. Believing that you can trust in the actions of your superiors and your fellows can sustain you even when all else fails. Most confident troops have that faith aplenty.

Fearless

In war there are always those who believe that the cause is bigger than themselves. Whether it's because they are fanatical zealots or just supremely confident, these troops are nearly unbreakable. They will fight to the last man, staying in battle until there is absolutely no choice but to withdraw. For fearless troops, incredible heroism is commonplace and fleeing from the enemy unthinkable.

Motivation Tests

In *Flames Of War* the courage and enthusiasm of your miniature troops is checked by making Motivation Tests.

To make a Motivation Test, roll a die and compare it to the platoon's Motivation rating on the table below. If the score equals or exceeds the score needed, you have passed the Motivation Test. If the score is lower, you have failed the Motivation Test.

Team's Motivation	Score Needed
Reluctant	5+
Confident	4+
Fearless	3+

Mixed-rating Platoons

In some cases a platoon will have teams with different skill or motivation ratings. This can occur in ad hoc battlegroups formed from bits and pieces of different platoons. It might also happen when a leader joins a platoon as well.

If a platoon has teams with different Skill or Motivation ratings, use the worst value in the platoon.

Soviet ISU-152 assault-guns

PLAYING FLAMES OF WAR

DIE ROLLS

Flames Of War uses the same standard six-sided dice that games like Monopoly and Yahtzee use.

When the rules say to roll a die, they give a number that you must equal or exceed, for example, 3+ (a roll of 3, 4, 5, or 6 means success), or 5+ (a roll of 5 or 6 means success). Any roll lower than the number means the attempt has failed.

In some cases, such as shooting at partly concealed targets, the number needed for success will be modified.

Add +1 to the required score for each of the modifiers that apply at the time. For instance, if you normally need a 3+ to hit the enemy, but the target was both (a) at long range and (b) concealed in a wood, the required score on each die would go up to 5+.

If the score needed ever goes above 6 then the attempt will automatically fail.

If the rules require you to roll more than one die, treat each roll as a separate success or failure.

RE-ROLLS

In some situations, where your first roll fails, you may be allowed a re-roll. A re-roll is just what the name says—you get to ignore the first attempt and roll the die again. The score on the second die roll is what counts. You never get more than one re-roll per situation.

MEASURING

Flames Of War gives game measurements in both inches (imperial) and centimetres (metric). You should agree on which system you and your opponent will use before the game begins—you must use one of these two systems, not switch between both. Generally, it's a good idea to use the system you are most familiar with.

Unlike some games, you are allowed to measure any distances on the battlefield any time you want to. You can measure how far your weapons can shoot, how far the opponent's weapons can shoot, or even whether or not you have enough movement to assault at the end of the turn. After all, your soldiers have maps, range-finders, and binoculars to help them work these things out.

DECLARATIVE MEASURING

You can make your game flow more easily by letting your opponent know what your intention is when moving your forces. If you tell them you are intending to stay out of range, or that you think your troops are completely out of sight behind a wood, it reduces disputes if a model gets bumped later.

UP TO HALF, AT LEAST HALF

At times *Flames Of War* allows or requires you to do something with up to half or at least half of your teams. When dealing with an even number of teams this is straightforward. With an odd number of teams, up to half means that the odd team is excluded, while at least half requires the odd team to be included. Either way, always use the current strength of the unit.

WYSIWYG

Flames Of War is a What You See Is What You Get, or WYSIWYG, game. One miniature represents one soldier or vehicle. In many cases you can resolve difficulties by remembering this and taking a look at the situation from a model's-eye view, down on the ground so to speak. Have a look at what your miniature could see from where they are or where they could go on the terrain as modelled.

American observer
US Signal Corps, NARA

READING THE RULES

To make the rules easier to read we have distinguished the explanations of the rules from the actual rules themselves. While the explanation may be useful in understanding and interpreting the rules, only the text printed in *italics* and in the accompanying tables are actually rules.

DIAGRAMS AND SUMMARIES

You'll find diagrams and summary boxes throughout the rules. These make it easier to understand the rules and refresh your memory of them at a glance when you are looking them up in a game.

Of necessity the diagrams and summary boxes show a shortened version of the rules and may not have all of the details that apply to your situation. Always go to the rules themselves if you have run into a problem and need to clarify the situation.

SPECIAL RULES

To keep things simple, the main part of the *Flames Of War* rules only cover the more common cases. Rules that are specific to certain weapons, vehicles, platoons or armies are given as special rules.

These special rules either add additional capabilities or allow the teams and platoons that use them to break the normal rules. When a special rule conflicts with the normal rules, apply the special rule.

WHEN THINGS HAPPEN

Normally turns in *Flames Of War* follow a straightforward sequence. However, some rules, particularly special rules, cause things to happen out of turn. An example of this would be reconnaissance troops disengaging when the enemy starts shooting at them.

When this happens, interrupt the normal turn sequence, resolve the unusual activity, then return to where you were and continue the turn.

General Eisenhower talking to US paratroopers on the eve of D-Day.
US Signal Corps, NARA

SPORTING PLAY

In a hobby such as wargaming, it's impossible to over emphasise the importance of being a good sport. Whether you are crushing your opponent or you are on the receiving end of an almighty pummelling, it's always good to remember that whatever the outcome of the battle, playing is all about having fun.

Some good basic rules are to play fair, follow the rules of the game, and treat your opponents with courtesy and respect. Oh, that and don't give up! The odds may look grim with your army set to be beaten, but hang in there. Some of the best stories are about heroic last stands and a few brave individuals turning the tide and holding out against the odds to finally snatch an unlikely victory.

Remember that whether you are facing a friend or a new opponent treat them just the way you would like to be treated, and you will get so much more from the hobby.

WORKING IT OUT

Lots of things happen in war, so naturally the *Flames Of War* rulebook may not cover every possible situation that can occur in your battles. If something unexpected happens, talk with the other players and try to come up with a good interpretation of what would happen.

If you can't come to an agreement quickly just roll a die:

- If you roll 4, 5, or 6, use your interpretation of the rule for the rest of the game.
- A roll of 1, 2, or 3, means that you have to accept your opponent's interpretation of the rule for the rest of the game.

After the game, when you have more time for discussion without holding up the battle, sit down and agree how you'll handle the situation in the future.

If you still aren't sure, you can always check out the forum at *www.FlamesOfWar.com* and ask other players how they would handle the problem.

TERRAIN

World War II was fought over almost every type of terrain. Battles ranged from the frozen arctic of northern Finland to the scorching heat of North African deserts, from the grassy steppes of the Ukraine to the dense forests of the German Reichswald, and from the hedgerows of France to the mountains of Italy.

Woods, hedges, bogs, bridges, rivers, lakes, rocks, rubble, and buildings all break up the terrain and complicate the battlefield. Sometimes this will be to your advantage, since your troops (whether riflemen, tanks, gunners, or trucks) can hide themselves among the clutter and put something solid between them and any bullets flying around. Other times these features will be a hindrance, as they impede your movement, slowing your advance to a crawl.

BUILDINGS

Man-made structures like buildings are different from natural terrain. They are solid, so troops can't be seen on the other side, but troops can enter them and fight through their openings, such as doors and windows.

AREA TERRAIN

Area Terrain, such as roads, rivers, forests, marshes, hills, snow, or mud, occupies an area of the table. Some types of Area Terrain like roads and hills can be easily modelled in a realistic fashion. Others like woods need a more representative approach.

OPEN SPACES

Open spaces are the areas of underlying table top around the other terrain features.

LINEAR OBSTACLES

Some terrain features like hedges, walls, and streams are Linear Obstacles forming a line running from one point to another. In game terms the chief characteristic of these terrain features is their lack of depth. A team can be on one side or the other of them, but never actually in or on them.

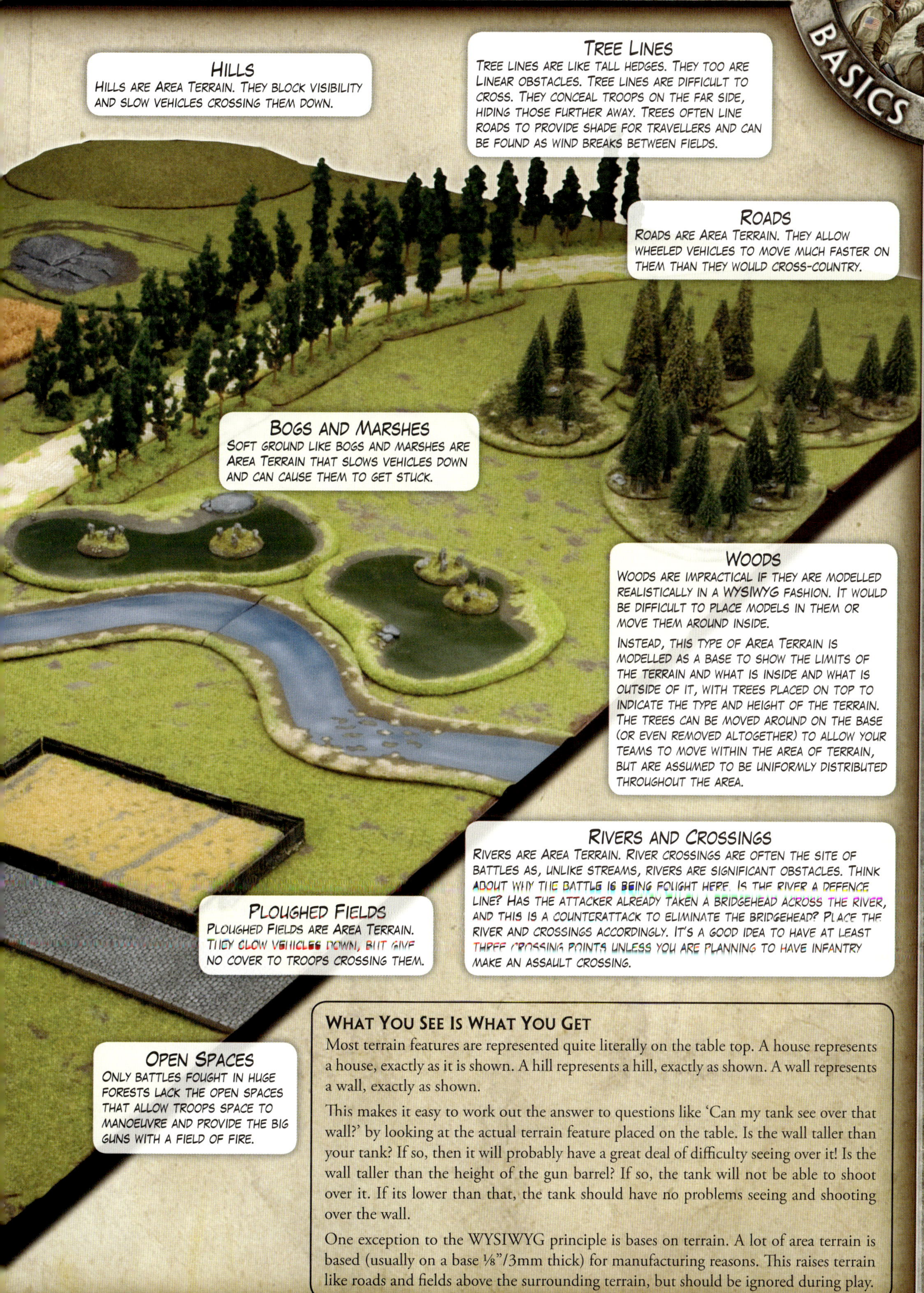

Hills
Hills are Area Terrain. They block visibility and slow vehicles crossing them down.

Tree Lines
Tree lines are like tall hedges. They too are Linear obstacles. Tree lines are difficult to cross. They conceal troops on the far side, hiding those further away. Trees often line roads to provide shade for travellers and can be found as wind breaks between fields.

Roads
Roads are Area Terrain. They allow wheeled vehicles to move much faster on them than they would cross-country.

Bogs and Marshes
Soft ground like bogs and marshes are Area Terrain that slows vehicles down and can cause them to get stuck.

Woods
Woods are impractical if they are modelled realistically in a WYSIWYG fashion. It would be difficult to place models in them or move them around inside.

Instead, this type of Area Terrain is modelled as a base to show the limits of the terrain and what is inside and what is outside of it, with trees placed on top to indicate the type and height of the terrain. The trees can be moved around on the base (or even removed altogether) to allow your teams to move within the area of terrain, but are assumed to be uniformly distributed throughout the area.

Rivers and Crossings
Rivers are Area Terrain. River crossings are often the site of battles as, unlike streams, rivers are significant obstacles. Think about why the battle is being fought here. Is the river a defence line? Has the attacker already taken a bridgehead across the river, and this is a counterattack to eliminate the bridgehead? Place the river and crossings accordingly. It's a good idea to have at least three crossing points unless you are planning to have infantry make an assault crossing.

Ploughed Fields
Ploughed Fields are Area Terrain. They slow vehicles down, but give no cover to troops crossing them.

Open Spaces
Only battles fought in huge forests lack the open spaces that allow troops space to manoeuvre and provide the big guns with a field of fire.

What You See Is What You Get
Most terrain features are represented quite literally on the table top. A house represents a house, exactly as it is shown. A hill represents a hill, exactly as shown. A wall represents a wall, exactly as shown.

This makes it easy to work out the answer to questions like 'Can my tank see over that wall?' by looking at the actual terrain feature placed on the table. Is the wall taller than your tank? If so, then it will probably have a great deal of difficulty seeing over it! Is the wall taller than the height of the gun barrel? If so, the tank will not be able to shoot over it. If its lower than that, the tank should have no problems seeing and shooting over the wall.

One exception to the WYSIWYG principle is bases on terrain. A lot of area terrain is based (usually on a base ⅛"/3mm thick) for manufacturing reasons. This raises terrain like roads and fields above the surrounding terrain, but should be ignored during play.

GROUND CONDITIONS

There are four categories of ground conditions that units can encounter: Roads, Cross-country, Rough Terrain, and Impassable. Rough Terrain is further divided into Slow going, Difficult Going, and Very Difficult Going.

ROADS

Whether concrete, brick, cobble, or dirt, a road provides a quick route from one place to another. Trucks and half-tracks travelling on a road move much faster than they do cross-country. Even tanks benefit from roads since they bridge or cut through most obstacles.

CROSS-COUNTRY

Terrain that is rated as cross-country is basically level and smooth enough that troops can cross it without much difficulty. It could be grassy or barren fields, expanses of firmly packed desert, or farmland.

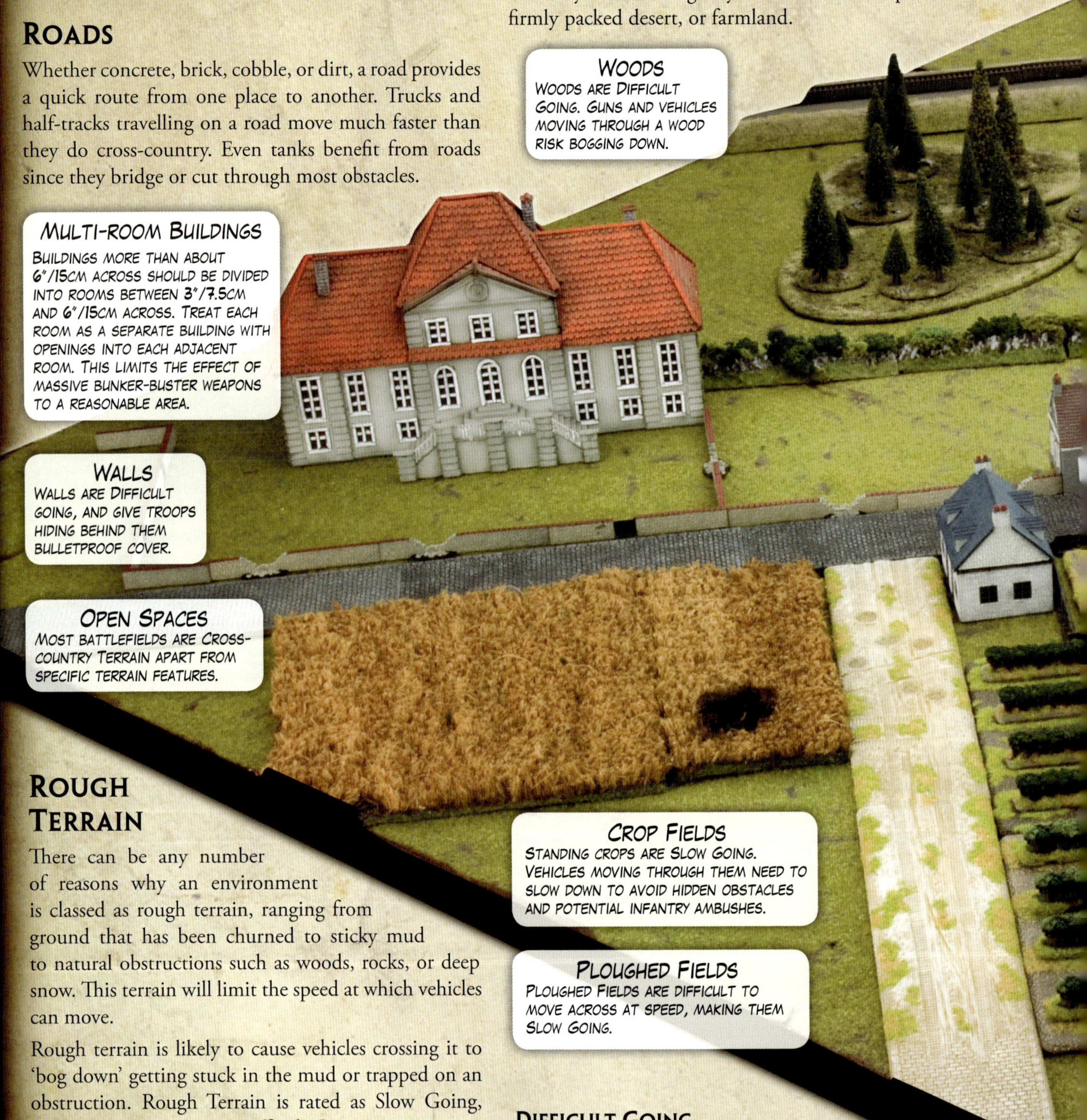

ROUGH TERRAIN

There can be any number of reasons why an environment is classed as rough terrain, ranging from ground that has been churned to sticky mud to natural obstructions such as woods, rocks, or deep snow. This terrain will limit the speed at which vehicles can move.

Rough terrain is likely to cause vehicles crossing it to 'bog down' getting stuck in the mud or trapped on an obstruction. Rough Terrain is rated as Slow Going, Difficult Going, or Very Difficult Going.

SLOW GOING

Slow going is a type of rough terrain that slows vehicles down, without any risk of them bogging down.

DIFFICULT GOING

Difficult going is rough terrain that presents a significant hindrance to movement. Vehicles attempting to move through this terrain must slow to a crawl and risk getting stuck if the driver isn't careful.

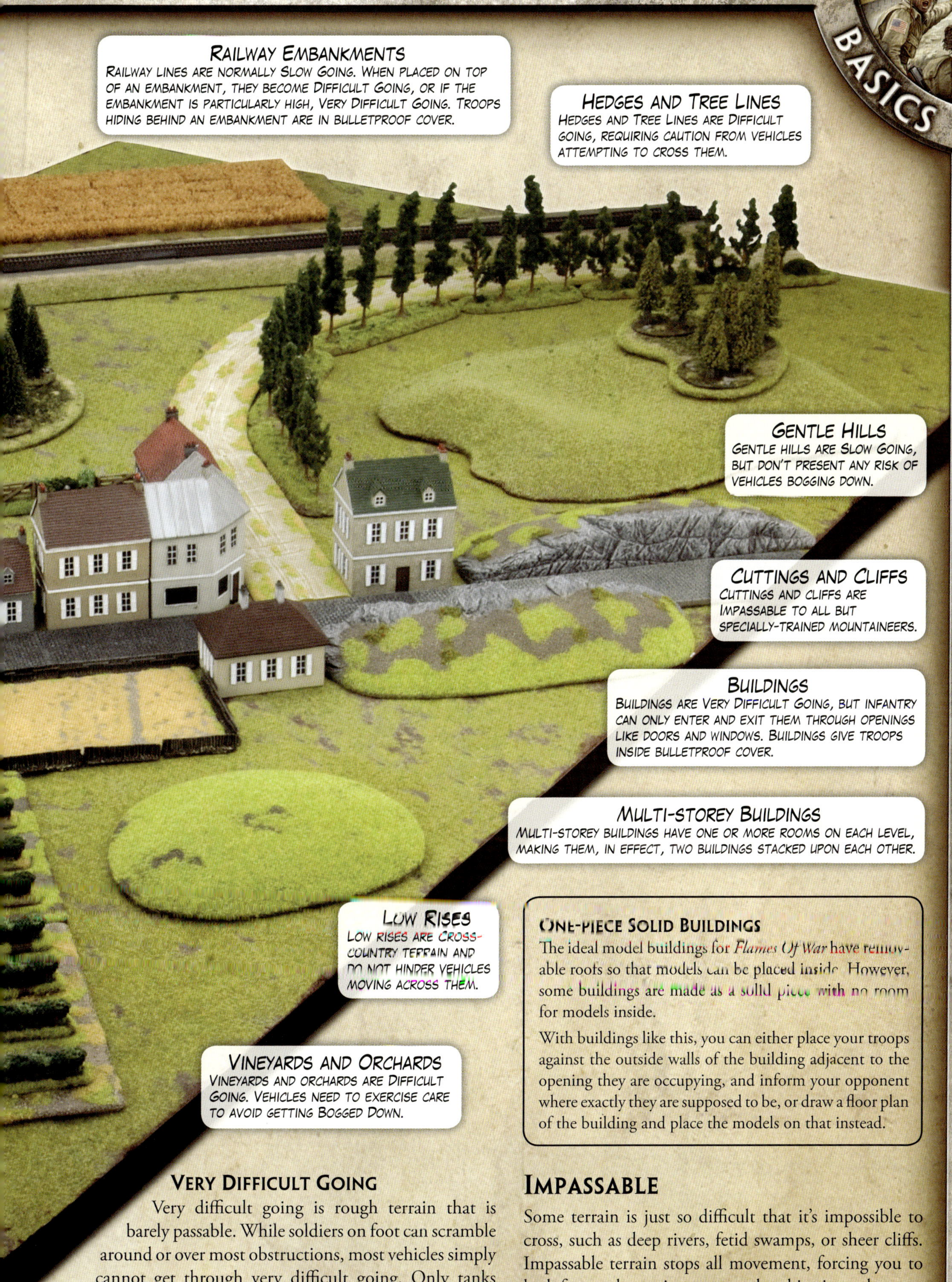

ONE-PIECE SOLID BUILDINGS

The ideal model buildings for *Flames Of War* have removable roofs so that models can be placed inside. However, some buildings are made as a solid piece with no room for models inside.

With buildings like this, you can either place your troops against the outside walls of the building adjacent to the opening they are occupying, and inform your opponent where exactly they are supposed to be, or draw a floor plan of the building and place the models on that instead.

VERY DIFFICULT GOING

Very difficult going is rough terrain that is barely passable. While soldiers on foot can scramble around or over most obstructions, most vehicles simply cannot get through very difficult going. Only tanks and other tracked vehicles are able to force their way through.

IMPASSABLE

Some terrain is just so difficult that it's impossible to cross, such as deep rivers, fetid swamps, or sheer cliffs. Impassable terrain stops all movement, forcing you to look for an alternative route to the objective unless you have special training or equipment.

EASTERN FRONT BATTLEFIELDS

Eastern Europe differs from Western Europe in being a lot more open and less densely cultivated. The steppes of central Russia are wide open grasslands of rolling hills broken by gullies and ravines where streams cut through the soft soil, flowing to wide, shallow rivers. Woods and scattered peasant villages linked by dirt roads break the monotony.

Modern Soviet Russia is overlaid on this timeless landscape with concrete cities of factories and apartment blocks, department stores and squares, collective farms, and railways linking them all together.

GULLIES

TRAVELLING ALONG THE FLOOR OF A GULLY IS SLOW GOING. THE SIDES ARE GENERALLY STEEP AND VERY DIFFICULT GOING WITH OCCASIONAL DIFFICULT GOING ACCESSES DOWN INTO IT.

STEEP HILLS

STEEP HILLS ARE DIFFICULT GOING AS ONLY VERY POWERFUL VEHICLES CAN SCALE THEIR SLOPES.

RIVERS

SHALLOW RIVERS UP TO 8"/20CM WIDE ARE VERY DIFFICULT GOING. DEEPER RIVERS ARE IMPASSABLE (ALTHOUGH INFANTRY CAN CROSS IN ASSAULT BOATS). RIVERS SHOULD HAVE AT LEAST TWO OR THREE ROAD OR RAIL BRIDGES TO ALLOW OTHER TROOPS TO CROSS.

MORE VARIED TERRAIN

Not all terrain needs to be the same.

One of the great things about *Flames Of War* is that you can introduce more variety into your battles by changing the terrain,

You might also like to bear in mind the season during which your *Flames Of War* battle is being fought, and adjust the effect of the terrain on your table accordingly. For example, you could adjudge that a shallow river that would normally be Very Difficult Going, has frozen over making it easier to cross and thus rated as only Difficult Going (maybe instead of bogging down, vehicles risk falling through the ice!). Or perhaps it is the spring melt, making the river an Impassable raging torrent!

Battles fought in particular places might have terrain that is slightly different than normal too, so German forests could be Very Difficult Going, focusing the action towards the tracks through them. At the other end of the spectrum, woods in Sicily might be so sparse that they are only Slow Going.

Don't get too carried away though, if the terrain is too difficult, the game will slow to a crawl as troops spend more time fighting the terrain than the opposition!

What Makes a Good Table?

A good table represents the real-life terrain in the area being fought over in the way it combines open space, linear obstacles, area terrain, and man-made features. The most important thing to consider is the way real-life terrain tends to clump. Houses form villages surrounded by crops, trees form woods, and boggy ground is found around rivers.

In the same way, open spaces are usually large as people clear space for crops and harvest wood. These open spaces aren't empty and are broken up by crop fields, or fenced or hedged grazing, but they do offer extensive lines of sight. As an example, most tank battles in Europe took place at ranges of half a mile (800m) or more (around 24"/60cm on a *Flames of War* battlefield), while ranges were even greater on the Eastern Front.

CITY TERRAIN

The Battle of Stalingrad was pivotal to the outcome of the Second World War and remains the standard for urban warfare. Like all combat in cities, the fighting was brutal, bloody, and at very close quarters. Whole battles were fought over single buildings as one side or the other tried to evict the enemy from their well-protected positions.

Only powerful guns firing at pointblank range, or desperate assaults with hand grenades and sharpened entrenching tools could clear a building room-by-room, floor-by-floor.

MULTI-ROOM BUILDINGS

BUILDINGS MORE THAN ABOUT 6"/15CM ACROSS SHOULD BE DIVIDED INTO ROOMS BETWEEN 3"/7.5CM AND 6"/15CM ACROSS. TREAT EACH ROOM AS A SEPARATE BUILDING WITH OPENINGS INTO EACH ADJACENT ROOM. THIS ALSO LIMITS THE EFFECT OF MASSIVE BUNKER-BUSTER WEAPONS TO A REASONABLE AREA.

CITY STREETS

BOMBING AND FIGHTING QUICKLY REDUCES A CITY TO A RUBBLE-STREWN MESS, MAKING HIGH-SPEED TRAVEL IMPOSSIBLE. STREETS IN A CITY THAT HAS BEEN FOUGHT OVER ARE SLOW GOING.

DISCUSS THE TERRAIN

It is important to discuss the terrain on the table with your opponent before you start your *Flames Of War* game. By agreeing on how each piece of terrain will work in the game, you reduce the possibility of confusion and misunderstanding during play. Most terrain will be fairly obvious from looking at the model and comparing it with the examples in this section. Some terrain is less obvious and will need some thought. If you can't reach an agreement, simply pick the most likely candidates and roll a die to choose between them.

Table Size

Most games of *Flames Of War* are played on 6'x4' (180cm x 120cm) tables, as this gives room for manoeuvre, while still being small enough for convenient storage. Battles fought in close terrain like cities and the Bocage of Normandy are usually played on a half-size 4' x 3' (120cm x 90cm) tables. This is useful as troops move more slowly and can only cover shorter frontages due to restricted lines of sight.

Larger tables, say 12'x6' (360cm x 180cm), suit bigger games with larger forces or multiple players.

Factories and Warehouses

Large industrial buildings like factories and warehouses often have huge spaces inside. Rather than treating this as a building, it works better to treat the interior as an open space surrounded by four walls.

Given the machinery and general clutter inside, Factories are Very Difficult Going and provide bulletproof cover to troops inside.

Ruins

Buildings require four walls, no matter how battered. Any structure with fewer walls is a ruin. Ruins are just an area of rubble, although the surrounding walls make it easier to hide in them.

Rubble

Piles of rubble are Area Terrain that is Very Difficult Going, blocking passage to all but Fully-tracked vehicles and soldiers on foot. Infantry and guns sheltering in rubble are concealed and in bulletproof cover.

TERRAIN SUMMARY

Terrain	Type	Ground Condition	Concealment	Bulletproof Cover
Open Spaces				
Grass or steppe	Open Space	Cross-country	✗	✗
Firm sand or thin snow	Open Space	Cross-country	✗	✗
Soft sand, snow or mud	Open Space	Slow Going	✗	✗
Deep snow or mud	Open Space	Difficult Going	✗	✗
Vegetation				
Ploughed field	Open Space	Slow Going	✗	✗
Crop field or open scrub	Area Terrain	Slow Going	✓	✗
Orchard or vineyard	Area Terrain	Difficult Going	✓	✗
Woods	Area Terrain	Difficult Going	✓	✗
Forest	Area Terrain	Very Difficult Going	✓	✗
Hedges and Walls				
Fence	Linear Obstacle	Slow Going	✓	✗
Hedge or line of trees	Linear Obstacle	Difficult Going	✓	✗
Wall	Linear Obstacle	Difficult Going	✓	✓
Hills				
Low rise	Area Terrain	Cross-country	✗*	✗
Gentle hill	Area Terrain	Slow Going	✗*	✗
Steep hill	Area Terrain	Difficult Going	✗*	✗
Rocky hill	Area Terrain	Very Difficult Going	✗*	✗
Banks, Gullies, and Cliffs				
Gully floor	Area Terrain	Slow Going	✗	✗
Gully accesses	Area Terrain	Difficult Going	✗	✗
Gully wall	Linear Obstacle	Very Difficult Going	✓	✗
Steep bank, or low sea wall	Linear Obstacle	Very Difficult Going	✓	✓
Cliff, cutting, or high sea wall	Linear Obstacle	Impassable	✓	✓
Water Features				
Ford across a stream	Area Terrain	Slow Going	✗	✗
Stream or ford across a river	Area Terrain	Difficult Going	✗	✗
Shallow river	Area Terrain	Very Difficult Going	✗	✗
Deep river	Area Terrain	Impassable	✗	✗
Bog	Area Terrain	Difficult Going	✗	✗
Marsh	Area Terrain	Very Difficult Going	✗	✗
Swamp or lake	Area Terrain	Impassable	✗	✗
Roads and Railway Lines				
Road or airfield	Area Terrain	Road	✗	✗
Track	Area Terrain	Cross-country	✗	✗
City streets	Area Terrain	Slow Going	✗	✗
Railway Line	Area Terrain	Slow Going	✗	✗
Low railway embankment	Linear Obstacle	Difficult Going	✓	✓
High railway embankment	Linear Obstacle	Very Difficult Going	✓	✓
Buildings				
Building	Building	Very Difficult	✓	✓
Rubble, ruin or factory space	Area Terrain	Very Difficult	✓	✓
Factory walls	Linear Obstacle	Impassable	✓	✓

* Hills block line of sight, concealing or hiding teams beyond them.

GAME TURNS

Like Chess, *Flames Of War* is played with each side taking turns to move and fight with their troops. In real life soldiers don't move one at a time, so you move and fight with your entire force in your turn, then your opponent moves and fights with their entire force.

TURN ORDER

A *Flames Of War* turn consists of one side playing their turn, then the other. When it's a player's turn, they will perform all of the actions available to them, then the turn will switch to the other player. The players keep alternating their turns like this until the game ends.

In *Flames Of War*, both players usually roll a die and whoever rolls the highest has the first turn. However, in some missions the attacker or defender always has the first turn.

PLAYING A TURN

To keep things organised, each player's turn is divided into four steps: the Starting Step, the Movement Step, the Shooting Step, and the Assault Step.

At the start of each of a player's turn they reorganise their troops and decide what they are going to do, then they move all of their platoons. After that, they shoot at the enemy, and finally they launch assaults on the enemy. When their turn is finished, the opposing player plays their turn in the same order.

ORDER OF A GAME TURN

A.	**Starting Step**	**Rally your forces, bring up reserves and air support, and spring your ambushes**
B.	**Movement Step**	**Manoeuvre all of your teams into position**
C.	**Shooting Step**	**Shoot the enemy from a distance**
D.	**Assault Step**	**Charge the enemy defences in fierce hand-to-hand combat**

A THE STARTING STEP

During the Starting Step you:	*page*
1. Check Sole Surviving Infantry Teams	176
2. Check Company Morale	175
3. Check Victory Conditions	274
4. Reveal Ambushes	266
5. Roll for Air Support	178
6. Roll for Reserves	268
7. Rally Pinned Down Platoons	104
8. Remount Bailed Out Vehicles	102
9. Free Bogged Down Vehicles	44
10. Remove Friendly Smoke Markers	107

B THE MOVEMENT STEP

During the Movement Step you:	*page*
1. Select a Platoon to Move	35
2. Bring Forward Transports	48
3. Move Teams in the Platoon	36
a. Dismount Passengers	47
b. Take Bogging Checks in Rough Terrain	43
c. Take Skill Tests to Enter Buildings	52
d. Move Transports after Mounting	46
4. Send Empty Transports to the Rear.	48
5. Return to 1 and Select the Next Platoon	

C THE SHOOTING STEP

During the Shooting Step you:	*page*
1. Select the Shooting Platoon	73
2. Select the Target Platoons	74
3. Decide Who will Shoot at each Platoon	74
4. Fire Smoke Ammunition	107
5. Check that the Target is Valid	75
6. Rotate to Face the Target	84
7. Check if the Target is Concealed	85
8. Roll to Hit	91
9. Allocate Hits to Target Teams	93
10. Roll Saves for Teams that were Hit	97
11. Roll Firepower Tests	97
12. Mark or Remove Destroyed Teams	103
13. Return to 1 and Select the Next Platoon	
14. Pin Down Platoons if Hit Five Times	104

D THE ASSAULT STEP

During the Assault Step you:	*page*
1. Select the Assaulting Platoon	143
2. Charge into Contact	145
3. Opponent Conducts Defensive Fire	152
4. Roll to Hit with Assaulting Teams	155
5. Roll Saves for Armoured Vehicles	175
6. Mark or Remove Destroyed Teams	103
7. Push into Enemy Positions	160
8. Has Assaulting Platoon Won (if so, Skip to 10)	161
9. Opponent Tests Motivation and either:	
• Counterattacks (Return to 2), or	162
• Breaks Off	165
10. Victor Consolidates	167
11. Return to 1 and Select the Next Platoon	

STARTING STEP

The Starting Step is the administrative step in *Flames Of War*. It is here that you check and update the status of the units under your command, rallying your troops and carrying out various other tasks depending upon the course of the battle. Because each of these tasks is just a small part of a bigger topic, for example Rolling for Air Support is a part of Air Support, we've left the explanation of them for their relevant section of the rule book. As you read on, you'll find each task fully explained in those sections.

Starting Step Sequence

1.	Check Sole Surviving Infantry Teams	176
2.	Check Company Morale	175
3.	Check Victory Conditions	274
4.	Place Ambushes	266
5.	Roll for Air Support	178
6.	Roll for Reserves	268
7.	Rally Pinned Down Platoons	104
8.	Remount Bailed Out Vehicles	102
9.	Free Bogged Down Vehicles	44
10.	Remove Friendly Smoke Markers	107

SS soldier
IWM EA48002

MOVEMENT

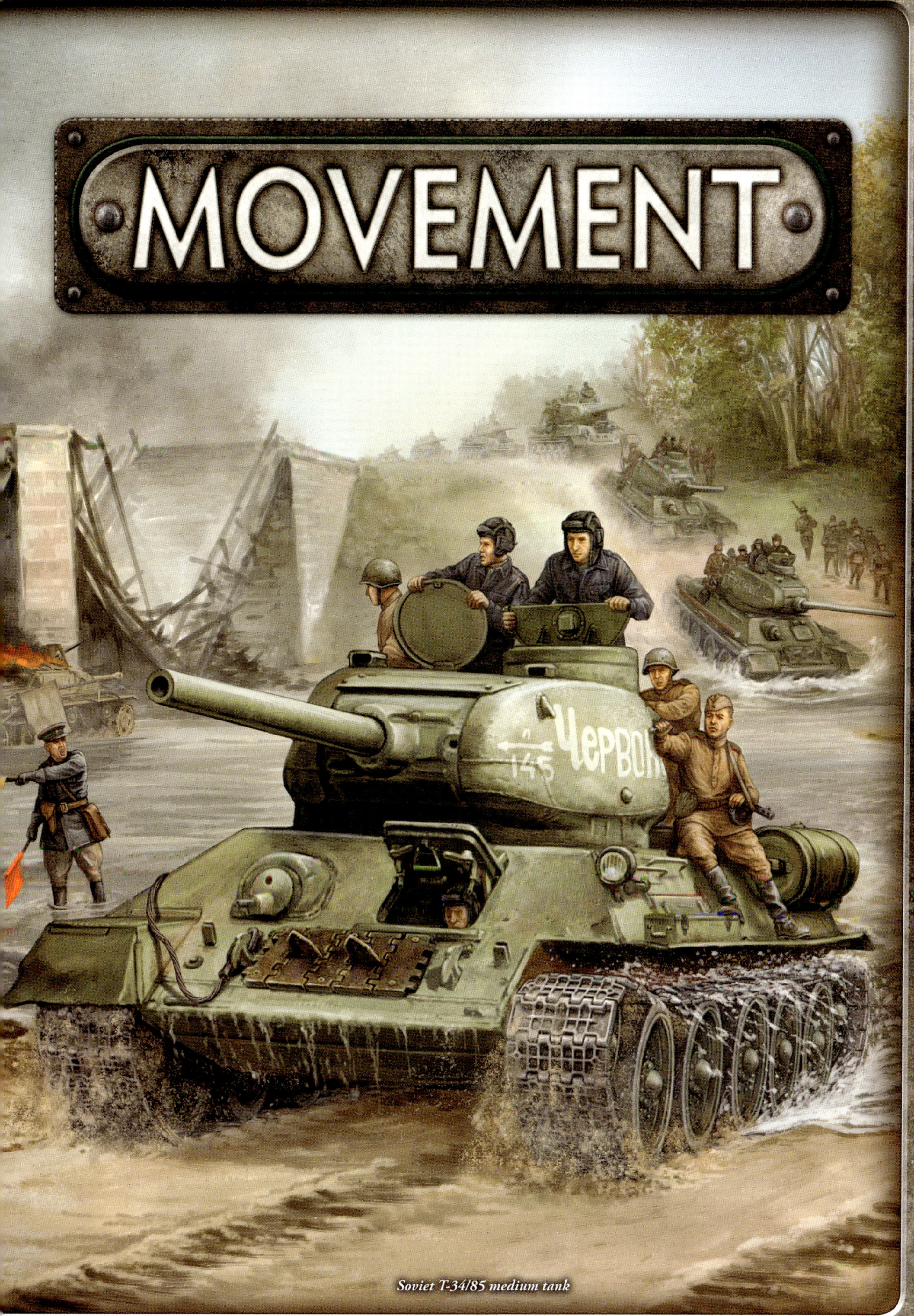

Soviet T-34/85 medium tank

While a battle may seem to be all about shooting, an intelligent commander quickly learns that movement is a crucial component of victory. After all, before you can shoot your enemy you have to put yourself into a tactical position that lets you do so!

While movement may seem a simple matter of getting in close and hitting your opponent with everything you have, it is often worthwhile to use fire and movement tactics, where one part of your force fires to cover the movement of another.

Where to advance is another important consideration. If you pick a place where the terrain is too dense and cluttered, your advance can be slowed to a crawl as your troops attempt to cross obstacle after obstacle. On the other hand, open ground can easily become a shooting gallery for your opponent's troops.

MOVEMENT SEQUENCE

1. Select a Platoon to Move
2. Bring Forward Transports
3. Move Teams in the Platoon
   a. Dismount Passengers before moving Transports
   b. Move Transports before or after Mounting Passengers
   c. Take Bogging Checks in Rough Terrain
   d. Take Skill Tests to Enter Contested Buildings
4. Send Empty Transports to the Rear
5. Return to 1 and Select the Next Platoon to Move

CONTENTS

SELECT A PLATOON TO MOVE

During your turn you are able to move each of your platoons one by one—though you don't have to move any at all. If you feel a platoon is in a good position there are advantages to keeping it stationary, but if their location isn't ideal they can be manoeuvred into a better position. It doesn't matter in what order you move your platoons, or the teams within each platoon, just remember to finish all of your movement with one platoon before moving on to the next one.

During the Movement Step you may move each of your platoons, one at a time. They may be moved in any order you wish, but do not need to be moved if you do not want to move them.

Once you have chosen a platoon, move any or all teams from that platoon one at a time.

After you have moved all teams from a platoon that you want to move, choose another platoon to move and repeat. When you have moved every platoon you wish to move, the Movement Step ends.

FIRE AND MANOEUVRE

MOVE TEAMS IN THE PLATOON

The amount of distance your team can move is determined by the type of troops that are moving. The more mobile the team, the further it can move.

The Movement Distance table gives the maximum distances teams can move over Cross-country Terrain.

Simply look up the relevant Arsenal to find the Mobility rating of the team that you are trying to move to find the maximum distance that the team can move.

Movement Distance	
Fully-tracked Tanks and Transports	
Standard Tank	12"/30cm
Light Tank	16"/40cm
Slow Tank	8"/20cm
Very Slow Tank	6"/15cm
Other Tanks and Transports	
Jeep, Motorcycle	16"/40cm
Half-tracked, Wheeled	12"/30cm
Slow Wheeled, Wagon	8"/20cm
Guns	
Man-packed and Light Guns	6"/15cm
Medium and Heavy Guns	4"/10cm
Immobile Guns	Cannot Move
Infantry	
Cavalry	10"/25cm
Infantry	6"/15cm

See page 62 for a summary of Movement Distances in all types of terrain.

British Sherman tank advancing through a French town
US Signal Corps, NARA

STANDARD TANKS ARE QUITE MOBILE, MOVING 12"/30CM CROSS-COUNTRY.

LIGHT TANKS HAVE POWERFUL ENGINES AND ARE MUCH FASTER, MOVING 16"/40CM.

HEAVY TANKS TEND TO BE SLOWER, MOVING 8"/20CM AS A **SLOW TANK**.

SOME REALLY OLD TANKS ADVANCE AT A WALKING SPEED AND MOVE 6"/15CM AS A **VERY SLOW TANK**.

ASSAULT GUNS MOVE LIKE TANKS. MOST MOVE 12"/30CM AS A **STANDARD TANK**.

SMALL TANKS LACK THE POWER OF FULL-SIZED TANKS, MOVING 12"/30CM AS **HALF-TRACKED** VEHICLES.

Tanks

Armoured cars with half tracks, half wheels, move 12"/30cm as **Half-Tracked** vehicles.

Most armoured cars are wheeled tanks. They move 12"/30cm as **Wheeled** vehicles.

Smaller, light weight armoured cars and big multi-wheeled vehicles move 16"/40cm as **Jeeps**.

The heaviest armoured cars are not as nimble, moving 8"/20cm as **Slow Wheeled** vehicles.

Truck-mounted guns fight as unarmoured tanks, moving 12"/30cm as **Wheeled** vehicles.

Jeeps and motorcycles often act as reconnaissance vehicles, moving 16"/40cm as **Jeeps**.

Infantry

Infantry are the mainstay of every army. They move 6"/15cm on foot.

Horsed cavalry still have a place in modern warfare. They move 10"/25cm as **Cavalry**.

Guns

Heavy machine-guns and mortars are carried by their crews, moving 6"/15cm as **Man-Packed Guns**.

Lightweight guns can be pushed by their crews. They move 6"/15cm as **Light Guns**.

Heavier guns can still be moved by their crews, moving 4"/10cm as **Medium** or **Heavy Guns**.

The heaviest guns need a tractor to move. They are **Immobile** and cannot move on their own.

Transports

Commanders often use fast jeeps as their personal transport, moving 16"/40cm as **Jeeps**.

Half-tracked transports give good cross-country mobility, moving 12"/30cm as **Half-Tracked** vehicles.

Trucks are cheap and still move 12"/30cm as **Wheeled** vehicles.

Heavy trucks move 8"/20cm as **Slow Wheeled** vehicles.

Although expensive, some armies use tracked transports. Most move 8"/20cm like a **Slow Tank**.

Horses are a major form of transport for European armies. They move 8"/20cm as **Wagons**.

Moving a Team

When you move a platoon, all of the teams in the platoon are moved separately. You can choose to have a team move in a different direction from the rest of the platoon or to move some teams in a platoon while you leave others in their current positions.

A team may move in any direction and end up facing any way you wish, just as long as the distance it covers in its complete movement is no further than the team's maximum allowed movement distance.

A team does not have to move in a straight line, and can deviate and zigzag as much as you like. Use the path travelled to determine the distance moved, rather than just the distance between the starting and end points.

Rotating Teams

Troops in combat tend to move slowly in fits and spurts, pausing between dashes to look out for enemy fire and time their sprints to avoid getting shot. After each dash they stop facing the enemy, ready to fight.

Teams can rotate to face in any direction at any time when they move, as long as this does not increase the total distance moved.

Although Immobile Guns cannot move any distance, they can still rotate about their centre as their movement.

Moving Through Friendly Teams

Soldiers and vehicles make way for friendly troops, and resume their positions once they pass.

Teams can move through other friendly teams, but a team cannot end its movement on top of another team.

Moving Near the Enemy

Movement towards an objective is quite a different manoeuvre than simply rolling your way across an open field. You must take care to ensure that you don't jeopardise your units or unnecessarily expose them to harm.

Infantry and Gun teams may not move closer than 2"/5cm to any visible enemy team and must stop moving when an unseen enemy team within 2"/5cm becomes visible to it (except in the Assault Step).

Vehicles can move within 2"/5cm of enemy vehicles (even passing through their position), but cannot end their movement on top of an enemy vehicle. However, vehicles may not move closer than 2"/5cm to an enemy Infantry or Gun team that is visible to it (except in the Assault Step).

Moving a Team

Moving Near the Enemy in Buildings

The walls of a building allow opponents to sneak up on each other. Troops only move up to an enemy-occupied building when they are ready to assault and clear it.

A team may move freely near an enemy Infantry or Gun team on the other side of the wall of a Building, except that it may not move within 2"/5cm of an enemy Infantry or Gun team measuring through an Opening within Line of Sight of your team (except, as usual, in the Assault Step).

As there is nothing to block Line of Sight, a team may not move within 2"/5cm of an enemy Infantry or Gun team that is in the same Building (again, except in the Assault Step).

Move Teams in the Platoon

SUMMARY

- Teams can move in any direction by any route as long as the distance covered is no more than its Movement Distance.
- Teams can rotate to face any direction as long as it stays within its Movement Distance.
- Teams can move through friendly teams.
- Infantry and Gun teams cannot move within 2"/5cm of enemy teams.
- Vehicles cannot move within 2"/5cm of enemy Infantry or Gun teams.
- Measure the distance to the enemy through Openings in Buildings.

WHEELED VEHICLES ON ROADS

Roads allow troops to avoid obstacles and move quickly from place to place. Roads are of particular benefit to wheeled vehicles that have relatively poor cross-country performance. Once on a road, the wheeled transport can actually use their high speed.

Jeep, Motorcycle, Half-tracked, Wheeled, Slow Wheeled, and Wagon vehicles move one and a half times as fast as normal when they spend their entire Movement Step on Roads.

All other types of teams, including Fully-tracked vehicles, Infantry (including Cavalry) and Gun teams, move at the same speed on Roads as they do Cross-country.

Wheeled and Half-tracked Vehicles Movement on Road

All Wheeled and Half-tracked vehicles move one-and-a-half times as fast on Roads.

Jeep, Motorcycle	24"/60cm
Half-tracked, Wheeled	18"/45cm
Slow Wheeled, Wagon	12"/30cm

See page 62 for a summary of Movement Distances in all types of terrain.

Wheeled Vehicles on Roads

German 15cm sFH18 howitzer being strafed by a P-51 Mustang fighter-bomber

MOVING THROUGH ROUGH TERRAIN

While tanks aren't generally fast, they are almost unstoppable. Their tracks and powerful engines allow them to plough through terrain that would immobilise a truck. Only troops on foot can match them in rough terrain.

Fully-tracked vehicles cannot move more than 8"/20cm if they start their movement in, enter or cross Rough Terrain (see page 24). Since Slow vehicles can only move 8"/20cm and Very Slow vehicles can only move 6"/15cm anyway, Rough Terrain does not slow them down at all.

Jeep, Motorcycle, Half-tracked, Wheeled, Slow Wheeled, and Wagon vehicles, and Guns (apart from Man-packed Guns) cannot move more than 4"/10cm if they start their movement in, or enter or cross Rough Terrain.

All other types of teams including Infantry and Man-packed Gun teams, move at the same speed in Rough Terrain as they do normally.

No Stopping on Linear Obstacles

Balancing models on top of hedges is messy!

A team may not end its movement on top of Linear Obstacles. It must be on one side or the other. If a team does not have enough movement to cross a Linear Obstacle, it stops on reaching it.

Moving through Mixed Terrain

To keep things simple, teams can only enter rough terrain if they move at the rough terrain speed for the whole turn.

A team may not enter Rough Terrain if it has already moved further than it is allowed to in Rough Terrain. Instead the team must stop at the edge of the Rough Terrain and wait until next turn to move into it.

Fully-tracked Vehicles Movement Distance in Rough Terrain	
Standard Tank	8"/20cm
Light Tank	8"/20cm
Slow Tank	8"/20cm
Very Slow Tank	6"/15cm

Other Vehicles Movement Distance in Rough Terrain	
All other vehicles	4"/10cm

See page 62 for a summary of Movement Distances in all types of terrain.

Moving Through Rough Terrain

Tactics

Move from Cover to Cover

Move from cover to cover whenever possible.

Don't stop in the open unless you absolutely have to, as you give the enemy a perfect target when you do.

Moving Through Gaps

Tactics

Taking the Shortest Route

Sometimes the shortest route is not the quickest. It's no good taking the shortest route to where you want to go, if that means a couple of teams from your platoon end up stuck, leaving the rest of your platoon unsupported and vulnerable to enemy attack.

Moving Through Gaps

Sometimes the gaps between obstacles are too narrow for a vehicle to pass through, forcing the driver to slow down and force their way through the obstacles.

If the gap between two pieces of terrain, or between a team or wrecked vehicle and terrain, is too small for a Tank, Transport, or Gun team to fit between, the team must move through one or both pieces of terrain to get through the gap.

If their vehicle and gun models can fit through the gap, the team does not need to pass through the Rough Terrain on either side, even if their base is wider than the gap.

Infantry teams can move through any gap at least ¼"/5mm wide.

Ignore any bases that vehicles, infantry, or guns are mounted on and assume that guns close their trails to move through gaps when determining if they can fit through.

Discuss Terrain Before the Game

Since it is physically impossible for two model terrain pieces to be perfectly touching, you should discuss with your opponent which pieces of terrain are supposed to be touching and which are supposed to have a gap. It may be a good idea to move pieces a little further apart where there is supposed to be a gap to make it clear.

Summary

Moving Through Rough Terrain

- **Reduce movement through Rough Terrain to 8"/20cm for Fully-tracked vehicles.**
- **Movement through Rough Terrain reduced to 4"/10cm for other vehicles and guns.**
- **Infantry and Man-packed Gun teams do not reduce their movement in Rough Terrain.**
- **Teams cannot enter Rough Terrain if they have already moved more than their Rough Terrain Movement Distance.**

Making Bogging Checks

As well as slowing down, vehicles moving through rough terrain run the risk of breakdown or getting stuck.

Vehicles in Rough Terrain

Even tanks, which are specifically designed to cross rough terrain, aren't immune to sinking deep into a marsh or getting hung up on a tree stump!

Bogging Down

Vehicles of all kinds have a habit of getting stuck or 'bogged down' when crossing rough terrain. The worse the going, the more likely they are to bog down.

Each time a vehicle attempts to cross Difficult Going or Very Difficult Going it must pass a Bogging Check to cross safely. Teams take a Bogging Check as they enter Area Terrain, start moving in Area Terrain, or attempt to cross a Linear Obstacle. Even if a vehicle's movement is just rotating on the spot in Area Terrain, it still needs to take a Bogging Check.

If a team attempts to cross multiple obstacles in the same turn, it takes a Bogging Check for each one.

Slow Going

Slow going forces drivers to slow down, but presents no real risk of getting stuck.

Slow Going is Rough Terrain and reduces the speed of vehicles crossing it accordingly, but does not require a Bogging Check to cross.

Difficult Going

Difficult going is the bane of vehicle drivers. No matter how carefully you proceed there is always the chance that you and your vehicle will become stranded.

Difficult Going is Rough Terrain and reduces the speed of vehicles crossing it, and can cause them to become Bogged Down. Each time a vehicle needs to take a Bogging Check for crossing Difficult Going, roll a die.

- *On a roll of 2+ the team continues moving without any problems.*
- *A roll of 1 means that the team has Bogged Down, and may not move any further until it is freed.*

Very Difficult Going

The only thing worse than crossing through muck that might get you stuck is going into stuff that you know will bog you down.

Very Difficult Going is Rough Terrain and reduces the speed of vehicles crossing it, and can cause them to become Bogged Down. Each time a Fully-tracked or Half-tracked vehicle needs to take a Bogging Check for crossing Very Difficult Going, roll a Skill Test (see page 18).

- *If they pass the Skill Test the team continues moving without any problems.*
- *If they fail, the team has Bogged Down, and may not move any further until it is freed.*

Other types of vehicles may not attempt to cross Very Difficult Going.

Bogging Down in Difficult Going

Guns in Rough Terrain

Gun crews have even more trouble manhandling their guns across rough terrain than tanks.

Guns in Difficult Going

Guns are manhandled into position, but if the terrain is difficult, they might find themselves stuck instead.

Light, Medium, or Heavy Gun teams must pass a Bogging Check to cross Difficult Going in the same way as vehicles.

No Guns in Very Difficult Going

While gunners can move their guns through some obstacles, they simply can't move through really difficult going at all.

Light, Medium, or Heavy Gun teams may not attempt to enter, exit, or cross Very Difficult Going, including when Limbered to a Transport team (see page 49).

However, Gun teams may begin the game in Very Difficult Going—their crews having spent the time to haul them into position before the battle begins. Once there, they cannot move, even to rotate on the spot, since it will take just as many hours to haul them out again. Gun teams, other than Man-packed Gun teams, may only be placed on the ground floor of a Building.

Infantry and Man-packed Guns in Rough Terrain

Unlike vehicles, troops on foot or horseback can go just about anywhere. They can cross almost any obstacle and make their way through all but truly impassable terrain.

Infantry teams (including Cavalry) and Man-packed Gun teams never become Bogged Down and do not need to take Bogging Checks regardless of the terrain encountered. They move at the same rate on Roads, and through Cross Country and Rough Terrain.

SUMMARY

Making Bogging Checks

- **Vehicles and Gun teams Bog Down if they roll a 1 when moving in Difficult Going.**
- **Fully-tracked and Half-tracked vehicles Bog Down if they fail a Skill Test when moving in Very Difficult Going.**
- **Other vehicles and guns (unless Man-packed) cannot move in Very Difficult Going.**
- **Infantry and Man-packed Gun teams never Bog Down.**

Bogged Down Teams

Once a vehicle is bogged down, the crew dismounts to fix the problem. They may be directing the driver from the ground, trying to wedge timber under the tread for traction, digging the wheels out of holes, or fixing a broken track. Whatever measures they are taking, they can't fight until they're going again.

Place a marker beside vehicles or Gun teams that have Bogged Down. They may not move or fight (including Shooting, firing Artillery Bombardments and fighting in Assaults) until the crew frees their vehicle or gun.

Bogged Down guns and vehicles end their movement at the point they had to take the Bogging Check. A team that Bogged Down entering a wood stops halfway into the woods, while one that Bogged Down within a wood stops where it was. A team that Bogged Down on a hedge stops as it reaches the hedge, and one that Bogged Down entering a Building stops as it reaches the Building.

Passengers may Dismount from a Bogged Down vehicle at the start of their next Movement Step as normal.

Freeing Bogged Down Teams

The problem isn't being stuck, it's getting free before your time runs out.

At the start of your turn, in the Starting Step, roll a Skill Test for each Bogged Down team.

- *If the test is successful, the crew manages to Free their vehicle or gun.*
- *If you fail the test, the crew are still trying to sort the problem out and remain Bogged Down. Roll again to free the team at the start of your next turn.*

A team that Frees itself can move, shoot and assault as normal that turn. If the team wishes to move through the same Rough Terrain again in the turn it Frees itself, it must take a new Bogging Check.

Bogged Down Command Tank

Officers don't have time to wait around while their crew get their tank back into operation after getting it bogged down, they simply commandeer someone else's tank.

If one of your Command Tank teams is Bogged Down, you may take over another tank using the Bogged or Bailed Command Tanks rule on page 105.

SUMMARY

- **Bogged Down teams stop immediately and cannot move or fight until Freed.**
- **Roll a Skill Test in the Starting Step to Free a Bogged Down team. Once Freed, it moves and shoots as normal.**

RECOVERY VEHICLES

Often it is easier, and more expedient, to simply have another vehicle pull a bogged vehicle out rather than leave the crew to fend for themselves. This greatly increases the odds of getting the vehicle unstuck and back on the move.

If a Recovery Vehicle that is not Bogged Down or Bailed Out ends the Movement Step touching a Bogged Down, Bailed Out, or Destroyed vehicle or Gun team, it can tow them instead of shooting.

Move the Recovery Vehicle and the team being towed up to 4"/10cm. The team being towed is Freed and no longer Bogged Down. If it does this, neither the Recovery Vehicle nor the team it towed may move further, shoot, or take part in an assault this turn.

If the Recovery Vehicle is in Rough Terrain when it starts towing the vehicle, it must take a Bogging Check before towing the vehicle.

Recovery Vehicles are Independent Teams

Recovery vehicles are manned by mechanics whose job is to keep everyone else moving. When they see a vehicle in trouble, they head off to fix it.

Recovery Vehicles are Independent teams, so are able to move wherever they need to go to do their job.

Bogged Down Marker

If one of your vehicles bogs down, place a marker next to it to remind you that it cannot move or shoot and to try to free it at the start of your next turn.

Improvised Vehicle Recovery

Almost any vehicle can be used to help a stuck vehicle, though they don't always have the proper tools and equipment to get the job done.

Any vehicle that is not Bogged Down or Bailed Out can attempt to tow a team as a Recovery Vehicle, provided that the model being towed is of the same size or smaller than the towing model.

When towing a team with a vehicle that is not a Recovery Vehicle take a Skill Test for the towing team.

- *If the Skill Test succeeds, the vehicle tows the team as if it were a Recovery Vehicle.*
- *Otherwise the team is not towed.*

Any attempt at towing, whether successful or not, leaves the improvised Recovery Vehicle and the team being towed unable to move further, shoot, or assault this turn.

SUMMARY

- **Recovery Vehicles touching a Bogged Down, Bailed Out, or Destroyed team may tow it up to 4"/10cm in the Shooting Step.**
- **Towed teams are no longer Bogged Down at end of the Shooting Step.**
- **Any vehicle may tow a team the same size or smaller like a Recovery Vehicle by passing a Skill Test.**
- **Towing or being towed prevents all further movement, shooting, and assaults that turn.**

Recovery Vehicles

TRANSPORTS AND PASSENGERS

Though troops on foot have their advantages, in general it is much easier, and more effective, to get soldiers to and from the battlefield in transport vehicles.

Carrying Capacity

A squad's vehicle is their home. It carries their personal belongings and spare ammunition, so naturally soldiers are reluctant to allow others to borrow their transport. Of course, if another squad's transport breaks down, they'll give them a lift, but there is no way another platoon is going to make off with their vehicles!

Transport teams may carry Infantry and Man-packed Gun teams as Passengers and are able to tow other types of Gun teams.

Transport teams may only be used to carry teams from their own platoon. Teams ride in their own section or squad's Transport teams. If their own Transport team is Destroyed, they must be evenly distributed across their platoon's other available Transport teams.

A Transport team can only carry a maximum of six teams as Passengers (including up to one towed Gun team). Pioneer, Supply, Ammo, Demolition Carrier, and Recovery vehicles may not carry any Passengers.

> It is important to keep track of which team is in what vehicle. You might do this by marking vehicles for particular squads, or by drawing a box for each vehicle on a piece of paper and placing teams in the boxes.

Independent Teams Ride Anywhere

While most of the time squads do their best to keep other people out of their transports, no one can say no when the 'Old Man' asks for a ride.

Independent and Warrior teams are able to ride in any Transport team capable of carrying them, from any platoon.

Ignore Passengers

While infantry on foot are well positioned to ambush a vehicle attempting to drive through them, once mounted in a vehicle, they have no ability to interfere with passing vehicles at all.

While mounted, Passengers do not stop their vehicle from moving within 2"/5cm of enemy vehicles, nor do they stop enemy vehicles moving within 2"/5cm of their vehicle.

Tank Escorts

Some tanks are particularly vulnerable to attacks by enemy infantry. They are given dedicated escorting infantry to protect them.

Tank Escorts are part of their Tank team, they are not separate teams and are not Passengers. Tank teams with Tank Escorts cannot carry Passengers.

Mounting Transports

When the time comes to move quickly, troops mount up and move out. If they have to wait for their transports to arrive first, things can take a lot longer.

Unless otherwise stated, teams can only Mount a Transport team in the Movement Step.

Only teams that started their turn Dismounted may Mount Transport teams. Teams that move far enough to reach a Transport team's passenger compartment can Mount it as Passengers.

If the Transport team has already moved when the Passengers Mount up, it cannot move any further.

If the Transport team has not yet moved when the Passengers Mount it, the Transport team can now move as normal. As long as the Passengers did not move At the Double (see page 50) to reach their vehicle, the Transport team can move At the Double after they Mount.

Mounting Transports

DISMOUNTING TRANSPORTS

DISMOUNTING TRANSPORTS

The whole point of transports is to get someone somewhere, and then for them to get out and fight!

Teams that started their turn Mounted may Dismount from Transport teams at the start of their Movement Step, prior to the Transport team moving. Unless otherwise stated, teams can only Dismount from a Transport team in the Movement Step.

When they Dismount, Passengers move as though they had begun their movement in the passenger compartment of the Transport team.

A Transport team cannot move before unloading Passengers and counts as moving, even if it does not move after the Passengers Dismount.

An empty Transport team (unless a Pioneer, Supply, Ammo, Demolition Carrier, or Recovery Transport team) must be Sent to the Rear when the last Passengers Dismount. Some German armoured half-tracks are an exception to this, remaining on table without passengers using the Mounted Assault special rule (see page 243).

TRANSPORT PLATOONS

Though some platoons have dedicated transports to support their activities, it is much more common to ask for a transport platoon when they need it.

A Transport Platoon operates as its own platoon. It must operate together picking up and dropping off other platoons as needed. Teams from a Transport Platoon can never be allocated out to other platoons.

Transport teams from Transport Platoons may carry or tow teams from any other platoons without restriction. They can even carry teams from several platoons at once if necessary.

Transport teams from Transport Platoons can each carry up to six Infantry or Man-packed Gun teams. They may tow one Gun team in place of one of their normal Passenger teams.

RIDING ON TANKS

Often infantry 'hitch a lift' on the engine decking of tanks. It's not a particularly safe means of getting about, and it certainly isn't comfortable, but it beats walking.

Tank teams can carry up to three Infantry or Man-packed Gun teams in the same manner as Transport teams carrying Passengers. Teams riding on tanks must be spread evenly across all tanks in the platoon.

A Tank team carrying Passengers must have infantry models, or some other identifiable token, placed on the rear deck of the tank to indicate that it is carrying passengers.

Passengers on Tank teams Mount and Dismount in the same way as Passengers in any other sort of transport.

Flame-throwing tanks may not carry Passengers—no sane infantryman can be convinced to ride on a 'mobile bomb'! They'd rather walk, no matter the discomfort.

Send Transports to the Rear

Because most transport vehicles are so vulnerable—lacking both firepower and armour—they are normally sent to the rear when their passengers dismount.

You must remove empty Transport teams (unless Pioneer, Supply, Ammo, Demolition Carrier, or Recovery Transport teams) from the table at the end of any Step. Transport teams removed in this fashion do not count as Destroyed.

When a Bogged Down (see page 43) or Bailed Out (see page 102) Transport team is Sent to the Rear, it ceases to be Bogged Down or Bailed Out.

The Mounted Assault special rule (see page 243) allows empty German armoured half-tracks to remain on table.

Bring Transports Forward

When their charges need them again, the transports come forward and pick them up.

Before moving a platoon, you may place all of its Transport teams (other than those that have been Destroyed) that have been Sent to the Rear or did not deploy on the table, back on the table.

The Transport teams must be placed within 4"/10cm of a team from their platoon, and may not be:

- *within 16"/40cm of any enemy team within Line of Sight, unless Concealed by Terrain from it, or*
- *within 4"/10cm of any enemy team, or*
- *within 8"/20cm of any enemy Recce team that is in Line of Sight (apart from Recce teams that are Bogged Down, Bailed Out, or moved at the Double).*

Once Brought Forward in this way, the Transport teams can mount Passenger teams and move in the normal way, but cannot shoot in the Shooting Step nor assault in the Assault Step. They may however move in either step if they have a special rule such as Avanti or Stormtroopers that allows them to do so.

Specialist Transport Platoons may be Brought Forward to load teams from any friendly platoon.

Transports and Passengers

SUMMARY

- **Transport teams carry up to six Infantry or Man-packed gun teams as Passengers.**
- **Dismounted teams move into a Transport team's passenger compartment to Mount. The Transport team can then move.**
- **Passengers move out of their Transport team's passenger compartment to Dismount. Passengers must Dismount before the Transport team moves. Remove all empty Transport teams.**
- **Tank teams without Tank Escorts may carry up to three Passengers.**
- **Bring a platoon's Transports Forward before it moves. Place each Transport team within 4"/10cm of its platoon. They cannot be placed within 8"/20cm of enemy Recce teams or 4"/10cm of other enemy if Concealed or out of sight, or within 16"/40cm if not Concealed. Passengers can then Mount and the Transport teams move as normal, but cannot shoot or assault.**

Bring Transports Forward

TOWING GUNS AND PORTEES

Pushing a gun is slow and backbreaking work. It is a lot quicker to limber the gun to a tractor (limbering is the gunner's term for hooking the gun to the tractor) and tow it to where you want to unlimber.

Transport teams can carry Gun teams as Passengers. While Man-packed Gun teams are carried in a vehicle like most Passenger teams, Light, Medium, Heavy, and Immobile Gun teams are towed behind the vehicle.

Towed Gun teams Limber and Unlimber their guns in the same way that other teams Mount and Dismount, except that each Transport team can only tow one Gun team. When a Gun team Unlimbers from its Transport team it starts its movement in its current location, and moves from there rather than from the passenger compartment.

Place Limbered Guns Behind Transports

A towing vehicle and its gun form a single entity when on the move. One is useless without the other until the crew dismount, unlimber their gun and go into action.

When it moves, a Towed Gun team is placed as though they were being towed behind the Transport team in which it is a Passenger. As Passengers, they do not need to take Bogging Checks separately from the vehicle.

The model of the Towed Gun and the Transport team towing it are both considered to be the Transport team when shot at, bombarded, assaulted and so forth.

Jeeps and Motorcycles Towing Guns

A jeep is barely able to tow a large gun and carry its ammunition, so it doesn't have room for the crew as well. As a result, the crew walk alongside, slowing progress.

The British and Americans sometimes used Bantam, Ford, and Willys jeeps to tow guns. The Germans used motorcycles and Kettenkrad tracked motorcycles in the same role. Any of these vehicles towing a Gun team can only move 8"/20cm on Roads and Cross Country.

Crash Action

Gun crews are trained to get their guns into action quickly. If a gun comes under fire while being towed, the crew leap out of their vehicle, unlimber the gun, and open fire.

A Gun team is not considered to have moved when it Unlimbers as long as it does not move other than rotating on the spot.

Dismounting Portee Guns

Some guns were carried '*en portée*' on the load bed of a truck rather than being towed to allow the gun to fire on the move.

A Tank team with the Portee attribute may Dismount its weapon by Sending the vehicle to the Rear and replacing it with a Gun team equipped with the same weapon, as if it were Unlimbering from a Transport team.

A Gun team Dismounted from a Portee may Mount again by Bringing Forward the vehicle as if it were a Transport team. Replace the Gun team with the Portee Tank team rather than placing the vehicle near the Gun team.

Portee guns may deploy as Dismounted Gun teams having already Sent their vehicle to the Rear.

SUMMARY

- **Man-packed Gun teams are carried as Passengers. Other Gun teams Limber and Unlimber in the same way other teams Mount and Dismount.**
- **Limbered Gun teams are placed behind their Transport teams, becoming part of the Transport team.**
- **Gun teams Unlimber in place and do not have to move.**

Towing Guns

MOVING AT THE DOUBLE

Sometimes speed is more important than safety. Maybe you have held a platoon in reserve waiting for that crucial breakthrough, and you want to move them fast once you know where it is going to happen. Maybe you're surrounded and the only option is a quick retreat. Regardless, a team can try to move at the double to gain this vital speed.

Any or all teams in a platoon that is not Pinned Down (see page 104) may elect to move At the Double. Those teams that move At the Double may move twice as far as normal.

When moving At the Double, teams may not:

- *Pass within 8"/20cm of an enemy team (other than an Independent team that is not a Warrior),*
- *Move through Rough Terrain (see page 41),*

Take the Most Direct Route

If you are moving fast you don't have time for clever tactical manoeuvres. You just point in the direction you need to go, and move!

Teams that move At the Double must follow the most direct route and may only change direction to avoid Rough Terrain, or coming within 8"/20cm of the enemy, or to follow a Road. They must end their movement facing in the direction they moved.

No Time for Delays

When moving at the double there isn't time for slow terrain, combat or clever tactics.

If a team moved At the Double, it may not take any further action this turn. It cannot move further, shoot, or assault. Other teams in the platoon can operate as normal.

Targets Moving at the Double

An enemy team moving at the double is not using concealment and has thrown caution to the wind.

Teams roll twice as many dice as normal when shooting at teams that moved At the Double. Artillery bombardments and air attacks against teams moving At the Double are no more effective than normal.

SUMMARY

- **At the Double, teams move up to twice as far as normal. They must take the most direct route and end facing the direction travelled.**
- **Teams must not be Pinned Down and may not move through Rough Terrain or move within 8"/20cm of the enemy.**
- **Teams moving At the Double cannot take any further action this turn.**

Moving At the Double

DIGGING IN

When riflemen halt, the first thing they do is dig themselves burrows in the earth for protection from enemy fire. They call their holes by many names: foxholes, slit trenches, slitties, and rifle pits. It's impossible to dig a proper slit trench in a battle situation, but a shallow shell scrape is almost as effective when you are desperate. Regardless of the name, they all minimise the soldier's exposure to enemy fire.

Rather than move, a platoon can use their Movement Step to attempt to Dig In. Platoons can Dig In while Pinned Down (see page 104). To Dig In, the platoon takes a Skill Test.

- *If the Skill Test succeeds, all Infantry and Gun teams in the platoon immediately dig themselves Foxholes.*
- *If the Skill Test fails, the ground is too rocky or hard, or they haven't dug deep enough yet and they remain unprotected.*

Regardless of whether they succeed or not, every team that attempted to Dig In is treated as having moved when determining its ROF if it shoots (see page 91), but not for any other purpose.

When a platoon Digs In, all Infantry and Gun teams in the Platoon that are not already in Bulletproof Cover must Dig In. Teams already in Bulletproof Cover and all vehicles and Cavalry, operate as normal since they do not need to Dig In.

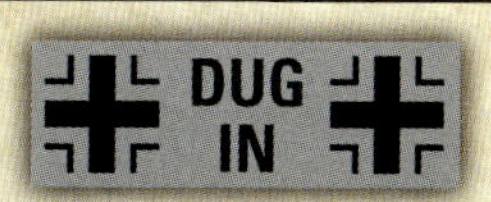

DUG IN MARKER

Show that teams in a platoon are in Foxholes by placing a marker with the Platoon Command team indicating that the whole platoon is Dug In or by putting Foxhole markers in front of the teams.

PIONEER SUPPLY VEHICLES

Pioneer supply vehicles carry stocks of picks, shovels, and explosives that make digging in much easier.

A platoon with a Pioneer Supply vehicle within 2"/5cm of the Platoon Command team, or any Independent team within 2"/5cm of a Pioneer Supply vehicle, may re-roll failed Skill tests to Dig In.

WHERE CAN'T YOU DIG IN

While infantry are very inventive, there are some places they just can't dig a foxhole—such as under water.

Teams that are in water terrain like streams, rivers, swamps and lakes, or on bridges or fords crossing them, cannot Dig In, so operate as normal.

DIGGING IN AND CONCEALMENT

As well as providing protection for the troops occupying them, foxholes make their occupants smaller targets. Unfortunately for most gun crews, their weapon is too big to quickly dig a pit for, so it remains standing tall giving their position away.

Dug In Infantry and Man-packed Gun teams are Concealed and in Bulletproof Cover. As they did not move, they are still Concealed in the Open (see page 89) if they failed their attempt to Dig In.

Dug In Light and Medium Gun teams (other than Anti-aircraft guns) are Concealed and in Bulletproof Cover.

Dug In Heavy and Immobile Gun teams, and Light and Medium Anti-aircraft Gun teams, are not Concealed, but are in Bulletproof Cover unless Concealed by Terrain.

Teams that Dug In or attempted to Dig In can Go to Ground (see page 90) if they do not shoot since they did not move.

LEAVING DUG IN POSITIONS

Though it is a miserable experience to dig a foxhole one minute and leave it the next, sometimes it has to happen. Other troops arriving later are unlikely to take up exactly the same positions, or even find well-concealed foxholes, so will have to dig new positions.

If a Dug In team moves in any way, other than rotating on the spot, it immediately ceases to be Dug In.

As an exception, you may mark the positions of the Dug In teams of a Defending platoon in an assault (see page 151) before moving them to Counterattack. Any team from that platoon that ends the Assault Step back in one of the marked positions becomes Dug In again. If a team cannot reach an unoccupied marked position at the end of the Assault Step, it is no longer Dug In. Remove any unoccupied markers remaining at the end of the Assault Step.

It is not necessary for teams to return to the specific foxholes they began in—only for the platoon to return to the foxholes they collectively dug.

SUMMARY

- **Platoons can Dig In instead of moving, requiring a Skill Test to do so.**
- **Dug In Infantry and Gun teams are in Bulletproof Cover. All Dug In teams, except Heavy, Immobile, and Anti-aircraft Gun teams, are Concealed. As they did not move, they can also Go to Ground.**
- **Teams cease to be Dug In if they move or assault, except when returning to their positions after being assaulted.**

MOVING IN BUILDINGS

Despite the fact that we live our lives in and around buildings, performing military manoeuvres within them can be incredibly challenging. Every attempt to move risks running into obstacles, and roundabout routes must be found to stay away from enemy fire.

OPENINGS

As in normal life, openings like doors and windows are essential for entering and exiting buildings. Even the toughest sergeant can't walk through walls.

Openings are gaps in the walls of Buildings that are big enough to move and shoot through. Windows, doors, and holes blown in the walls are all Openings.

CHECKED BUILDINGS

Soldiers don't just dash into a building without checking it first. They send scouts forward to see who's holding the building, then they either dash inside or plan an assault to push the enemy out.

A Building is a Checked Building if it either contained a friendly team, or a friendly team was touching an Opening into the Building at the start of the current Step. Note that a Building can be Checked even if there is an enemy team inside.

CONTESTED BUILDINGS

Soldiers only stay alive by being cautious. Any building not known to be clear of the enemy has to be assumed to be occupied by the enemy until checked out.

A Building that is not Checked is Contested. A Contested Building can be either empty or occupied by the enemy.

ENTERING BUILDINGS

Entering a building in a combat situation isn't just a matter of walking up and knocking on the door.

ENTERING CHECKED BUILDINGS

It is easy enough to get into a building held by friends. They will have unbarred the door or help drag the new arrivals in through the window.

An Infantry or Man-packed Gun team can move into a Checked Building through any ground-floor Opening. Measure the team's movement up to the Opening and into the Building, just like moving across any other form of terrain.

ENTERING CONTESTED BUILDINGS

An unoccupied building also presents difficulties. Even if the door isn't bolted or barricaded by the owners hoping to protect their possessions, approaching infantry need to be prepared just in case it does turn out to be occupied—by the enemy!

When a moving Infantry or Man-packed Gun team attempts to enter a Contested Building through an Opening that they were not touching at the start of their movement, roll a Skill Test.

- *If it passes the Skill Test, the team enters the Building through the Opening and the Building is now Checked for the rest of the Step.*
- *Otherwise it failed the Skill Test and the team ends its movement for the Step outside the Building touching the Opening it attempted to enter. This blocks further*

ENTERING CHECKED BUILDINGS

troops from using the same Opening this turn. Other teams may still attempt to enter and Check the Building through other Openings.

If a modelled Opening is wider than the Checking team's base, it only blocks its base width of the Opening if it fails its Skill Test, allowing another team to attempt to enter through the remaining part of the Opening.

EXITING BUILDINGS

Once a building has been checked out, troops can pass through it at will as the occupying troops guide them through the maze of rooms to the appropriate exit.

Infantry or Man-packed Gun teams can move through and out of Checked Buildings using a ground-floor Opening.

MOVING ACROSS ALLEYWAYS

Moving Across Alleyways

Soldiers in one building can easily check out a building across a narrow alleyway without exposing themselves too much. If the other building turns out to be unoccupied, they can quickly nip across the alley and into the other building.

If two Buildings are separated by an alleyway that is too narrow to fit a team, treat the two Buildings as being adjacent when crossing the alleyway. If an Infantry or Man-packed Gun team fails to enter a Contested Building across such an alleyway, it remains at the Opening in its own Building since it cannot be placed in the alleyway.

Moving Up or Down

Many buildings have two or more floors or levels. Stairs run between the floors, allowing troops to move up and down. If the stairs have collapsed, soldiers will use rubble and ladders to move up and down instead.

Infantry and Man-packed Gun teams can move up or down by a total of two floors at any time during their movement. This is additional to the normal Movement Distance, so a team can move its full Movement Distance and still move up or down two floors.

If your Buildings don't have any Openings modelled between floors, simply assume that there is a ladder or sufficient rubble to climb up to an Opening in the ceiling of each room.

Guns in Buildings

Getting small, team-carried guns into a building is fairly easy, but it takes a huge amount of effort to get a bigger gun inside.

Man-packed Gun teams enter and exit Buildings like Infantry teams.

Other Gun teams may not enter, exit, or move in a Building during a game, but they can be deployed on the ground floor of a Building at the start of the game.

MULTI-STORY BUILDINGS

Driving Through Buildings

A tank will never fit through a door, but that doesn't matter at all—it simply makes its own opening. Tanks can go almost anywhere, until they fall into a cellar or have the whole house collapse on top of them!

Fully-armoured vehicles are the only type of vehicles that can enter Buildings. Other types of vehicles cannot enter a Building or be deployed in one at the start of the game.

Fully-armoured vehicles do not need an Opening (and cannot use Openings) to enter a Building, they simply drive straight through. As Buildings are Very Difficult Going, they still need to pass a Skill Test to enter, exit, or move within or through a Building.

The debris from falling walls and ceilings immediately closes off the hole smashed by the tank, leaving no Opening for infantry or other vehicles to follow.

Summary

Moving in Buildings

- Buildings are either Checked or Contested. Checked Buildings contain a friendly team or have a friendly team at an opening.
- Infantry teams can freely move through Openings in Checked Buildings, but must pass a Skill Test to move into a Contested Building, and block the Opening if they fail.
- Teams can climb or descend up to two floors in a Building while moving.
- Man-packed Gun teams move through Buildings as Infantry. Other Gun teams cannot move in Buildings, but can be Deployed there.
- Fully-armoured vehicles treat Buildings as Very Difficult Going. Other vehicles cannot move through Buildings.

American soldiers with a .50 cal machine-gun entering a building
IWM EA53096

CROSSING RIVERS

When a river crossing was expected, special equipment was moved forward to assist the effort. Boats, rafts and other floatation devices helped the men get across. When a crossing was unexpected, the unit would use any means available to hastily cross the river. This would include local boats, rafts, or even stringing a rope across the river.

Paddling Across the River

When the infantry set out across the river, each was given a landing point on the opposite bank.

A wide River or canal is normally Impassable. However Infantry (including Cavalry) and Man-packed Gun teams can paddle across Impassable Rivers up to 8"/20cm wide. To do so an Infantry or Man-packed Gun team must begin its Movement Step square against the edge of the River.

In the Movement Step the team moves directly across the River to touch the opposite bank. It is placed in the River to show that it is still crossing.

If crossing the River would put the team within 2"/5cm of an enemy team, the team cannot cross the River. The team must either move further along the bank and cross in a subsequent turn, or wait until the enemy is cleared from the far bank.

No Shooting or Assaulting

While paddling their assault boats across the river, the men have one goal in mind—get to the other side as fast as possible. They are too busy making their way across to do anything else!

While crossing the River, teams may not shoot, move, assault, or be assaulted, and take no part in any assault happening around them.

Sitting Ducks

Sitting in a boat is not the best place to be in a fight. There is nowhere to grab cover or dodge incoming fire.

Teams cannot be Concealed in the Open (see page 89) or Gone to Ground (see page 90) while in a River. The exception to this is that Smoke markers have their normal effect of making teams seen through them Concealed and Gone to Ground (see pages 107 and 137)

Teams crossing a River do not have their normal Infantry or Gun Save. Instead, roll a die for each hit:

- *If the result is 5+, the team manages to avoid any casualties despite their exposed position.*
- *Otherwise, the team has been cut down during the crossing and is Destroyed.*

Pioneers

Pioneers have trained extensively on crossing rivers and may have assault boats with outboard engines, allowing them to cross quickly and with little difficulty.

Pioneer Infantry teams ignore the Sitting Ducks rule, and retain their normal 3+ Infantry Save.

Landing on the Other Side

As soon as the soldiers got to the other side they moved quickly to clear the bank for the follow-up troops.

In the turn after entering the River, a team that began the turn in the River completes its crossing.

The team moves as normal movement from its landing point on the River bank.

Soviet Infantry attacking across a river.

Crossing Rivers

A Contested Crossing

Since you cannot enter the river if there are enemy within 2"/5cm of your intended landing point, you may have to use firepower to make a gap before you can cross the river.

If your opponent moves troops up to contest your crossing after you have entered the river, they still can't stop you crossing as they can't come within 2"/5cm of the crossing team and cannot assault into the river. On the other hand, your teams can assault out of the river as they land, opening the way for others to cross after them.

Summary

- **Infantry, Cavalry and Man packed Gun teams can cross Impassable Rivers up to 8"/20cm wide if they start their Movement Step touching the bank.**
- **Move crossing teams directly across the River until they are touching the far bank (but not within 2"/5cm of the enemy).**
- **While crossing, teams can't shoot, assault or be assaulted and, unless Pioneer teams, pass saves on a 5+ instead of 3+.**
- **Next turn crossing teams move out of the River, but can't move At the Double.**

NORMANDY HEDGEROWS

Fighting in the *Bocage* is essentially the same as fighting anywhere else. However, the restricted fields of fire and the difficulty of manoeuvre require careful tactics to overcome.

The *Bocage* is an area covering the southern and western part of Normandy. It is made up of many small irregular fields bordered by the hedgerows that give the area its name. *Bocage* hedgerows have thick stone banks, formed when the fields were cleared in antiquity, topped by dense hedges of trees and bushes. While the hedgerows are excellent for keeping cattle from straying, they are almost impassable to vehicles and even to troops on foot they present a major obstacle.

The area is rural, so most roads are small lanes designed for horse-drawn carts, barely wide enough for a motorised vehicle. The main roads between the towns are wider and more modern, but few and far between. Roads are usually banked up on both sides and lined with trees that often meet overhead.

The farm buildings are usually made of the same grey stone as the hedgerow banks. The tile-roofed houses are rather plain with little in the way of decoration to break their square lines.

The farmers of the area mostly raise cattle to make the famous cheeses of the region and grow apples to make into potent Calvados brandy. Crops like corn and wheat are mainly restricted to the flatter open areas around Caen.

Bocage on the Tabletop

The *Bocage* extended 60 miles (100 km) from north to south, and over half of that east to west. Apart from farmhouses, small villages, enclosed orchards, and occasional woods, the entire area of a battle fought in the *Bocage* should be covered in *bocage* hedgerows. *Bocage* fighting requires far more troops to defend the same frontage and slows down forward movement dramatically. As a result, you will need to fight over a half-sized table (4'x3'/120cm x 90cm or 4'x4'/120cm x 120cm).

Bocage fields typically scale out to be 6-12"/15-30cm across by 8-16"/20-40cm long. They are usually entirely surrounded by *bocage* hedgerows with few gates through the banks. Some fields do not have a gate at all, just an opening barely wide enough to allow a wheelbarrow or cow to pass through.

Placing small patches of *bocage* terrain on a normal gaming table does not tend to work well as it essentially becomes impassable terrain for tank forces and slows down infantry battles. In this situation, it is better to treat *bocage* hedgerows as tall normal hedgerows as this could be anywhere in Europe.

Bocage Hedgerows

Hedgerows are the defining feature of the *bocage*. They make cross-country movement a nightmare and give the enemy plenty of cover and concealment.

Crossing Bocage Hedgerows

The banks of *bocage* hedgerows are stone walls 6 feet (1.8m) or more tall and up to twice as thick. The roots of the trees growing on the banks bind them together into an impenetrable mass.

Bocage Hedgerows are Very Difficult Going, but only Infantry and Man-packed Gun teams on foot, and Fully-tracked vehicles can cross them at all.

In addition, the hedgerows are so overgrown that teams must stop their movement on reaching a Bocage Hedgerow, ready to cross next turn. A team must start their movement touching a Bocage Hedgerow to cross it. This can result in disjointed movement with a platoon taking several turns to cross a hedgerow as each echelon moves up to the hedgerow and crosses in turn.

Like any Linear Obstacle, teams cannot end a Step sitting on a Bocage Hedgerow. They must be on one side or the other and clearly either touching the Hedgerow or back from it.

Moving Through Gates in Bocage

While gates are much easier to travel through, they are narrow and overgrown, making negotiating them slow and tricky.

Gates in Bocage Hedgerows are Difficult Going. Like the Bocage Hedgerows, teams must start their movement touching a Gate to use it, and must stop their movement upon reaching a Gate in a Bocage Hedgerow.

Belly Up!

Tanks stuck on *bocage* hedgerows usually found themselves stranded with their nose pointing to the sky—and their belly pointing to the enemy!

Any Armoured vehicle Bogged Down on a Bocage Hedgerow uses its Side armour rating as its Front armour rating when hit from the front. The hit still counts as being on the Front armour, just with a lower armour rating.

Normandy Bocage from the air

NARROW LANES

The narrow lanes often found in *bocage* country are easier going than the hedgerows, but are dangerous since any advance must be on a one team frontage. They present additional problems for vehicles as they can neither pass nor turn in them.

A Narrow Lane is a Road with some additional rules to reflect the practical need to model a Narrow Lane wider than it really should be to enable things like artillery pieces mounted on large bases to fit down it.

A team in a Narrow Lane is considered to be touching the Bocage Hedgerows on both sides of the road. Vehicles must face along a Narrow Lane and cannot turn their hull to the side without crossing the Bocage Hedgerow into the adjacent field. Vehicles and Gun teams cannot pass other Gun teams and vehicles in a Narrow Lane. They have to detour into the neighbouring field.

SUMMARY

- **Bocage Hedgerows are Very Difficult Going, but only Infantry and Man packed Gun teams on foot and Fully-tracked vehicles can cross Bocage Hedgerows. Gates in Bocage Hedgerows are Difficult Going.**
- **Teams must start the Movement Step touching Bocage Hedgerows or Gates to cross them.**
- **Tanks Bogged Down on Bocage Hedgerows use their Side amour rating as their Front armour rating.**
- **Gun teams and vehicles on a Narrow Lane must face along the Road and can't pass other Gun teams and vehicles.**

CROSSING BOCAGE HEDGEROWS

LEAVING THE BATTLEFIELD

There are times when discretion is most definitely the better part of valour and troops must leave the battlefield. It might be because they are so badly battered that they can no longer effectively contribute to the fight. It might be because they find themselves so badly outgunned and outnumbered that retreat is the only viable option. Or it could be that they have just performed their mission and are no longer required.

Withdrawing is always a risk though. Inexperienced troops seeing friendly troops leaving the battlefield are all too likely to take that as a sign that they should leave too. Only well-handled veterans can pull it off without confusion and potential disaster.

Any team that moves off one of the table edges (either partially or entirely) is removed from the game and cannot return.

Any time that teams from a platoon move off the table edge, the platoon must take a Skill Test.

- *If they pass the Skill Test, they understand the tactical significance of the withdrawal and are unaffected.*
- *If they fail the Skill Test, the entire platoon is Destroyed as the remaining teams think they have been abandoned and follow the departing teams.*

If the platoon remains on table, they do not count teams that left through their own Deployment Area or the table edge where their Reserves arrive as Destroyed, they are simply no longer part of their platoon. Teams that exit from a table edge other than their Deployment Area are always Destroyed, even if the rest of the platoon remains on the table.

SUMMARY

- **If a team moves off the table, the platoon must pass a Skill Test or be Destroyed.**
- **If a team moves off a table edge outside its Deployment Area or Reserves arrival area, it is Destroyed.**
- **Teams that move off the table can't return.**

LEAVING THE BATTLEFIELD

Germans surrendering to British soldiers in Normandy
US Signal Corps, NARA

MOVEMENT SPECIAL RULES

The following rules represent the battlefield performance of teams with unusual characteristics and supersede the normal movement rules for these teams. The Arsenals list which attributes apply to a particular team.

Amphibious

Amphibious vehicles are designed to swim, carrying their passengers across rivers or lakes.

Amphibious vehicles treat all Impassable water terrain as Difficult Going instead of Impassable. If Passengers are forced to Dismount for any reason while in Impassable water, they drown and count as Destroyed.

Fast Tank

Tanks based on Christie's design are built around exceptionally powerful engines and flexible suspensions and can really move when the throttle's opened up.

Fast tanks can move up to 32"/80cm At the Double. However, they still only go 12"/30cm during normal movement.

Mountaineers

Some infantry are trained as mountaineers. They can scale cliffs that are impassable to normal infantry.

Mountaineers treat steep hills as normal Cross-country Terrain (they can move At the Double across them) and rocky hills as Difficult Going.

Mountaineers can cross Impassable cliffs and similar obstacles (but not Impassable terrain in general). To do so they must start the Movement Step touching the obstacle and not be Pinned Down (see page 104).

Roll a Skill Test for each team instead of moving in the Movement Step.

- *If they succeed, the team crosses the obstacle, halting at the top or bottom of the cliff.*
- *If they fail, the team remains where it is.*

A team that attempts to cross an Impassable obstacle cannot shoot this turn, although it can assault.

Overloaded

Super-heavy tanks and heavily-laden assault guns often overload their engines and suspensions, making them very poor at crossing obstacles.

When required to take a Bogging Check to cross Difficult Going, an Overloaded vehicle becomes Bogged Down on a roll of 1 or 2, rather than the usual 1.

An Overloaded vehicle must re-roll successful Skill Tests to cross Very Difficult Going.

Unreliable

Whether poorly designed, unsuitable for the conditions, or requiring more maintenance than current supply considerations will allow, these vehicles have a significant chance of breakdown when pushed too hard.

If an Unreliable vehicle attempts to move At the Double, roll a die. On a roll of 1 the vehicle becomes Bogged Down.

Wide Tracks

Some excellent tank designs have successfully utilised wider tracks, allowing them to cross almost any terrain.

If a vehicle with Wide Tracks becomes Bogged Down while attempting to cross Rough Terrain, roll again. On a roll of 4+ the vehicle immediately frees itself and continues moving.

FAST TANKS

MOVEMENT SUMMARY

1 Select the Moving Platoon

Select a platoon to Move.

2 Bring Forward Transports

Place a platoon's empty Transport teams back on the table, ready to mount up and move out. The Transport teams cannot shoot or assault.

3 Move All Teams in a Platoon

Move each team up to its Movement Distance.

If moving across multiple terrain types, use the slowest Movement Distance.

Passengers can Dismount before they or their Transport team moves.

Transport teams can move before or after Mounting Passengers.

Teams moving in or across Rough Terrain may need to take a Bogging Check.

Teams must pass a Skill Test to Enter a Contested Building, but may enter a Checked Building freely.

4 Send Empty Transports to the Rear

All empty Transport teams must be removed and Sent to the Rear.

5 Return to 1 and Select the Next Platoon to Move

In the Starting Step

Free Bogged Down Vehicles

Pass a Skill Test in the Starting Step to Free a Bogged Down vehicle.

Type	Movement Distances: Cross Country	Road	Rough Terrain
Fully-tracked Tanks and Transports			
Standard Tank	12"/30cm	12"/30cm	8"/20cm
Light Tank	16"/40cm	16"/40cm	8"/20cm
Slow Tank	8"/20cm	8"/20cm	8"/20cm
Very Slow Tank	6"/15cm	6"/15cm	6"/15cm
Other Tanks and Transports			
Jeep, Motorcycle	16"/40cm	24"/60cm	4"/10cm*
Half-tracked	12"/30cm	18"/45cm	4"/10cm
Wheeled	12"/30cm	18"/45cm	4"/10cm*
Slow Wheeled, Wagon	8"/20cm	12"/30cm	4"/10cm*
Infantry			
Cavalry	10"/25cm	10"/25cm	10"/25cm**
Infantry	6"/15cm	6"/15cm	6"/15cm**
Guns			
Man-packed Guns	6"/15cm	6"/15cm	6"/15cm**
Light Guns	6"/15cm	6"/15cm	4"/10cm*
Medium and Heavy Guns	4"/10cm	4"/10cm	4"/10cm*
Immobile Guns		Cannot Move	

* Cannot move in Very Difficult Going   ** No Bogging Checks required

British infantry marching across the French countryside
US Signal Corps, NARA

COMMAND

British Sherman V and Firefly VC medium tanks

Soldiers without leadership are like ants without a queen. Without orders and direction, they will tend to wait around doing as close to nothing as possible. As soon as they are properly led, they become a deadly fighting unit. In a *Flames Of War* battle it is important for teams to remain close enough together to be able to receive orders from their officers.

CONTENTS

US Infantry in Normandy

COMMAND DISTANCE

The ability of a platoon to spread out effectively will depend on its training and experience. Battle-hardened veterans have learned to spread out without losing their cohesion. Less experienced troops need to be closer together so their officers can supervise them more closely.

The Command Distance table gives the maximum distance a team may be from another to be within Command Distance of it. If two teams have different Command Distances, take the lower Command Distance to determine if they are within Command Distance of each other.

COMMAND DISTANCE

Experience	Tank Teams	Others
Conscript	4"/10cm	2"/5cm
Trained	6"/15cm	4"/10cm
Veteran	8"/20cm	6"/15cm

IN COMMAND

In a *Flames Of War* battle, a team may be either in command or out of command.

A team is In Command if it is either:

- *within Command Distance of its Platoon Command team, or*
- *within Command Distance of another team from the platoon that is itself In Command, thereby forming a chain back to the Platoon Command team.*

If neither of these applies to a team, then that team is Out of Command.

SUMMARY

- **Teams are In Command if they are within Command Distance of their Platoon Command team or within Command Distance of another team that is In Command.**
- **Take the lower Command Distance if two teams have different Command Distances.**

IN COMMAND

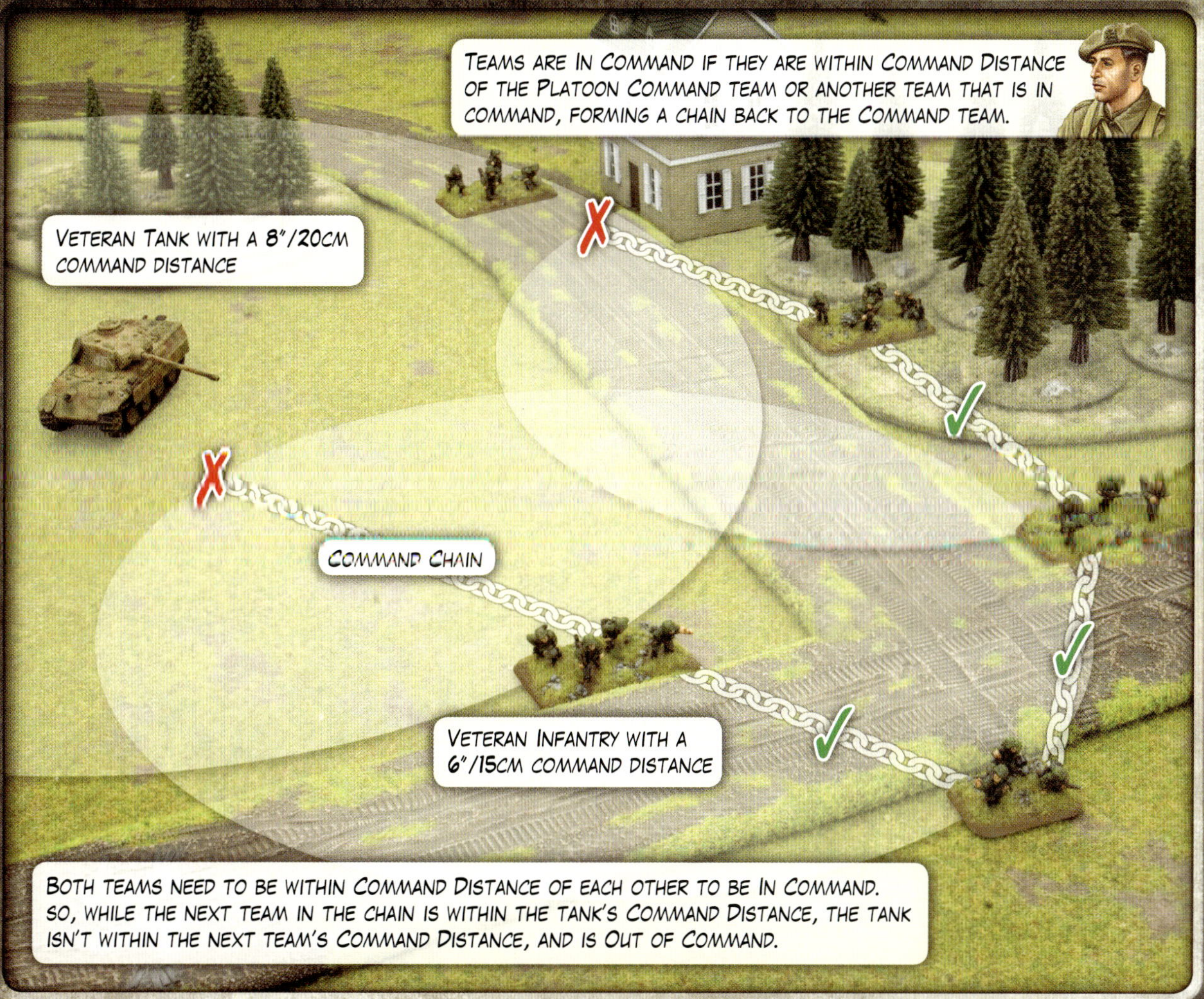

COMMAND AND MOVEMENT

MOVING WHILE IN COMMAND

MOVING WHILE IN COMMAND

A platoon moves together as a group. All of the soldiers stay close enough to receive new orders. If necessary, the platoon commander can order individual teams or vehicles to halt and provide covering fire while the rest of the platoon advances.

When moving, a team may either:

- *Move so as to be In Command at the end of the Movement Step, or*
- *Remain in place without moving.*

This allows you to leave teams in place to shoot while others move off under their protection.

MOVING WHEN OUT OF COMMAND

It is sometimes useful to leave a team to guard a flank or provide covering fire for your advance. Once the team's task is complete, it must return to its unit to receive new orders. Once they see where the rest of the platoon is going, they hasten to catch up.

Movement by teams that start the Movement Step Out of Command takes place after all teams in their platoon that started In Command have moved.

When a team that was Out of Command moves, it must do so as to be In Command, or as close to being In Command as possible, at the end of the Movement Step. This does not require a team to move At the Double, although it may do so if the owning player wishes it to.

If the platoon does not have a Command team, its teams cannot move to be In Command, so cannot move at all.

MOVING WHEN OUT OF COMMAND

STAY TOGETHER

An officer's job is to lead his unit, not to run off on his own leaving them wondering what to do. While a good officer will sometimes order a team or two to sit back and cover the rest, they'll quickly regroup with the platoon if their own party takes too many casualties.

Should an officer find themselves cut off from their surviving troops, they will work their way back to their unit to take them under command once again.

A Platoon Command team that moves must end the Movement Step with at least half of the teams in their platoon (not counting Transport teams) In Command.

If this is not possible, the moving Platoon Command team must move directly towards teams that are Out of Command (avoiding enemy teams and Rough Terrain if they wish) so as to bring at least half of the teams in their platoon (not counting Transport teams) In Command or as close to In Command as possible.

SUMMARY

- **Moving teams must stay In Command.**
- **Out of Command teams move last and must move to be In Command if they move at all.**
- **A Platoon Command team must take at least half of the platoon with it when it moves.**

British Sherman tanks
IWM B008276

WARRIOR TEAMS

Some soldiers stand out from the rest. Their outstanding performance in combat and strong leadership marks them out as warriors. Most warriors operate independently, roving the battlefield, while others are part of a platoon, fighting their battle with their comrades.

Although they are not a platoon, Warrior teams that are not permanently part of a platoon move as a platoon on their own. They do not need to remain within Command Distance of any other teams.

Warriors that are Transport teams are never Sent to the Rear nor removed from the table unless they are Destroyed.

2iC, Company, and Higher Command teams are always Warrior teams.

Warrior teams are not Independent teams (see page 70).

Joining Platoons

While mostly free to operate on their own, a warrior will often want to join one of their platoons to lead it through a critical part of the battle.

Warriors may Join friendly platoons at any time in either player's turn. A Warrior team can Join one friendly platoon within Command Distance in each Step. Once they Join, they remain Joined until the end of the Step, at which point they automatically leave the platoon. They can Join the same or a different platoon in the next Step.

A Warrior team that is a permanent part of a platoon cannot Join another platoon or team.

Joining Other Warriors

Sometimes a leader finds themselves with no friendly platoons to call upon for assistance. In that case they gather any nearby troops and form an ad hoc platoon.

A Warrior team can Join any friendly Independent teams and Warrior teams within Command Distance instead of Joining a platoon. If they do so, they become the Platoon Command team of a temporary platoon that exists until the end of the Step. Other Warrior teams can then Join the temporary platoon in the same way they would Join a normal platoon.

Only Join Own Company

While captains and majors lead their own company, colonels and generals command the whole battle, welding their commands into a single seamless whole.

Most Warrior teams can only Join platoons from their own company, but cannot Join an Allied platoon (see page 70) supporting their company. As an exception, Higher Command teams can Join platoons from any friendly company, again excepting Allied platoons.

Warrior's Transport also Joins

A warrior's vehicle is essential for them to do their job. They stay with their leader come hell or high water.

A Transport team belonging to a Warrior always Joins the same platoon as the Warrior, but remains dedicated to that Warrior. It cannot carry teams from the Joined platoon.

Joining Platoons

WHO'S IN CHARGE?

Company commanders can order anyone in their company to do whatever is needed at the time. They simply walk over, give the order, and leave again.

When a Warrior Command team Joins a platoon that does not have a Platoon Command team, they become the platoon's Command team leading the platoon in place of the normal Platoon Command team.

COMMAND LEADERSHIP

The 'Old Man', has the experience to know just how critical the situation is and the leadership to encourage his troops to hold out for just a little longer.

A Company or Higher Command team always re-rolls failed Motivation Tests that it is required to take, except when taking Company Morale Checks, unless the team is Bailed Out (see page 102).

A platoon or a team, unless Allied, from a platoon Joined by a Company or Higher Command team may re-roll any Motivation Tests it is required to take, unless the Company or Higher Command team is Bailed Out.

JOIN AT ANY TIME

A Warrior team can Join a platoon at any time. This means that it can Join a platoon that has just failed a Motivation Test before that failure takes effect, and allow it to re-roll the failed test. Since it is now part of the platoon (until the end of the Step), it will be affected by the outcome of the success or failure.

However, no matter when a Warrior team Joins a platoon, neither it nor the platoon can benefit from a roll made previously by the other. So, the Company Command team could not Join a platoon that had passed its test to make a Stormtroopers move (see page 241) and then make a Stormtroopers move with them.

USE PLATOON'S MOTIVATION RATING

While the 'Old Man' may be able to inspire troops to fight harder, the main factor in whether a platoon will stand or fall in a crisis is their own belief in their abilities and their cause.

Platoons always use their own Motivation rating, rather than the Warrior's Motivation rating, when taking Motivation Tests, unless the Warrior's special rules state otherwise.

WARRIOR SPECIAL RULES

Warriors are by their very nature extraordinary, capable of feats barely considered by common soldiers.

Warriors have their own special rules, and unless otherwise specified in the special rule, Warrior teams are not affected by the special rules of a platoon that they Join, and conversely the platoon is not affected by the Warrior team's special rules.

SUMMARY

- **2iC, Company, and Higher Command teams are Warrior teams**
- **Warrior teams can Join a platoon within Command Distance at any time, leaving the platoon again at the end of the Step.**
- **Use the platoon's Motivation rating, rather than the Warrior's for Motivation Tests.**
- **Re-roll Motivation Tests if Joined by Company or Higher Command teams.**

INDEPENDENT TEAMS

Independent teams are teams like company commanders and artillery observers that do not operate as permanent members of any platoon. Instead their roles require them to move between platoons as the battle progresses, or even to head off on their own.

Although they are not a platoon, Independent teams move as a platoon on their own. They do not need to remain within Command Distance of any other teams.

INDEPENDENT TEAM'S TRANSPORT

Commanders often have their own personal transport in order to move around the battlefield quickly. This vehicle is theirs and theirs alone.

If an Independent team has a Transport team, the Transport team operates as part of the same platoon as its Independent team.

If the Independent team is Destroyed, the Transport team is also Destroyed, but the Destruction of the Transport team has no effect on the Independent team itself.

A Transport team belonging to an Independent team cannot carry any Passengers other than Independent teams. If its Independent team Dismounts, all other Passengers must also Dismount, and the Transport team must be Sent to the Rear. It can be Brought Forward again later if the Independent team needs it again.

SUMMARY

- **Independent teams move as a platoon with their transport.**
- **If the Independent team is Destroyed, its Transport team is also Destroyed.**

ALLIED PLATOONS

Sometimes—in situations where this occurred historically—forces will contain platoons from allied armies fighting alongside your main force. While allied platoons have to obey your orders, they only answer to their own commanders.

An Allied platoon is one of a different nationality from the Company HQ (or a different branch of service under the German Reich Divided special rule on page 242).

Warrior teams and Independent teams may not voluntarily Join an Allied platoon, and cannot Spot for Allied Artillery Batteries (see page 126).

The exception to this is that US and British teams can Spot for each other's Artillery Bombardments, and German teams can Spot for German Artillery Bombardments, regardless of branch.

SUMMARY

- **Platoons of different nationalities are Allied Platoons.**
- **Warriors and Independent teams cannot voluntarily Join Allied Platoons.**
- **The exception is that US and British teams can Spot for each other's Artillery Bombardments, and German teams ignore branch when Spotting for Artillery Bombardments.**

Russian Maxim heavy machine-gun and riflemen take cover in the open.
[IWM HU89822]

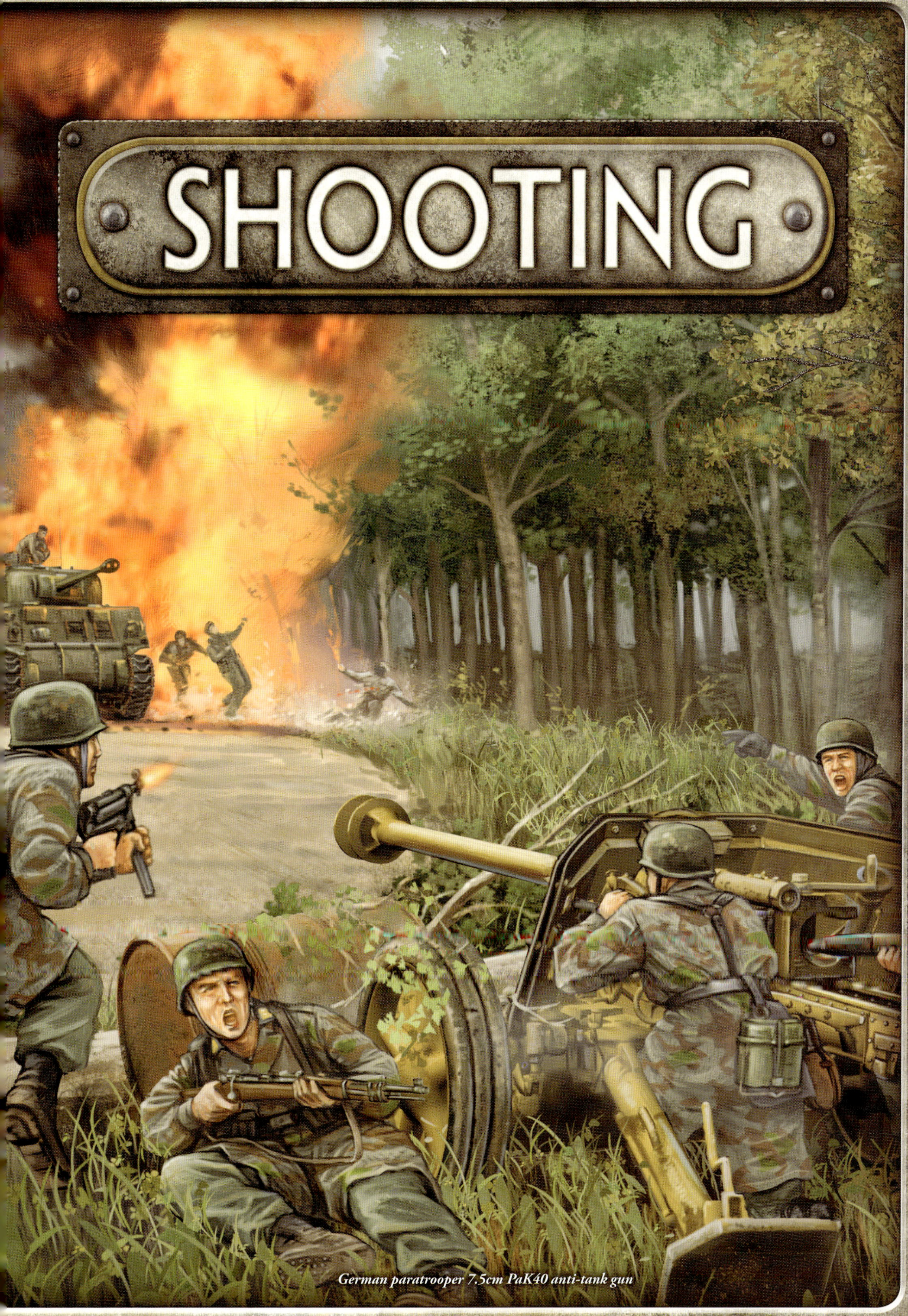

German paratrooper 7.5cm PaK40 anti-tank gun

Modern warfare is all about guns. The entire array of weapons equipping an army are designed to destroy the enemy and win the day for your side. Once you have finished all of your movement, it's time to shoot.

SHOOTING SEQUENCE

1. Select the Shooting Platoon
2. Select the Target Platoons
3. Decide Who will Shoot at each Platoon
4. Check that the Target is Valid
   a. Check Line of Sight
   b. Check Range
   c. Check Field of Fire
5. Rotate to Face the Target
6. Check if the Target is Concealed
7. Roll to Hit
8. Allocate Hits to Target Teams
9. Roll Saves for Teams that were Hit
10. Roll Firepower Tests for Armoured Teams and Teams in Bulletproof Cover
11. Mark or Remove Destroyed Teams
12. Return to 1 and Select the next Shooting Platoon
13. Pin Down Platoons that were Hit Five Times

CONTENTS

WHO CAN SHOOT

Shooting is not as simple as just ordering your soldiers to 'Fire!' It is about maximising the effectiveness of every weapon at your disposal. Pick your targets carefully—not every enemy soldier is worth expending your firepower upon. Choose your moment well—sometimes holding your fire will pay dividends.

Who can Shoot

Unsurprisingly, almost all of the soldiers on a battlefield are capable of shooting at the enemy. The few exceptions to this are troops with a specialist job, for example truck drivers, or weapons which have been developed to use a very specific method of attack, like rocket launchers which cannot shoot directly at the enemy, but can only fire bombardments.

Any team with weapons listed in their Arsenal is eligible to shoot at the enemy during the Shooting Step.

Some teams may also have a line listing their characteristics for firing bombardments. Although this type of fire is conducted during the Shooting Step, it is distinct from normal shooting and must be conducted using the Artillery rules (see page 121).

No Shooting At the Double

When troops move at the double, reaching their new position is their only concern, leaving no time to shoot accurately.

If a team moved At the Double, it may not shoot.

SUMMARY

- **Any team can shoot with the characteristics listed in their Arsenal.**
- **Teams that moved At the Double cannot shoot.**

SELECT THE SHOOTING PLATOON

Although to the untrained observer fire on a battlefield may look chaotic and uncontrolled, it is in fact usually well-coordinated and timed to achieve maximum effect. No soldier has the luxury of an unlimited ammo supply and the freedom to shoot at anything that moves!

In the Shooting Step, you shoot with any or all of your platoons one by one. When a platoon shoots, each team that wants to shoot in the platoon shoots its weapons at the enemy.

Once you've finished shooting with one of your platoons, move on to the next until all of the platoons that you want to shoot with have shot.

The important thing to remember is that you must finish shooting with the whole platoon before moving on to shoot with other platoons.

Not every platoon must shoot. Sometimes it is better to hold your fire and go to ground rather than make yourself a target by shooting.

SUMMARY

- **Choose a platoon and finish all of its shooting before selecting the next one.**
- **Shoot with any or all of the teams in that platoon.**

German '88' (8.8cm FlaK36) anti-aircraft gun

SELECT THE TARGET PLATOON

In the excitement and confusion of battle, it's not usually possible for your troops to pick out specific targets. They shoot at whatever they can see. To reflect this, teams shoot at enemy platoons rather than at specific teams.

You must select an enemy platoon or Independent team to shoot at with the platoon that is shooting.

Splitting Your Platoon's Fire

Although your troops will usually concentrate their fire on the most dangerous enemy platoon, you may occasionally want to split the fire of one platoon across several enemy platoons.

A platoon may split its fire to shoot at more than one enemy platoon. To do so you must declare which of your teams will shoot at each enemy platoon before your platoon begins shooting.

A team must shoot all of its weapons at the same enemy platoon, so a tank firing its main gun and machine-guns must shoot them all at the same enemy platoon. If some of a team's weapons can't damage the target or are out of range, then you usually won't shoot with them.

Shooting at Isolated Groups

Sometimes your opponent will split their platoons into several groups, each covering a different avenue of approach. When they do this, you can direct your fire at the most dangerous group and ignore the rest.

If an enemy platoon is sufficiently spread out that a part of it is not within Command Distance of the rest, then the platoon is broken into two or more Isolated Groups (one of which has the Platoon Command team).

You may choose to shoot at an Isolated Group rather than the whole platoon. If you do so, treat the Isolated Group as if it were a separate enemy platoon. You must declare that you are only targeting the Isolated Group before you roll the dice.

Warrior & Independent Teams

Commanders aren't stupid. When moving around the battlefield they try to make sure they don't become sitting ducks for enemy fire. By staying close to their men they make it difficult to be picked out from the ordinary soldiers and any shooting will have to target the whole group.

When a Warrior team that has not already Joined a platoon this Step is selected as the target for the enemy's shooting, it must, if possible, immediately Join a friendly platoon (see page 68). It must Join a platoon with a team of the same type (Tank, Transport, Infantry, Gun) if one is available, otherwise it Joins any friendly platoon.

When an Independent team (such as an artillery observer or recovery vehicle) is selected as the target for the enemy's shooting, it must Join a platoon (if it can) as if they were a Warrior team.

Shooting is then resolved against the combined platoon, including the Warrior and Independent teams.

Sharing the Risks

Sometimes a commander needs to take a few risks to be an effective leader.

As well as being forced to Join a platoon when targeted by enemy shooting, a Warrior team that has not Joined a platoon this Step and is within Command Distance of a friendly platoon that is selected as the target for the enemy's shooting may Join the platoon if the owning player wishes.

SUMMARY

- **A team must shoot all its weapons at the same platoon, but different teams in a platoon may shoot at different enemy platoons.**
- **You may choose to shoot at an Isolated Group of enemy teams instead of the whole enemy platoon.**
- **Warrior and Independent teams must Join a friendly platoon within Command Distance when shot at.**

A British soldier with a Projector Infantry Anti-Tank (PIAT for short)
(IWM B008913)

CHECK THAT THE TARGET IS VALID

Before you shoot, you need to make sure your troops actually have some chance of hitting the target.

For each team in the shooting platoon check that the target platoon is within:

- *Line of Sight,*
- *Range, and*
- *Field of Fire.*

At least one team from the target platoon must fulfil all of these criteria for the platoon to be a valid target. If there are no valid targets in the target platoon, select another platoon for that team to shoot at.

Ideally, all of the teams in your platoon will be able to fire their weapons at the target platoon. If some cannot, either select a different target for those teams or don't fire with them this turn.

CHECK YOUR LINE OF SIGHT

Put yourself in the place of your soldiers—lying flat on your belly trying to be as inconspicuous as possible. You can't see much of what is in front of you, and you definitely can't see what is beyond the next hill or in the middle of those woods over there.

A Line of Sight is the imaginary line along which your team sees the enemy. If the Line of Sight is blocked by terrain, the target is not valid.

What You See Is What You Get

The easiest way of deciding whether a miniature can see another is to physically get down to the level of the miniature and take a look at what the miniature could see from its current position. So if, while looking from directly behind one of your tanks, you are unable to see some enemy tanks because some miniature houses on your tabletop are in the way, then it is safe to assume that your tank commander could not see them either.

If you are still not sure after getting down and looking, ask your opponent to have a look and get their opinion. If you can't come to a quick agreement, it's obviously too close to call, so roll a die—1,2,3 you have Line of Sight, 4,5,6 you don't.

Looking to and from Infantry and Guns

Infantry and gunners operate as part of a close-knit team. Individual soldiers aren't as important as the team as a whole. The specific location of the individuals doesn't matter as much as the location of the whole team.

Trace the Line of Sight of an Infantry or Gun team to or from any figure or weapon in the team. In addition, Line of Sight can be traced to and from the space that would be occupied by a standing figure anywhere on the base (as if the figures on the base stood up and moved around).

Ignore protruding gun barrels, extra bases holding loading crews, and the like. Treat teams modelled with decorative terrain as if the figures were standing on the base.

Looking to and from Vehicles

Vehicles fight as individuals, each standing alone, rather than as teams occupying a general area.

Trace the Line of Sight of a vehicle's weapon from the weapon's mounting point on the miniature. Trace Line of Sight to any point on a vehicle model, ignoring protruding gun barrels, bases, loading crews, and other accessories except trailers and Towed Gun teams.

Line Of Sight

INTERVENING TERRAIN

The world is not flat like a billiard table. Hills, gullies, woods, hedges, crops, and buildings abound, breaking up the line of sight of your troops.

Terrain that is taller than both the shooting team and its target blocks the Line Of Sight of teams looking across it.

TEAMS AGAINST OBSTACLES SEE THROUGH

No matter how tall a hedge is, troops that come right up to it will be able to find gaps and see what's on the other side. In doing so, they give the enemy the opportunity to spot them too.

A team placed with a base edge or face of the model square against a Linear Obstacle that would normally block Line of Sight, can see anything on the other side of the Obstacle, even if the enemy is also touching the same Obstacle further along it.

A team at the intersection of two Linear Obstacles can see across either of them, including across the corner into the field diagonally across from itself.

TEAMS CAN BE SEEN OVER LOWER TERRAIN

If the opponent is tall enough, they can be seen sticking out above hedges and standing crops.

Terrain does not block Line of Sight if either the shooting team or its target are taller than it.

TEAMS ON HIGH GROUND SEE MORE

A team occupying a hill or similar high ground (such as a church tower) has a much better field of view than a grunt hugging the ground below.

A team on higher ground may be able to see across Terrain that would normally block its Line of Sight. The only way to check whether they have a Line of Sight is to look from the miniature's position and see if it can see the enemy.

TEAMS AGAINST OBSTACLES SEE THROUGH THEM

Check your Line of Sight

Tall terrain blocks the Line of Sight of all troops.

Teams square up against Linear Terrain can see and be seen through it.

Terrain shorter than one or both teams can be seen over by both teams.

Teams shorter than terrain cannot see each other as the terrain blocks their Line of Sight.

Teams on higher ground can see and be seen over Terrain.

LOOKING INTO AREA TERRAIN

THE 6" RULE—LOOKING INTO AREA TERRAIN

Woods don't just block visibility to troops on the far side, they also hide troops within them as well.

Any team that straddles the edge of Area Terrain can be seen by troops on the same side of the Area Terrain, but is out of Line of Sight to teams on the far side of the Area Terrain.

Teams completely within Area Terrain that is taller than both the shooting team and the target cannot see or be seen by teams more than 6"/15cm away. Any team beyond this distance is out of Line of Sight.

LOOKING THROUGH GAPS

While a soldier might get a glimpse of the enemy through a small gap in the terrain, it won't be enough to positively identify the target as enemy.

You must have a gap of at least 1"/2.5cm between two Terrain Features to trace Line of Sight through it. Any narrower gap requires you to see through or over the terrain instead.

BOCAGE HEDGEROWS

In the *Bocage* even the gates are massively overgrown, making them just as difficult to see through.

Bocage Hedgerows, and gates and other gaps through them, are overgrown Linear Obstacles and block Line of Sight.

LOOKING THROUGH GAPS

Not Enough to Shoot At

There are quite often times when you look to see if you have line of sight to an enemy team and can only see a tiny part of the team. This isn't enough to shoot at, as even if you did shoot at it, you wouldn't hit anything critical.

If only a small part of the enemy team, such as a tank's gun barrel or mudguard, or part of an infantry figure, is in Line of Sight, then it is not a valid target and cannot be shot at. Conversely, it cannot shoot back either.

Talk to Your Opponent

Because terrain and scenery are one of the most variable things in miniature wargaming we can't give hard and fast rules about what your troops can and cannot see. These pages contain some guidelines but in the end it is going to come down to your imagination and common sense. Be reasonable in this. For example, if a tank is almost completely hidden by a building, and only has a bit of its track or gun barrel showing, it's not really enough to shoot at. If in doubt, tell your opponent whether you think your tank is hidden or not when you move it into position. Likewise, it is a good idea to tell your opponent your intention when you position a vehicle hull down behind a hill or a low rise.

Summary: Check Your Line of Sight

- **Check for Line of Sight from the shooting vehicle's weapons or from any figure or weapon on the shooting Infantry or Gun team's base to the target team.**
- **Terrain taller than the shooting and target teams block Line of Sight, unless one or both teams are square up against it.**
- **Teams can see teams entirely within Area Terrain up to 6"/15cm away.**
- **Gaps must be at least 1"/2.5cm wide to see through.**

An American soldier looks on as an M10 3" GMC tank destroyer engages the enemy
US Signal Corps, NARA

SHOOTING NEAR FRIENDLY TEAMS

It is not enough to be able to see the enemy, you need to be able to shoot them without hitting friendly troops.

Shooting Through Enemy Teams

You can always shoot through the position of an enemy team to hit another behind it. Your soldiers don't care if they accidentally hit enemy soldiers they weren't aiming at and the team in the way quickly gets out of the line of fire, thankful that you're not shooting at them instead.

A team may shoot through any enemy team at another team beyond it.

No Shooting Through Friendly Teams

Although it is possible to see through your own troops—they don't interfere with visibility like a hill or a building does—it would be foolish to try firing through them as the risk of hitting them is too great.

A team may not shoot through a friendly team. If you cannot draw a Line of Sight to the enemy team without passing through a friendly team, you may not shoot at the enemy team, although you can still see it to Spot for an Artillery Bombardment (see page 126).

A team may fire over friendly troops at targets on higher or lower ground, provided that the Line of Sight clearly passes above the heads of the friendly team.

Shooting Between Friendly Teams

For the same reason, soldiers are reluctant to fire through gaps between friendly units unless the gap is sufficiently wide to guarantee they won't hit their own men.

A team may only shoot between two friendly teams or a Terrain Feature and a friendly team if they are at least 1"/2.5cm apart.

Shooting Over Stationary Infantry

Shooting through your own troops is too risky, but shooting over them is okay if they have hit the dirt.

Vehicles, Gun teams, and Bunkers can shoot over friendly Infantry (but not Cavalry) teams that did not move.

Infantry teams shooting at vehicles can shoot over friendly Infantry (but not Cavalry) teams that did not move.

Shooting Down Narrow Lanes

The narrow lanes often found in *bocage* country are dangerous as any advance must be on a one-team frontage.

A team in a Narrow Lane is considered to be square up against the Bocage Hedgerows on both sides of the Lane, so friendly teams cannot shoot past it down the Lane.

A vehicle in a Narrow Lane can fire turret-mounted weapons freely, but can only fire hull-mounted weapons at targets in the Lane or touching the Lane's Hedgerows.

SUMMARY

- **Check that no friendly teams block the Line of Sight.**
- **Teams can shoot through gaps at least 1"/2.5cm wide.**
- **Infantry can shoot at vehicles over stationary infantry, while other teams can always shoot over stationary infantry.**

SHOOTING THROUGH FRIENDLY TEAMS

Shooting over Stationary Infantry

CHECK THE RANGE

Although modern weapons have the potential to fire over very long distances, on the battlefield amidst all the noise and confusion, the effective distance of a weapon is usually much shorter. The key is not how far they can shoot, but how far away they can actually see their target. Your troops will not waste their precious ammunition shooting at targets they have almost no chance of hitting. Doing so would probably only result in drawing unwanted enemy fire upon themselves!

Check the range from each team in the shooting platoon to the teams in the target platoon.

Teams cannot hit enemy teams beyond the maximum range of their weapons given by their Range characteristic in their Arsenal listing.

Measure the range to or from the nearest point on a vehicle model, ignoring protruding gun barrels, bases, loading crews, and other accessories except trailers and Towed Gun teams.

Measure the range to or from an Infantry or Gun team to or from any point on the team's base. Ignore protruding gun barrels, any extra bases holding loading crews, and the like.

SUMMARY

- **Check that the target is in Range measuring between the nearest points of the shooting and the target teams.**

Check The Range

Fields of Fire

CHECK YOUR FIELD OF FIRE

Your troops must be pointing their weapons at the enemy to be able to shoot at them. Mostly that's not a problem, but if someone sneaks up from behind, you could be in trouble. It's easy enough to swing a rifle around to shoot at someone behind you, but it's a lot harder with an anti-tank gun weighing over a ton.

A weapon's Field of Fire is the arc through which it may easily fire at the enemy.

Check the Field of Fire for each team in the shooting platoon. A team can only hit teams that are at least partly within their weapon's Field of Fire.

Infantry Weapons

Infantry weapons are light and handy enough that they are quick to fire at enemy attacking from any direction.

Infantry teams have no limits on their Field of Fire. They can fire at enemy teams in front of them, behind them, or to the side of them.

Tank Turrets

Most tank weapons are mounted in turrets that allow them to be brought to bear upon targets in any direction, giving them great flexibility.

Vehicle turrets have no limits on their Field of Fire.

Deck Turrets

In the 1930's, a number of designers envisioned tanks as battleships on land and covered them in machine-gun turrets placed on the top deck of the tank.

Guns and machine-guns mounted in Deck Turrets have an all-round Field of Fire, except where their rotation is blocked by the vehicle's superstructure.

Hull-mounted Guns

Some tanks mount weapons in the front of the hull instead of in a turret to save weight or to make them easier to produce.

A hull-mounted weapon mounted in the front of a vehicle has a 180-degree Field of Fire covering everything in front of a line drawn across the front of the vehicle.

If the weapon is mounted at the rear of the vehicle, the Field of Fire covers everything to the rear of a line drawn across the rear of the vehicle.

Side-mounted Guns

Half-tracks sometimes mounted weapons on the sides as well as the front of the crew compartment.

A side-mounted weapon on a vehicle has a 180-degree Field of Fire covering everything beyond a line drawn down the side of the vehicle from straight ahead to straight behind.

Guns

Most guns have a limited field of fire unless the crew pick up the trails and move the whole gun to face a different direction.

Gun teams (including Man packed Gun teams like HMG teams) have a Field of Fire covering everything in front of a line drawn across the front of the base.

Guns on Turntables

Some guns, mostly anti-aircraft guns, are mounted on turntables allowing them to turn in any direction.

Gun teams on Turntables can fire in any direction.

SUMMARY

- **Turret-mounted weapons, guns on turntables, and Infantry teams can shoot in any direction.**
- **Other weapons can only shoot targets in front of them.**

ROTATE TO FACE THE TARGET

Before they fire, all of your weapons must be brought to bear on the enemy. Your gunners traverse their weapons, aim, and fire.

After determining your Field of Fire, but before they shoot, Rotate your teams to point directly at any team in the enemy platoon they are shooting at. Rotating a team within its Field of Fire like this does not count as movement, so teams in Rough Terrain don't need to take Bog Checks to do this.

Tank Turrets

The whole point of a tank turret is that it can rotate without the whole vehicle needing to move. Sometimes though, it is better to turn the whole vehicle to face the enemy, bringing thicker front armour to bear.

Vehicles firing weapons mounted in turrets may either:

- *rotate just the turret to point at the target, or*
- *treat the turret weapon as a hull-mounted weapon and Rotate the whole vehicle (with the turret pointing straight ahead) to point at a target within the field of Fire of a hull-mounted weapon.*

No Room to Rotate

You may not be able to rotate models in close terrain, so they remain as they are.

If a team is square against a wall or similar item of terrain, Dug In, or in a Building or Entrenchments (see page 215), it does not need to, and may not, rotate to face the target. The team remains where it is without rotating, but can still shoot.

If a team is touching a wall or similar item of terrain, or the table edge, it may need to be moved slightly to allow it to rotate, but should remain touching the terrain or table edge. If there is still not room for it to rotate, it cannot shoot at that target.

A Gun team (unless a Man-packed Gun team) in Very Difficult Going does not need to, and may not, rotate to face the target. The team remains where it is without rotating, but can still shoot.

SUMMARY

- **After checking Fields of Fire, rotate each team (or just its turret) to point at one of the enemy teams they are shooting at.**
- **Teams square up against terrain don't rotate, but they can still fire.**

Rotate to Face the Target

CHECK IF THE TARGET IS CONCEALED

The ability to conceal your troops from the enemy is critical to victory. The deadly accuracy, long range and firepower of modern weapons force soldiers to adopt ingenious camouflage schemes and to make use of all available cover on the battlefield.

You may know that the enemy is shooting at you from the edge of the woods, that doesn't mean that you can actually find the individual guns and hit them. Even quite large guns can be difficult to locate when firing from concealment.

Concealing Terrain is any terrain feature on the tabletop that provides Concealment to troops behind or within it.

An enemy team that is within Line of Sight, but at least half hidden by terrain, is Concealed. Teams suffer a +1 penalty to shoot at or Range In an Artillery Bombardment on targets that are Concealed.

DON'T LEAVE TEAMS HANGING OUT TO DRY

If there isn't enough concealed firing positions for the entire platoon, it's often a good idea to leave some of the platoon in reserve out of sight to the rear. Doing so ensures that anyone attempting to shoot at your platoon will suffer a penalty to hit them because the only teams they can see are all concealed, whereas even a single team sitting out in the open gives away the positions of the whole platoon.

CONCEALED BY TERRAIN

Concealed by Linear Obstacles

Fields throughout the world are bounded by lines of trees, hedges, and stone walls. Although these are of varying dimensions, in general they obstruct the view of anyone trying to see beyond them.

Teams seen through or across Linear Obstacles are generally Concealed. As usual, the best method of confirming this is to look from a model's-eye perspective.

The main exception to this is that a team placed with a base edge or face of the model square against a Linear Obstacle can see anything on the other side of the Obstacle clearly. The team itself will be concealed, but teams seen through the Linear Obstacle will not be.

Concealed by Hills

Hills are probably the most significant terrain features on any battlefield, and are certainly the largest.

Hills provide Concealment in the same way as Linear Obstacles. If the hill is just a low rise, teams can see over it and will be Concealed.

Teams can usually adopt a 'hull-down' position on a hill where they are Concealed to teams on the far side, but can see clearly over the hill.

The easiest way to determine if this is so is to look from the viewpoint of each model and check what it can see.

Concealed by Hills

US M18 Hellcat GMC tank destroyer

Concealed by Area Terrain

Unlike solid objects like walls and hills that completely block line of sight, trees, bushes, and standing crops are harder to see into the further the target is inside them. If we made a model wood with a realistic number of trees and a lifelike amount of scrub and undergrowth, there would be no room for our models, so the usual visibility rule of looking from the model's position doesn't work well with a miniature wood or forest.

Teams at least half in Area Terrain, but straddling the edge, are Concealed, but can see out of the Area Terrain without hindrance. Teams less than half in Area Terrain, are not Concealed by it. If they are entirely within the Area Terrain, then both they and the enemy will be Concealed.

Concealed by Area Terrain

TACTICS

Stick to Cover

Using concealment well is one of the keys to success on the battlefield. Remember, it's not just about inflicting as much damage on your opponent's forces as possible, you need to protect your own troops at the same time. The commander who makes best use of available concealing terrain on the tabletop goes a long way to ensuring their victory.

Why Can't I Hide Behind My Own Tanks?

People often think that it would be a lot safer for infantry to advance behind tanks than to spread out around them.

While it sounds good in theory, there are a lot of reasons why it doesn't work in reality. The biggest problem is that infantry can't really stay close enough to the tank to actually get any protection from enemy machine-guns spread out across the battlefield. Even if they did, they would be a prime target, being bunched up and easy to hit with a single burst.

On top of this, tanks are bullet magnets. They are big and obvious and attract a lot of fire, far more than infantry advancing in open order. Unfortunately for the infantry trying to hide behind the tank, they don't have the tank's armour to stop most of these shots.

If this isn't enough for the poor infantry, they run a serious risk of being run over by the tank. Tanks can't see infantry close to them and change direction or even go into reverse without warning, squashing any infantry standing too close.

In practice, infantry are much safer advancing in open order with the tanks. That way they are spread out, and if shot at can hit the dirt and take cover. The experienced Canadians tried to tell the Highland Division this at the Battle of Cambrai in 1917. The Highlanders refused to listen and learned the lesson the hard way.

Concealed when Dug In

One of the reasons for digging foxholes is to put a lot of dirt between you and the enemy's bullets. Another reason is simply to get out of sight so they don't even shoot you! Unfortunately, some guns are just so big that there is no way of hiding them short of digging a full-on gun pit as part of a fortified position.

Dug In Infantry teams and Man-packed, Light, and Medium Gun teams (other than Anti-aircraft guns) are Concealed.

Dug In Heavy and Immobile Gun teams and all Anti-aircraft guns are not Concealed unless Concealed by Terrain.

Concealed in the Open

Infantry and small infantry support weapons like heavy machine-guns make use of every little dip and hollow, bush and shrub to conceal themselves from the enemy. Most of these features are too small to be shown on the tabletop but they are still there and can be of benefit to your troops.

Infantry teams and Man-packed Gun teams are Concealed in the following enemy turn if they don't move or assault in their own turn, even if they are in the open and aren't hidden from enemy view by any Concealing Terrain.

These teams remain Concealed if they shoot, as long as they don't move or assault.

Looking Through Multiple Features

What matters is whether or not you can see the target. It does not matter if the terrain that the target is hiding behind is itself hidden by other, closer terrain, you can still either see the target or you can't.

It does not matter how many terrain features lie between the shooting team and its target. As long as the target can reasonably be seen and is more than half hidden by the terrain features it is Concealed. Additional intervening terrain features, such as several walls between the shooting team and the target, provide no additional benefit.

Summary: Check if the Target is Concealed

- **Teams in Line of Sight but at least half hidden by Terrain are Concealed.**
- **Teams entirely within Area Terrain are Concealed, and all enemy are Concealed to them as well.**
- **Look from the model's perspective to check what is Concealed and what is not.**
- **Dug In Infantry, Man-packed, Light, and Medium Gun teams (except Anti-aircraft guns) are Concealed.**
- **Infantry and Man-packed Gun teams that didn't move or assault are Concealed even if in the open.**
- **Teams suffer a +1 to hit when shooting at Concealed enemy platoons.**

Concealment Status Summary

Team	Moving in Open	Stationary* in Open	Dug In	Concealed by Terrain
Infantry	✗	✓	✓	✓
Man-Packed Gun	✗	✓	✓	✓
Light Gun	✗	✗	✓	✓
Medium Gun	✗	✗	✓	✓
Heavy Gun	✗	✗	✗	✓
Immobile Gun	✗	✗	✗	✓
Vehicle	✗	✗	—	✓

*Including when attempting to Dig In.

GONE TO GROUND

Infantry go to ground by stopping shooting and hugging the dirt. Vehicles and guns use tree branches and camouflage nets to hide themselves, as well as simply remaining immobile in the shadows.

Teams that did not move, shoot, or assault in their own turn are Gone to Ground. In addition, all teams are Gone to Ground at the start of the game unless otherwise specified.

Teams suffer a +1 penalty to shoot at or bombard enemy troops that are both Concealed and Gone to Ground in addition to the +1 penalty for the target being Concealed, for a total penalty of +2. If a team is Gone to Ground, but is not Concealed, the only benefit it receives is a better Gun Save (see page 99).

Place a marker with any Gone to Ground platoon or team to remind you that it did not move, shoot, or assault.

SUMMARY

- **Teams that did not move, shoot, or assault in their own turn are Gone to Ground.**
- **Teams suffer an additional +1 penalty to shoot or bombard targets that are both Concealed and Gone to Ground.**
- **Gun teams that are Gone to Ground have a 3+ Gun Save.**

GONE TO GROUND

TACTICS

DIG IN AND GO TO GROUND

INFANTRY REMAIN CONCEALED IN THE OPEN WHILE THEY DIG IN. THIS LEAVES THEM TWO CHOICES IN THE SHOOTING STEP. THEY CAN EITHER OPEN A HASTY FIRE (LIMITED BY THE FACT THEY COUNT AS MOVING FOR SHOOTING AFTER HAVING DUG IN), OR HOLD THEIR FIRE AND GO TO GROUND. THIS OPTION IS VERY USEFUL IF THEY FAILED TO DIG IN AS IT MINIMISES THEIR CASUALTIES UNTIL NEXT TURN WHEN THEY CAN TRY AGAIN.

ROLL TO HIT

Having selected your target and checked that it is in range and that you can see it, you need to roll to see if you can hit it. The roll to hit not only includes the actual firing of your troops' weapons at the enemy as you'd expect, but also considers such things as visibility, communications and plain old luck. That is, a missed roll to hit may mean that your troops didn't see the target clearly enough to get a good shot, or they maybe didn't see the target at all and never even shot! Or maybe their machine-gun jammed on them and it took most of the turn to get it cleared. Anything can happen on a battlefield!

When rolling to hit the first steps are to:

- *work out how many dice each team's weapons give you to shoot with, and then*
- *work out the score you need to hit with each die.*

Then you:

- *roll the dice and count up your hits.*

Different teams in a platoon may need different scores to hit depending on the targets available to them. Work out the score to hit for each shooting team depending on its circumstances.

HOW MANY DICE?

A weapon's rate of fire (ROF) rating reflects the number of rounds a weapon can shoot in a turn.

When a team shoots, roll one die for each point of ROF.

There are some exceptions to this rule, such as that which reduces the ROF of vehicle MG's when firing with other weapons (see page 112).

SHOOTING WHILE MOVING

When moving, troops have less time to shoot accurately. While they can fire from a quick halt, the number of shots they can get off is dramatically reduced.

A team that moved reduces the ROF of all of its weapons by half as shown in the ROF when Moving table

ROF WHEN MOVING

ROF	ROF when Moving
1 to 3	1
4 or 5	2
6 or more	3

If some of the teams in your platoon did not move, then those teams still shoot at their full rate of fire, even if other teams moved.

PASSENGERS CANNOT SHOOT

Shooting accurately from the back of a crowded, swaying truck is impossible, a soldier needs solid ground beneath his feet to fire effectively.

Passenger teams cannot shoot while Mounted in or on vehicles, but can fire Passenger-fired MG's (see page 119).

PASSENGERS CANNOT BE TARGETED

Transport vehicles are much bigger targets than their passengers, so it makes sense to shoot at the vehicle and simply catch the passengers in the same burst of fire.

Passenger teams cannot be the target of shooting. You must shoot at the vehicle carrying them rather than at the Passengers themselves. Passengers can be hit if their vehicle is hit or Destroyed (see page 101).

Remember, the Gun team towed by a Transport team can be shot at as part of the Transport team (see page 49).

TARGETS MOVING AT THE DOUBLE

An enemy team moving at the double is not using concealment and has thrown caution to the wind, making it and any friendly troops nearby an easy target.

Double the number of dice you roll To Hit if any valid target in the enemy platoon moved At the Double.

SUMMARY

- **Teams roll one die per point of ROF, halving this when they move.**
- **Passengers cannot shoot or be shot at.**
- **Double the number of dice rolled if any valid target team moved At the Double.**

SPEEDING THINGS UP

Shooting can involve lots of dice rolls. Don't panic though—you don't always have to roll for each team separately. Because most platoons have the same weapons in each team and often all need the same score to hit, you can generally roll all the dice for a platoon's shooting at the same time.

For a platoon of tanks with both guns and machine-guns you could use two different coloured dice. Declare which colour is for each type of weapon, and roll the whole lot together.

If your opponent agrees, you can usually roll all of the dice for a platoon's shooting at once and simply leave your opponent to allocate the hits to eligible teams regardless of which exact team scored the hit.

In some cases however, taking it slowly and resolving the shooting one team at a time makes complicated situations much simpler than they appear at first glance.

SCORE TO HIT

The single biggest factor in determining how many casualties a platoon takes is battlefield experience. Less experienced troops haven't learned how to use terrain to their advantage and often don't recognise the danger they are in until it is too late. It only takes one soldier moving about at the wrong time to give the whole unit's position away.

The score required for your team to hit the enemy depends upon the targeted team's Skill rating modified as shown in the Roll to Hit table.

- *A successful roll means that the shooting team located the target (not always easy to do) and managed to hit it and its platoon with one or more rounds.*
- *A failed roll means either that the shooting team could not find the target or were unable to hit it.*

ROLL TO HIT

Target Team's Skill	Score Needed to Hit
Conscript	2+
Trained	3+
Veteran	4+

Add +1 to the score to hit for each of the following:

- The range to the targeted team is over 16"/40cm.
- Target team is Concealed.
- Target team is Gone to Ground while Concealed.
- Shooting weapon has ROF 1 and moved.

MOVING WITH ROF 1

Slow-firing guns take time to load, limiting their ability to take snap shots on the move.

If the shooting weapon team has a ROF of 1 and moved earlier in the turn, add +1 to the score required to hit.

TARGETS REQUIRING DIFFERENT SCORES

The hardest part is finding the enemy. Once you have found one of them, you know where to look for the rest.

If the target platoon has teams that would require different scores to hit, select the easiest team to hit (out of the valid targets) to calculate the score that a team needs to hit. Remember, each shooting team calculates its score to hit separately. Once you have calculated the score to hit the easiest team, all of that team's rolls to hit require the same score, but may hit any valid target in the platoon.

IMPOSSIBLE SHOTS

Remember, if the score required to hit is more than 6, then the shooting team cannot score any hits.

SUMMARY

- **Score to hit depends on the target team's Skill rating, the range, whether it is Concealed and if it is also Gone to Ground.**
- **Teams with ROF 1 that move and shoot add +1 to the score required to hit.**
- **Each shooting team selects the easiest target team when calculating their To Hit score.**

SCORE TO HIT

ALLOCATE HITS TO TARGET TEAMS

When an important soldier like a bazooka gunner is hit, the platoon commander will attempt to keep the weapon in action by ordering another soldier to take over the weapon. This is reflected by the targeted player allocating the hits to the more expendable elements of their platoon first. However, if there is enough incoming fire, the valuable weaponry will be at risk too.

Your opponent allocates the hits you scored on their platoon to the teams in that platoon.

There are some restrictions though:

- *Only teams that are valid targets—within Line of Sight, Range, and Field of Fire of the shooting team—can be allocated hits.*
- *Hits must be allocated evenly across all of the eligible teams so as to maximise the number of teams that have hits allocated to them.*
- *Hits must be allocated to other teams before teams that are Gone to Ground.*
- *Hits must be allocated to operational teams and other teams (including Gone to Ground teams) before Bogged Down or Bailed Out teams.*

Your opponent allocates all of the hits from your platoon's shooting before any rolls to see the effect of your hits.

If after applying all of the above rules, there is still a choice of teams to allocate the hit to, then teams closer than 16"/40cm to the shooting team must be allocated hits before those beyond 16"/40cm.

ALLOCATING MIXED RATINGS

The enemy aren't stupid, they spread their heavy firepower around, seeking out those valuable targets rather than pounding the same spot over and over again.

If you are allocating hits with different Anti-tank or Firepower ratings, you must allocate the hits of each type as evenly as possible, subject to the normal hit allocation rules. This means that no team takes a second hit from the same type of weapon until all have taken one hit from that weapon.

If you were shooting with weapons that have different Firepower or Anti-tank ratings, it is important to keep track of which hits were scored by which weapons as these will have different effects on the teams they hit.

OVERKILL

Sometimes a well-armed platoon will score more hits than there are targets available.

If a platoon scores more hits than it has valid targets, allocate one hit to each team, then apply the hit allocation procedure again to allocate the remaining hits.

SMOKE GRENADES AND SMOKE DISCHARGERS

Most armies equip their soldiers with smoke grenades and dischargers. As a company commander, it's not your job to tell a private when to throw a smoke grenade, it's just part of their training. In part that's why the target's skill is the biggest factor in hitting the enemy. Veteran troops make full use of tricks like smoke grenades, while conscripts may not even know how to use them.

ALLOCATE HITS TO TARGET TEAMS

SHOOTING AT MIXED PLATOONS

Shooting at Mixed Platoons

Some platoons combine troops or vehicles of different types such as an armoured rifle platoon with both infantry and their half-tracks. Troops firing at these platoons have little difficulty in picking out the best target for their weapon, firing anti-tank weapons at the vehicles and machine-guns at the infantry.

Before rolling to hit, you may nominate a Priority target type for each shooting team. The Priority target type can be either Tank, Infantry, Gun or Transport teams. A team can only have one Priority target even if it has multiple weapons.

Your opponent must allocate hits from that team to teams of the Priority target type before other types of target, subject to the usual rules about allocating hits. Exactly which teams of that type are hit is at your opponent's discretion.

Targeting Man-packed Gun Teams

While it is easy to spot a large gun sitting amongst an infantry platoon, machine-guns and anti-tank rifles are hard to pick out with rifles and machine-guns that rely on volume of fire rather than accuracy for effect.

When allocating hits from weapons with Firepower 5+ or 6 using the Shooting at Mixed Platoons rule, the opponent can allocate hits to Man-packed Gun teams as if they were either Infantry teams or Gun teams. This rule only affects hit allocation, it has no effect on Gun Saves.

Allocating Firepower

The big guns usually target the most dangerous opponents while the riflemen and machine-gunners keep everyone else's heads down.

If hits are being allocated to both the chosen Priority target type and other teams, hits allocated to the Priority type must be the hits with the best Firepower.

ALLOCATING FIREPOWER

Hit Weakest Armour First

Hit Weakest Armour First

When given the option of shooting at thick front armour or thinner side armour, soldiers take the easier shot.

If hits are being allocated to vehicles, they must be allocated to Unarmoured vehicles before Armoured vehicles, and Armoured vehicles with the lowest Armour rating before those with higher Armour ratings, subject to all previous rules about allocating hits.

Mixed Anti-tank Ratings

If given the choice, troops direct their most effective anti-tank weapons against armoured vehicles saving their small arms for unprotected targets.

If hits are being allocated to both Armoured vehicles and other teams, hits allocated to the Armoured vehicles must be the hits with the highest Anti-tank rating, even if they have lower Firepower ratings. If hits with different Anti-tank ratings are being allocated to Armoured vehicles, the hits with the lower Anti-tank ratings must be allocated to targets with the lowest Armour ratings, subject to all previous rules about allocating hits.

Which Armour Rating to Use

If a tank only gives a gunner a partial shot at its weak side armour, they'll still take it over the thicker front.

If the shooting team can hit both the Front and Side armour of a tank (see page 98), treat it as having the weaker of the two when allocating hits. Hits must be placed against teams with only their weaker armour showing before they can be allocated to teams with both Front and Side armour showing.

Mixed Anti-tank Ratings

GUN TANKS

OTHER EXAMPLES OF DISTINGUISHABLE TANKS

CHURCHILL IV WITH 6 PDR VS. CHURCHILL VI WITH 75MM GUN—SAME CHASSIS, DIFFERENT GUN.
PANZER III N WITH 7.5CM KWK36 GUN AND A PANZER IV F1 WITH 7.5CM KWK36 GUN—SAME GUN, DIFFERENT CHASSIS.
PANZER III J (LATE) AND A PANZER III M—SAME GUN, SAME CHASSIS, BUT SPACED ARMOUR ON PANZER III M.

EXAMPLES OF INDISTINGUISHABLE TANKS

CHURCHILL IV (NA75), CHURCHILL VI, AND CHURCHILL VII—MINOR DIFFERENCES IN HATCHES AND TURRET SHAPE DON'T MATTER.
TIGER II (HENSCHEL) AND TIGER II (PORSCHE)—MINOR DIFFERENCES IN TURRET SHAPE DON'T MATTER.
M4A1 SHERMAN WITH 75MM GUN VS. M4A3 SHERMAN (LATE) WITH 75MM GUN—SAME GUN, SAME CHASSIS.

GUN TANKS

Distinguishing different marks or models of tanks from one another on the battlefield can sometimes be difficult for your average soldier. However, even a raw recruit can tell a giant Tiger tank from a tiny Luchs reconnaissance tank, or tell that a Sherman tank with a long 76mm gun is better armed than one with a short 75mm gun.

On the Flames Of War *battlefield your troops are able to distinguish between different marks or models of tanks if their chassis are different from one another, or if their chassis are the same but they mount a different Main Gun from each other, or if they differ in major fittings like German* Schürzen *skirting or dozer blades.*

Before you shoot at a platoon that contains Tank teams, you may state that you wish to hit one particular mark or model of tank that is distinguishable from the others in the platoon.

After rolling to hit, take a second roll for each hit scored.

- *If you roll a 5 or 6, you can choose which mark or model of tank you are shooting at.*
- *Otherwise, the hits are allocated as normal.*

Even when you do get to choose which mark or model of tank is hit, your opponent still gets to choose which specific vehicle of that type was hit.

When used, the Gun Tank rule overrides all other rules about hit allocation except those regarding valid targets, although all of the hit allocation rules apply to how hits are allocated within tanks of each mark and model.

BUNKER BUSTERS AGAINST TANKS

Huge bunker-busting guns have great difficulty in hitting moving targets, especially when moving themselves.

Hits from a Bunker Buster that moved cannot be allocated to a vehicle unless it is Bogged Down or Bailed Out.

ALLOCATE HITS TO TARGET TEAMS

SUMMARY

- **All hits from a shooting platoon are allocated by the target player at the same time.**
- **Only valid targets can be allocated hits.**
- **Hits of each type must be allocated evenly.**
- **Hits must be allocated to operational vehicles before Bogged Down or Bailed Out.**
- **Teams within 16"/40cm are hit before teams outside 16"/40cm.**
- **The shooting player may choose to hit Tank, Infantry, Gun or Transport teams first. These teams must be allocated the hits with the best Firepower rating.**
- **Hits on Armoured vehicles are allocated to weakest armour first, with the lowest Anti-tank rating going to the weakest armour.**
- **The shooting player may roll 5+ per hit to target a specific type of tank.**
- **Moving Bunker Busters can't hit vehicles unless Bailed Out or Bogged Down.**

ROLL SAVES FOR TEAMS THAT WERE HIT

Now that your hits are allocated to the enemy teams, the next step is to determine the effects of your shooting. Like the roll to hit, the roll to save can represent a number of different things. For example, when a heavily armoured tank makes a successful save from a direct hit, it may be that the shell struck the tank at such an acute angle that it bounced right off the thick steel plating without penetrating. Likewise a burst of fire might have passed between the soldiers of an infantry team without actually hitting anyone. Use your imagination when thinking about what may have happened to your miniature troops on the battlefield!

Rolling to save is done in two parts:

- *your opponent rolls to save their teams from the worst effects of your hits, then*
- *if they failed to save their teams, you roll to destroy them, although unprotected targets are destroyed outright if they fail their save.*

Armoured Vehicle Saves

For each hit on an enemy tank, your opponent rolls an armour save to see if their tank's armour stopped the shot.

When a hit is scored on an Armoured vehicle, the owning player takes an Armour Save. They roll a die and add:

- *The vehicle's Armour rating.*
- *An additional +1 if the range between the team that scored the hit and the team making the save is over 16"/40cm.*

Exceeds Anti-tank Rating

If your opponent's Armour Save roll is greater than your weapon's Anti-tank rating, their Armour Save is successful. The shot has no effect having bounced harmlessly off the tank's armour.

Equals Anti-tank Rating

If your opponent's Armour Save roll exactly equals your weapon's Anti-tank rating, they failed their Armour Save. Although your shot didn't penetrate the tank's armour, it might still have some effect.

To determine the effect of the hit you must take a Firepower Test. Roll another die.

- *If the roll equals or exceeds your weapon's Firepower rating, the crew panic and Bail Out.*
- *If the roll is lower than your weapon's Firepower rating the shot has no effect and the tank continues in action unharmed.*

Less than Anti-tank Rating

If your opponent's Armour Save roll is less than your weapon's Anti-tank rating they failed their Armour Save.

To determine the effect of the hit you must take a Firepower test. Roll another die.

- *If the roll equals or exceeds your weapon's Firepower rating, the tank is Destroyed.*
- *If the roll is lower than your weapon's Firepower rating the shot failed to do significant damage to the vehicle but the crew still Bails Out of the tank fearing that the next shot might do worse.*

ARMOURED VEHICLE SAVES

HITTING THE HULL OR TURRET

FRONT OR SIDE ARMOUR

The thickest armour on a tank is at the front. Smart troops will outflank an enemy tank to shoot its side or rear where their shots will penetrate more easily.

When the shooting player hits a turreted vehicle, they roll a die.

- *On a score of 4+, the shot hits the turret.*
- *Otherwise, it hits the hull.*

Hits on turretless vehicles always hit the hull.

When rolling their Armour Save, the opponent uses their vehicle's Front armour rating if the Line of Sight of the firing team is in front of a line drawn across the front of the hull or turret (whichever was hit). Otherwise the Side armour rating is used.

If the firing team is in the front or side of both the hull and turret, there is no need to roll to see which was hit.

FRONT OR SIDE ARMOUR

Unarmoured Vehicle Saves

Soft-skinned vehicles like trucks and jeeps have no armour at all. This makes them particularly vulnerable.

When you hit an Unarmoured vehicle team (a Tank or Transport team with a Top armour rating of '-'), your opponent must take an Unarmoured Vehicle Save to see if your shot caused any serious damage. The opposing player rolls a die.

- *If the result is 5+, the vehicle survives unharmed apart from some holes in the bodywork*
- *Otherwise, the vehicle is automatically Destroyed.*

Gun Shields Protect Vehicles

When there aren't enough armoured self-propelled anti-tank guns to go around, soldiers start mounting guns on trucks to get mobility instead. While these portee mounts aren't armoured, at least the gun shield might give some protection.

If an Unarmoured Tank team with a Gun Shield on its weapon is hit by a weapon firing from in front of a line drawn across the gun shield, the vehicle does not have a save at all. Instead, the shooting player must take a Firepower Test for each hit.

- *If the roll equals or exceeds the weapon's Firepower rating, the vehicle is Destroyed.*
- *Otherwise, the Gun Shield protects the vehicle and crew from harm.*

If hit in any other fashion, the vehicle has its usual 5+ Unarmoured Vehicle Save

Recce and Warrior Vehicle Saves

Reconnaissance jeeps and motorcycles are small and their crews are trained to move stealthily and take cover quickly under fire.

Unarmoured vehicles that are Warrior, Independent, or Recce teams (including all Motorcycle Reconnaissance teams) save on a roll of 3+ instead of the usual 5+.

Infantry Saves

Infantrymen rely upon whatever cover they can find, or improvise, to protect them from the effects of hits. Fortunately, even an apparently open battlefield has many places in which troops can take temporary cover—dips and hollows, or dense patches of undergrowth—and soldiers are trained to do just that!

For each hit on an enemy Infantry team, your opponent must take an Infantry Save to see if your shot caused any serious damage. The opposing player rolls a die.

- *If the result is 3+, the team survives largely unharmed.*
- *Otherwise, unless the team is in Bulletproof Cover, it is Destroyed.*

Gun Saves

While gunners can hit the dirt, they have to get up again and move about to load and fire the gun, making them more vulnerable than infantry.

When you hit an enemy Gun team, your opponent must take a Gun Save to see if your shot caused any serious damage. The opposing player rolls a die.

- *If the result is 5+, they escape without serious injury.*
- *Otherwise, unless the team is in Bulletproof Cover, it is Destroyed.*

Gone to Ground Gun Saves

When working their gun, gunners are forced to clump together more than infantry. However, if they go to ground, they can spread out and take full advantage of cover, making them much less vulnerable.

Any Gun teams that are Gone to Ground (that is, did not move and did not shoot), even if not Concealed, have a 3+ save instead of a 5+ save. This does not apply to teams that are only Gone to Ground because they are behind a Smoke Marker. Remember, hits must be allocated to other teams before teams that are Gone to Ground.

Unarmoured Vehicle Saves

No Saves from Big Guns

Some weapons are just so powerful that there is no chance of surviving a hit from them. These heavy guns are often mounted in tanks and self-propelled guns designed to break through enemy defensive lines.

Infantry teams, Gun teams, Passengers, and Unarmoured vehicles automatically fail their Saves when hit by a Breakthrough Gun or a Bunker Buster. This does not apply to Artillery Bombardments (see page 121).

Bulletproof Cover

One of the chief advantages of infantry is their ability to make the maximum use of any available cover. Although unprotected infantry are vulnerable, infantry in trenches or other bulletproof cover can be very difficult to kill. Although soft cover like trees and hedges conceals your teams, making them harder to hit, it won't stop a bullet and does nothing to protect them once hit.

A Dug In Infantry or Gun team, or one in a Building, crater, Trench Line, Gun Pit, or similar bulletproof terrain is in Bulletproof Cover. Likewise, an Infantry or Gun team Concealed by a Building, stone wall, Bocage hedgerow, or similar bulletproof terrain is in Bulletproof Cover.

If the target Infantry or Gun teams are in Bulletproof Cover, the cover might protect them, even though they failed their save. To determine the effect of the Bulletproof Cover, take a Firepower Test.

- *If the roll equals or exceeds your weapon's Firepower rating, your weapon blew through the cover and the target team is Destroyed.*
- *If the roll is lower than your weapon's Firepower rating, the cover protects the team from harm.*

Gun Shields give Bulletproof Cover

Manning a gun in the thick of battle is a hazardous job. To offset the increased vulnerability of gun crews to enemy fire, many guns have a bulletproof gun shield.

Gun Shields provide your Gun teams with Bulletproof Cover from shots fired from in front of a line drawn across the front of the team's base. Shots fired from behind this line hit the unprotected crew behind it.

Gun Shields do not provide cover to teams moving At the Double, nor from artillery bombardments.

Unprotected Teams are Hit First

Troops in the open are always targeted by enemy fire before those in cover.

When you are shooting at a platoon that has some teams in Bulletproof Cover and others that are not, your opponent must allocate hits to the unprotected teams before allocating hits to those in Bulletproof Cover, subject to the usual rules for allocating hits. The exception to this is that a hit from a weapon with the Bunker Buster attribute must always be allocated to a team in a Building before a team outside a Building.

Mixed Firepower Ratings

Troops will always direct the fire of their heaviest weapons against any enemy that are sheltering behind bulletproof cover.

If hits are being allocated to both teams in Bulletproof Cover and unprotected teams, hits allocated to the teams in Bulletproof Cover must be those with the best Firepower rating.

If Infantry or Gun teams are the Priority Target Type (see page 94), then the Allocating Firepower rule has precedence, otherwise the Mixed Anti-tank Rating rule (see page 95) has precedence.

Passengers in Transports

Passengers in Transports

Transport vehicles are not intended to fight. They might be armoured, but even then they know they don't stand much chance in a fight, so they run when shot at.

Armoured Transports

Armoured vehicles, such as half-tracks, may consider hanging around under fire as they do have a reasonable chance of surviving.

Armoured Transport teams roll saves in the same way that Armoured Tank teams do. If you Destroy an Armoured Transport team, every Passenger carried by the Transport team must pass a 5+ Passenger Save or be Destroyed. Any surviving Passenger teams immediately Dismount Under Fire and their platoon is now Pinned Down (see page 104).

If any Armoured Transport teams in a platoon were Bailed Out or Destroyed, the platoon must take a Motivation Test at the end of the Shooting Step.

- *If it passes, all Bailed Out Armoured Transport teams in the platoon immediately Remount (see page 102), ceasing to be Bailed Out.*
- *Otherwise, all Passenger teams immediately Dismount Under Fire and the platoon's Transport teams are Sent to the Rear.*

Unarmoured Transports

When 'soft-skin' transport vehicles come under fire, the drivers drop their cargos and high tail it to safety.

When you hit an Unarmoured Transport team (whether or not you Destroy it), every Passenger carried by the Transport team must pass a 5+ Passenger Save or be Destroyed. If all of the Passengers in a Transport team are Destroyed but the vehicle is not, the Transport team is Sent to the Rear immediately.

If any Transport teams in the platoon were Destroyed, then all surviving Passenger teams mounted in Unarmoured Transport teams immediately Dismount Under Fire and all Unarmoured Transport teams in the platoon are Destroyed and removed from the table. Their platoon is now Pinned Down (see page 104).

Dismounting Under Fire

Sometimes troops will be forced to dismount from their vehicles as they come under heavy fire.

If its transport is Destroyed or removed as a result of shooting, any surviving Passenger teams must immediately Dismount, moving up to 4"/10cm, but no closer to the shooting teams as it does so.

If necessary, Transport teams (other than Wrecks of Armoured Transport teams) can be removed first to create space for the Passengers to Dismount. If there is no room for a Passenger team to Dismount, then the Passenger team is Destroyed.

Passengers on Tanks

While the armour may protect it and its crew, even bullets and ricochets can sweep unprotected men from its exterior.

If you hit a Tank team carrying Passengers, every team carried by the Tank team is also hit by the same weapon and your opponent must take a 5+ Passenger Save for each of them instead of their usual Infantry or Gun Save. The Passengers are not in Bulletproof Cover, so no Firepower Test is needed to Destroy them.

If the Tank team receives multiple hits from the same platoon's shooting, each Passenger team takes one hit for each hit on their vehicle.

All surviving Passenger teams immediately Dismount Under Fire and their platoon is now Pinned Down (see page 104).

SUMMARY

Roll Saves for Teams that were Hit

Armoured Vehicle saves

- **Roll a die and add:**
  - **Vehicle's Armour rating.**
  - **+1 if range to target is over 16"/40cm.**
- **Compare result to Anti-tank rating:**
  - **If greater, vehicle is unharmed.**
  - **If equal, Firepower Test to Bail Out.**
  - **If less, Firepower test to Destroy, if fail the vehicle is Bailed Out.**
- **Hit hull on 1, 2, or 3, turret on 4, 5, or 6.**

Unarmoured Vehicle saves

- **Unarmoured vehicles pass a save on a 5+. Unarmoured Vehicles that are Warrior, Independent or Recce teams save on a 3+.**
- **Unarmoured portees don't save hits from in front of a Gun Shield. Shooting team takes a Firepower Test instead.**

Infantry and Gun saves

- **Infantry teams save on 3+. Gun teams save on 5+, unless Gone to Ground when they save on 3+. Riders on tanks save on 5+.**

Cover, Passengers, and Big Guns

- **A Firepower Test is required to Destroy teams in Bulletproof Cover.**
- **Passengers in Unarmoured transports or Destroyed Armoured transports must pass a Passenger Save of 5+. Survivors immediately Dismount and are Pinned Down.**
- **Infantry teams, Gun teams, and Unarmoured vehicles automatically fail their Saves when hit by a Breakthrough Gun or a Bunker Buster.**

BAILED OUT VEHICLES

Tanks are a thick metal shell filled with flammable fuel and explosive ammunition and their crews like being burnt alive about as much as the next guy. So when they hear a round penetrate their tank, they usually jump out as fast as possible. After they're sure the tank isn't going to burn they'll get back in and carry on.

In *Flames Of War*, we describe any armoured vehicle that isn't operational, but at the same time isn't obviously destroyed, as bailed out.

This covers a wide range of situations. A tank may be completely wrecked, but because it's not burning neither side can tell what's happening, or the crew could still be unharmed inside the tank, but stunned from the impact of high-velocity shells. Mostly, bailed out means that the crew have abandoned their tank and are waiting to see if it is going to explode, or whether it is safe to get back in.

Place a marker to indicate that an Armoured vehicle has been Bailed Out. Bailed Out vehicles may not move or fight (including Shooting, firing Artillery Bombardments and fighting in Assaults) until the crew Remount the vehicle.

Passengers may Dismount from a Bailed Out vehicle at the start of their next Movement Step as normal.

Bailed Out a Second Time

It takes guts to keep fixing your vehicle under fire. Most troops simply cut and run when the enemy starts scoring hits.

Each time a vehicle that is already Bailed Out or Bogged Down would be forced to Bail Out again (whether shooting or from assault or any other reason), take an immediate Motivation Test instead of placing a second marker.

- *If the test is passed, the shot has no effect.*
- *If the test is failed, the crew decides that it's too dangerous to Remount their vehicle and the vehicle is Destroyed.*

Remounting Bailed Out Vehicles

A crew that has bailed out of its tank is understandably nervous about getting back in again. It might yet explode, and even if it doesn't, the enemy have its range and could easily put another round into it if it shows signs of life again. However, once a brave crew has taken a moment to establish that the vehicle is not going to blow up on them, they will get back in and continue to fight.

During the Starting Step at the start of your turn, roll a Motivation Test for each Bailed Out Armoured vehicle.

- *If the test is successful, the crew Remounts their vehicle. Remove the Bailed Out marker. The vehicle can now act as normal this turn.*
- *If you fail the Motivation Test, the crew is still too shaken to fight, and you'll have to wait until the start of your next turn to roll again.*

SUMMARY

- **Bailed Out vehicles may not move or fight until they Remount.**
- **A Bailed Out or Bogged Down vehicle must pass a Motivation Test for each hit that forces it to Bail Out again or be Destroyed.**
- **Take a Motivation Test at the start of your turn to Remount a Bailed Out vehicle.**

Soviet T-34/85 obr 1943

DESTROYED TEAMS

In *Flames Of War*, a team is destroyed when, for whatever reason, it can no longer function. This does not necessarily mean that all its soldiers are dead. For example, tank crews often survive their tank getting knocked out. An infantry team may have been so terrorized by an artillery bombardment that they have become psychological casualties and have fled to the rear areas to recover. These guys will be back, but not before the *Flames Of War* battle is long over. Whatever the damage, the destroyed team is out of action for the duration of the battle.

Remove all destroyed Infantry and Gun teams and Unarmoured vehicles from the table.

Destroyed Armoured Vehicles

The abandoned wrecks of destroyed tanks litter the battlefield, often still burning.

Leave Destroyed Armoured vehicles on the table. Mark them as Destroyed by placing a plume of smoke on the model representing smoke and flame from internal fires.

A Destroyed Armoured vehicle is not Terrain, but does have some similar effects to Terrain.

Destroyed Armoured vehicles are Slow Going. Teams may not end their Movement on top of a Destroyed Armoured vehicle.

A Destroyed Armoured vehicle Conceals any team seen through it (ignoring the smoke plume), and provides Bulletproof Cover to teams immediately behind it in the same way as a Linear Obstacle.

Like teams facing each other across a wall in an assault, teams touching the wreck count as being in Contact with teams on the other side of the wreck in an assault (see page 148).

SUMMARY

- **Remove all Destroyed Infantry and Gun teams and Unarmoured vehicles.**
- **Leave Destroyed Armoured vehicles on the table as wrecks, which are Slow Going and Conceal any team seen through them.**

Destroyed Armoured Vehicles

German Panzer IV H

PINNED DOWN PLATOONS

Even if you don't manage to kill the enemy with your shooting, the weight of fire may pin them down. For soldiers under such intense fire, forward progress is impossible, and even shooting is difficult. Soldiers keep as low a profile as possible, only popping up occasionally for a quick shot before ducking back under cover.

A platoon that takes at least five hits in a single Shooting Step becomes Pinned Down. These hits can be from any source or combination of sources, as long as all five hits were inflicted in the same Shooting Step. In addition, a platoon that takes a single hit from an Artillery Bombardment (see page 121) or Air Attack (see page 177) also becomes Pinned Down.

Place a Pinned Down marker with the Platoon Command team to show that a platoon is Pinned Down.

MOVING WHILE PINNED DOWN

Troops either hit the dirt or retire when the incoming fire gets too heavy. On the other hand, armoured vehicles are relatively unaffected by incoming fire.

Infantry and Gun teams and Unarmoured vehicles in a Pinned Down platoon may not move closer to any enemy team in Line of Sight, nor move into Line of Sight of any other enemy team. Armoured vehicles in a Pinned Down platoon may move freely.

SHOOTING WHILE PINNED DOWN

Pinned-down troops can still shoot, but at reduced effect from having to duck the enemies' bursts of fire.

Infantry and Gun teams and Unarmoured vehicles in a Pinned Down platoon can still shoot, provided they do not move. While Pinned Down teams reduce their ROF by half as shown in the ROF When Moving Table on page 91, or if they started with ROF 1, add a +1 penalty to the score to hit the target.

Armoured vehicles (whether Fully-armoured or Open Topped) do not reduce their ROF when Pinned Down.

Pinned down teams cannot fire Artillery Bombardments (see page 121) unless they are Armoured vehicles.

WARRIORS AND INDEPENDENTS

Senior officers and artillery observers are relatively inconspicuous targets and can move about and take cover quite freely, even under heavy fire.

Warrior teams and Independent teams cannot be Pinned Down except while they have joined a platoon.

A Warrior team or Independent team that has joined a platoon is Pinned Down if the platoon they have joined is Pinned Down, but ceases to be Pinned Down when they leave the platoon at the end of the Step.

RALLYING FROM PINNED DOWN

When the attack grinds to a halt, the men need to regather their wits and courage, and get moving again.

If your platoon is Pinned Down, you may attempt to Rally it in the Starting Step at the start of your turn. Roll a Motivation Test for the platoon.

- *If the test is successful, the platoon recovers fully and is immediately ready to continue the battle. Remove the Pinned Down marker.*
- *Otherwise, the platoon remains Pinned Down.*

Since armoured vehicles are unaffected by being pinned down, there is no need to record that a platoon consisting solely of armoured vehicles is pinned down.

SUMMARY

- **Platoons that take at least five hits in a Shooting Step are Pinned Down.**
- **Armoured vehicles are not affected.**
- **Other teams cannot move closer to visible enemy and reduce their ROF by half. If it was already 1, they add +1 to hit. They cannot fire Artillery Bombardments.**
- **Take a Motivation Test at the start of your turn to Rally from being Pinned Down.**

PINNED DOWN PLATOONS

COMMAND CASUALTIES

PLATOONS WITH NO COMMAND TEAM

The platoon commander is responsible for seeing that their platoon carries out its part in the overall battle plan. If the platoon's command team is wiped out, leaving a platoon leaderless, the platoon's advance stalls. It will fight on bravely, but it will fight where it stands.

A platoon that does not have a Platoon Command team cannot move in the Movement Step but its teams can still rotate on the spot, Dismount, or Dig In.

Platoons can continue to fight and take Motivation Tests as normal without a Platoon Command team.

BOGGED OR BAILED COMMAND TANK

When an officer's tank gets stuck or damaged, they simply swap it with some luckless junior tank commander and carry on.

If one of your Command Tank teams is Bogged Down or Bailed Out, you may, at the end of any Step in your turn, take over another tank (after any Platoon Morale Checks you need to take). Designate another Tank team that is within Command Distance of the old Command team as the new Command team.

Higher Command teams may take over any friendly tank. Company and 2iC Command teams may take over any tank in their company (including attached supporting platoons). Platoon Command teams may only take over a tank from their own platoon. However, none can take over a tank from an Allied platoon (see page 70)

The Bogged Down or Bailed Out tank remains in play. However, it is no longer the Command tank. Instead it becomes part of the platoon the taken-over tank came from.

Since the Command team takes their own crew with them to crew their new tank, giving their old tank to their new tank's crew, both teams retain their own Motivation and Skill ratings and their own special rules. Any special abilities such as the German Tiger Ace skills (see page 244) transfer with the Command team to their new vehicle, and the platoon applies its skills to the vehicle they gained from the Command team.

Unless both vehicles are Recce teams (see page 193), neither vehicle is a Recce team after the transfer.

NO RE-ROLL WHILE BAILED OUT

When a commander is forced out of his vehicle, his influence on the battle is temporarily curtailed.

While a Higher or Company Command Tank team is Bailed Out, it no longer allows the platoon it is leading to re-roll failed Motivation Tests. However, in the Starting Step the Command Tank team may attempt to Remount their own tank first (see page 102), then if successful grant the re-roll to the remainder of the platoon.

APPOINTING NEW COMMANDERS

When an attack stalls due to the loss of leaders, a senior officer can go over and appoint a new leader to get them moving again.

If your Company or 2iC Command team does not Join any platoon in the Shooting Step and does not shoot, it may appoint any Tank, Infantry, or Gun team that is within Command Distance, and from a platoon in their own company (including attached supporting platoons) that does not have a Platoon Command team, as the platoon's new Platoon Command team.

If the appointed team is a Tank team, it becomes the new Platoon Command team. If the team is an Infantry or Gun team, replace it with the original Platoon Command team if that was an Infantry team, or a spare Command Rifle team otherwise.

The new Platoon Command team is appointed at the start of the Shooting Step. The new Platoon Command team can shoot this Step, only the Company or 2iC Command team is prevented from shooting while appointing a new command team.

HIGHER COMMAND TEAMS

Senior officers have the authority to appoint commanders for any platoon in the force.

A Higher Command team may appoint a new Platoon Command team in the same way as a Company Command team.

However, while a Company Command team may only appoint a Platoon Command team for their own company, a Higher Command team may appoint a Platoon Command team to any platoon in the force that they can Join.

SUMMARY

- **Platoons without a Command team cannot move except to Rotate, Dismount or Dig In.**
- **Bailed Out or Bogged Down Command tanks can take over another tank within Command Distance at the end of any step.**
- **Higher or Company Command teams can't re-roll Motivation Tests while Bailed Out.**
- **Higher, Company, and 2iC Command teams appoint a new Command team instead of shooting.**

WARRIOR CASUALTIES

Teams are made up of a group of soldiers all of whom work together to do their job. If several are killed or wounded, the remaining individual soldiers are unable to continue alone, so carry the wounded to the rear or join another team.

Experienced officers however, are a different matter. Their individual fate matters—a lot. There is a good chance that an officer will survive the destruction of their command team and their experience allows them to reform it from nearby soldiers and continue with their job.

Heroic soldiers are similar. Unlike normal soldiers, they don't stop just because the soldiers around them do. They simply gather more soldiers together and carry on. The only way to stop them is to actually kill them.

> **REMEMBER**
> Company and 2iC Command teams are Warrior teams and take advantage of the Warrior Casualties rules

WARRIOR TANK TEAM CASUALTIES

Unless a lucky shot kills or seriously wounds the warrior, the loss of their tank won't stop them. They simply walk over to another tank and take it over from its previous commander.

If you Destroy an enemy Warrior that is a Tank team by shooting or assault (but not as a result of a failed Platoon Morale Check), roll a die.

- *On a roll of 4+ you killed or seriously wounded the warrior and the team is Destroyed.*
- *Otherwise, the owning player may designate any other friendly Tank team that is within Command Distance of the Warrior team for the warrior to take over as the new Warrior team. The tank that the warrior took over now counts as Destroyed to the platoon it came from. If there are no suitable Tank teams, the Warrior is Destroyed.*

Since the warrior takes their own crew with them to crew their new tank, they retain their own Motivation and Skill ratings and their own special rules. Unless the tank they take over is also a Recce team, the Warrior team is no longer a Recce team if they were before.

WARRIOR INFANTRY TEAM CASUALTIES

Warriors fighting on foot still fight as part of a team with other soldiers covering them and supplying extra grenades and ammunition. While most teams cease to function after a few casualties, a warrior is not so easily deterred. As long as they aren't actually disabled, they simply gather a new team to themselves and carry on.

If you Destroy an enemy Warrior that is an Infantry team by shooting or assault (but not as a result of a failed Platoon Morale Check), roll a die.

- *On a roll of 4+ you killed or seriously wounded the warrior and the team is Destroyed.*
- *Otherwise, the owning player Destroys any other friendly Infantry team that is within Command Distance of the Warrior team instead as the warrior calls them over to form a new team. If there are no suitable Infantry teams, the Warrior is Destroyed.*

WARRIOR GUN TEAM CASUALTIES

Gunners need guns. Warriors are too hard-fighting to let something minor like the loss of their own gun stop them. If their own gun is knocked out, they run to the next gun in the unit and take command of it instead.

If you Destroy an enemy Warrior that is a Gun team by shooting or assault (but not as a result of a failed Platoon Morale Check), roll a die.

- *On a roll of 4+ you killed or seriously wounded the warrior and the team is Destroyed.*
- *Otherwise, replace any other friendly Gun team equipped with the same weapon that is within Command Distance of the Warrior team with the Warrior Gun team. The Gun team that the warrior replaced is Destroyed. If there are no suitable Gun teams, the Warrior is Destroyed.*

WARRIOR TRANSPORT TEAM CASUALTIES

The leadership of senior officers is more important than their combat ability. They ride in jeeps or half-tracks to get to where they are needed quickly. Fortunately, there isn't much of a jeep that actually needs to keep working for it to function. It can be riddled with bullet holes and still get the officer to where they need to be.

If you Destroy an enemy Warrior that is a Transport team by shooting or assault (but not as a result of a failed Platoon Morale Check), roll a die.

- *On a roll of 4+ you killed or seriously wounded the warrior and the team is Destroyed.*
- *Otherwise, the Warrior's vehicle is riddled with bullet holes, but is still driveable. The Warrior team continues on unharmed and is not Destroyed.*

SUMMARY

- **A Warrior team Destroyed by shooting or assault is only Destroyed on the roll of a 4+, otherwise the owning player chooses another team of the same type within Command Distance to take over as the Warrior team.**
- **Warrior Transport Teams do not replace other teams but continue unharmed.**

SMOKE AMMUNITION

Sometimes your weapons won't destroy the enemy quickly enough to prevent them from wreaking havoc on your own troops first. One way to protect your troops in the meanwhile is to fire smoke at the enemy to temporarily impair their vision.

Only weapons listed as having the Smoke attribute in their Arsenal may fire smoke. Some weapons can also fire Smoke Bombardments (see page 136).

Shoot Smoke First

Smoke screens take time to develop. If you don't fire them at the first opportunity, the enemy will shoot back while you are still waiting for your screen to form.

Weapons shooting Smoke must shoot before other weapons in the same platoon.

Firing Smoke Ammunition

Smoke ammunition is used much like any other, except that when it hits it doesn't explode but gives off a dense cloud of white smoke instead.

Use the normal shooting rules to determine the number of hits scored. Unlike normal shooting, the shooting player may choose which teams out of the valid targets were hit when firing smoke ammunition.

For each hit scored, place two Smoke markers 2"/5cm in diameter and 2"/5cm tall (balls of cotton wool work well), one on either side of a line running between the centre of the shooting model and the centre of the target model, to form a 4"/10cm wide screen directly in front of the selected target team. The hit has no other effect.

You can only fire smoke at enemy teams. While firing smoke at friendly teams may seem like a good idea, the likelihood of confusion and friendly casualties is too high to make it worthwhile.

Effect of Smoke

It takes more smoke ammunition than most weapons have to produce a screen dense enough and long-lasting enough to completely block vision.

A team cannot see another team at over 16"/40cm if all Lines of Sight between them enter or pass through Smoke Markers.

If all Lines of Sight from a Shooting or Spotting team to an enemy team pass through Smoke markers, the enemy team is both Concealed and Gone to Ground, regardless of all other considerations, except in Defensive Fire where it only Conceals (see page 152).

If any Line of Sight from a Shooting or Spotting team to the enemy team does not pass through a Smoke Marker, the Smoke Screen has no effect.

A Smoke Screen is not a Terrain Feature.

Smoke Disperses

Smoke shells don't burn for long so the smoke drifts away quite quickly. Within a few minutes the target will be able to shoot again, so make sure you are ready when it happens.

In the Starting Step at the start of your next turn, remove all Smoke markers that you fired.

SUMMARY

- **Smoke must be fired before other shooting.**
- **When a team is hit with smoke, place two Smoke markers in front of it to form a 4"/10cm wide screen between the target and the shooting team.**
- **Teams cannot see through Smoke at over 16"/40cm, and the target is Concealed and Gone to Ground at shorter ranges.**

SMOKE AMMUNITION

BUILDINGS

Buildings are big solid objects. You can't see through them, but you may be able to see over them.

Buildings block Line of Sight through them. Troops on one side of a Building are completely out of sight of any enemy on the other side, unless of course they are positioned high enough to see over the top.

Shooting From a Building

Though buildings provide exceptional cover, they greatly restrict the visibility of those taking refuge inside—leaving large blind spots.

Teams in Buildings only have Line of Sight to teams outside if they are square up against one or more Openings. The Field of Fire of a team firing out an Opening is everything in front of a line drawn along the wall that the Opening is in.

An Infantry team has a Field of Fire through any or all of the Openings it is square up against, regardless of its normal Field of Fire. Gun teams can only shoot out an Opening in front of them.

Only one team can have Line of Sight through an Opening, unless the modelled Opening is wider than the team's base. For wider Openings, as many teams as can fit completely into the Opening together can use it at the same time, with an additional team using the remaining space in the Opening if there is any.

Tanks Shooting From a Building

If a tank wants to shoot out of a building, it simply drives out through a wall, swings its gun to the front, and backs into the hole it just made.

The front of a Tank team must be square up against a wall to shoot through it. Treat that wall as having an Opening through it that is occupied by the tank. The tank can only shoot through this Opening. It cannot Rotate its turret, so must move to shoot through a different wall.

Loopholes

While troops cannot dig foxholes in a building, they can knock loopholes in the walls to give them a better field of fire.

Infantry teams that Dig In (see page 51) while in a Building do not create foxholes. Instead they Loophole the walls, giving them Line of Sight through all walls they are square against as if they were at an Opening. As with any Digging In, if the team moves, they lose the benefits of their Loopholes.

Enemy teams shooting at a team that has Loopholed a wall also shoot as if there were Openings in all walls that the team is square up against.

Loopholes cannot be used for any other purpose. You cannot move or assault through them.

Shooting at Teams in a Building

It is almost impossible to distinguish the occupants of a dark building from outside, so most shooting is at the openings rather than a specific occupant.

Teams with a Line of Sight to an Opening into a Building have Line of Sight to every team in the Building. Teams in a Building always count as Concealed and in Bulletproof Cover, even to teams in the same Building, except against Defensive Fire during assaults (see page 152).

Shooting From a Building

SHOOTING AT A BUILDING

BUNKER BUSTERS SHOOTING BUILDINGS

While buildings provide excellent protection from most weapons, some guns are big enough to make the building a deathtrap. One hit is likely to kill everyone inside.

When a weapon with the Bunker Buster attribute scores a hit on a team in a Building, it also scores a hit on every other Infantry or Gun team in the Building. If the Building has multiple rooms, or the target platoon is occupying several Buildings, the shooting player may choose which room and Building is hit by each shot.

SHOOTING AT TANKS IN BUILDINGS

Tanks make a total mess of a building when they drive through it, smashing walls and bringing down half of the ceiling.

Because of the damage it has done to the Building while moving in, a Tank team can be seen through any wall of the Building it is in (but remains Concealed), even if there is no Opening modelled in that wall.

SUMMARY

- Teams inside Buildings can see out if they are square against an Opening.
- Teams in Buildings are Concealed and in Bulletproof Cover.
- Teams with Line of Sight to an Opening can see all teams inside. No Opening is needed to see a Tank team in a Building.
- When a Bunker Buster scores a hit on a team in a Building, it hits every team in it.

SHOOTING AT TANKS IN BUILDINGS

SNIPERS

Snipers, solitary hunters with telescopic sights on their rifles, are the stuff of legends. They usually work in pairs. One shoots while the other spots, telling them if they were high, low, left, or right. The pair spends hours lying hidden, unable to move, waiting for their prey to come into their sights. Then, with one shot they bring the enemy down.

Although snipers don't kill as many soldiers as a machine-gun, the personal nature of their shooting makes them far more fearsome than an indiscriminate machine-gun. A leader can rally his men to advance into machine-gun fire, but even the act of waving your men forward means death in the face of a skilled sniper.

All Snipers have the following characteristics. Snipers are Independent Infantry teams and always rated as Confident Veteran. Although Snipers are Independent teams, they may not Join platoons.

Snipers are armed with a sniper rifle.

Weapon	***Range***	***ROF***	***Anti-tank***	***Firepower***
Sniper rifle	*16"/40cm*	*1*	*0*	*4+*

SNIPER'S HIDE

Snipers sneak out in the darkness before dawn, moving stealthily into their chosen hide. Once in position they wait patiently for their prey.

Sniper teams are never deployed at the start of the game. Instead, they are held off table in a Sniper Pool. Immediately before you Roll for Reserves in the Starting Step, you may place any of your Sniper teams in any Terrain Feature in your own Deployment Area or No Man's Land such that the Sniper team is not within 4"/10cm of any enemy team.

ALTERNATE HIDES

If the tactical situation changes or a sniper's hide has been discovered, they will sneak off and occupy a previously reconnoitred alternative position.

During the Movement Step you may attempt to remove a Sniper team from the table. To do this, roll a die:

- *On a roll of 4+, you can remove the Sniper and put it back into your pool of Snipers ready to be placed again in a future turn.*
- *Otherwise, the Sniper cannot move safely at the moment and remains where they are.*

Aside from being removed like this, once positioned a Sniper team cannot move for any reason. If they have to move for any reason, they are Destroyed and removed from the game.

PERFECTLY CAMOUFLAGED

A good sniper's hide is chosen so that the sniper will remain invisible, even when they shoot.

Sniper teams are Concealed and Gone to Ground, even when they shoot. They are also in Bulletproof Cover.

A Sniper team may not fire if there are any friendly teams within 4"/10cm, as the presence of these troops will give away their hide.

EXPERT SHOT

Snipers are excellent shots, shooting anyone who moves, making it difficult to keep up the momentum of attacks.

A Sniper may re-roll any failed Roll to Hit. Any platoon hit by a Sniper team is automatically Pinned Down.

DRIVEN OFF

If the enemy discover the sniper's hide, a smart sniper realises the game's up and gets out.

If a Sniper team is Destroyed, the player that Destroyed it rolls a die.

- *On a score of 4+, they knock out the sniper.*
- *Otherwise, the Sniper team slips away and is placed back into your pool of Snipers ready to return later.*

Sniper teams cannot be assaulted. Instead, if a team that can Charge into Contact is within 4"/10cm of an enemy Sniper team during the Assault Step (see page 141), it can attempt to catch the Sniper. To do so, the player rolls a die:

- *On a score of 4+, they knock out the sniper, removing the team from the game.*
- *Otherwise, the Sniper team slips away and is placed back into your pool of Snipers ready to return later.*

Attempting to catch the Sniper does not prevent the team from taking part in an assault later in the Assault Step.

SUMMARY

- **Snipers are placed at least 4"/10cm from all enemy. They are always Concealed, Gone to Ground, and in Bulletproof Cover.**
- **Snipers can't move but can be returned to the Sniper pool on the roll of a 4+.**
- **Snipers re-roll any misses and any target hit is Pinned Down, but they cannot shoot if friendly teams are within 4"/10cm.**
- **Roll a die for a Sniper that is Destroyed or within 4"/10cm of the enemy in the Assault Step. On a 4+ it is Destroyed, otherwise it returns to the Sniper pool instead.**

VEHICLE WEAPONS

Most tanks have a main gun mounted in their turret and numerous machine-guns.

MAIN GUNS

A big main gun is important if a tank is going to knock out other tanks and shoot up infantry in fortified positions.

A Main Gun is any vehicle-mounted weapon other than the Vehicle Machine-guns listed on the following pages. Some tanks are only armed with machine-guns and do not have a Main Gun.

TURRET MOUNTED

Most main guns are mounted in rotating turrets allowing them to engage any target they can see. Unless otherwise indicated all main guns are turret mounted.

Turret-mounted guns have an all-round Field of Fire.

HULL MOUNTED

Expense, the weight of the gun, or the size of the vehicle can force a tank to have its main gun mounted in the hull with a limited field of fire.

A Hull-mounted weapon has a 180-degree Field of Fire either in front of a line drawn across the front or to the rear of a line drawn across the rear of the vehicle (depending on where the gun is mounted).

MULTIPLE WEAPONS

Some tanks, such as the US M3 medium tank (Grant in British service), mount more than one main gun. This is not as useful as it may seem, since the gunners rely on the commander to give them targets and he can only do one thing at a time!

Vehicles with multiple Main Guns may fire both guns at the same time, at either the same platoon or different enemy platoons.

When firing multiple Main Guns, you may choose which Main Gun fires at its normal ROF. All other Main Guns have ROF 1.

Tanks do not have to fire all of their guns at once. They may fire only some, one or even none of their weapons.

Remember, if a tank moves the ROF of its main gun drops to 1. Since any other main guns that fire already have ROF 1, they must add +1 to the score needed to hit.

CHOOSE THE BEST WEAPON FOR THE JOB

MACHINE-GUNS

Though every army has its own designs of vehicle machine-guns, they are all essentially the same.

Vehicle machine-guns have a range of 16"/40cm, a ROF of 3, an Anti-tank rating of 2, and a Firepower rating of 6.

The main exceptions to this are the various heavyweight .50 cal (half-inch) machine-guns used by some countries for their extra knockdown power against aircraft and light armoured vehicles.

.50 cal vehicle machine-guns have a range of 16"/40cm, a ROF of 3, an Anti-tank rating of 4, and a Firepower rating of 5+.

FIRING ON THE MOVE

One of the advantages of mounting a machine-gun on a vehicle is that they tend to provide good shooting platforms. As a result vehicle machine-guns do not reduce their ROF when moving.

Vehicle machine-guns do not reduce their ROF when moving or Pinned Down.

FIRING WITH OTHER WEAPONS

A tank won't get the full benefit of its machine-guns if it is busy firing other weapons as well.

Only one vehicle machine-gun can fire at its full ROF 3 at a time and only if the vehicle isn't firing its Main Gun. Under all other circumstances, vehicle machine-guns reduce their ROF to 1.

All of a vehicle's machine-guns must shoot at the same platoon that the Main Gun is engaging.

COMMON VEHICLE MACHINE-GUNS

Weapon	Range	ROF	Anti-tank	Firepower	Notes
Vehicle MG	*16"/40cm*	*3*	*2*	*6*	*ROF 1 if other weapons fire.*
.50 cal Vehicle MG	*16"/40cm*	*3*	*4*	*5+*	*ROF 1 if other weapons fire.*

MACHINE-GUN MOUNTINGS

Machine-guns are mounted on vehicles in many different ways, each of which has its own advantages and limitations.

Both the normal vehicle MG and the heavier .50 cal MG can be mounted on vehicles in the following ways.

AA MG (ANTI-AIRCRAFT MG)

Many vehicles are fitted with anti-aircraft machine-guns to protect the crews from strafing and dive-bombing aircraft. These are fired by the crew from the open hatches of their vehicles. Manning the anti-aircraft machine-gun during an assault invites a grenade through the open hatch if the defensive fire isn't effective.

An AA MG has an all-round Field of Fire and is a Self-defence Anti-aircraft weapon (see page 182) allowing it to engage aircraft as well as targets on the ground. However, firing an AA MG leaves the vehicle more vulnerable. In assaults a tank that fired an AA MG in this or the previous player's turn has a Top armour rating of 0.

Anti-aircraft machine-guns can be fired at the same time as other machine-guns, but not at the same time as a Main Gun, since the commander and gun crew cannot do two things at once.

CO-AX MG

Coaxial or co-ax machine-guns are mounted beside the main gun and aim along the same axis. This allows a gunner to keep shooting at the enemy using the co-axial machine-gun while he waits for the loader to reload the main gun.

Co-axial machine-guns may fire at the same time as the Main Gun it is mounted with, but only have ROF 1 if the Main Gun fires.

CUPOLA MG

Some tanks have their machine-guns mounted in a small turret or cupola above the main turret.

Cupola machine-guns have an all-round Field of Fire. They may fire at the same time as other machine-guns, but not at the same time as the turret's Main Gun.

DECK TURRET MG

In the 1930's a number of designers envisioned tanks as battleships on land. Covered in guns, they would steam forward into enemy formations to wreak serious havoc. All of these extra weapons were mounted in deck turrets placed on the top deck of the tank. The biggest of the land battleships, the Soviet T-35 had four deck turrets in addition to its main turret!

Guns and machine-guns mounted in Deck Turrets have an all-round Field of Fire, except where their rotation is blocked by the vehicle's superstructure. Ignore the facing of Deck Turrets when determining if a shot hits the Front or Side armour.

HULL MG

Most tanks mount a machine-gun in the front of the hull for extra firepower.

The field of fire of a Hull MG includes everything in front of a line across the front of the vehicle's hull.

A Hull MG cannot fire at the same time as a hull-mounted Main Gun.

HULL-REAR MG

Some armoured cars mounted a machine-gun in the rear of the hull to cover their withdrawal if necessary.

The field of fire of a Hull-rear MG includes everything behind a line across the rear of the vehicle's hull.

TURRET-FRONT MG

A turret-front MG is mounted beside the main gun, but unlike a co-ax MG the gunner must shift positions in the tank to operate it.

A Turret-front MG has an all-round Field of Fire, but cannot fire at the same time as the vehicle's Main Gun.

TURRET-REAR MG

While not very practical for long-range shooting, a machine-gun mounted in the back of the turret is perfect for discouraging boarders in an assault.

A Turret-rear MG may not shoot, it is purely defensive.

In assault combat, if a hit from an Infantry or Gun team is allocated to a Tank team armed with a Turret-rear MG, the team that scored the hit must take another Skill Test.

- *If they pass the second Skill Test, the assaulting team gets past the machine-gun to hit the tank and the tank must take an Armour Save as normal.*
- *If they fail the second Skill Test, the machine-gunner managed to keep the infantry at bay and protect the tank, and the assaulting team fails to score a hit.*

Bailed Out Tank teams do not benefit from their Turret-rear MG.

TWIN MG

A twin MG is simply two machine-guns mounted side by side, doubling the effective firepower of the mounting.

A Twin MG functions as a standard vehicle MG but has ROF 4 when firing on its own or ROF 2 if the vehicle fires any other machine-guns at full ROF, or its Main Gun.

TWIN MG TURRETS

Some tank designs from the early 1930's had two machine-gun turrets mounted side-by-side making them lethal against infantry.

Twin MG Turrets are Deck Turrets. Both turrets can fire at their full ROF 3 at the same time, either at the same platoon or each at a different enemy platoon.

INFANTRY WEAPONS

Though the preference for any army is to use a combined arms attack, as often as not, the real work falls on the 'Poor Bloody Infantry'. Limited to what they can carry on their backs, the perpetual trial of foot soldiers is to try to solve their problems using only what they have with them.

RIFLE TEAMS

At the start of the Twentieth Century, infantry were all armed with simple bolt-action rifles. They are typically slow to operate and only able to lay down a limited amount of fire, although modern semi-automatic rifles can make rifle teams surprisingly flexible.

Rifle teams have a ROF of 1. Because their rate of fire is already 1, if a Rifle team moves or is Pinned Down, it adds +1 to the score required to hit a target.

RIFLE/MG TEAMS

Much more common is a combination of rifles and light, bipod-mounted squad machine-guns like the German MG34 or the British Bren gun. Each squad combines the firepower of an MG team with the flexibility of a Rifle team to form a pair of hybrid Rifle/MG teams.

Rifle/MG teams have a ROF of 2. Like other teams, if a Rifle/MG team moves or is Pinned Down, its ROF is reduced to 1.

MG TEAMS

Mechanised troops can move lots of ammunition and heavier weapons in their vehicles. Some units use this capability to give every team a light bipod-mounted squad machine-gun.

This gives them immense firepower when stationary, but as they cannot fire their machine-guns while moving, their rate of fire drops dramatically when doing so. It is often a good idea to leave some teams halted to pin the enemy with their full ROF while the rest of the platoon advances into an assault.

MG teams have a ROF of 3. If a MG team moves, its ROF is reduced to 1 as usual. However, unlike other teams, the sheer amount of fire they can kick out gives them ROF 2 when they are Pinned Down.

SMG TEAMS

A submachine-gun, or SMG, is a small, compact, automatic weapon designed for lightning-fast, close-range engagements. They sacrifice long range for the ability to fire from the hip in assaults.

SMG teams only have a range of 4"/10cm compared with the 16"/40cm range of Rifle teams. The advantage they have is that their ROF remains at 3, whether they moved or not. However, if they are Pinned Down, their ROF drops to 1.

RIFLE/MG TEAMS

The differences between Rifle, Rifle/MG, and MG teams can be a bit confusing for new players. Historically, the distinction is the number of machine-guns carried by a squad of two teams. Rifle squads have none, Rifle/MG squads have one machine-gun per squad, while MG teams have two machine-guns issued to each squad.

If this was represented literally in Flames Of War, it would mean that Rifle/MG squads would have one MG team and one Rifle team. The problem with this is keeping track of the two types of teams. Every time you moved or shot you would have to look carefully at each team to make sure that you had the right type of team.

Needless to say, it is much easier to simply average the two types into Rifle/MG teams. Two Rifle/MG teams are almost the same as one Rifle team and one MG team, without the extra hassle of keeping track of two different types of team.

COMMON INFANTRY TEAMS

Team	Range	ROF	Anti-tank	Firepower	Notes
Rifle	16"/40cm	1	2	6	
Rifle/MG	16"/40cm	2	2	6	
MG	16"/40cm	3	2	6	ROF 2 when Pinned Down.
SMG	4"/10cm	3	1	6	Full ROF when moving.
Assault Rifle	8"/20cm	3	1	6	Full ROF when moving.
Light Mortar	16"/40cm	1	1	4+	Can fire over friendly teams.
Flame-thrower	4"/10cm	2	-	6	Remove after shooting.
Boys anti-tank rifle	16"/40cm	1	4	5+	Tank Assault 3.
Bazooka	8"/20cm	1	10	5+	Tank Assault 4.

Assault Rifle Teams

An assault rifle attempts to marry the range of a rifle with the automatic fire of a sub-machine-gun. It uses a full length barrel, but has a smaller and lighter cartridge than a rifle round, making fully-automatic fire possible.

Assault Rifle teams have a ROF of 3 and a range of 8"/20cm. Like SMG teams, movement doesn't affect the ROF of Assault Rifle teams, so they shoot at a ROF of 3 even if they move, but drop to ROF 1 if Pinned Down.

Light Mortar Teams

Infantry have difficulty knocking out dug-in heavy machine-guns with their rifles and machine-guns, but cannot advance into their hail of fire until they do. One answer is the light mortar. These grenade launchers throw small bombs in a high arc aiming to get one into the machine-gun pit and knock it out.

Light Mortar teams have a Firepower rating of 4+ making them excellent for knocking out teams in Bulletproof Cover.

Though they do not fire bombardments, light mortars are considered to be lobbing their rounds in a high trajectory and so can fire over friendly teams as an exception to the normal Line of Sight rules.

Infantry Anti-tank Teams

Ever since the first tanks rolled across the battlefields of Europe, armies have been trying to give their infantry light anti-tank weapons to destroy or disable them. The first versions were anti-tank rifles, oversized rifles capable of punching through the armour of a light tank. As armour got thicker, a new invention came along, the Bazooka, a rocket launcher firing a high-explosive anti-tank (HEAT) round capable of knocking out any tank.

The characteristics of infantry anti-tank weapons like anti-tank rifles and bazookas vary greatly from weapon to weapon. The precise characteristics are given in their army's Arsenal. Some infantry anti-tank weapons like the Panzerfaust are additional equipment for Rifle or other teams. Teams equipped with this type of weapon can either fire their normal weapons or fire the additional weapon.

Other Infantry Weapons

Although the basic infantry teams are the same in every army, there are also numerous weapons that are unique to each army. The Arsenal for an army describes its weapons and their effects.

MAN-PACKED GUNS

Man-packed guns are the infantry's own supporting weapons. They are small and light enough to operate with the infantry in the front line, but too big and cumbersome to take part in close-quarters fighting in assaults.

Heavy Machine-guns (HMG)

One weapon common to almost every army is the HMG, a tripod-mounted heavy machine-gun, firing standard rifle bullets. They have water-cooling jackets or quick-change barrels and plenty of ammunition so they can keep up an immense rate of fire almost indefinitely. Even when under heavy fire, an HMG team can keep up a good rate of fire making them ideal defensive weapons.

HMG teams have a ROF of 6. Because of its high rate of fire, an HMG team fires with ROF 3 when Pinned Down or moving.

Light Machine-guns (LMG)

Light machine-guns are heavy machine-guns lightened up by dropping the water-cooling for an air-cooled jacket. This makes them more suitable for close infantry support, but reduces their ability to keep up a high volume of fire at long range.

LMG teams have a ROF of 5. With a lower sustained rate of fire than an HMG, an LMG team fires with ROF 2 when Pinned Down or moving.

Mortars

Mortars are light enough to allow infantry to carry their very own artillery wherever they go, giving them fast accurate fire as required. The simplicity of operation allows them to be fired as quickly as new rounds can be dropped down the tube. Of course the guy that has to carry the base-plate may have other ideas about how light they really are. Lighter mortars like the US M2 60mm and M1 81mm mortars can be used as direct-fire grenade launchers as well as firing bombardments.

Mortars lob their rounds in a high trajectory and so can fire over friendly teams as an exception to the normal shooting rules.

When firing directly at a target rather than firing an Artillery Bombardment, mortar teams (whether Gun teams or on self-propelled mountings as Tank teams) have a minimum range of 8"/20cm.

The characteristics of mortars vary greatly from weapon to weapon and are given in their army's Arsenal.

Light Anti-tank Weapons

Before the war many countries developed giant anti-tank rifles with calibres up to 20mm to overcome the increasingly thick armour of the enemy tanks. While much smaller and more mobile than a true anti-tank gun, they are still cumbersome weapons barely able to be carried by their crews. With the invention of the recoilless gun, a new generation of heavy infantry anti-tank weapons appeared using high-explosive anti-tank (HEAT) rounds.

The characteristics of light anti-tank weapons vary greatly from weapon to weapon. The precise characteristics of each weapon are given in their army's Arsenal.

Sample Man-packed Guns

Weapon	Range	ROF	Anti-tank	Firepower	Notes
Machine-guns					
M1917 HMG	24"/60cm	6	2	6	ROF 3 when moving or Pinned Down.
M1919 LMG	16"/40cm	5	2	6	ROF 2 when moving or Pinned Down.
Mortars					
M2 60mm mortar	24"/60cm	2	1	3+	Minimum range 8"/20cm.
Firing bombardments	*32"/80cm*	-	*1*	*6*	
8cm GW34 mortar	24"/60cm	2	2	3+	Smoke, Minimum range 8"/20cm.
Firing bombardments	*40"/100cm*	-	*2*	*6*	Smoke bombardment
Light Anti-tank Weapons					
PTRD anti-tank rifle	16"/40cm	2	5	5+	Tank Assault 3.
2.8cm sPzB41 AT rifle	16"/40cm	3	7	5+	No HE.
8.8cm RW43 (Püppchen)	16"/40cm	1	11	5+	

LARGER GUNS

Guns have many roles. They drop shells and rockets on enemy infantry and tanks miles away, defend the skies against incoming aircraft, and punch holes in enemy armour so their army can advance. The range of different guns in use is vast. Every country has their own designs with their own characteristics.

ANTI-TANK GUNS

Anti-tank guns fire high-velocity armour piercing shots directly at tanks. Most anti-tank guns can also fire explosive, fragmenting rounds against infantry targets if necessary. Every army developed its own range of anti-tank guns as it sought to gain an edge on enemy armour. The table below shows two typical anti-tank guns. Each army's Arsenal describes their anti-tank guns.

ANTI-AIRCRAFT GUNS

Anti-aircraft guns are principally designed to shoot down aircraft, but their high rate of fire and the velocity of their shot makes them excellent, if rather large, anti-tank guns. Once again, the Arsenal has the details of each army's anti-aircraft guns.

ARTILLERY

The main function of artillery is bombarding the enemy from a distance. They rely on pounding an area for long enough to hit the enemy, rather than specifically trying to hit them with each shot. Artillery bombardments are explained in more detail on page 121.

GUNS AND HOWITZERS

Guns and howitzers are the most common form of artillery. These are conventional guns lobbing heavier shells than anti-tank guns over longer ranges. They aren't as accurate, but given time they can be more destructive. As with anti-tank guns, each army fielded its own range of artillery pieces. Again, the Arsenals give the full details. Below is a sample selection.

HEAVY MORTARS

Heavy mortars are just scaled up versions of their man-packed cousins. With calibres from 4.2" (107mm) to 160mm (6.3"), they pack a powerful punch for such simple and cheap weapons.

ROCKET LAUNCHERS

Rocket launchers were one of the secret weapons of the Red Army at the start of World War Two. By the end of the war every army had their own version of these lightweight weapons capable of delivering a stunning volume of fire and saturating the target area with explosives. Each army's Arsenal describes their rocket launchers.

GUN TEAMS CAN FIRE AS RIFLES

Gunners are usually equipped with rifles and the occasional machine-gun for self-defence. If they are attacked by infantry and don't have time to bring their weapons to bear, or their weapon is not going to have any effect against infantry, they leave the gun where it is, pick up their rifles, and open fire.

Gun teams (including Man-packed Gun teams) can fire as Rifle teams instead of shooting their main weapon. If they do this, they have an all-round Field of Fire, but do not rotate to face the target they are shooting at.

SAMPLE GUNS

Weapon	Mobility	Range	ROF	Anti-tank	Firepower	Notes
Anti-tank Guns						
OQF 6 pdr gun	Medium	24"/60cm	3	10	4+	Gun shield.
7.5cm PaK40 gun	Medium	32"/80cm	2	12	3+	Gun shield.
Anti-aircraft Guns						
20/65 gun	Light	16"/40cm	4	5	5+	Anti-aircraft, Turntable.
Artillery						
M2A1 105mm howitzer	Immobile	24"/60cm	1	9	2+	Breakthrough Gun, Gun shield, Smoke.
Firing bombardments		*72"/180cm*	-	*4*	*4+*	*Smoke bombardment.*
Heavy Mortar						
120-PM-38 mortar	Light	56"/140cm	-	3	3+	
Rocket Launcher						
15cm NW41 rocket launcher	Light	64"/160cm	-	3	4+	Smoke bombardment.

SHOOTING SPECIAL RULES

The following rules represent the battlefield performance of weapons with unusual characteristics and supersede the normal shooting rules. The Arsenals list which attributes apply to a particular weapon or vehicle.

Awkward Layout

Some tank designs have such an awkward internal layout that it is difficult for the crew to fire on the move. In the Archer, for example, the gun recoils into the driver's position, requiring them to vacate before firing.

Tank teams cannot shoot any weapons with Awkward Layout in their own Shooting Step if they move in the Movement Step. They may still shoot at Aircraft in the enemy's Shooting Step (see page 181).

HMG Carrier

When they board their HMG carrier, the machine-gunners mount their machine-gun on their carrier so they can fire the gun while mounted.

An HMG team that started the turn as a Passenger in an HMG Carrier may fire the carrier's hull-mounted vehicle machine-gun as an HMG team at their full ROF of 6 and a range of 24"/60cm as long as the vehicle does not move. However when moving, the weapon is reduced to the usual ROF 3 and 16"/40cm range of a vehicle hull-MG. While firing the machine-gun as an HMG team, it counts as the vehicle's Main Gun.

The HMG team that fires cannot Dismount in the same turn, except to escape the destruction of their vehicle.

Horse Artillery

Horse artillery has a long tradition of galloping the guns to the fore. Within 30 seconds of the order 'Crash Action!' being given, the well-drilled crews have the guns unlimbered and are delivering fire. Trading their horses for mechanical gun tractors has changed the drill a little, but crash action remains.

A Gun team rated as Horse Artillery that started its turn Mounted may Unlimber at the end of its movement, unless it moved At the Double. The Gun team remains exactly where it ended its movement, and the Transport vehicle is Sent to the Rear.

If they do this, they can shoot on the move. However, they cannot fire Artillery Bombardments in the turn they Unlimber.

Improvised Armour

It was not uncommon for tank crews to add their own improvised armour—made of sandbags, tank tracks or whatever they could find—to the outside of their vehicle for additional protection against short-range infantry anti-tank weapons.

If vehicles with Improvised Armour fail an Armour Save against weapons with a Firepower rating of 5+ or 6, roll another die.

- *On a roll of 5+ the Improvised Armour stopped the shot. Ignore the failed save.*
- *Otherwise, the results of the failed Armour Save stand.*

Improvised Armour has no effect against Flame-throwers, Artillery Bombardments, or Aircraft. In assaults, it only protects against hits from Gun teams using the Tanks Hit by Gun Teams rule on page 157.

Limited Vision

In order to pack more into small tanks, some tank designers reduced the crew to a minimum and severely limited the number of vision devices. Thus, the tanks require the commander to operate as a somewhat vision-impaired gunner as well.

Tanks with Limited Vision add +1 to the score required to hit when shooting any weapon except an AA MG at targets that are entirely behind a line drawn across the front of the tank's turret before they rotate their turret to face the target.

Tanks with Limited Vision must rotate their turret to point straight ahead when they move.

No HE

Some weapons come equipped only with armour-piercing ammunition, and have no high explosive ammunition at all, reducing their effectiveness against infantry and 'soft' targets.

Hits from weapons with No HE cannot be allocated to Infantry or Gun teams. If only Infantry and Gun teams are valid targets, all hits from weapons with No HE are ignored completely as the anti-tank gun has no targets.

Gun teams with No HE are not completely helpless against Infantry teams though as they can shoot as Rifle teams if necessary (see page 117).

One-man Turret

French tanks retain the one-man turret of their First World War forebears. Although this is sufficient for infantry-support, in tank-versus-tank clashes the commander is faced with the impossible task of finding new targets, and loading and firing the gun, while directing the driver as well.

Any tank with a One-man Turret that moves adds +1 to the score required to hit when shooting with its turret Main Gun. Machine-guns and Flame-throwers do not suffer this penalty.

In addition, a tank with a One-man Turret may not fire both the turret Main Gun and the turret machine-gun in the same turn.

Limited Vision

Passenger-fired Weapons

Some transport vehicles come equipped with an on-board machine-gun, but are only crewed by the driver, meaning the weapon can only be fired when passengers are mounted in the vehicle.

Vehicles with Passenger-fired weapons can only shoot those weapons if a Passenger team is Mounted in the vehicle. A single Passenger team can fire all of a vehicle's Passenger-fired weapons.

A team that fires a Passenger-fired weapon cannot Dismount in the same turn, except to escape the destruction of their vehicle.

Protected Ammo

Many tanks are destroyed not by the enemy shell but by their own ammunition being hit by white-hot fragments of armour and exploding. The chances of this were minimised by providing a safe place for stowing ammunition within the vehicle such as an armoured compartment or inside a water-filled jacket.

If forced to bail out, crews of tanks with protected ammunition are far more confident when it comes to remounting their vehicle quickly.

Tanks with Protected Ammo re-roll all failed Motivation Tests to Remount Bailed Out vehicles in the Starting Step (see page 102).

Recoilless Guns

Paratroops need light artillery. One solution is recoilless guns. These weapons vent propellant gasses from the rear of the gun to counteract the recoil of the shell being fired. Although this creates a large cloud of dust and flying debris behind the gun, it does allow it to do away with the heavy recoil-absorbing carriage of most artillery.

Recoilless guns never count as Concealed if they fired in their last Shooting Step as the dust cloud gives away their position.

Because of the danger from flying debris, you cannot fire a Recoilless gun when any part of a friendly team is directly behind and within 2"/5cm of the Gun team. Recoilless guns cannot fire from within Buildings.

Slow Traverse

Most tanks were either fitted with power traverse or had turrets that were light enough to be quickly swung by hand. Some designs suffered from heavy turrets lacking power traverse.

Tanks with slow traverse add +1 to the score required to hit when shooting any turret-mounted weapon except an AA MG at targets that are entirely behind a line drawn across the front of the tank's turret before they rotate their turret to face the target.

Stabiliser Jacks

Heavy anti-aircraft guns are much more mobile when mounted on trucks, but they need outriggers and stabiliser jacks to stop them from tipping over when they fire. The addition of a gun shield makes them useful anti-tank weapons too.

Vehicles with Stabiliser Jacks have a Gun Shield for the Main Gun and use the Gun Shields Protect Vehicles rule (see page 99).

SHOOTING SUMMARY

1 Select the Shooting Platoon

Select one platoon to shoot with.

2 Select the Target Platoons

Select the enemy platoons to shoot at.

3 Who will Shoot each Platoon

Decide which enemy platoon each team will shoot at.

4 Fire Smoke Ammunition

Smoke must be fired before the rest of the platoon shoots.

5 Check that the Target is Valid

A valid target must be:

- *in Line of Sight,*
- *in Range, and*
- *in Field of Fire.*

6 Rotate to Face the Target

Turn the weapon to face a team in the target platoon.

7 Check if the Target is Concealed

- *Targets at least half hidden by terrain are Concealed.*
- *Infantry and Man-packed Guns are always Concealed if they don't move.*
- *Teams that did not move, shoot, or assault are Gone to Ground.*

8 Roll to Hit

Roll one die per point of ROF for each shooting team.

- *Teams that moved reduce their ROF by half.*

ROF	*ROF when Moving*
1 to 3	*1*
4 or 5	*2*
6 or more	*3*

Score required to hit based on easiest team to hit in target platoon.

Target Team's Skill	*Score Needed*
Conscript	*2+*
Trained	*3+*
Veteran	*4+*

Add +1 to the score to hit for each of the following:

- *Range is over 16"/40cm.*
- *Target team is Concealed.*
- *Target team is Gone to Ground while Concealed.*
- *Shooting weapon has ROF 1 and moved.*

9 Allocate Hits to Target Teams

Opponent allocates hits to teams within target platoon. Hits must be allocated:

- *to valid targets.*
- *evenly across teams.*
- *to operational vehicles before Bailed Out or Bogged Down ones.*
- *to targets closer than 16"/40cm before those beyond.*
- *to lowest Armour first.*

10 Roll Saves for Teams that were Hit

Opponent rolls a die and adds the Armour rating of Armoured vehicles and compares the result to the Anti-tank rating:

Roll is	*Result*
Greater	*No effect*
Equal	*Firepower test to Bail Out*
Less	*Firepower test to Destroy otherwise Bail Out*

Roll 5+ save for Unarmoured vehicles, except 3+ save for Warrior, Independent, and Recce teams.

Roll 3+ save for Infantry teams.

Roll 5+ save for Gun teams, unless Gone to Ground, then 3+ save.

11 Roll Firepower Tests

Roll Firepower Tests to Destroy Armoured vehicles, Infantry teams, and Gun teams in Bulletproof Cover.

12 Mark or Remove Destroyed Teams

Mark Destroyed Armoured vehicles as Wrecks.

Remove other Destroyed teams.

13 Return to 1 to Select your next Shooting Platoon

14 Pin Down Platoons Hit Five Times

Platoons that take five or more hits in a Shooting Step are Pinned Down.

In the Starting Step

Rally Pinned Down Platoon

Pass a Motivation Test in the Starting Step to Rally a Pinned Down platoon.

Remount Bailed Out Vehicles

Pass a Motivation Test in the Starting Step to Remount a Bailed Out vehicle.

ARTILLERY

British BL 5.5" gun.

The ancient science of artillery reached its destructive pinnacle in the bloody stalemate of the First World War. There the armies of Europe learned the art of massed artillery fire to smash enemy defences and cut them off from their reserves. Their technique was slow and methodical, but extremely deadly.

ARTILLERY SEQUENCE

1. Select the Aiming Point
2. Nominate the Spotting Team
3. Check that the Target is Valid
   a. Check Line of Sight
   b. Check Range
   c. Check Field of Fire
4. Rotate to Face the Target
5. Check if the Target is Concealed
6. Roll to Range In on the Target
7. Position the Template
8. Roll to Hit Teams Under the Template
9. Roll Saves for Teams that were Hit
10. Mark or Remove Destroyed Teams
11. Pin Down all Platoons that were Hit

CONTENTS

ARTILLERY

Artillery weapons are the big guns of the army. Most troops must be able to see their enemy to shoot. Artillery allows you to quickly concentrate a lot of firepower anywhere on the battlefield, way beyond the range of normal weapons. This is particularly useful for taking out troublesome machine-guns and anti-tank guns.

Bombardments saturate the target area with high-explosive shells rather than hitting one specific target, making it especially useful against densely-packed enemy formations as all of them are hit at the same time. Being on the receiving end of a bombardment is terrifying. Shells exploding everywhere tends to keep soldiers' heads down. This makes an artillery bombardment the ideal precursor to an all-out assault on the enemy position.

ARTILLERY TEAMS

Firing an artillery bombardment is a very specialised task. It requires the right equipment and training, not to mention literally tons of ammunition!

Only Artillery teams can fire Artillery Bombardments. Artillery teams are those listed in the Arsenals with a line giving characteristics for firing Bombardments.

Some mortars and rocket launchers cannot fire directly at a target and therefore only have a single line in the Arsenals that lists their characteristics for firing Bombardments. These are also Artillery teams.

Light Mortar teams are Infantry teams and cannot fire bombardments, their characteristics are for normal shooting.

FIRING A BOMBARDMENT

When are Bombardments Fired

Artillery batteries fire their long-range bombardments while other troops are engaging the enemy with direct fire at shorter ranges.

Artillery teams fire Artillery Bombardments in the Shooting Step at the same time as other weapons.

Artillery teams cannot fire Artillery Bombardments as Defensive Fire during the Assault Step. The enemy is already too close to your own troops for a bombardment to be effective.

Who Can Fire a Bombardment

It takes a lot of work to prepare a bombardment, and it takes even more time to fire enough rounds to make the bombardment effective. There is no way guns can fire an artillery bombardment from the move.

To fire a bombardment an Artillery team must either:

- *spend the whole turn stationary, or*
- *Unlimber in the Movement Step provided the Gun team remains where it started the turn aside from rotating.*

Pinned Down

It is difficult to load and fire an artillery piece under fire, and impossible to fire fast enough to maintain an effective bombardment. Only self-propelled guns can keep firing while under heavy fire.

Only Armoured vehicles can fire Artillery Bombardments when their platoon is Pinned Down. Other types of teams cannot fire a bombardment while Pinned Down.

One Bombardment Per Turn

Organising and firing a bombardment is too time consuming to allow an artillery battery to engage multiple targets in a short space of time.

An Artillery platoon can only fire one Artillery Bombardment per turn.

No Splitting of Artillery Fire

The time required for a battery to coordinate a bombardment forces it to ignore all other targets.

When a platoon fires an Artillery Bombardment, its Artillery teams cannot fire any other weapons this turn. If they do not fire in the Artillery Bombardment they cannot shoot at all.

Non-artillery teams cannot fire Bombardments, so are free to conduct normal Shooting.

Ranging Artillery

An artillery bombardment begins with the spotter giving a map reference for the target to the plotting team at the gun position. They calculate the bearing and range and the gunners fire a round at that map reference.

Usually, between difficulties in precisely locating the target on a map, the round will land close, but not right on target. The spotter calls back a correction such as 'Down 200, right 100.' The gunners correct and fire another round. If this lands on target, the spotter calls 'On target, four rounds, fire.' Each gun fires four rounds dropping a salvo on the target. Fire mission complete!

Summary

- **Bombardments are fired at the same time as other shooting.**
- **Artillery teams must spend the whole turn stationary to fire a Bombardment, and only Armoured vehicles can fire a Bombardment if the platoon is Pinned Down.**
- **If a platoon fires a Bombardment, all Artillery teams must participate or not shoot at all. A platoon can only fire one Bombardment per turn.**
- **Remember, Bogged Down and Bailed Out teams may not participate in a Bombardment.**

Who can fire a Bombardment

SELECT THE AIMING POINT

Although the idea of shelling every suspicious bush, rock, or house makes perfect sense to the trooper at the front line, it doesn't work out that way in the real world. The amount of ammunition needed would be massive, even if there were enough time to wait for endless bombardments. Before the gunners will expend their precious shells and sweat firing a bombardment, they have to be sure that there is a target worth the effort.

The Aiming Point of an Artillery Bombardment must be the centre of a specific enemy team. Place a suitable marker with the enemy team to mark the Aiming Point of the Bombardment.

Maximum Bombardment Range

While guns firing bombardments shoot at high angles of elevation to achieve longer ranges than normal shooting, there is still a limit to how far they can throw a shell.

An Artillery team may not fire in an Artillery Bombardment where the Aiming Point is further than their Bombardment Range away.

Measure the range from the closest part of the Artillery team (excluding gun barrels) to the nearest part of the enemy team (excluding gun barrels) that is the Aiming Point.

Check the range separately for each Artillery team in the firing platoon. This may result in some teams not firing while the rest conduct the bombardment without them.

Minimum Bombardment Range

If the enemy gets too close to your guns, firing a bombardment becomes impractical.

Only Artillery teams that are more than 8"/20cm from the Aiming Point can fire an Artillery Bombardment.

Field of Fire

Most artillery weapons have limited-traverse mountings that restrict the targets they can engage without completely realigning the guns, a rather time-consuming operation.

An Artillery team may not fire in an Artillery Bombardment where the Aiming Point is outside its Field of Fire (see page 82).

Rotate to Face Target

Before they fire, all of your weapons must be brought to bear on the enemy. Your gunners traverse their weapons, aim, and fire.

After determining your teams' Fields of Fire, but before they fire the Bombardment, rotate your teams to point directly at the Aiming Point in the same way that teams rotate to face their target in normal shooting (see page 84).

Firing Over Troops And Terrain

Artillery weapons lob their shells in an arc high overhead. It is this high trajectory that gives them their longer range and allows them to shoot at a distant enemy not even visible to the artillery crews themselves.

Artillery teams can fire a Bombardment over intervening troops or terrain. They do not need a Line of Sight to the Aiming Point as long as their Spotting team has a Line of Sight.

Select the Aiming Point

Firing over Terrain

Firing over Buildings

High obstacles such as buildings are a hazard for artillery crews. They need to have sufficient clearance to lob their shells over the buildings. One of the advantages of mortars is that their steep trajectory allows them to fire over buildings more easily than other artillery pieces.

An Artillery team cannot fire an Artillery Bombardment if the Line of Sight between the Artillery team and the Aiming Point passes through a Building closer to the team than the height of the Building.

Mortar teams are an exception to this and may fire over any Building more than 4"/10cm away from them, no matter how tall the Building is.

Artillery teams can never fire an Artillery Bombardment from within a Building.

Firing over Woods

When positioning their weapons artillery crews are careful not to get too close to intervening trees. If they set up too close, their shells will hit the trees and blow the battery to pieces!

An Artillery team cannot fire an Artillery Bombardment if the Line of Sight between the Artillery team and the Aiming Point passes through trees (such as woods or tree lines) or Bocage Hedgerows within 4"/10cm of the team. This prevents Artillery teams from firing Artillery Bombardments from completely within a Wood.

Summary

- **The Aiming Point of an Artillery Bombardment is an enemy team.**
- **Artillery teams must be more than 8"/20cm from the Aiming Point and within Bombardment Range of the target team.**
- **The Aiming Point does not need to be in Line of Sight, but must be in the Artillery team's Field of Fire.**
- **As for normal shooting, teams Rotate to face the Aiming Point.**
- **Artillery cannot fire over a Building if it is closer than its height. Mortars may fire over any building at least 4"/10cm away.**
- **Artillery cannot fire over trees or a Bocage Hedgerow within 4"/10cm.**

SPOTTING TEAMS

In order to range the guns in on the aiming point, someone has to spot the fall of shot and report the necessary corrections back to the gunners.

Every Artillery Bombardment requires a Spotting team. This can be one of the Artillery teams firing the bombardment, the Platoon Command team or Staff team of the platoon firing the bombardment, any Company or Higher Command team, or a specialist Observer team.

A Spotting team can only Spot for one Artillery platoon and an Artillery platoon can only have one Spotting team Spot for it each turn, even if they fail to Range In.

The Spotting team must have a Line of Sight to the enemy team that is the Aiming Point, must not have moved in the Movement Step, must not shoot in the Shooting Step other than to participate in this Artillery Bombardment, and may not assault in the Assault Step.

Spotting While Pinned Down

Observers do not need to expose themselves much to do their job. They can continue to perform their task, even under heavy enemy fire. However, they still need their radios, so if they abandon their tank, they can't call for bombardments.

Spotting teams can Spot while Pinned Down, but not if they are in a Bogged Down or Bailed Out vehicle.

Spotting with Company Command Teams

Experienced officers can spot for any artillery under their command. They have less training in directing bombardments though, so their bombardments will tend to be less accurate than that of a properly trained spotter.

Company and Higher Command teams can act as the Spotting team for any Artillery platoon under their command, but can only Spot for one platoon per turn.

When acting as a Spotting team, they suffer an additional +1 penalty to the score required to Range In due to their lack of training.

SUMMARY

- **Every Bombardment requires a Spotting team: either a team firing the Bombardment, the commander or Staff team of the Artillery Battery, a Company or Higher Command team, or an Observer team.**
- **The Spotting team must have a Line of Sight to the Aiming Point, and must not move, shoot or assault.**
- **Teams can Spot while Pinned Down, but not while Bogged Down or Bailed Out.**

SPOTTING TEAMS

TACTICS

EYE OF GOD

OBSERVERS NEED A GOOD VIEW TO DO THEIR JOB. PLACE THEM IN CHURCH STEEPLES OR ON HIGH HILLS AT THE START OF THE GAME WHERE THEY CAN HIDE WHILE DIRECTING FIRE ON THE ENEMY.

OBSERVER TEAMS

Artillery can fire much further than it can see so it makes sense to have the weapons placed well back, safely behind friendly lines, and send out small parties known as observer teams to seek out enemy targets in the front lines. Once the observers have found a target they use radios or telephone lines to communicate with their artillery batteries to bring devastating fire down upon unsuspecting enemy troops.

Observer teams are Independent teams and are either Infantry teams, such as Observer Rifle teams, or Tank teams, such as an Observer Sherman tank.

An Observer team can act as the Spotting team for their own platoon from anywhere on the battlefield.

MULTIPLE OBSERVER TEAMS

Large artillery platoons often have two or more observer teams. This allows them to have eyes all over the battlefield to ensure that the enemy has nowhere to hide. However, the artillery platoon can still only respond to one call for fire at a time.

A platoon with multiple Observer teams can only use one of them as a Spotting team each turn.

SPOTTING FOR OTHER PLATOONS

Staff teams are linked to each other by radio or telephone lines so as to form an effective communications network on the battlefield. This practice means that observer teams can call for fire from any battery within range.

An Observer team from an Artillery platoon with a Staff team may act as the Spotting team for another Artillery platoon with a Staff team (aside from an Allied platoon, see page 70) instead of its own platoon. When doing this they can still only Spot for one platoon per turn.

OBSERVERS MOVE CAUTIOUSLY

Observers are trained to make the best use of any cover, even when on the move. This allows them to get right up close to the enemy positions so they can watch their every move and report it back to the artillery battery.

Observer teams and their transports use the Cautious Movement rule on page 193 like a Recce team.

DISMOUNTING OBSERVERS FROM TANKS

Sometimes a good observation post such as a church steeple is more important than armour protection and mobility. In that case, the observer will dismount taking a portable radio and send their tank away.

You may Dismount an Observer Tank team that is not Bailed Out as an Observer Rifle team. To do so, remove the Tank team at the start of your Movement Step or when Deploying the team at the start of the game, and replace it with an Observer Rifle team placed anywhere under the area covered by the Tank team.

When a Bogged Down (see page 44) Observer Tank team Dismounts, it immediately ceases being Bogged Down and is removed.

Observer Tank teams may only Dismount if you have an Observer Rifle team to replace it, otherwise, it must stay in the vehicle.

SUMMARY

- **Observer Teams are Independent teams that can Spot for their Artillery Battery. They also have the Cautious Movement ability.**
- **Artillery Batteries can only use one Observer to Spot for them each turn.**
- **Observers may Spot for other Artillery Batteries if both their platoon and the Artillery Battery have Staff teams.**
- **Observer Tank teams Dismount by swapping the tank for an Observer Rifle team.**

US M7 Priest 105mm GMC.

STAFF TEAMS

A staff team is an important component of large artillery platoons. The staff team's job is to take the target's map reference, radioed to them by the spotter, and convert it to angles and elevations for the artillery weapons. Their technical expertise allows the staff to perform complex calculations and communicate the results to the rest of the artillery platoon quickly.

Mortar platoons and rocket batteries lack artillery staff because their operation does not permit prolonged bombardments and sophisticated artillery tactics.

Staff Teams

To do their job, a staff team needs lots of maps, plotting boards, charts and tables, not to mention radios and telephones. All this equipment prevents them from being very mobile or effective in combat.

Although they are an Infantry team, Staff teams are part of their Artillery platoon and move slowly as if they were a Heavy Gun team. A Staff team can shoot as a Rifle team, but cannot function as a Staff team in the turn it does so.

A Staff team can function just as well when it is mounted in its own Transport team as it can when Dismounted (as long as it is not Bailed Out or Bogged Down), but cannot function at all when mounted in another Transport team.

All Guns Repeat!

If the spotter successfully ranged the artillery in last turn, the staff team can order all of their guns to repeat the bombardment on exactly the same place. The target coordinates for a repeat bombardment are exactly the same as the previous bombardment, meaning all weapons can fire again quickly and effectively.

An Artillery platoon with a Staff team may Repeat an Artillery Bombardment fired in the previous turn.

Because a Repeated Bombardment Ranged In on a previous turn, it automatically Ranges In on the first attempt this turn.

The Repeated Bombardment must use the same Spotting team as the original Artillery Bombardment, and it must still meet the other requirements for a Spotting team (see page 126).

All Artillery teams that fired the original Bombardment that still can must fire in the Repeated Bombardment, and no other teams may be added to the Bombardment.

The Repeated Bombardment must use the same Template (see page 130) as the previous turn's Bombardment, unless there are insufficient weapons still firing.

The Repeated Bombardment is centred on the original Aiming Point, regardless of whether or not the enemy team that was originally targeted is still there or not.

SUMMARY

- **Staff teams are Infantry teams that move as a Heavy Gun and shoot as a Rifle team.**
- **Artillery platoons with a Staff team may Repeat a Bombardment fired in the previous turn.**
- **A Repeated Bombardment must use the same Spotting team and Aiming Point, and automatically Ranges In.**

US M1 155mm Howitzer

ROLL TO RANGE IN ON THE TARGET

Having selected the aiming point, the artillery must range their guns in before they can fire the bombardment.

As with direct shooting, the most difficult part of ranging the artillery in is finding the enemy in the first place.

A Spotting team may make three attempts to Range In an Artillery platoon each turn.

- *If any roll to Range In is successful, the Artillery platoon Ranges In on the Aiming Point, and can now fire the Bombardment.*
- *Otherwise the Artillery teams fire their ranging shots (counting as shooting), but have no effect on the target.*

The score required for your Artillery to Range In depends on the enemy's Skill rating as shown in the Score Needed to Range In table.

Score Needed to Range In

Target Team's Skill	Score Needed to Hit
Conscript	2+
Trained	3+
Veteran	4+

Add +1 to the score to range in for each of the following:

- Target team is Concealed.
- Target team is Gone to Ground while Concealed
- Spotting team is a Company or Higher Command team.

Mortars Re-roll First Attempt

Mortars are closer to the scene of the action and fire much more rapidly than guns. This allows them to range in quicker and deliver an effective bombardment almost immediately.

If an Artillery Bombardment is only being fired by Mortar teams, you may re-roll the first failed attempt to Range In.

If it fails on the re-roll, you still have two more Ranging In attempts left as normal. The mortars do not get a re-roll on their second and third attempts.

Locating and Hitting the Target

Ranging in an artillery bombardment requires a similar score to that needed to hit the target with normal shooting. In both cases the trickiest part is actually locating the target as opposed to actually hitting it once it is located.

Once the spotter has located the target, it is then up to the skill of the gunners to deliver a timely and concentrated bombardment on the target. Skilful gunners will have the rounds landing quickly in a tight pattern. Conscripts on the other hand, take time to get on target, and even then splatter shells across the landscape.

Summary

- **Scores to Range In depend on the target team's Skill rating and concealment.**
- **A Spotting team may make three attempts to Range In. If any attempt is successful, the Artillery platoon Ranges In. Otherwise it counts as shooting but has no effect.**
- **Mortars may re-roll their first attempt to Range In if it fails.**

Ranging In

Tactics: Targets Moving At the Double

One of the most effective countermeasures against artillery is getting out of the danger zone as fast as possible. The artillery either has to keep shifting their fire or cease fire. This makes moving at the double through artillery fire a viable tactic. It doesn't reduce casualties, but it does reduce the time you are exposed to artillery bombardments.

POSITION THE TEMPLATE

Artillery bombardments differ from normal shooting in that the gunners are attempting to hit all targets in an area centred on the target team. The artillery is raining huge explosive power down upon the target and the surrounding area. Anyone close is likely to suffer.

Place the Artillery Template (a square measuring 6"/15cm on each side) centred over the Aiming Point. The sides of the Template must be lined up pointing towards the centre of the Bombarding platoon. If several platoons are combining to fire a Bombardment, by using the Hit 'em With Everything You've Got rule on page 240 for example, choose one of the Bombarding platoons and line the Template up with it.

All of the Artillery weapons in a Bombardment are firing at the same target point, so you only use one Template, no matter how many weapons the battery has.

DOUBLE-WIDTH TEMPLATES

If you get enough guns firing, you can cover a much larger area. This is useful when pounding an enemy platoon that is dispersed over a wide area.

A Double-width Template is a rectangle measuring 12"/30cm wide by 6"/15cm deep. Align the Template so that it is centred over the Aiming Point with one 6"/15cm square template on each side of the line running back to the Bombarding platoon.

DEVASTATING BOMBARDMENTS

Massed rocket launchers can saturate a huge area making a normal artillery bombardment look paltry. The sheer area covered makes up for the lack of accuracy of each launcher.

A Devastating Bombardment Template is a square measuring 12"/30cm on each side. The sides of the Template must be lined up pointing towards the Bombarding platoon.

SUMMARY

- **Centre the Artillery Template on the Aiming Point lined up towards the Bombarding platoon.**
- **If multiple platoons are firing, then align the Artillery Template with one of the firing platoons.**
- **Artillery Templates are 6"/15cm square.**
- **Double-width Templates are 12"/30cm wide by 6"/15cm deep.**
- **Devastating Bombardment Templates are 12"/30cm square.**

POSITION THE TEMPLATE

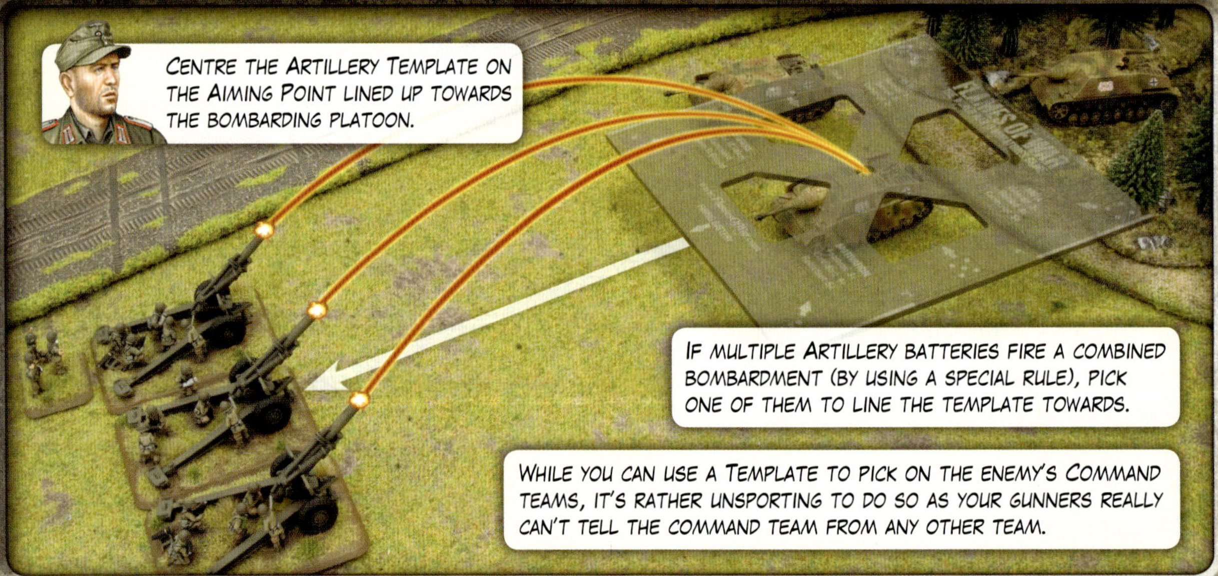

WHY ARE ARTILLERY TEMPLATES SQUARE?

While the danger area for a single artillery shell is anything but square (more of a butterfly shape in reality), the danger area for an artillery battery is generally considered to be a square. This reflects the way the aiming points of the individual guns are spread out, and the dispersion of the individual shells landing within the target area. We use the same size template for artillery of all calibres because, although heavy artillery fires huge shells, while lighter weapons fire many more, smaller shells, the overall effect is to create a similar-sized danger area, either from a few big explosions or lots of smaller ones.

BIGGER AND SMALLER BATTERIES

Not all artillery bombardments are created equal. A bombardment by one or two small guns is unlikely to cause serious harm, while a massed bombardment by a dozen or more heavy guns will smash almost any target to pulp in short order.

Single-gun Batteries

Good luck hitting anything with a bombardment if you only have one weapon firing!

If the Bombarding platoon has only one weapon firing, you must use a standard Artillery Template and add +1 to the score required to hit any target in addition to re-rolling successful rolls To Hit.

Two-gun Batteries

If you only have a few weapons firing, there are not going to be as many shells hitting the target and the casualties will be a lot less.

If the Bombarding platoon has two weapons firing, you must use a standard Artillery Template and re-roll successful rolls To Hit to confirm your hits.

Three to Five-gun Batteries

Once you get sufficient weapons firing, a bombardment starts to take full effect on the enemy.

If the Bombarding platoon has three to five weapons firing, use a standard Artillery Template.

Six to Eight-gun Batteries

The more weapons you have firing, the more shells you can fire, the more explosives you deliver onto the target area, and therefore the more likely you are to destroy your target.

If the Bombarding platoon has six to eight weapons firing, you may either re-roll failed rolls To Hit, or use a Double-width Template.

Nine to Thirteen-gun Batteries

At a certain point the sheer number of guns firing allows you to spread your fire over a larger area while retaining maximum effectiveness.

If the Bombarding platoon has nine to thirteen weapons firing, you may either use a Double-width Template and re-roll failed to hit rolls, or use a Devastating Bombardment Template.

Fourteen or More-gun Batteries

Gigantic bombardments are devastating. Everything in the entire area is pulverised.

If the Bombarding platoon has fourteen or more weapons firing, use a Devastating Bombardment Template and re-roll failed to hit rolls.

Mixed Bombardments

Some artillery battalions have a heavy battery with a different type of weapon, or flexible fire control that allowed batteries from different units to coordinate their fire. While the effect of the heavy weapons is diluted by the lighter weapons, the mixed bombardment is still more deadly than the light weapons alone.

When an Artillery Bombardment is fired by a combination of different Artillery weapons use the worst Skill rating, the lowest Anti-tank rating, and the worst Firepower rating of all the types of weapon.

If at least one third of weapons firing have a better Anti-tank rating than the worst weapons, add +1 to the lowest Anti-tank rating, using this rating for the whole Bombardment.

If at least one third of weapons firing have a better Firepower rating than the worst weapons, improve the worst Firepower rating by -1, using this rating for the whole Bombardment.

Example

If a Soviet artillery battalion with four 122mm howitzers (Anti-tank 4, Firepower 3+) and eight 76mm guns (Anti-tank 3, Firepower 6) fires a bombardment, it does so with an Anti-tank rating of 4 and a Firepower rating of 5+. If there were only two howitzers, the whole bombardment would have the ratings of the 76mm guns instead.

Summary

- **Single-Gun Bombardments add +1 to the score and re-roll successful rolls To Hit.**
- **Two-Gun Bombardments re-roll successful rolls To Hit.**
- **Six to Eight-Gun Bombardments either re-roll failed rolls To Hit, or use a Double-width Template.**
- **Nine to Thirteen-Gun Bombardments either use a Double-width Template and re-roll failed rolls To Hit, or use a Devastating Bombardment Template.**
- **Fourteen or more-Gun Bombardments use a Devastating Bombardment Template and re- roll failed rolls To Hit.**
- **Mixed bombardments use the worst Skill rating, the worst Firepower rating and the lowest Anti-tank rating. If a third of the weapons have better Anti-tank and Firepower ratings than the worst, improve these ratings by 1.**

ROLL TO HIT TEAMS UNDER THE TEMPLATE

Once the guns are ranged in on the target point, they all open fire, saturating the target area, but the results all depend on how quickly and accurately the gunners can shell the target. Experienced gunners deliver a devastating, concentrated bombardment, while poorly trained conscripts scatter shells ineffectively over a wide area.

Rather than rolling one die per point of ROF as teams do when shooting normally, count up the number of teams at least partly under the Template, and roll that number of dice. Roll hits separately for each platoon under the Template.

The score needed to hit is based on the bombarding teams' Skill rating, modified by the time taken to locate and Range In on the target as detailed in the Score Needed to Hit table.

- *A successful to hit roll means a team was hit by the Bombardment.*
- *A failed to hit roll means that the team was lucky and escaped harm from the Bombardment.*

Multiple Target Types

Although soldiers can be ordered to man other weapons, a destroyed gun cannot be replaced with a truck!

Roll to hit each Type of team (Tank, Infantry, Gun, and Transport teams) in the platoon separately.

A Six Always Hits with Artillery

A bunch of poorly-trained conscripts trying to get artillery on target isn't the most impressive sight, but with enough shells, close enough is good enough.

The score to hit a team under an Artillery Bombardment is never more than 6, provided two or more weapons are firing.

Score Needed to Hit

Firing Platoon's Skill	Score Needed to Hit
Conscript	5+
Trained	4+
Veteran	3+

Add +1 to the score to hit if:
- The artillery ranged in on the second attempt.

Add +2 to the score to hit if:
- The artillery ranged in on the third attempt.

Add +1 to the score to hit if:
- Only one weapon is firing.

SUMMARY

- **Roll one die for each team at least partly under the template. Roll separately for each platoon and each type of team.**
- **Scores to Hit depend on the firing team's Skill rating and the time taken to Range In.**
- **A score of 6 always hits as long as two or more weapons are firing.**

Multiple Target Types

ALLOCATE HITS TO TEAMS

Commanders order soldiers to replace casualties in weapons teams to keep important weapons in action.

Your opponent allocates hits to teams of the appropriate type under the Template from the platoon that was hit, subject to the following rules in order of priority.

- *Each team may only be allocated one hit.*
- *Unprotected teams must be allocated hits before teams in Bulletproof Cover.*
- *Hits must be allocated to operational vehicles and other teams (including Gone to Ground teams) before Bogged Down or Bailed Out vehicles.*
- *Unarmoured vehicles must be allocated hits before Armoured vehicles.*
- *Hits must be allocated to Armoured vehicles with lower Top armour ratings before those with higher Top armour ratings.*
- *Hits must be allocated to other teams before teams that are Gone to Ground.*

Riding on Tanks

Riding on a tank is dangerous under artillery fire.

Do not roll to hit Infantry or Man-packed Gun teams riding on a tank separately from their tank. Instead, if the Tank team is hit, all teams riding on it are also hit.

Hitting Teams in Buildings

Artillery fire on buildings is the same as any other—those caught in the danger zone are at risk.

Check the teams' positions in the Building to determine which ones are under the Template of an Artillery Bombardment in the same way as if they were outside the Building.

Friendly Fire

Artillery is indiscriminate and everyone under the bombardment, whether friend or foe, suffers. Unfortunately this means that your own troops may be hit if they are too close to the enemy when the bombardment is requested!

If any friendly teams are under or partially under the Artillery Template during an Artillery Bombardment, you must roll to hit them exactly as you would for enemy teams. If a friendly team is unlucky enough to be hit during a bombardment the effects will be exactly the same as for an enemy team!

SUMMARY

- **Target player allocates hits.**
- **Each team may only be allocated one hit.**
- **Hits must be allocated to unprotected teams before teams in Bulletproof Cover.**
- **Hits must be allocated to Unarmoured vehicles before Armoured vehicles.**
- **Hits must be allocated to other vehicles before Bogged Down or Bailed Out ones.**
- **Hits must be allocated to Armoured vehicles with the lowest Top armour first.**
- **Hits must be allocated to other teams before teams that are Gone to Ground.**
- **If a tank is hit by a Bombardment, any teams riding on it are also hit.**

PIN DOWN ALL PLATOONS THAT WERE HIT

With shells exploding and shrapnel flying everywhere, it takes an exceptionally brave soldier to stick his head out of his hole under an artillery bombardment.

If a platoon takes one or more hits from an Artillery Bombardment, it is automatically Pinned Down *(see page 104).*

SUMMARY

- **Any platoon hit by an Artillery Bombardment is automatically Pinned Down.**

British Bren gun team under fire in Tunisia
IWMna2165

ROLL SAVES FOR TEAMS THAT WERE HIT

A hit means that a shell has landed close enough to an enemy team to be dangerous. The roll to save determines if the shell did any serious damage.

Armoured Vehicle Saves

Mostly the shells falling everywhere explode near the tanks, and shake up the crew. If a shell does actually hit a tank it falls on the thin top armour.

When you hit a tank, the opposing player rolls a die and adds the vehicle's Top armour rating. Compare their result with your weapon's Anti-tank rating for Bombardments.

Exceeds Anti-tank Rating

If your opponent's Armour Save roll is greater than your weapon's Anti-tank rating for bombardments, their Armour Save is successful, and the shot has no effect having bounced harmlessly off the tank's armour.

Equals Anti-tank Rating

If your opponent's Armour Save roll exactly equals your weapon's Anti-tank rating for bombardments, they failed their Armour Save. Although your shot didn't penetrate the tank's armour, it might still have some effect.

To determine the effect of the hit you must take a Firepower Test. Roll another die.

- *If the roll equals or exceeds your weapon's Firepower rating, the crew panic and Bail Out.*
- *If the roll is lower than your weapon's Firepower rating the shot has no effect and the tank continues in action unharmed.*

Less than Anti-tank Rating

If your opponent's Armour Save roll is less than your weapon's Anti-tank rating for bombardments, they failed their Armour Save.

To determine the effect of the hit you must take a Firepower Test. Roll another die.

- *If the roll equals or exceeds your weapon's Firepower rating, the tank is Destroyed.*
- *If the roll is lower than your weapon's Firepower rating the shot failed to do significant damage to the vehicle but the crew still Bails Out of the tank fearing that the next shot might do worse.*

Unarmoured Vehicle Saves

Unarmoured vehicles have no protection from artillery. Their only hope of survival is that the exploding shells will do only minor damage.

When your bombardment hits an Unarmoured vehicle team (a Tank or Transport team with a Top armour rating of '-'), the opposing player rolls a die.

- *If the result is 5+, the vehicle escapes unharmed.*
- *Otherwise, the vehicle is automatically Destroyed.*

Recce and Warrior Vehicle Saves

Small jeeps and motorcycles are fast-moving targets and tend to get out of the bombardment area or into hollows and out of danger quickly.

Unarmoured vehicles that are Warrior, Independent or Recce teams (including all Motorcycle Reconnaissance teams) save on a roll of 3+ instead of the usual 5+.

Infantry Saves

Infantry caught in the open have very little protection against the shells whistling down on their position. Their only hope is to hit the dirt, and fast! If the shelling continues, they should move out of the barrage as fast as possible.

Infantry in bulletproof cover is a different matter. They are very hard to dig out.

When your bombardment hits an Infantry team, the opposing player rolls a die.

- *If the result is 3+ the team escapes with no serious injury.*
- *Otherwise, unless the team is in Bulletproof Cover, it is Destroyed.*

Gun Saves

Guns are even more endangered by artillery bombardments than infantry, as the guns and crews are less able to disperse to avoid the falling shells. However, if the guns are dug in, they can be tough to destroy as only a direct hit will wipe out the whole crew.

When your bombardment hits a Gun team, the opposing player rolls a die.

- *If the result is 5+ the team escapes with no serious injury.*
- *Otherwise, unless the team is in Bulletproof Cover, it is Destroyed.*

Gone to Ground Gun Saves

When working their gun, gunners are forced to clump together more than infantry. However, if they go to ground, they can spread out and take full advantage of cover, making them much less vulnerable.

Any Gun teams that are Gone to Ground have a 3+ save instead of a 5+ save. This does not apply to teams that are only Gone to Ground because they are behind Smoke.

Bulletproof Cover

A bombardment renders cover that only protects from one direction useless.

Linear Obstacles like walls or Bocage Hedgerows, and Gun Shields do not provide Bulletproof Cover against Bombardments, although other Bulletproof Cover (including being Dug In or in Entrenchments) does.

If the target Infantry or Gun teams are in Bulletproof Cover, take a Firepower Test.

- *If the roll equals or exceeds your weapon's Firepower rating, your weapon blew through the cover and the target team is Destroyed.*
- *If the roll is lower than your weapon's Firepower rating, the cover protects the team from harm.*

Passengers in Transports

Transports are not intended to fight. They get out of the battle when shot at.

Armoured Transports

Armoured half-tracks were conceived as a way of getting troops safely through the artillery zone and into combat. They won't stop under artillery fire while they can still move.

Armoured Transport teams roll saves in the same way that Armoured Tank teams do. However, they automatically Remount (see page 102) immediately when Bailed Out by an Artillery Bombardment.

If you Destroy an Armoured Transport team, every Passenger carried by the Transport team must pass a 5+ Passenger Save or be Destroyed. Any surviving Passenger teams immediately Dismount Under Fire and the platoon is now Pinned Down (see page 104).

Unarmoured Transports

The best thing to do under artillery fire is keep driving and pray that you don't get hit.

When you hit an Unarmoured Transport team (whether or not you Destroy it), every Passenger carried by the Transport team must pass a 5+ Passenger Save or be Destroyed. If all of the Passengers in a Transport team are Destroyed but the vehicle is not, the Transport team is Sent to the Rear immediately. The platoon is now Pinned Down (see page 104).

Surviving Unarmoured Transport teams still carrying Passengers remain on table after an artillery bombardment, even if other Transport teams in the platoon were Destroyed.

Dismounting Under Fire

When an artillery round wrecks their vehicle, the survivors leap out seeking cover in the folds of the ground.

If its transport is Destroyed or removed as a result of a Bombardment, any surviving Passenger teams must immediately Dismount, moving no closer to the shooting teams as it does so.

If necessary, Transport teams (other than Wrecks of Armoured Transport teams) can be removed first to create space for the Passengers to Dismount. If there is no room for a Passenger team to Dismount, then the Passenger team is Destroyed.

Passengers on Tanks

If riding in a vehicle is unsafe, clinging to the outside of a tank under fire is even more dangerous.

Infantry or Man-packed Gun teams riding on a tank must take a 5+ Save instead of their usual Infantry or Gun Save when hit. The Passengers are not in Bulletproof Cover, so no Firepower Test is needed to Destroy them.

All surviving teams immediately Dismount Under Fire and the platoon is now Pinned Down (see page 104).

SUMMARY

Roll Saves for Teams that were Hit

Armoured Vehicle Saves

- **Roll a die, add the vehicle's Top armour, and compare result to Anti-tank rating:**
  - **If greater, vehicle is unharmed.**
  - **If equal, Firepower Test to Bail Out.**
  - **If less, Firepower test to Destroy, if fail the vehicle is Bailed Out.**

Unarmoured Vehicle Saves

- **Unarmoured vehicles pass a save on a 5+. Unarmoured vehicles that are Warrior, Independent or Recce teams save on a 3+.**

Infantry and Gun Saves

- **Infantry teams save on 3+. Gun teams save on 5+, unless Gone to Ground when they save on 3+. Riders on tanks save on 5+.**

Bulletproof Cover and Passengers

- **A Firepower Test is required to Destroy teams in Bulletproof Cover. Linear Obstacles and Gun Shields do not provide Bulletproof Cover against Bombardments.**
- **Passengers in Unarmoured transports that were hit or Destroyed Armoured transports must pass a Save of 5+. Survivors immediately Dismount and are Pinned Down.**

SMOKE BOMBARDMENTS

A smoke screen is created by firing shells filled with chemicals that burn quickly, giving off clouds of dense white smoke. Enormous amounts of these shells must be fired onto a small area to create a smoke screen large and dense enough to provide complete concealment for your troops. Impromptu smoke screens of the type called down by a commander during a battle, while still impressive and quite effective, are nowhere near as dense and complete and cannot be maintained indefinitely.

Only weapons listed as having the Smoke Bombardment attribute in their Arsenal listing may fire a Smoke Bombardment.

FIRING SMOKE BOMBARDMENTS

Artillery follows the same process when firing smoke as when firing normal ammunition, the only difference is that smoke rounds can't hurt the target.

When firing a Smoke Bombardment, use the normal Artillery Bombardment rules to Range In using an enemy team as the Aiming Point as usual. If any roll to Range In is successful, place a Smoke Screen. The Bombardment has no other effect.

FIRE SMOKE BOMBARDMENTS FIRST

Smoke bombardments require many shells and considerable time to take full effect. If you do not give them priority, they will not be effective in stopping the enemy from shooting the troops you are trying to screen.

Smoke Bombardments must be fired at the beginning of the Shooting Step before all other shooting.

NO REPEAT BOMBARDMENTS

Firing a smoke bombardment requires a different set of computations than firing a normal bombardment. Even when artillery fires a smoke bombardment on the same target, the delay in bringing up more specialist smoke ammunition and minor changes in wind speed and direction mean new calculations.

Artillery firing a Smoke Bombardment may not use the All Guns Repeat! rule to repeat a previous Bombardment. Smoke Bombardments must be Ranged In anew every turn they are fired, even when the Aiming Point is the same.

SMOKE DISPERSES

The shells generating the smoke don't burn for very long and the wind will blow the smoke away fairly quickly.

In the Starting Step at the start of your next turn, remove all Smoke Screens that you have fired.

SIZE OF A SMOKE SCREEN

The size of the smoke screen created by a smoke bombardment is directly related to the number of weapons firing the bombardment. This smoke screen is then blown downwind of the target area.

When placing a Smoke Screen on the table, centre the 6"/15cm square Artillery Template on the target team, but instead of lining the sides up with the firing battery the Template sides are positioned parallel to the Wind Direction.

- *If two weapons are firing, the Smoke Screen covers the area of the Template.*

SMOKE SCREENS

- *If three to five weapons are firing, the Smoke Screen may be extended to cover the area of the Template and another Template downwind of and adjacent to it.*
- *If six or more weapons are firing, the Smoke Screen may be extended to cover the area of the Template and another one or two Templates downwind of it.*
- *If only one weapon is firing, the smoke disperses as fast as the weapon can fire it, so there is no Smoke Screen produced.*

The Smoke Screen occupies all of the Templates and is 2"/5cm high. Fill each Artillery Template with nine Smoke markers 2"/5cm in diameter and 2"/5cm tall (balls of cotton wool work well) or a single large Smoke marker 6"/15cm square and 2"/5cm tall.

Effect of a Smoke Screen

The thick blanket of smoke generated by a bombardment is difficult to see through.

A team cannot see another team at over 16"/40cm if all Lines of Sight between them pass through Smoke Markers.

If all Lines of Sight from a Shooting or Spotting team to an enemy team enter or pass through Smoke markers, the team is both Concealed and Gone to Ground, regardless of all other considerations, except in Defensive Fire where it only Conceals (see page 152).

If any Line of Sight from a Shooting or Spotting team to the enemy team does not pass through a Smoke Marker, the Smoke Screen has no effect.

A Smoke Screen is not a Terrain Feature.

Wind Direction

Since smoke tends to drift downwind, one of the major factors to consider when firing a smoke bombardment is which way the wind is blowing.

Either player can find out what the wind direction is at any time. If not done so beforehand, a player must determine the Wind Direction when they fire the first Smoke Bombardment of the game.

Align the Artillery Template so that it points to one of the short table edges. The defending player rolls a die and compares it to the Template to determine the Wind Direction. The attacking player may re-roll the wind direction, reflecting their ability to choose the timing and direction of the attack. If they do, this roll is final, even if less favourable than the first. Once determined, this is the wind direction for the duration of the game.

Summary

- **Range In as normal when firing a Smoke Bombardment, but only teams with the Smoke Bombardment attribute can do so.**
- **Smoke Bombardments must be fired before all other shooting.**
- **Remove Smoke Screens in the Starting Step.**
- **Place the first Artillery Template of a Smoke Screen parallel to the wind direction, then others downwind of that.**
- **Two-gun batteries create a Smoke Screen the size of the an Artillery Template.**
- **Three- to Five-gun batteries create a Smoke Screen two Artillery Templates long.**
- **Six-or-more-gun batteries create a Smoke Screen three Artillery Templates long.**
- **Teams cannot see through Smoke at over 16"/40cm, and the target is Concealed and Gone to Ground at shorter ranges.**

Wind Direction

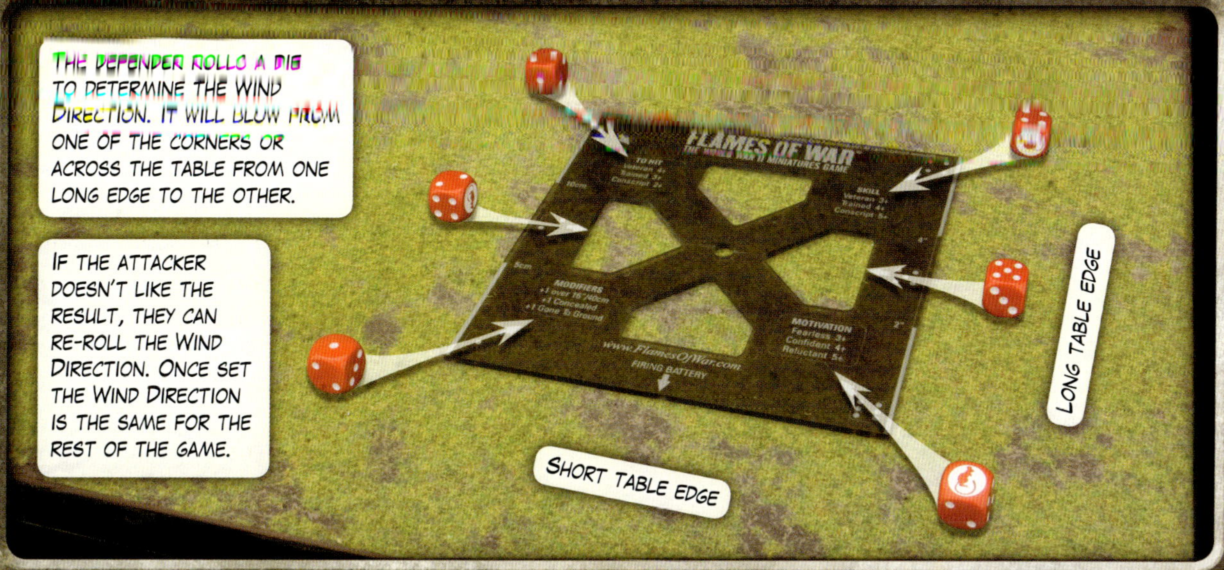

ROCKET LAUNCHERS

Salvo rocket launchers fire bombardments just like any other artillery, but with one key difference. After ranging in as usual (usually by firing a single rocket at a time, just like ordinary artillery), they fire all of their rockets in one massive salvo.

If an Artillery Bombardment is only being fired by Rocket Launcher teams, it does not suffer a To Hit penalty if they Ranged In on their second or third attempt.

Big Rocket Batteries

Rockets are notoriously difficult to control in flight. Without any on-board guidance system the rockets of World War II could not hope to match the accuracy of conventional artillery and very big salvoes would simply be spread across a wider area.

If an Artillery Bombardment is being fired by six to eight Rocket Launcher teams, you must use a Double-width Template rather than re-rolling failed rolls To Hit.

If an Artillery Bombardment is being fired by nine to thirteen Rocket Launcher teams, you must use a Devastating Bombardment Template rather than re-rolling failed rolls To Hit.

An Artillery Bombardment fired by fourteen or more weapons, uses a Devastating Bombardment Template and re-rolls failed To Hit rolls.

Fire in the Sky

Salvo rocket launchers leave long smoke trails through the sky when they fire. Unfortunately, the smoke trails give away the weapons' position, allowing enemy artillery to range in on the rough area.

Place a Smoke Trail marker (a ball of cotton wool or similar) to the rear of each Rocket Launcher team that fires (including failed attempts to Range In).

Spotting teams do not need a Line of Sight to Rocket Launcher teams marked by a Smoke Trail to Range In on them as the smoke trails rise above all terrain. However, if the Spotting team does not have a Line of Sight to the Aiming Point, the target team counts as being Concealed, because the smoke doesn't give away the rocket launchers' precise location.

Remove all smoke trail markers on your Rocket Launcher teams in the Starting Step of your next turn.

SUMMARY

- **Bombardments fired by Rocket Launchers do not modify their To Hit rolls for Ranging In on the second or third attempt.**
- **Six to Eight-Rocket Launcher Batteries use a Double-width Template.**
- **Nine to Thirteen-Rocket Launcher Batteries use a Devastating Bombardment Template.**
- **Fourteen or-more-Rocket Launcher Batteries use a Devastating Bombardment Template and re-roll failed To Hit rolls.**

Soviet BM-13 Katyusha.

AIR OBSERVATION POSTS

Flying low over the front line, an American L4 'Grasshopper' or British Auster liaison aircraft operating as an air observation post (AOP) is the bane of German soldiers. Any movement at all is instantly spotted and radioed back to the field artillery, who respond in their usual brutal fashion by pounding the target until all movement ceases. By D-Day, every American and British division had light aircraft operating as AOP's giving them unequalled artillery observation capability.

An Air Observation Post (AOP) is an Independent Observer team, but may never Join another Independent team or platoon. An AOP is not treated as an aircraft, except for shooting at it and Fighter Interception.

The AOP carries no weapons and cannot shoot, assault, or be assaulted.

An AOP cannot operate at night. If the mission uses the Dawn rules (see page 273), the AOP will move on to the table in its first daylight turn. If the mission uses the Dusk rules (see page 273), the AOP will leave the table in its first night turn.

Moving an AOP

The AOP flies low over the front looking for the enemy and reporting their positions. Although slow compared to fighter (or even bomber) aircraft, an AOP is still extremely fast compared to its earth-bound compatriots.

An AOP does not have a Movement Distance. Simply place the AOP where you want it to be in the Movement Step.

An AOP may be placed within 2"/5cm of an enemy team, and enemy teams may move within 2"/5cm of an AOP.

Artillery Observer

The main role of an AOP aircraft is artillery observation, using its mobility to find targets and avoid enemy anti-aircraft fire. It flies low to avoid enemy fighter aircraft, making it more like a ground vehicle than an aircraft.

An AOP is an Observer team that can act as the Spotting team for any Artillery platoon that has a Staff team. An AOP Spots like a ground vehicle, drawing Line of Sight to and from the aircraft model, ignoring its flight stand.

Unlike other Observer teams, an AOP can Spot for artillery while moving. When using the All Guns Repeat! special rule on page 128, an AOP can move, but must still be in a position to Spot the Aiming Point from the previous turn.

Due to the difficulties in flying an aircraft and locating targets at the same time, the AOP aircraft model (ignoring the flight stand) must be within 16"/40cm of the Aiming Point. Line of Sight from an AOP is taken from any part of the aircraft model.

The AOP benefits from its height by allowing it to re-roll the third attempt to Range In if it failed on that attempt.

Shooting at an AOP

Even though they are flying low, an AOP is still moving too fast and high for anything but an anti-aircraft gun to hit.

An AOP can only be shot at using the rules for Conducting Anti-aircraft Fire on page 181 as if it was an Aircraft. Self-defence Anti-aircraft weapons can shoot at an AOP, even if not attacked by it. As with all Anti-aircraft Fire, the AOP is shot at in its own Shooting Step, not the enemy Shooting Step.

Fighter Interception

AOP pilots relied on being inconspicuous to survive in their defenceless light aircraft. Sometimes it worked, and sometimes it didn't.

If your opponent has Air Support, they can roll for Fighter Interception instead of Ground Attack at the beginning of their own turn. If they receive their Fighter Interception, the AOP is shot down and Destroyed.

If the AOP player also has Air Support, they may roll for Fighter Interception (as if the opponent had rolled for Ground Attack) to stop the opponent's fighters before they shoot down the AOP.

SUMMARY

- **Place an AOP anywhere on the table as its movement.**
- **An AOP can act as an Observer for any Artillery platoon that has a Staff team. It can act as a Spotting team while moving, and must be within 16"/40cm of its Aiming Point to Spot.**
- **An AOP re-rolls its third attempt to Range In if it failed on that attempt.**
- **Shoot at an AOP using the Conducting Anti-aircraft Fire rules.**
- **Aircraft can attempt to shoot down an AOP instead of providing a Ground Attack mission.**

American Grasshopper Air Observation Post

ARTILLERY SUMMARY

1 Select the Aiming Point

Select an enemy team as the aiming point.

2 Nominate the Spotting Team

Select one of the weapons firing, the Platoon Command or Staff team, the Company or a Higher Command team, or an Observer team as the Spotting team.

3 Check that the Target is Valid

Target must be in Line of Sight, Range, and Field of Fire.

4 Rotate to Face the Target

Turn the artillery to face the target of its bombardment.

5 Check if the Target is Concealed

- *Targets at least half hidden by terrain are Concealed.*
- *Infantry and Man-packed Guns are always Concealed if they don't move.*
- *Teams that did not move, shoot, or assault are Gone to Ground.*

6 Roll to Range In on the Target

Three attempts to range in.

Target Team's Skill	*Score Needed*
Conscript	*2+*
Trained	*3+*
Veteran	*4+*

Add +1 to the score to range in for each of the following:
- *Targeted team is Concealed.*
- *Targeted team is Gone to Ground while Concealed.*
- *Spotting team is a Company or Higher Command team.*

Mortars may re-roll a failed first attempt to Range In.

7 Position the Template

Centre the template over the Aiming Point.

Weapons Firing	*Template*	*Re-rolls*
1	*6"/15cm x 6"/15cm*	*Re-roll hits*
2	*6"/15cm x 6"/15cm*	*Re-roll hits*
3 to 5	*6"/15cm x 6"/15cm*	*No re-rolls*
6 to 8 or	*6"/15cm x 6"/15cm* *12"/30cm x 6"/15cm*	*Re-roll misses* *No re-rolls*
9 to 13 or	*12"/30cm x 6"/15cm* *12"/30cm x 12"/30cm*	*Re-roll misses* *No re-rolls*
14 or more	*12"/30cm x 12"/30cm*	*Re-roll misses*

8 Roll to Hit

Roll one die per team under the template.

Firing Platoon's Skill	*Score Needed*
Conscript	*5+*
Trained	*4+*
Veteran	*3+*

Add +1 to the score to hit if:
- *The artillery ranged in on the second attempt.*

Add +2 to the required score to hit if:
- *The artillery ranged in on the third attempt.*

Add +1 to the score to hit if:
- *Only a single weapon is firing.*

Artillery with 2+ weapons firing always hits on a 6.

9 Roll Saves for Teams that were Hit

Artillery hits the Top armour of Armoured vehicles. Opponent rolls a die and adds their Top armour rating and compares the result to the Artillery Anti-tank rating:

Roll is	*Result*
Greater	*No effect*
Equal	*Firepower test to Bail Out*
Less	*Firepower test to Destroy otherwise Bail Out*

Roll 5+ save for Unarmoured vehicles, except 3+ save for Warrior, Independent, and Recce teams.

Roll 3+ save for Infantry teams.

Roll 5+ save for Gun teams, unless Gone to Ground, then 3+ save.

Roll Firepower Tests to Destroy Infantry teams, and Gun teams in Bulletproof Cover.

10 Mark or Remove Destroyed Teams

Mark Destroyed Armoured vehicles as Wrecks.

Remove other Destroyed teams.

11 Pin Down Platoons that were Hit

Any hit on a platoon from a Bombardment means the platoon is Pinned Down.

ASSAULTS

German infantry under assault by Soviet infantry and T-34/85 tanks

Although you'd think that the firepower of machine-guns and artillery would be more than enough to deal with the most stubborn enemy, experience has repeatedly shown that well dug-in infantry in trenches and bunkers can withstand a heavy bombardment. In the end, the only way to take their position is to get up close and personal with bayonets and hand grenades.

ASSAULTS SEQUENCE

1. Select the Assaulting Platoon
2. Test for Tank Terror
3. Charge into Contact
4. Opponent Conducts Defensive Fire
5. Roll to Hit with Assaulting Teams
6. Roll Saves for Armoured Vehicles
7. Mark or Remove Destroyed Teams
8. Push into Enemy Positions
9. Has Assaulting Platoon Won (if so, Skip to 11)
10. Opponent Tests Motivation and either:
    - Counterattacks, or
    - Breaks Off
11. Victor Consolidates
12. Return to 1 and Select the Next Platoon

CONTENTS

Readying grenades, your soldiers rise to their feet, the sun glinting off their bayonets, and charge towards the enemy positions. The decisive moment has come. While some of the fighting in an assault is hand-to-hand with bayonets and sharpened spades, much is simply close-quarters combat with submachine-guns and grenades.

In the Assault Step, you launch a series of assaults. To keep things simple, each assault is fought in turn before the next assault begins.

In each assault, you select one of your platoons to charge the enemy. Each assault pits one of your platoons against one or more of your opponent's platoons.

Your assaulting platoon charges into contact with the enemy, then the defenders conduct defensive fire in an effort to pin the assaulting platoon down and stop it.

If they fail, all assaulting teams attack in a lethal flurry of bayonets and grenades.

After this terrifying onslaught, the defender tests their willingness to counterattack with their own wave of bayonets and grenades. Otherwise the defenders break off and the assault succeeds.

Should the defender fight back, the assaulting platoon needs to test their willingness in turn. If they are ready to carry on, they counterattack and the process continues until one side or the other breaks off.

When you have completed one platoon's assaults, you select another platoon to Launch an Assault and charge in.

SELECT THE ASSAULTING PLATOON

Your troops need to manoeuvre themselves to within striking distance of the enemy to launch an assault.

Select one of your platoons or a Warrior team as the Assaulting platoon. It must be able to get into base-to-base contact with an enemy team when it Charges into Contact *(see page 145)**.*

Pinned Down Platoons Can't Assault

One of the easiest ways to stop the enemy from assaulting is to keep their heads down with heavy fire.

You may not select a Pinned Down platoon containing Infantry teams as the Assaulting platoon since they aren't allowed to move closer to the enemy.

A Pinned Down platoon containing only Armoured Tank teams can be selected as the Assaulting platoon since being Pinned Down does not affect Armoured Tank teams.

British infantry

Leaderless Platoons Cannot Assault

Without someone to lead the way into the enemy positions, nothing happens.

You may not select a platoon without a Platoon Command team as the Assaulting platoon, although such a platoon can still Counterattack *(see page 163)**.*

Tank Terror

Infantry avoid assaulting tanks as they lack weapons that can penetrate these well-armoured beasts.

If any Assaulting Infantry team is within 6"/15cm of an enemy Armoured Tank team, the platoon must take a Motivation test before it can assault.

- *On a successful roll, your infantry get up and assault the enemy.*
- *On a failed roll, they do not launch the assault, preferring to remain where they are.*

Ignore Bogged Down or Bailed Out Tank teams and Independent teams (but not Warrior teams) when determining if an Assaulting platoon needs to take a Motivation Test to assault.

SUMMARY

- **Assault with one platoon at a time, then select another. An Assaulting platoon must be able to reach the enemy when it Charges into Contact.**
- **Pinned Down platoons cannot assault unless they are all Armoured Tank teams.**
- **Platoons without a Command team cannot assault.**
- **A platoon with Infantry teams within 6"/15cm of a tank must pass a Motivation Test to assault.**

ASSAULTING AND NON-ASSAULTING TEAMS

While a smart officer tries to maximise the strength of their assaulting force, sometimes they have to leave teams behind.

All of the Infantry and Armoured Tank teams in the Assaulting platoon are Assaulting teams, aside from those that are identified as Non-assaulting teams.

The assaulting player may declare any teams from the Assaulting Platoon to be Non-assaulting teams.

MUST BE IN COMMAND

If the order to charge doesn't reach some of your troops in time, they won't be involved in the assault.

Teams that are Out of Command are Non-assaulting teams.

TOO FAR AWAY

Troops can only charge so far. If the enemy is further away, they can only watch the fight awaiting its outcome.

Teams more than 8"/20cm from all Defending teams are Non-assaulting teams. The Soviet Quality of Quantity special rule (see page 251) extends this to 12"/30cm in some circumstances.

MUST SHOOT ON THE MOVE TO CHARGE

In order to assault, troops need to work their way into a good jump-off position, close to the enemy. You cannot do this while blazing away flat out at the enemy.

Teams that shoot with more than half of their ROF in the Shooting Step are Non-assaulting teams, unless they have a rule allowing them to shoot at their full ROF while moving.

CANNOT ASSAULT AT THE DOUBLE

The effort required to get your troops across the battlefield quickly means that there is simply not enough time left to organise an assault after moving at the double.

Teams that moved At the Double are Non-assaulting teams.

TANKS CANNOT CHARGE TANKS

Tanks do not assault other tanks, they shoot them. Instead, they charge down the infantry, hoping that the defending tanks won't kill them first.

Tank teams cannot Charge into Contact with Tank or Transport teams. They must Charge into Contact with Infantry or Gun teams instead.

SOFTSKINS CANNOT CHARGE

Charging the enemy in a 'softskin', or unarmoured vehicle, or even a lightly armoured transport, is a good way to 'buy the farm'.

Unarmoured Tank teams and any Transport teams in the Assaulting platoon are Non-assaulting teams.

An exception to this is German armoured half-tracks that can charge into contact using their Mounted Assault special rule (see page 243).

GUNS AND ROCKETS CANNOT CHARGE

The domain of gunners is shooting, not launching wild bayonet charges.

Gun teams (including Man-packed Gun teams), self-propelled armoured Rocket Launchers, and Staff teams in the Assaulting platoon are Non-assaulting teams. However, they may end up fighting the enemy as the result of an enemy assault or Counterattack.

ANTI-AIRCRAFT FIRE

Troops shooting at aircraft are too busy with that task to launch an assault.

Teams in the Assaulting platoon that Conducted Anti-aircraft Fire during the enemy turn are Non-assaulting teams. See page 181 for rules on shooting at aircraft.

WARRIOR TEAMS MUST JOIN BEFORE ASSAULT

Heroic leaders don't sit back and watch while their troops attack, they get stuck in and lead from the front.

In order to Join the Assaulting platoon as an Assaulting team, a Warrior team must Join it before it Charges into Contact. Any Warrior team that Joins the Assaulting platoon after it has Charged into Contact is a Non-assaulting team.

SUMMARY

- **Only Infantry and Armoured Tank teams can assault. In addition they must:**
  - **be In Command,**
  - **be within 8"/20cm of an enemy team,**
  - **not have stopped to fire at full ROF, and**
  - **not have Moved at the Double.**
- **Tanks can't assault Tanks or Transports.**
- **Teams that fired at Aircraft in the enemy turn cannot assault.**
- **Warrior teams must Join before the assault begins if they want to assault.**

CHARGE INTO CONTACT

The assaulting troops break into a run and charge the enemy, bayonets glinting. Racing across the intervening distance, the charging soldiers seek to get to grips with the enemy as fast as possible to minimise the amount of fire they take from the defenders. Troops in the second wave spread out to finish off any remaining resistance.

When Charging into Contact, you move the Assaulting teams of the Assaulting platoon (or Counterattacking teams of the Counterattacking platoon, see page 163) into contact with the enemy in the following steps. Non-assaulting teams cannot Charge into Contact.

1. Move Closest Teams into Contact

1. Move Closest Team into Contact

Those closest to the enemy lead the way, closing rapidly with the nearest defenders. The troops following tackle whoever they can reach.

Move the Assaulting (or Counterattacking) Infantry or Tank team that is closest to the enemy up to 4"/10cm into base-to-base contact with the nearest enemy team.

2. Move Other Teams into Contact

Move all remaining Assaulting (or Counterattacking) teams that can contact an enemy team. These teams may move up to 4"/10cm to contact an enemy team. You must move as many of the Assaulting (or Counterattacking) teams as possible into contact, and must contact as many enemy teams as possible.

2. Move Other Teams into Contact

3. Move Remaining Teams

When all of the teams from the Assaulting (or Counterattacking) platoon that can move into contact with enemy teams have done so, move all remaining Assaulting (or Counterattacking) teams that are within 8"/20cm of a Defending team. Move these teams 4"/10cm towards either any team that has already been contacted by one of your teams, or the nearest enemy team that has not been contacted by one of your teams.

3. Move Teams into Assault Range

The Most Direct Route

Troops want to get into contact as fast as possible, but not at the cost of getting stuck on the way. They will divert slightly to avoid obstacles.

Teams Charging into Contact must take the shortest, most direct route into contact with the team they are charging. This means that if there are no obstacles between them and the enemy, they must move in a straight line towards the enemy. If there is an obstacle between them and the enemy, they may either move straight towards the enemy over the obstacle, or take the shortest route around the obstacle to get to the enemy.

Teams may go around or through a friendly team that has already finished its Charge into Contact if this will get them closer to the team that they are charging.

Teams that contact an enemy team rotate at the end of their movement so that they are square up against a contacted enemy team.

Do Not Need to Remain In Command

Once they get the order to charge, soldiers don't need to be told what to do.

Assaulting teams do not need to remain In Command when Charging into Contact.

Ignore Teams that are Out of Reach

While soldiers will hunt out enemy hiding behind buildings or in woods, there isn't much that they can do about enemy troops up an impassable cliff.

When Charging into Contact, teams ignore enemy teams that they cannot reach due to terrain that is impassable to them.

Moving Near the Enemy

Assaults are all about closing with the enemy. Unlike normal movement where you must keep your distance, you can move right up to the enemy when assaulting.

Your Assaulting (or Counterattacking) teams may move within 2"/5cm of enemy teams when they Charge into Contact, but may not move over or through an enemy team nor end their movement with their base overlapping any other team's base. An Assaulting team may not pass through gaps between enemy teams less than its own base width.

US soldiers fighting in a French village
IWM KY30309

Most Direct Route

Charge Who You Shot At

Sometimes a platoon intending to assault will need to split its fire to engage several platoons at once.

When Charging into Contact an Assaulting team that shot in the Shooting Step must charge a team that was within 8"/20cm of a team from the platoon that it shot at. If it cannot do this, it is a Non-assaulting team and cannot Charge into Contact at all.

What if I Destroyed My Target?

If there is a risk that your shooting will destroy the only enemy team within 8"/20cm of the platoon that you want to assault with, mark the position of the destroyed team in the Shooting Step to make it clear that you can still assault your intended target using the Assaulting Abandoned Positions rule on page 150.

Summary: Charge into Contact

- Starting with the nearest, move Assaulting teams up to 4"/10cm directly in to contact with as many enemy teams as possible.
- Move remaining Assaulting teams 4"/10cm towards either the nearest uncontacted enemy team or any team already contacted.
- Teams must move by the shortest route, but can avoid obstacles and friendly teams.
- Teams that shot can only charge teams within 8"/20cm of the platoon they shot at.

Charge Towards Who You Shot

Tactics

Fire on the Move

If you want to assault, be sure to shoot with your teams at the reduced ROF for moving (unless you have assault weapons like SMG's), even if you don't need to move.

CHARGING INTO TERRAIN

Linear Obstacles

It is obviously impossible for your teams to be placed in physical contact with an enemy team defending an obstacle like a wall or hedge. In this case close enough is good enough.

A team in contact with a Linear Obstacle, the Wreck of a Destroyed vehicle, an Opening in a Building, or any other Obstacle that physically prevents it from being placed closer to an enemy team is deemed to be in contact with any enemy teams immediately across the obstacle from it.

If there isn't enough space between the enemy team and the Linear Obstacle for the Assaulting team to be placed physically in touch with the enemy, it is still in contact with the enemy from the other side of the Obstacle.

Area Terrain

Many types of area terrain are modelled with things like trees and rocks on them that limit where teams can be positioned. Once again, close enough is good enough.

If a team in Area Terrain is unable to contact an enemy team due to the way the terrain is modelled, it counts as being in contact if it is as close as it can get and is within 2"/5cm of the enemy team.

Charging a Building

Once an assaulting team gets to the doors and windows of a building, they can throw in grenades and attempt to clear the enemy out.

Infantry teams charge through unoccupied Openings using the normal rules for entering Checked or Contested Buildings (see page 52).

If there is no space for the charging team inside the Building, it Charges into Contact with the nearest Opening, counting as being in contact with the nearest enemy team inside. If there is no space beside the Opening because of another nearby Building forming an alleyway, the charging team remains at the Opening in its own Building leading into the alleyway or at the end of the alleyway, but still counts as being in contact with the nearest enemy team inside.

If a team inside a Building is unable to contact an enemy team due to the construction of the Building, it counts as being in contact if it is as close as it can get and is within 2"/5cm of the enemy team.

Charging into Terrain

Tanks Assaulting Into Terrain

Tanks In Terrain

If the enemy is trying to hide in terrain, your tanks have to go in after them.

The normal rules for crossing or entering Rough Terrain apply while Charging into Contact. Tank teams must make the appropriate Bogging Checks as required.

Even if the Tank team doesn't actually enter or cross Rough Terrain, it must make a Bogging Check as if entering or crossing the Rough Terrain when it Charges into Contact with an enemy team in or across Rough Terrain, unless it is also within 2"/5cm of another enemy Infantry or Gun team that is not in or across Rough Terrain.

Tanks Charging Buildings

Tanks are not really designed for fighting in built up areas, but if they have to, they can attempt to bring the building down around the infantry hiding in it.

Only Fully-armoured Tank teams (see page 8) can assault teams in Buildings. Other vehicles cannot assault teams in Buildings as they cannot enter Buildings. The rules for Tanks Assaulting into Terrain apply to Tank teams Assaulting (or Counterattacking) teams in Buildings. Since Buildings are Very Difficult Going, the Tank team will need to pass a Skill Test to avoid Bogging Down.

Unlike Infantry teams, Tank teams do not need an existing Opening to assault into a Building. Instead, they treat all walls as Openings. In all other respects Fully-armoured Tank teams assault into Buildings in the same way that Infantry teams do.

Tank teams cannot move up stairs, so they do not need to move into Contact with Infantry teams on the upper levels of a Building to assault them, but do have to move as close as possible.

Assault Always Continues

Sometimes your leading troops will find themselves stopped by obstacles before they reach the enemy, leaving them exposed to enemy fire and counterattacks.

Once you Launch an Assault, the assault continues, even if no Assaulting (or Counterattacking) teams actually make contact with an enemy team when Charging into Contact (because all of your tanks Bogged Down or your infantry got hung up on barbed wire for instance). This means that the defenders will still conduct Defensive Fire (see page 152).

SUMMARY

- **If terrain or vehicle wrecks prevent teams from actually contacting the enemy, they are considered to be in contact.**
- **Tanks take Bogging Checks when assaulting teams that are in Rough Terrain.**
- **Fully-armoured Tank teams are the only vehicles that can assault teams in buildings.**
- **The assault continues even if no teams actually contact the enemy due to terrain.**

ASSAULTING ABANDONED POSITIONS

If your shooting was so successful that it destroyed the enemy teams that you were about to assault, the assault can still take place as the assaulting platoon moves forward and occupies the abandoned enemy position unopposed. Sometimes a similar thing will happen when two platoons assault side by side. If the first platoon to assault the position pushes the enemy back, the second platoon to assault will be left with an easy walk to victory.

If a team from your platoon that was in a position to Launch an Assault at the start of the Shooting Step is able to Launch an Assault in the Assault Step, but cannot because the enemy teams that it would have assaulted are no longer there, your platoon may still Launch its Assault.

Instead of Charging into Contact with enemy teams, the Assaulting teams must Charge into Contact with the missing enemy teams as if the enemy teams were still where they were at the start of the Shooting Step.

Mark Destroyed Enemy Positions

If you plan to use the Assaulting Abandoned Positions rule, it can be helpful to mark the positions of the teams that you destroyed in the Shooting Step so that you can charge them in the Assault Step.

Still Enemy Close Enough to Assault

If the enemy platoons you were intending to assault still have teams close enough to assault, you can continue the assault as normal, even though you won't make contact with any enemy teams.

If at least one of your Assaulting teams is within 4"/10cm of an enemy team after their Charge into Contact, the assault is conducted as normal. If there are no enemy teams within 2"/5cm, the Assaulting teams cannot score any hits, but the Defending platoons must still take a Motivation Test to Counterattack (see page 162).

No Enemy Close Enough to Assault

If your shooting was spectacular or the enemy was widely dispersed, your troops may be able to simply walk in and take the enemy positions unopposed.

If none of your Assaulting teams can get within 4"/10cm of an enemy team by Charging into Contact, the Assaulting platoon still makes its Charge into Contact move to contact the positions of the vanquished enemy. It suffers Defensive Fire (see page 152) as usual, and if it doesn't Fall Back from the Defensive Fire, automatically Wins the Assault and Consolidates (see page 167).

SUMMARY

- **A platoon in position to launch an assault in the Shooting Step may still assault, even if the enemy are no longer there, taking Defensive Fire as usual.**
- **If any enemy are within 4"/10cm, they must take a Motivation Test to Counterattack, otherwise the Assaulting platoon automatically wins and Consolidates.**

You Must Have Been Able to Assault

The Assaulting Abandoned Positions rule does not allow you to just move at will after sitting still and shooting at their full rate. The assaulting teams would still have needed to fire at the reduced rate of fire for moving to be able to do this, as otherwise they are not eligible to charge into contact. In *Flames Of War* you can't just decide to take the positions after you've shot all of the enemy!

Assaulting Abandoned Positions

WHICH PLATOONS ARE DEFENDING

Generally anyone near enough to know what is happening will open fire on the attacking troops before fixing bayonets ready to see the enemy off. Those too far away to distinguish friend from foe can only watch and hope.

Any enemy platoon that has teams within 8"/20cm of an Assaulting team is a Defending platoon. A platoon does not need to be in contact with the enemy to be a Defending platoon.

Determine which platoons are Defending platoons after the Assaulting platoon has Charged into Contact.

NON-ASSAULTING TEAMS

No one wants to expose themselves to fire unnecessarily, so only troops being charged will open fire. Those faced with troops giving covering fire will just lie low.

Enemy teams within 8"/20cm of Non-assaulting teams are not being assaulted unless an Assaulting team is also within 8"/20cm.

WHO CAN DEFENSIVE FIRE

The enemy won't take your charge lying down. When they see your soldiers bearing down on them, they will redouble their fire in an effort to stop your troops from reaching them. After the attacking platoon has launched their assault, the defenders get one last chance to stop your attack with their defensive fire.

After the Assaulting player Charges into Contact, the defending player conducts Defensive Fire against the Assaulting platoon.

Only teams within 8"/20cm of an Assaulting team can shoot in Defensive Fire.

NO DEFENSIVE FIRE AT THE DOUBLE

Troops moving at the double are focused on reaching their goal quickly and are not ready for combat.

A Defending team that moved At the Double in its previous Movement Step cannot conduct Defensive Fire.

NO FLAME-THROWERS IN DEFENSIVE FIRE

Flame throwers are offensive weapons. They take time to prepare and cannot react quickly when surprised.

Teams cannot shoot Flame-throwers in Defensive Fire. Infantry Flame-thrower teams can still shoot as Rifle teams (see page 198).

SUMMARY

- **Any enemy platoon that has a team within 8"/20cm of an Assaulting team is a Defending platoon.**
- **Defending teams within 8"/20cm of an Assaulting team may Defensive Fire, unless they moved At the Double or are Flame-thrower teams.**

DEFENDING PLATOONS

OPPONENT CONDUCTS DEFENSIVE FIRE

Shooting an enemy charging you, bayonets fixed, is much the same as shooting any other enemy, aside from the dire consequences of failing to shoot their charge down!

Defensive Fire uses the normal shooting procedure (including checking that the team is a valid target, rolling to hit, rolling saves, and rolling to destroy, etc.) with the following changes.

DEFENSIVE FIRE AT SHORT RANGE

There is no time to pick your targets when the enemy is charging, you just shoot what's in front of you.

Only Assaulting teams within 8"/20cm are valid targets in Defensive Fire, so hits must be allocated to Assaulting teams within 8"/20cm of the shooting team.

DEFENSIVE FIRE FROM THE HALT

Even though they only have a short time to shoot, modern weapons can pour on the lead when necessary.

Teams shooting in Defensive Fire do not count as moving, even if they moved in their previous turn, instead they fire at their full ROF. However, a team from a Pinned Down platoon still reduces their ROF for being Pinned Down.

CONCEALMENT FROM DEFENSIVE FIRE

Unless the defender is in the middle of a wood or the like, your attacking troops are going to be in clear view as they charge across the last gap and into the enemy.

Defensive Fire is conducted on the Assaulting teams where they are after Charging into Contact, so they only benefit from Concealment they occupy at that point. In most cases this means that Assaulting teams will be in the open and unprotected. However, an assault in a wood or through a smoke screen would count as Concealed for instance.

ASSAULTING THROUGH SMOKE

Although a swirling smoke screen hides the enemy at long range, they are clearly visible silhouetted against the pale smoke as they charge into contact.

As Defensive Fire is conducted at pointblank range, Assaulting teams are only Concealed, but not Gone to Ground when seen through Smoke Markers.

WHO CAN BE HIT

If you are being charged, you naturally shoot at the troops charging you.

Hits from Defensive Fire must be allocated to Assaulting teams, and may not be allocated to Non-assaulting teams. Aside from this, hits are allocated using the normal shooting rules.

NO BULLETPROOF COVER

Your troops have to leave the safety of their own positions to charge into contact with the enemy, rendering them more vulnerable to defensive fire.

As Defensive Fire is conducted on the Assaulting teams as they charge, they never benefit from Bulletproof Cover, even in terrain that gives Bulletproof Cover.

SHOOTING OVER INFANTRY

A well laid out infantry position is likely to have machine-guns and anti-tank guns supporting the infantry.

As with other shooting, vehicles and Gun teams can shoot over Infantry (but not Cavalry) teams, as can other Infantry teams shooting at vehicles (see page 80).

CONCEALMENT FROM DEFENSIVE FIRE

SNEAKING UP ON TANKS

TANKS AND DEFENSIVE FIRE

Tanks have turrets so they can engage close-in threats from the flanks in a way that assault guns cannot.

TANK GUNS IN DEFENSIVE FIRE

Rapid-firing machine-guns and turret-mounted weapons are the most effective weapons a tank has for halting infantry assaults.

As well as its machine-guns, a vehicle can use any turret-mounted weapons to shoot at Infantry teams in Defensive Fire.

All hits in Defensive Fire from other vehicle-mounted weapons must be allocated to Tank teams. If only Infantry, teams are valid targets, those hits are completely ignored.

SNEAKING UP ON TANKS

One of the weaknesses of tank design is that they have a huge blind area close to the tank making them vulnerable to infantry attack. Tanks have to be very wary of driving into terrain occupied by infantry as the enemy can sneak up and blind it with smoke grenades, mud, or flour bombs, before the crew even know that they are under attack. Once blinded, they are virtually defenceless against infantry.

A Defending vehicle may not Defensive Fire at all if it is in contact with an assaulting Infantry team that Sneaked Up on it.

An Infantry team can Sneak Up on a vehicle if the team:

- *did not move in the Movement and Shooting Steps,*
- *did not shoot in the Shooting Step, and*
- *started its Charge into Contact Concealed by Terrain.*

DEFENSIVE FIRE HITS SIDE ARMOUR

At point blank range, anti-tank weapons are much more effective. Their rounds hit harder and the gunners will target vision slits, tracks and other vulnerable spots making them much more likely to penetrate the tank.

Tanks use their Side armour for any Armour Saves against Defensive Fire, even when the model is facing the shooting team.

SUMMARY

- **Defensive Fire can only be fired at Assaulting teams within 8"/20cm, and is always fired as if stationary.**
- **Assaulting teams cannot be Gone to Ground and never have Bulletproof Cover.**
- **Infantry can shoot at vehicles over other infantry, while other teams can always shoot over infantry.**
- **Tanks can only use machine guns and turret-mounted weapons to shoot at infantry in Defensive Fire.**
- **Vehicles cannot Defensive Fire if contacted by infantry that did not move or shoot and started its Charge into Contact Concealed.**
- **Defensive Fire always hits the side armour of assaulting tanks.**

FORCING THE ASSAULT TO FALL BACK

Fall Back from Five Hits

Charging into a wall of bullets is not a winning proposition. If the defender's fire is heavy enough, the assaulting platoon will break off the assault and fall back. Although throwing more troops at a problem normally just results in more casualties, there are occasions when extra numbers can make a difference.

If the total number of hits from Defensive Fire is five or more, the Assaulting platoon is immediately Pinned Down and must Fall Back. Their assault is now over.

The Soviet Quality of Quantity special rule (see page 251) requires ten hits to force infantry to Fall Back in some circumstances.

Tanks Fall Back from Two Effective Hits

While infantry and open-topped vehicles can be driven off by a hail of bullets, battle tanks just wade on through anything that doesn't knock them out.

If all of the Assaulting teams are Fully-armoured vehicles (other than Recce teams), they do not Fall Back if they take five or more hits from Defensive Fire.

However, if two or more Armoured vehicles (whether Open-topped or Fully-armoured) are Bailed Out or Destroyed by Defensive Fire, the platoon must Fall Back.

Falling Back

If soldiers are unable to close with the enemy, they will hit the dirt just outside of grenade range.

If an Assaulting platoon Falls Back from Defensive Fire, all teams within 2"/5cm of an enemy team immediately move by the most direct route until they are more than 2"/5cm away from the enemy, ending facing the enemy.

If friendly teams are occupying the position that a team needs to Fall Back to, the friendly teams Fall Back the shortest distance required to make space for the Falling Back team, pushing any teams in their way back in turn.

Vehicles do not need to take Bogging Checks for Rough Terrain while Falling Back. Any tanks that Bogged Down or were Bailed Out within 2"/5cm of the enemy, either during the Charge into Contact or by Defensive Fire still Fall Back until they are more than 2"/5cm from the enemy as they never got that close in the first place. If the Fall Back takes a Bogged Down tank back out of the Rough Terrain it Bogged Down in, it is no longer Bogged Down.

A Charge Too Far

Sometimes the defenders' fire mows down the assaulting troops before they get close enough to fight.

If there are no surviving Assaulting teams within 2"/5cm of any enemy team after Defensive Fire, the Assaulting platoon is Pinned Down and the assault over (even if the Assaulting platoon was not forced to Fall Back), unless it was Assaulting Abandoned Positions (see page 150).

SUMMARY

- **Assaulting platoon must fall back outside 2"/5cm of all enemy teams, if it takes five or more hits. If the platoon is all Fully-armoured Tank teams, it Falls Back if two or more tanks are Bailed Out or Destroyed.**
- **If the Assaulting platoon is left with no teams within 2"/5cm of the enemy, the assault is over and they are Pinned Down.**

Forcing the Assault to Fall Back

ROLL TO HIT WITH ASSAULTING TEAMS

Assault combat is quick, brutal, and confusing. Your soldiers use anything that comes to hand—submachine-guns, grenades, bayonets and even sharpened spades—as they set about clearing the enemy position.

Roll to Hit with all of the Tank, Infantry, and Gun teams that are in within 2"/5cm of a Defending team that is in their Line of Sight.

Assaulting (or Counterattacking) teams can fight through any friendly team and do not need to have a target within their Field of Fire to be able to Roll to Hit as they are close enough to be able to avoid hitting their friends and to use personal weapons if necessary.

Assaulting Gun teams will not be within 2"/5cm of the enemy during the initial assault, but may come within 2"/5cm of the enemy as a result of a counterattack.

Transport teams and teams carried as Passengers cannot fight in an assault and do not Roll to Hit. An exception to this is German armoured half-tracks that can fight using the Mounted Assault special rule (see page 243).

FIGHTING IN BUILDINGS

Assaulting into a building is a difficult prospect as it is hard to bring numbers to bear on the enemy.

Infantry and Gun teams can only fight into or out of a Building through Openings they are touching. Only one team can fight through an Opening unless the Opening is wider than a stand width, in which case additional teams can fight alongside the first until the Opening is full. Teams fighting through an Opening or within a Building must still be within 2"/5cm of the enemy to fight.

Tank teams do not need Openings into a Building to fight as they can make their own.

SCORE NEEDED TO HIT

Once you have determined which of your assaulting teams can fight, you need to roll to see if they can score a hit. A successful roll shows that your team beat the enemy to the punch. A missed roll could be a dud grenade or jammed gun, inability to find the enemy in the smoke and confusion, or the enemy parrying a bayonet with their entrenching tool. Assaults are a confusing swirl of events where anything can happen.

Each team fighting in the assault rolls a Skill Test to hit the enemy. There are no modifiers to this roll.

- *If successful, the team has hit an enemy team.*
- *Otherwise, they failed to score a telling blow and have no effect.*

SCORE TO HIT

Assaulting Team's Skill	Score Needed to Hit
Conscript	5+
Trained	4+
Veteran	3+

SUMMARY

- **Roll one Skill Test to hit with each Assaulting team within 2"/5cm of a visible Defending team.**
- **Only one Infantry or Gun team can fight through each Opening in a Building. Fully-armoured tanks create their own Openings.**

ROLL TO HIT WITH ASSAULTING TEAMS

ALLOCATE HITS TO DEFENDING TEAMS

It is relatively easy for a brave soldier to keep the enemy away from a valuable weapon, at least until they die!

The player receiving the hits allocates each hit to any of their teams within 2"/5cm and in Line of Sight of the team that caused the hit.

The following restrictions apply:

- *Hits must be allocated evenly across all of the eligible teams so as to maximise the number of teams that have hits allocated to them.*
- *Teams that are Bogged Down or Bailed Out are only hit after teams that are still fighting.*
- *Hits must be allocated to Tank, Infantry, or Gun teams (even those that are Bogged Down or Bailed Out) before Transport teams.*
- *Hits must be allocated to Armoured vehicles with lower Top armour ratings before those with higher Top armour ratings.*

Allocate all of the hits from an assault before rolling to see the effect of the hits.

ASSAULTING MIXED PLATOONS

A well planned assault will see each squad given specific orders about the target of their attack.

Before rolling to hit, you may nominate a Priority target type for each Assaulting (or Counterattacking) team. The Priority target type can be either Tank, Infantry, or Gun teams.

Your opponent must allocate hits from that Assaulting team to Defending teams of the Priority target type if possible, although hits must still be allocated evenly across teams of all types. Exactly which teams of that type are hit is at your opponent's discretion, subject to the usual rules about allocating hits.

ALLOCATING HITS ACROSS PLATOONS

At close quarters it is easy for a squad to dash to the rescue of a nearby team to save a valuable weapon.

The player being assaulted (or Counterattacked) may allocate hits to teams from any platoon, just as long as the team being allocated the hit is close enough to be hit by that Assaulting (or Counterattacking) team.

ALLOCATING HITS IN BUILDINGS

Only a few troops can fight at a time in the restricted confines of a building.

Hits from a team fighting into a Building through an Opening must be allocated to teams in the Building. Hits from a team fighting out of a Building through an Opening must be allocated to teams within 2"/5cm of the Opening. Hits from a team fighting within a Building must be allocated to teams in the same Building.

TANKS ASSAULTING BUILDINGS

If the enemy is trying to hide in buildings, your tanks have to go in after them.

Hits from Fully-armoured Tank teams (and their Tank Escorts) can be allocated to any team in a Building within 2"/5cm. Hits from other types of Tank teams cannot be allocated to teams in Buildings at all. Ignore any hits for which there is no valid target.

TANKS CANNOT HIT TANKS

Tanks can't charge tanks, so all of their hits must be allocated to the guns and infantry that are their targets.

A hit from a Tank team or its Tank Escorts cannot be allocated to a vehicle. If only vehicles are available to allocate the hit to, then ignore the hit.

IGNORE OUT OF REACH

There isn't much that a soldier can do about enemy troops up an impassable cliff.

A hit from an Assaulting (or Counterattacking) team cannot be allocated to a team that the Assaulting (or Counterattacking) team cannot reach due to terrain that is impassable to it.

SUMMARY

- **Hits must be allocated to visible teams within 2"/5cm. They must be allocated:**
  - **evenly across eligible teams,**
  - **to other teams before Transport teams,**
  - **to active vehicles before Bogged Down or Bailed Out vehicles, and**
  - **vehicles with lower Top armour before higher Top armour, with the highest Anti-tank ratings going to the best armoured.**
- **The Assaulting player may prioritise hits to Tank, Infantry, Guns or Transport.**
- **Hits can be allocated to any valid target, regardless of platoon.**
- **Hits from Tank teams cannot be allocated to vehicles.**

ROLL SAVES FOR ARMOURED VEHICLES

Tanks Hit by Infantry Teams

While a tank's armour is still a problem for infantry, a big advantage of getting close to a tank is that you can hit it where it really hurts, its thin top armour.

When you hit an Armoured vehicle with an Infantry team in an assault, the owning player takes an Armour Save using its Top armour rating. The owning player rolls a die for each hit scored on an Armoured vehicle and adds the vehicle's Top armour rating to get their Armour Save.

Exceeds Tank Assault Rating

If the Armour Save exceeds the Infantry team's Tank Assault rating, their Save succeeded and the team was unable to find any weakness in the vehicle's armour and their attack has no effect.

Equals Tank Assault Rating

If the Armour Save matches the Infantry team's Tank Assault rating exactly, they failed the Save and the infantry manage to temporarily blind and immobilize the vehicle. Count the crew as having Bailed Out, although they are actually cowering in the bottom of their vehicle.

Is Less than Tank Assault Rating

If the Armour Save is less than the Infantry team's Tank Assault rating, they failed the Save and the vehicle is Destroyed.

Firing Anti-aircraft Machine-guns

A tank has to keep its hatches open to fire anti-aircraft machine-guns, leaving the tank vulnerable to assaults.

Any vehicle that fired an AA MG or .50 cal AA MG in their previous Shooting Step, at Aircraft in this Shooting Step, or in Defensive Fire treats their Top armour as 0 when making Armour Saves in assaults. However, it does not become Open-topped as a result.

Mixed Armour Ratings

Tank-hunters go for the easiest targets first.

If hits are being allocated to vehicles, they must be allocated to Unarmoured vehicles before Armoured vehicles, and Armoured vehicles with the lowest Armour rating before those with higher Armour ratings, subject to all previous rules about allocating hits.

Tank Assault Ratings

Infantry tank hunters use grenades and Molotov Cocktail fire bombs rather than their normal weapons.

All Infantry and Gun teams have an Tank Assault rating for use against Armoured vehicles. This is always 2, regardless of the normal Anti-tank rating of the weapon, unless they have special rules that change it.

Mixed Tank Assault Ratings

Specialist tank hunters seek out the most dangerous foes, leaving the easier targets to regular soldiers.

If hits are allocated to Armoured vehicles and other teams, the hits allocated to the Armoured vehicles must be those with the highest Tank Assault ratings, with the hits with the lower Tank Assault ratings must be allocated to targets with the lowest Armour ratings.

Tanks Hit by Gun Teams

Infantry stalk tanks, but guns just keep shooting as long as they can. Anything but the biggest and most cumbersome gun is still deadly at pointblank range.

Gun teams that hit an Armoured vehicle in an assault can make it take its saves with its Side armour rather than its Top armour. To do this, the Gun team must have a ROF of 2 or more (ignoring any effects of being Pinned Down), or be a Man-packed Gun team (other than a mortar), and the vehicle must be in its Field of Fire.

Which Teams Are Hit

Tanks Hit by Gun Teams

If a Gun team does this, these hits must be allocated to armoured vehicles with lower Side armour ratings before higher Side armour ratings (rather than Top armour ratings).

Exceeds Anti-tank Rating

If your opponent's Armour Save roll (using their Side Armour rating) is greater than your weapon's normal Anti-tank rating, their Armour Save is successful, and the shot has no effect.

Equals Anti-tank Rating

If your opponent's Armour Save roll (using their Side Armour rating) exactly equals your weapon's normal Anti-tank rating, they failed their Armour Save.

To determine the effect of the hit you must take a Firepower Test. Roll another die.

- *If the roll equals or exceeds your weapon's Firepower rating, the crew panic and Bail Out.*
- *If the roll is lower than your weapon's Firepower rating the shot has no effect.*

Less than Anti-tank Rating

If your opponent's Armour Save roll (using their Side Armour rating) is less than your weapon's normal Anti-tank rating they failed their Armour Save.

To determine the effect of the hit you must take a Firepower Test. Roll another die.

- *If the roll equals or exceeds your weapon's Firepower rating, the tank is Destroyed.*
- *If the roll is lower than your weapon's Firepower rating the shot has no effect. The tank is not Bailed Out, and continues in action unharmed.*

Fighting as Infantry

Gunners taken from the flank, or crewing weapons too heavy to engage targets at pointblank range, are forced to fight as riflemen rather than using their guns.

If the Gun team is unable to or the assaulting player elects not to hit a vehicle in the Side armour, it hits the Top armour with its Tank Assault rating as usual.

Summary

- **Armour Saves use Top armour against the assaulting team's Tank Assault rating. No Firepower Test is required to Destroy or Bail Out a vehicle that failed its save.**
- **Tank Assault rating is always 2 unless a special rule changes it.**
- **Gun teams with ROF of 2 or more, and Man-packed Guns (other than mortars) may use their normal Anti-tank rating against Side armour instead. If it does so, a Firepower Test is required to Destroy or Bail Out the vehicle. Failed Firepower tests result in no effect at all.**

OTHER TEAMS DO NOT ROLL SAVES

Unarmoured Vehicles

Unarmoured vehicles are perhaps the most vulnerable in an assault. One grenade is sufficient to turn them into flaming pyres.

Unarmoured vehicles do not get any save in an assault. When hit they are Destroyed and removed from the battlefield.

Infantry And Gun Teams

Hitting the dirt might protect you from a rifleman hundreds of metres away, but it is useless against close-range shots, grenades, and bayonet thrusts. At short range every hit is lethal.

There are no saves for Infantry or Gun teams hit in an assault. These teams are Destroyed and removed from the battlefield.

Bulletproof Cover

Bulletproof cover is of no value once things get down to grenade range. Troops hiding in cover can generally be dislodged with a grenade, and in a confined space the fragments are even more deadly than in the open.

> **Speeding Things Up**
>
> As with shooting, the details of which team hit which team are usually unimportant, so although an assault involves lots of die rolls you don't always have to roll for each team separately.
>
> If your opponent agrees, you can usually roll all of the dice for a platoon's assault at once and simply leave your opponent to allocate the hits to eligible teams regardless of which exact team scored the hit.
>
> In some cases however, taking it slowly and resolving the assault one team at a time makes complicated situations much simpler than they appear at first glance.

Bulletproof Cover does not grant any protection in an assault. Assaulting (or Counterattacking) teams do not need to make a Firepower Test against teams in Bulletproof Cover.

Passengers

Vehicles are deathtraps in close-combat. The assaulting force simply cuts down the passengers and crew attempting to escape their burning vehicle.

Passengers in a vehicle (whether Armoured or not) that is Destroyed in an assault are also Destroyed.

It's a good idea to dismount from a vehicle well away from the enemy so that you can't be hit by a surprise assault while still mounted up.

Passengers Riding on Tanks

While an armoured half-track may protect its passengers, tank riders on the outside of a tank are bunched together and totally unprotected. They will be easily wiped out by troops attacking the tank.

Passengers riding on top of a Tank team are Destroyed if the vehicle they are riding on is hit in an assault, even if the vehicle is unharmed.

> **SUMMARY**
>
> - **Infantry, Guns, and Unarmoured vehicles are all automatically Destroyed when hit.**
> - **Bulletproof cover has no effect.**
> - **Passengers in a Destroyed vehicle or on a Tank team that is hit are Destroyed.**

German tank-hunters prepare to assault Soviet KV-1s heavy tanks

PUSH INTO ENEMY POSITIONS

Having disposed of the enemy immediately in front of them, your assaulting teams can now swarm forward across obstacles and into buildings to fight the enemy in their own positions.

An assaulting team that was in contact with an enemy team across a Linear Obstacle or through an Opening in a Building may, if they choose to, immediately occupy the position of an enemy team it Destroys in an assault.

If there is insufficient space for the team to occupy the position, they may shunt the teams in the Building aside to make space. If there is still insufficient space, the team must Destroy more teams to make a big enough space.

Push Over Linear Obstacles

Push into Buildings

HAS THE ASSAULTING PLATOON WON

Your men have done their best, tearing into the enemy and ripping them apart. If they have killed or captured everyone in the vicinity, they have won the assault. If not, the enemy may counterattack trying to regain their positions.

You have won the assault if, after all hits have been allocated, saves made, and any teams pushing into enemy positions have done so, you have:

- *no enemy teams within 4"/10cm of any Assaulting teams, or*
- *the only enemy teams within 4"/10cm of any Assaulting teams are Bailed Out or Bogged Down Tank teams or Transport teams.*

Once you have won, you must Consolidate your position (see page 167).

If you have not won, your opponent will test their Motivation to Counterattack and the fighting continues back and forth until one side is destroyed or runs away.

TANKS CAN'T ASSAULT TANKS

Since tanks can't assault tanks, when your tank platoon assaults a platoon of mixed tanks and infantry, the assault is over once all of the infantry are wiped out.

If the only enemy teams that are within 4"/10cm of an Assaulting team are Tank or Transport teams, and the only Assaulting (or Counterattacking) teams within 4"/10cm of any enemy teams are Tank teams, you have won the assault.

WINNING ASSAULTS IN BUILDINGS

Infantry cannot see through solid walls, so it is entirely possible for opposing soldiers to be on different sides of a wall and unable to fight.

Measure the distance to the enemy teams through an Opening when measuring to see if you have won an assault in a Building. Measure the distance to Fully-armoured Tank teams in a straight line as they can drive straight through walls.

SUMMARY

- **You have won if there are no enemy teams within 4"/10cm of any Assaulting teams that are not Transport teams or Bailed Out or Bogged Down Tank teams.**
- **If you have won, you must Consolidate.**
- **Otherwise your opponent takes a Motivation test to Counterattack.**

HAS ASSAULTING PLATOON WON

OPPONENT TESTS MOTIVATION

Having survived the initial onslaught, the defenders look to fight back, throwing hand grenades and fighting those attackers that have reached their positions.

If you have not won the assault, the Defending player rolls a single die. They then compare the score of this die with the Motivation rating of each Defending platoon.

- *If the score is at least as high as the Defending platoon's Motivation rating, that platoon may choose to either Counterattack or Break Off.*
- *If the score is less than the Defending platoon's Motivation rating, that platoon must Break Off.*

Re-rolls to Counterattack

Some troops have a reputation for stubbornness, refusing to give ground unless they absolutely have to.

If a special rule gives a re-roll to Motivation Tests, work out which platoons passed on the original roll, then re-roll the die and apply the outcome to any platoons affected by the rule that failed the original roll.

No Test if Assault Scores No Hits

If the enemy is so unsuccessful that they do not score any hits at all, your soldiers have nothing to fear.

If none of the Assaulting (or Counterattacking) teams scored a hit (whether or not it actually Destroyed a team), all of the Defending platoons automatically pass their Motivation Tests to Counterattack or Break Off and can simply choose which to do.

Must Test if Assaulted by Tanks

Even if tanks just rumble around without actually causing any damage, they still scare infantry.

If any Assaulting (or Counterattacking) team is an Armoured Tank team, all Defending platoons must take their Motivation Test to Counterattack or Break Off, even if none of them actually suffered any hits. This is not an additional test, just a requirement to take the test whether or not the enemy scored any hits.

Unarmoured Tanks Must Break Off

While a real tank may scare infantry, the infantry terrify the unprotected crews of guns mounted on trucks.

A Defending platoon that has Unarmoured Tank teams within 4"/10cm of an enemy team may not Counterattack. It must Break Off instead.

Independent Teams Must Break Off

Only strong leaders and heroic warriors hang round when the grenades start flying. Observers and recovery vehicles get out of the way as fast as they can.

Independent teams (but not Warrior Teams) must Break Off rather than Counterattack, immediately leaving any platoon that they had Joined.

SUMMARY

- **The defender rolls a single die to see who may Counterattack. All platoons compare their Motivation rating to that die roll. They may Counterattack if they pass, otherwise they must Break Off.**
- **If a special rule allows re-rolling failed Motivation tests, re-roll the die and apply the new result to the platoons affected by the roll.**
- **The Motivation Test is automatically passed if the Assaulting platoon did not score any hits, unless any of the Assaulting teams is an Armoured tank.**
- **Unarmoured Tank teams and Independent teams must Break Off.**

Opponent Tests Motivation

COUNTERATTACKING

Once the defenders are over the initial shock of the assault they are going to fight back viciously. If your assault doesn't destroy the defenders outright or force them to run, your opponent will usually attempt an immediate counterattack to regain their positions.

If any of the Defending platoons passed their Motivation Tests and chose to Counterattack rather than Break Off, both sides change roles.

The Assaulting (or Counterattacking) platoon (or platoons if they are Counterattacking) now become Defending platoons and the Defending platoon or platoons become Counterattacking platoons.

The platoons that are now Counterattacking now have their turn to assault the platoons that previously assaulted them.

MULTIPLE PLATOONS COUNTERATTACKING

While coordinating a large-scale assault is difficult, everyone who is attacked will fight back.

If the defender has more than one platoon engaged in the assault, any Defending platoons that Counterattack do so simultaneously.

CHARGING INTO CONTACT

The enemy is upon your platoon. Now the rest of your platoon must charge into the fray, provided of course, that they are close enough to know what's happening.

Any teams in the Counterattacking platoon within 8"/20cm of a Defending team that are not already in contact with a Defending team move as if they were Charging into Contact. Teams that are more than 8"/20cm from all Defending teams cannot Charge into Contact and remain where they are.

Counterattacking teams may only charge teams from platoons that are or have been involved in the assault (the Defending platoons and any that have previously Broken Off). Counterattacking teams cannot move within 2"/5cm of teams from other enemy platoons not involved in the assault.

You may elect to have teams become Non-assaulting teams instead of Charging into Contact.

IGNORE PINNED DOWN

Once the general melee begins, the attacking enemy troops mask the fire that was keeping the defenders pinned down, allowing them to counterattack.

Teams from Pinned Down platoons may still Counterattack, ignoring the effect of being Pinned Down while Counterattacking.

NO COUNTERATTACK IF NOT ASSAULTING

The assault is so confused, with friendly and enemy everywhere, that troops not involved in the initial assault cannot take part in on-going counterattacks.

Non-assaulting teams (see page 144) may not Charge into Contact when Counterattacking, although they can fight if any enemy teams come close enough.

GUN TEAMS CANNOT MOVE

Once the fighting starts, the role of guns and machine-guns is over. All they can do now is watch and wait.

Gun teams and Staff teams cannot move to Counterattack, so must remain where they are, although they can fight if any enemy are close enough.

SIT TIGHT IN BULLETPROOF COVER

If you are occupying a building when a tank drives down the street, it might be wiser to wait for it to come to you rather than fixing bayonets and charging down the street at it.

Infantry teams in Bulletproof Cover do not need to Charge into Contact if they Counterattack. They may remain where they are and still Roll to hit against enemy teams within 2"/5cm.

Knocked out German Panzer IV tank
US Signal Corps, NARA

Tanks Assaulting into Terrain

Although the models may not be moving, any team that stays still for long in an assault is a dead one.

Tank teams must still take Bogging Checks for Charging into Contact with troops in Rough Terrain (see page 41), as they do when Charging into Contact, even if it started the Counterattack in contact with the enemy.

Passengers Must Dismount

Sitting in a truck while the enemy is throwing grenades is not much fun. Troops prefer to jump out of their vehicles and storm into the enemy.

Transport teams must either Break Off, or their Passengers must Dismount (see page 47) to Counterattack. They do this at the start of their Charge into Contact movement as if this was the Movement Step.

An exception to this is that Passengers in German half-tracks using the Mounted Assault special rule (see page 243) can remain Mounted to fight.

No Defensive Fire

In an assault, troops are already too heavily engaged in the ebb and flow of the combat to pick out the enemy with so many friends close by.

In a Counterattack, a Defending platoon does not get any Defensive Fire at the Counterattacking troops as they close.

Fighting In Counterattacks

Once battle is joined, the fight swirls on until one side or the other is victorious.

After Charging into Contact, the sequence of events for a counterattack is the same as for the original assault. If the counterattacking side hasn't won, then the original attackers will counterattack, and so forth.

Counterattack

SUMMARY

- **All Defending platoons that pass the Motivation Test Counterattack and the Assaulting platoon becomes the Defending platoon. All Defending platoons Counterattack at the same time.**
- **Counterattacks are the same as Assaults, except there is no Defensive Fire.**
- **Infantry and Armoured Tank teams within 8"/20cm Charge into Contact, even if Pinned Down. They can not go within 2"/5cm of enemy teams not involved in the assault.**
- **Gun teams cannot move and Infantry teams in Bulletproof Cover can opt not to move, but both fight any enemy within 2"/5cm.**

BREAKING OFF

Sometimes discretion is the better part of valour and running away to live and seek revenge later is the best choice. Of course, a ferocious attack may leave you no choice if your soldiers lose their nerve and run anyway.

If a platoon Breaks Off, any or all teams in the Defending platoon that are within 8"/20cm of an Assaulting team may move up to a full move away from the Assaulting teams.

Teams do not have to move their full move when Breaking Off, but any movement they make must be, as much as possible, directly away from the Assaulting platoon.

The movement may not take the team closer than 4"/10cm to any enemy team in Line of Sight, nor closer to any enemy team already within 4"/10cm and in Line of Sight. Ignore enemy teams that are Bogged Down, Bailed Out, or that moved At the Double.

A platoon that is Breaking Off, ignores any movement restrictions due to being Pinned Down.

Teams that are Breaking Off must attempt to remain In Command or return to being In Command at the end of this movement. Any teams that move off the table while Breaking Off are Destroyed.

Tanks and Guns in Rough Terrain

The hazards of difficult going don't end when it breaks off, it still risks bogging down and getting captured.

If a Defending vehicle or Gun team starts its Break Off movement in Rough Terrain (as opposed to in contact with a team in Rough Terrain), or crosses Rough Terrain while Breaking Off, it must make a Bogging Check as normal for moving in Rough Terrain.

Platoons Break Off Separately

It is entirely possible for a brave platoon to fight back while another breaks off and flees the fight.

Each platoon Breaks Off separately. The Assaulting (or Counterattacking) platoon does not win until all Defending platoons have Broken Off or been Destroyed.

Captured if too Slow

Sometimes troops find themselves trapped with nowhere to run. Maybe they have their backs to a river or an impassable cliff. In that case, there is nothing to do but surrender.

At the end of their Break Off movement, any Defending teams that remain within 4"/10cm and in Line of Sight of an Assaulting team (aside from an Assaulting Transport or Bogged Down or Bailed Out Tank team) are immediately Captured and Destroyed.

Only Assaulting (or Counterattacking) teams can capture Breaking Off teams. Other enemy teams can block their movement, but cannot Capture them.

Guns Fight or Die

It's too late to pack up a gun and get it away once the enemy get within grenade range. The only option then is to keep firing, hoping to drive the enemy off. If that fails, they must abandon the gun and run for it.

A Gun team within 2"/5cm of an Assaulting team that could Capture it may not move to Break Off and is automatically Captured and Destroyed. Any remaining Gun teams must Break Off as normal or be Captured.

Break Off

Tanks Can't Capture Tanks

A tank's weapon is its gun. While the threat of this is enough to make infantry and guns surrender, an enemy tank protected by armour plate is likely to be less impressed by another tank.

If the only Assaulting (or Counterattacking) teams that are within 4"/10cm of a Defending Tank team are Tank teams, the Defending Tank team is not captured and so is not Destroyed.

Dismounting to Break Off

Troops in transports usually fight dismounted, but are sometimes caught by surprise still in their vehicles. Dismounting, whether to counterattack or break off was usually the top priority.

Infantry teams carried as Passengers may Dismount at the start of their Break Off movement as if this was the Movement Step. Gun teams carried as Passengers may not Dismount as part of their Break Off movement. Teams may not Mount vehicles while Breaking Off.

Cannot Counterattack

Once a platoon starts running, it won't stop until the enemy stops chasing it.

Sometimes when a platoon Breaks Off while other Defending platoons Counterattack, the Assaulting (or Counterattacking) platoon can end up back within 4"/10cm of the platoon that Broke Off. If this happens, the platoon that Broke Off may not choose to Counterattack, but must Break Off again.

Once the assault is over, the platoon catches its breath and is able to fight as normal against other enemy platoons later in the Assault Step.

Pinned Down If Break Off

Breaking off from an assault is fraught with danger and is an admission of defeat. A platoon requires time to properly reorganise its defences after breaking off.

A platoon that Breaks Off is immediately Pinned Down, unless it took no hits in the entire assault, other than from Defensive Fire.

Opponent Wins

Leaving the fight concedes victory to your opponent.

If all of the Defending platoons Break Off, the Assaulting (or Counterattacking) platoons win the assault and Consolidate *(see page 167)**.*

Break Off through the Enemy

Tank teams don't have to retreat in order to break off combat. Being virtually unstoppable, tanks can simply drive through infantry positions when they break off.

Tank teams in a platoon that passed their Motivation Test to Counterattack, but chose to Break Off instead may move in any direction when they Break Off. They may even move straight through the enemy platoons they were fighting in the assault, but they cannot end their movement within 2"/5cm of an enemy Infantry or Gun team.

If the platoon failed the Motivation Test and was forced to Break Off, it must move away from the enemy as normal rather than passing through them.

Summary

Breaking Off

- **Platoons that Break Off move all teams within 8"/20cm of an Assaulting team up to their full move distance away from the Assaulting platoon. Teams cannot move closer than 4"/10cm to enemy teams.**
- **Teams that are left within 4"/10cm of an Assaulting team are Destroyed, except that Tank teams cannot capture Tank teams.**
- **Gun teams within 2"/5cm are automatically Destroyed.**
- **Infantry may Dismount to Break Off.**
- **Once a platoon has Broken Off, it cannot Counterattack until the assault is over.**
- **If all Defending platoons Break Off, the assault is over.**
- **Tanks that pass the Motivation Test to Counterattack may elect to Break Off in any direction including through enemy.**

German infantry advancing supported by a StuG assault gun
IWM HU5151

VICTOR CONSOLIDATES

After the hammering of machine-guns, the crack of grenades and the shouts and screams of the troops locked in combat, the sudden silence at its end is shocking. As fast as the assault began, it ends, and the victors set about regrouping to defend their new positions.

If the Assaulting (or Counterattacking) platoon won the assault, they now Consolidate.

Consolidation Movement

After the helter-skelter of an assault, your platoon will need to reorganise itself to prepare for the next assault or to organise a counterattack. If the disorganised remnants of the defeated enemy are in the way, they are simply brushed aside.

You may move any or all surviving teams from the victorious Assaulting (or Counterattacking) platoon, including Non-assaulting teams, up to 4"/10cm in any direction. Platoons can Consolidate in any direction, even if they are Pinned Down.

This movement may take Assaulting (or Counterattacking) teams, but not Non-assaulting teams, within 2"/5cm of Defending teams. However, no team can move within 2"/5cm of any team from a platoon that was not a Defending platoon.

Command and Consolidation

With their job done, any teams left behind run to catch up with the platoon to consolidate their gains.

All teams that move while Consolidating must remain In Command, or attempt to return to being In Command, at the end of their Consolidation movement.

Platoons that do not have a Command team cannot move while Consolidating.

Consolidating in Rough Terrain

Tanks have to take care when assaulting troops in rough terrain as even after defeating the enemy, they could still be defeated by the terrain itself.

The normal rules for crossing or entering Rough Terrain apply to movement while Consolidating, so vehicles and Gun teams must make the appropriate Bogging Checks as required.

Defending Teams Retreat

The defeated enemy are in no position to interfere with your reorganisation. If your troops get too close to them, they simply melt back further, hoping to avoid another thrashing.

If the Consolidation movement ends with an Assaulting team within 2"/5cm of a Defending team, if it can the Defending team must move the minimum distance necessary so as to be more than 2"/5cm from your Consolidating team. Teams must take any Bogging Checks necessary for this movement.

If the Defending team cannot move more than 2"/5cm from the Assaulting team, or Bogs Down within 2"/5cm of, the Defending team, it is Captured and Destroyed.

Tanks Can't Capture Tanks

Tanks are more concerned by an enemy tank's gun than its tracks. Even if they cannot fall back far enough to break clean away, they still aren't going to surrender to another tank.

If the only Consolidating teams that are within 2"/5cm of a Defending Tank team are Tank or Transport teams, the Defending Tank team is not captured and so is not Destroyed.

Victor Consolidates

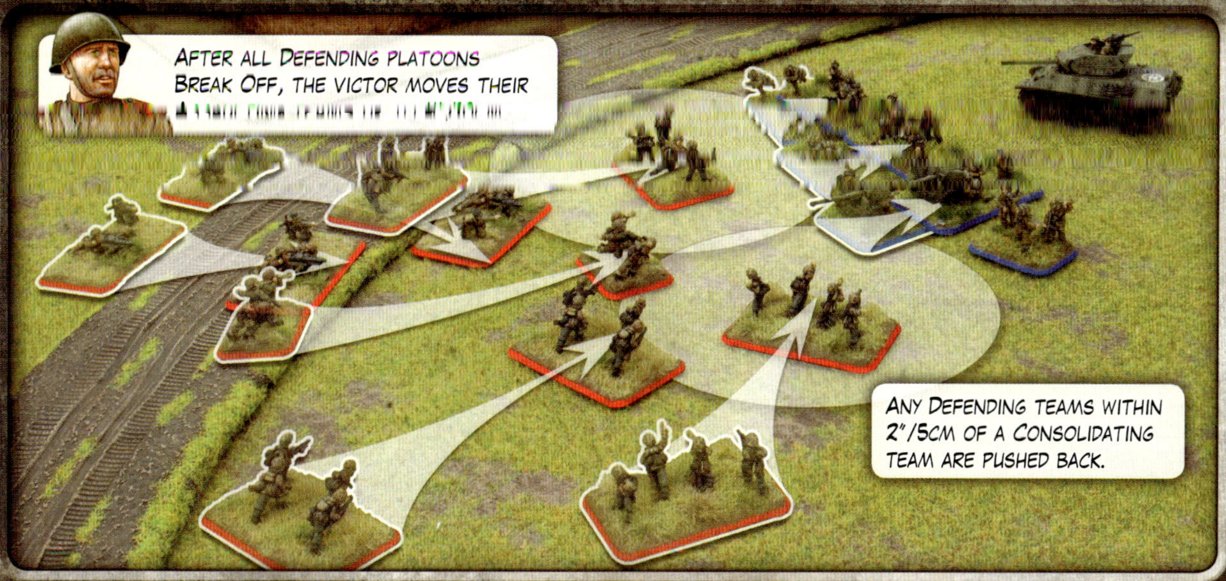

Dismount to Consolidate

Having somehow chased off the enemy, troops quickly dismount and set up a defensive position to stop any following attacks.

Passenger teams may Dismount at the start of their Consolidation movement as if this was the Movement Step, moving up to 4"/10cm as they do so. Teams may not Mount vehicles while Consolidating.

Victor is Pinned Down

It takes time to regain control of a platoon after a victorious assault. The attacking troops are scattered and disorganised, vulnerable to a counterattack.

A victorious platoon is immediately Pinned Down after it Consolidates, unless it took no hits in the entire assault (other than from Defensive Fire).

Armoured Transports Remount

Having survived intense close-range combat, surviving transports and their passengers rejoin their platoon.

Any Bailed Out Armoured Transport teams in the Assaulting (or Counterattacking) or Defending platoons Remount their Bailed Out vehicles (see Remounting Bailed Out Vehicles on page 102) after Consolidation is completed. Any Dismounted Passengers remain Dismounted.

SUMMARY

Victor Consolidates

- **Teams from the winning platoon move up to 4"/10cm in any direction, remaining or returning to be In Command.**
- **This movement may take Assaulting teams within 2"/5cm of Defending teams, but not teams from other platoons.**
- **The Defending teams must then move outside of 2"/5cm or be Destroyed.**
- **Consolidating platoons are Pinned Down unless they took no hits in the Assault.**

British infantry surprise a German StuG G assault gun

WARRIORS AND INDEPENDENT TEAMS

Some officers take the heroic approach of leading from the front, fighting at the head of their soldiers in every fight. Others prefer a more considered approach planning the battle from the rear where they can see everything and issue the appropriate orders.

Independent Teams cannot Assault

Independent teams have their own tasks to perform, leaving the cut and thrust of close combat to others.

Independent teams cannot Charge into Contact at all, and must Break Off at the earliest opportunity, immediately leaving any platoon that they had Joined.

Warriors May Assault Alone

The lead-from-the-front type of fire eater takes every opportunity to lead their troops into battle.

A Warrior team can Charge into Contact on its own, or if it is not already part of a platoon, it can Join a platoon to Launch an Assault along with it.

SUMMARY

- **Independent teams cannot Charge into Contact and must Break Off.**
- **Warrior teams can Charge into Contact alone or after Joining a platoon.**

US M8 Scott HMC howitzer and M4A1 (76mm) Sherman tank
US Signal Corps, NARA

ASSAULT SPECIAL RULES

A number of units have unusual equipment and training allowing them to perform better in assaults. The following special rules reflect this. Each army's Arsenal indicates which of their teams use these special rules.

Tank Assault

While most troops have basic training in combating tanks, they have little experience and even fewer weapons to make the theory a reality. However, some troops are specifically trained and practised in tank-hunting and have specialised anti-tank grenades making them deadly in close combat against tanks.

Teams with a Tank Assault rating listed use this rating in assault combat, e.g. Tank Assault 3 has an Tank Assault rating of 3. This has no effect on their normal Anti-tank rating used in shooting.

Improvised Tank Assault

Some of the anti-tank grenades issued in World War Two were almost as dangerous to the troops using them as to the tanks they attacked. A good example of this is the British 'Grenade, Hand, No 74', commonly known as the 'Sticky Bomb'.

If a team with the Improvised Tank Assault attribute rolls a 1 when rolling to hit in an assault combat, the team scores an 'own goal' and is Destroyed.

A team armed with Improvised Tank Assault weapons may, before rolling to hit, choose not to use them if the target does not justify the risk involved. In this case, the team reverts to its normal Tank Assault rating of 2.

ASSAULT SUMMARY

1 Select the Attacking Platoon

Select one platoon to assault.

- *Must pass a Motivation Test to assault Tank teams.*

2 Charge into Contact

Move nearest team 4"/10cm to contact enemy team.

Move remaining teams 4"/10cm to contact enemy teams.

Move all teams within 8"/20cm of the enemy 4"/10cm toward nearest unengaged enemy or any contacted enemy.

3 Opponent Conducts Defensive Fire

All Defending teams within 8"/20cm of the Assaulting team conduct Defensive Fire.

Defensive Fire uses normal shooting procedure except:

- *Full ROF even if moved, but not if Pinned Down,*
- *Tanks use Side armour for Armour Saves.*

If Assaulting platoon takes 5 hits or two Tank teams Bailed Out or Destroyed from Defensive Fire, it falls back until 2"/5cm away from the enemy.

4 Roll To Hit with Teams in Contact

All Assaulting teams (apart from Transport teams) within 2"/5cm of the enemy roll a Skill Test to hit.

Assaulting Team's Skill	*Score Needed to Hit*
Conscript	*5+*
Trained	*4+*
Veteran	*3+*

5 Allocate Hits to Target Teams

Opponent allocates hits to teams in target platoon within 2"/5cm. Hits must be allocated:

- *evenly across teams.*
- *to operational vehicles first.*
- *to other targets before Transport teams.*
- *to lowest Armour first.*

6 Roll Saves for Teams that were Hit

No save for Unarmoured vehicles, Infantry, or Gun teams in assaults and no Firepower Test to Destroy them.

When Armoured vehicles are hit, the opponent rolls a die and adds the Top armour rating and compares the result to the Tank Assault rating (normally 2):

Roll is	*Result*
Greater	*No effect*
Equal	*Bail Out*
Less	*Destroy*

Gun teams with ROF 2 or more and Man-packed Gun teams (other than mortars) can use their normal Anti-tank rating against Side Armour rating instead. In this case, a Firepower Test is required to Bail Out or Destroy the target.

7 Mark or Remove Destroyed Teams

Mark Destroyed Armoured vehicles as Wrecks.

Remove other Destroyed teams.

8 Push into Enemy Platoons

Teams can advance into position of Destroyed enemy team across Linear Obstacle or into Building.

9 Has Assaulting platoon Won

Assaulting platoon wins if no Defending teams left within 4"/10cm.

- *Ignore Bogged Down and Bailed Out enemy vehicles and Transport teams.*

If won, Victor Consolidates.

10 Opponent Tests Motivation

Opponent makes Motivation Test using the same die roll for all Defending platoons.

- *If pass, choose to Counterattack, or Break Off.*
- *If fail, must Break Off.*

If no teams were hit, pass Motivation Test automatically unless assaulting Tank teams.

11 Counterattack

Defending platoons become Assaulting platoons and Charge into Contact without receiving Defensive Fire.

12 Break Off

Gun teams left within 2"/5cm of the enemy are Destroyed. All other teams move to get at least 4"/10cm away from enemy. Any teams left within 4"/10cm of assaulting teams are Destroyed.

Breaking Off platoons are Pinned Down.

13 Victor Consolidates

Move victorious teams up to 4"/10cm to Consolidate. Push any Defending teams within 2"/5cm away. Consolidating platoons are Pinned Down.

14 Return to 1 to Select your next Assaulting Platoon

MORALE

American M4A1 76mm Sherman

Almost any force will stand firm while their losses are light. But once the casualties mount, even the most battle-hardened soldiers question the wisdom of staying in the fight, deciding that discretion is the better part of valour. You can never be sure when this is going to happen. Some particularly stubborn, brave, or perhaps foolhardy troops fight on long after others would have given up, while others break and run at the first sign of trouble.

CONTENTS

PLATOON MORALE CHECKS

CHECK AT THE END OF THE SHOOTING STEP

With the bullets flying and your buddies dropping around you, it can take an iron will to stand tough.

You must make a Platoon Morale Check for a platoon at the end of a Shooting Step if:

- *the platoon has more teams Destroyed than still fighting, and*
- *it had teams Destroyed or forced to Bail Out during the Shooting Step.*

CHECK AT THE END OF THE ASSAULT STEP

While fighting, soldiers have no idea of their losses. Once they stop and learn the situation, they may break.

You must make a Platoon Morale Check for a platoon at the end of an Assault Step if:

- *the platoon has more teams Destroyed than still fighting, and*
- *it had teams Destroyed or forced to Bail Out during the Assault Step.*

PLATOON MORALE CHECK AFTER ASSAULTS

Do not make Platoon Morale Checks until the end of the Assault Step. This check is separate from the Motivation Tests that you take to Counterattack and only occurs after all assaults are over. Your platoons could be reduced to having more dead than still fighting in an assault, continue fighting, and even win the assault, only to abandon the field when the fighting ends and they realise the extent of their losses.

PLATOON MORALE CHECKS

Checking Platoon Morale

Though the nerve of your soldiers plays a large part in whether they fight or flee, ultimately it comes down to the discipline of their training and a bit of luck.

When you need to make a Platoon Morale Check roll a Motivation Test for that platoon.

- *If you pass the Motivation Test, the platoon grits its teeth and continues fighting.*
- *If you fail the Motivation Test, the entire platoon is removed from the table and is considered Destroyed.*

Leave the wrecks of Destroyed Armoured vehicles in place when a platoon fails its Platoon Morale Check. If any of its Armoured vehicles are Bailed Out or Bogged Down, leave them in place as Destroyed Wrecks as well.

More Teams Destroyed than Still Fighting

There is always a point in the battle when an officer or NCO takes stock of what's left of his fighting force and decides whether or not to go on.

Ignore Bogged Down and Bailed Out

Bogged down and bailed out vehicles are not destroyed, but they are also not capable of fighting. They are neither a source of encouragement, nor a source of discouragement like a destroyed tank.

When deciding whether a platoon has more teams Destroyed than still fighting, do not count Bogged Down or Bailed Out teams as either Destroyed or as capable of fighting. They do not come into the equation at all.

A platoon does not need to take a Platoon Morale Check if it doesn't have any Destroyed teams, even if every team in it is Bailed Out. It may not have anything still fighting, but it also doesn't have anything Destroyed.

However, having a team Bailed Out is still a trigger for Checking Platoon Morale if you have more dead than still fighting.

A platoon can have more teams destroyed than still fighting (i.e. the number of tanks destroyed exceeds the number of tanks still capable of fighting), and then return to having more teams fighting than destroyed again as bailed out crews remount their vehicles, increasing the number of tanks capable of fighting.

Ignore Transport Teams

Trucks and gun tractors are not intended to fight, and the infantry and gunners don't expect them to hang around once they have dropped off their passengers. Even armoured infantry half-tracks usually only fight against light opposition. Against anti-tank weapons, the half-tracks are just too vulnerable.

Ignore Transport teams, whether they are Destroyed or still operational, when determining whether a platoon has more teams Destroyed than still fighting.

Motivation Tests and Morale Checks

The term Motivation Test is used when you are required to roll a die and compare it with a team's or platoon's Motivation rating. This happens under a variety of circumstances ranging from Rallying from being Pinned Down to stirring up the courage to charge the foe.

A Morale Check happens when a platoon or company has suffered heavy casualties and may flee the battle. Taking a Morale Check requires a Motivation Test, but aside from this they are two very different, though occasionally confused, concepts.

Ignore Bogged Down and Bailed Out Tanks

US infantry pass a burning German Sd Kfz 250 half-track
US Signal Corps, NARA

Ignore Teams not on the Table

Sometimes it is sensible to send troops to safety in the rear, rather than keep them unnecessarily exposed to danger. With them gone, the remaining troops know they no longer have their support.

Teams that are removed from the table but not Destroyed are ignored in Platoon Morale Checks. They do not count as Destroyed, but neither are they on the table to contribute to the platoon's fighting strength.

Ignore Pre-game Losses

While attrition from preliminary bombardments and other misfortunes is demoralising, the soldiers' spirits inevitably rise once the chance to fight back arrives.

In certain missions it is possible for a force to incur casualties before the first turn of the game. Any teams removed or Destroyed before the first turn of the game never count as Destroyed when determining whether a platoon has more teams Destroyed than still fighting. They are completely ignored in Platoon Morale Checks.

Warrior and Independent Teams

Soldiers care more about their own than any officer that joins them in their position.

Ignore Warrior teams that are not permanently part of the platoon and Independent teams when determining if a platoon has more teams Destroyed than still fighting. Whether fully operational or Destroyed, neither the Warrior teams nor the Independent teams are counted.

Loss of Warrior or Independent Teams

On the other hand, if they are already a bit shaky, the loss of a visiting officer can serve as a potent reminder that it could easily have been them that took the bullet.

Despite being ignored in determining if the platoon has more teams Destroyed than still fighting, a Warrior or Independent team that was Destroyed or Bailed Out will trigger a Platoon Morale Check in a platoon that it has Joined if that platoon already has more teams Destroyed than still fighting.

Carried Away in the Rout

Senior officers can use their authority to steady the nerves of a jumpy platoon and keep it fighting, but should they fail, they can easily be swept away in the ensuing rout.

Warrior teams and Independent teams that have joined a platoon are Destroyed if the platoon fails a Platoon Morale Check. Warrior and Independent team must still make a Platoon Morale Check for the platoon they have Joined, if they are the only teams left in the platoon at the end of the Step.

SUMMARY

Platoon Morale Checks

- **Check Platoon Morale for any platoon that took casualties and has more teams Destroyed than still fighting at the end of the Shooting or Assault Step.**
- **A platoon taking a Platoon Morale Check must pass a Motivation Test or the whole platoon is Destroyed.**
- **Ignore Bogged Down and Bailed Out vehicles and Transport teams when deciding if a platoon has more teams Destroyed than still fighting.**
- **Any teams Destroyed before the game began or removed from the table during the game, but not Destroyed, are also ignored.**
- **Ignore Warrior and Independent teams when deciding if a platoon has more teams Destroyed than still fighting.**
- **Warrior and Independent teams that have joined a platoon are Destroyed if the platoon fails a Platoon Morale Check.**

COMPANY MORALE CHECKS

WHEN TO CHECK

Confusion reigns on the battlefield and often forces are only aware of what is happening immediately beside them. So when a platoon retreats, neighbouring platoons may see that as the whole situation devolving and follow suit.

This could come from the feeling that their flanks have been left too exposed by the retreat of their fellow platoons. Or perhaps they mistake the retreat for an order to withdraw. Regardless, once you start losing platoons, the chances of your company falling apart increases exponentially.

You must make a Company Morale Check in the Starting Step at the start of every one of your turns that your company has more platoons destroyed than still fighting.

CHECKING COMPANY MORALE

The key figure in holding the company together in a crisis is the company commander. While the commander stands firm, the company fights. One slip, one hesitation, however, and the company's faith is lost.

When you need to make a Company Morale Check roll a Motivation Test for the Company Command team.

- *If you pass the Motivation Test, your commander's leadership holds the company together.*
- *If you fail, your shattered forces retreat from the field of battle and the game is over. You have lost the battle.*

Command teams never re-roll failed Company Morale Checks unless specifically allowed to by a special rule.

If you are required to make a Company Morale Check and the Company Command team has already been Destroyed, or is not on the table, the 2iC Command team may take the Company Morale Check instead. If both are Destroyed or not on the table, the game ends immediately as the Motivation Test is automatically failed.

USING HIGHER COMMAND TEAMS

When a senior officer is on the field, it is their confidence in victory that matters. If they are willing to continue sacrificing a company to win, the troops have no choice but to fight on. If the losses are too heavy for the officer to stomach, they will order a retreat.

If a Higher Command team is on the table, they take the Motivation Test for a Company Morale Check, not the Company Command or 2iC Command team.

MORE PLATOONS DESTROYED THAN STILL FIGHTING

Losses are an unfortunate reality of war, but it's when those losses begin to pile up that the spirit of an army can break.

WHEN IS A PLATOON DESTROYED

Even though they may be bloody and battered, a good commander won't count a unit out of the fight until they have nothing left. Even a small cadre of survivors are enough to rebuild the unit again after the battle.

A platoon is Destroyed when the last surviving team on the table is Destroyed. If the only teams left in the platoon are Warrior or Independent teams that have Joined it, the platoon is Destroyed at the end of the Step when the Warrior and Independent teams leave the platoon (having survived a Platoon Morale Check).

It doesn't matter how weak or battered a platoon is, so long as it still has one team on the table, it is still a functioning platoon.

German Infantry Platoon

Ignore Platoons not on the Table

Once a platoon is out of battle, it will start to recover its strength as stragglers and lightly wounded soldiers return to the colours.

Platoons that are not Destroyed, but not on the table for any reason (such as platoons that have been sent to the rear or are held in reserve) are simply ignored when working out if your company has more platoons Destroyed than still fighting.

Ignore Transport Platoons

Nobody expects transport units to fight, but their loss implies long marches on foot or shortages of food and ammunition in the future.

Ignore Transport Platoons when working out whether a company has more platoons Destroyed than still fighting. They are ignored in Company Morale Checks.

Ignore Pre-game Losses

Some things, like the losses your force suffers in the lead up to battle, just can't be helped. You just have to make a new plan and fight on.

Any platoons removed or Destroyed before the first turn of the game never count as Destroyed when determining whether a company has more platoons Destroyed than still fighting. They are completely ignored in Company Morale Checks.

Ignore Warrior and Independent Teams

Though the 'Old Man' and other key teams are vital assets to any force, one individual simply can't make up for the loss of an entire platoon.

Ignore Warrior and Independent teams when determining whether your company has more platoons Destroyed than still fighting.

More Than One Company

If you are fielding more than one company in your force, the other companies, seeing one falling back, decide that things must be worse than they thought and retreat too.

The game ends when any company in a force fails its Company Morale Check, regardless of how many other companies are still fighting.

SUMMARY

- **Check Company Morale at the start of each of your turns once your company has more platoons Destroyed than still fighting.**
- **A company taking a Company Morale Check must pass a Motivation Test or the whole company is Destroyed.**
- **A Higher Command team takes the Motivation Test in place of the Company Command team.**
- **Ignore Transport platoons and Warrior and Independent teams when deciding if a company has more platoons Destroyed than still fighting.**
- **Any platoons Destroyed before the game began or removed from the table during the game, but not Destroyed are also ignored.**

Sole Surviving Infantry Team

Even a single squad can still be somewhat effective under the right circumstances, but when a platoon is reduced to just a single team, the survivors have to weigh up how much they can achieve against the high probability of becoming casualties.

If a platoon has been reduced by casualties to no more than a single Infantry team and any number of Transport teams, it must make a sole survivor Motivation Test at the start of each of your Starting Steps before making Company Morale Checks.

- *If they pass the Motivation Test, they continue to fight and function as normal.*
- *If they fail the test, the team flees from the table and the platoon is Destroyed.*

A team that passes its Motivation Test can voluntarily leave the battlefield by moving off the table (see page 60).

Warriors Fight On Alone

Heroic soldiers are famous specifically because they fight on when others leave the fight.

If the sole surviving Infantry team is a Warrior team, it does not need to take a Motivation Test. It can always fight on alone.

SUMMARY

- **Any platoon reduced to just one Infantry team must pass a Motivation Test at the start of each turn or be Destroyed.**
- **Warriors will fight on alone.**

AIRCRAFT

US P-47 Thunderbolt 'Rough and Ready'

CONTENTS

AIR SUPPORT LEVEL

In *Flames Of War*, aircraft come in two main types: ground-attack aircraft and fighters. Ground-attack aircraft bomb, rocket, or strafe the enemy on the ground. Fighters protect your troops by shooting down enemy aircraft. When you have air support, both types of aircraft operate with your company, supporting it on the ground and protecting it from enemy aircraft.

Air Support Pool

The air force isn't directly under the army's control. You will make requests for air support, but it's entirely up to the air force whether you get it or not. Since there are never enough aircraft to go around, the amount of air support you get depends on your priority in the overall battle plan.

When you are organising your company for a battle, you can choose to have Air Support if your Intelligence Briefing provides it. There are three levels of Air Support:

- *Priority Air Support,*
- *Limited Air Support, and*
- *Sporadic Air Support.*

The level of Air Support you have determines the number of dice in the Air Support Pool you use to request Ground-attack Aircraft and Fighter Interception.

A force only ever has one Air Support Pool shared across all of its companies. If multiple companies are playing on a side, take the best level of Air Support as the level of Air Support for the entire force.

Priority Air Support

Your mission has been accorded the highest priority at headquarters. All available air support will support you.

With an Air Support level of Priority Air Support you have seven dice in your Air Support Pool.

Limited Air Support

Despite your efforts your mission has been allocated a lower priority by the air force. It doesn't have enough aircraft to support you fully.

With an Air Support level of Limited Air Support you have five dice in your Air Support Pool.

Sporadic Air Support

Your air force has few resources to support your mission. Either the aircraft are committed elsewhere or are simply not available.

With an Air Support level of Sporadic Air Support you have three dice in your Air Support Pool.

No Air Support

Many battles are fought without air support, either by choice or simply because none is available.

If you have no Air Support, you have no dice in your Air Support Pool and can never receive support from aircraft.

ROLL FOR AIR SUPPORT

Air support requires considerable coordination and planning. Even the best air support could take an hour or more to organise.

All requests for Ground Attack Aircraft and Fighter Interception happen at the beginning of the turn in the Starting Step.

GROUND ATTACK

If you have air support, the air force will attempt to send ground-attack aircraft to support you when you request them.

If you choose to request Ground-attack Aircraft, roll all of the dice in your Air Support Pool. A die roll of 5+ on any of the dice results in a Flight of Ground-attack Aircraft arriving this turn to support your operations. You only receive one Flight no matter how many dice roll 5+.

Every request (successful or not) for Ground-attack Aircraft permanently removes one die from your Air Support Pool, although your pool cannot be reduced below one die.

HOW MANY AIRCRAFT

The air support that you receive will be a flight of one to three ground-attack aircraft.

When Ground-attack Aircraft arrive to support you, roll on the How Many Aircraft Table to determine how strong the Flight is.

HOW MANY AIRCRAFT

Score	Strength of Flight
1 or 2	1 aircraft
3 to 5	2 aircraft
6	3 aircraft

FIGHTER INTERCEPTION

Your fighters attempt to intercept the enemy aircraft before they reach the battlefield.

Each time your opponent receives Ground-attack Aircraft you may attempt to intercept his planes. If you decide to do so, roll all of the dice in your Air Support Pool. Any die roll of 6 is a success resulting in the enemy Aircraft being chased off or shot down so that your opponent gets no Ground-attack Aircraft this turn.

Every request (successful or not) for Fighter Interception permanently removes one die from your Air Support Pool, although your pool cannot be reduced below one die.

There is no need to put fighter aircraft on the table as this air combat takes place many miles away.

FIGHTER INTERCEPTION ONLY

Some air forces did not provide ground-attack support to their army, attacking the enemy air force instead.

Some Air Support is Fighter Interception Only, in which case it cannot be used for Ground Attack.

SUMMARY

- **Roll the dice in your Air Support Pool in the Starting Step to request Ground Attack Aircraft. Any roll of 5+ succeeds.**
- **Remove one die from the Air Support Pool after each attempt.**
- **Roll to see how many aircraft arrive.**
- **If your opponent has Ground Attack Aircraft, you may roll the dice in your Air Support Pool. Any roll of 6 shoots down the enemy Ground Attack Aircraft.**
- **Fighter Interception Only support cannot be used for Ground Attack.**

British Bofors 40mm light anti-aircraft gun standing to
IWM B5647

SELECT THE TARGET AND PLACE AIRCRAFT

Once your aircraft have arrived over the battlefield, the next step is to nominate the target that they will attack. It is important to pick your targets carefully as aircraft cannot safely attack close to your own troops.

Select any enemy team as the target team.

PLACE AIRCRAFT

Aircraft move incredibly fast and can move anywhere on the table without hindrance. Their biggest concerns are setting up an accurate attack on the target while minimising incoming anti-aircraft fire and making sure they don't accidentally bomb the wrong side.

Place the Aircraft so that it is within 4"/10cm of and facing towards the target team (ignoring the flight stand).

The Aircraft may be placed anywhere that its flight stand can fit on the table, but may not be placed so that it's flight stand overlaps any team, a Linear Obstacle or wood, or is on a Building.

Place an Aircraft die on the flight stand to indicate the Strength of the Flight.

SUMMARY

- **Pick an enemy team as the target. Place the aircraft within 4"/10cm of the target enemy team.**
- **Place an Aircraft die on the flight stand to indicate the Strength of the Flight.**

SELECT THE TARGET

US M1 90mm anti-aircraft gun
US Signal Corps, NARA

CONDUCT ANTI-AIRCRAFT FIRE

Facing anti-aircraft fire is one of the worst experiences a pilot will ever face. No matter how skilful the pilot is, the need to keep straight and true during an attack run means that survival is pretty much pure luck—you can't take evasive action, you just have to hope you don't get hit.

Anti-aircraft Fire is conducted by the opposing player after all other shooting is complete, but before the Aircraft makes their attack. It does not matter that the Anti-aircraft weapons are firing out of turn.

WHO CAN SHOOT

Shooting at aircraft requires a special anti-aircraft mounting to allow the weapon to shoot at high angles and rotate rapidly to track fast-moving aircraft.

Only weapons with the Anti-aircraft, Heavy Anti-aircraft, or Self-defence Anti-aircraft attribute can fire at Aircraft. Anti-aircraft weapons that are still being towed by or carried as Passengers in Transport vehicles cannot shoot at Aircraft.

Anti-aircraft weapons must have a Line of Sight and be within Range to shoot at Aircraft.

Any teams that shoot at Aircraft can't move At the Double, Dig In, Shoot or Assault in their next turn.

Any weapons (other than Self-defence Anti-aircraft weapons) that shoot at Aircraft cannot conduct Defensive Fire if assaulted later in this turn.

LINE OF SIGHT TO AIRCRAFT

Aircraft dive steeply at the target, or make a low-level strafing run directly over their target, making them almost impossible to spot in time to engage if they are concealed by tall trees or buildings.

The Line of Sight and Range to Aircraft are measured to the Aircraft model (ignoring the flight stand).

Smoke Markers block Line of Sight to Aircraft, even if the Aircraft is within 16"/40cm. However, if the Anti-aircraft weapon is far enough away, from the Smoke Markers it may be able to see over them, just like any other terrain.

LINE OF SIGHT TO AIRCRAFT

Anti-aircraft Range

Aircraft are easy to engage at long range as intervening terrain does not get in the way.

Anti-aircraft weapons firing at Aircraft can fire 8"/20cm further than their normal Range characteristic.

Anti-aircraft Range

Range	Anti-aircraft Range
16"/40cm	24"/60cm
24"/60cm	32"/80cm
32"/80cm	40"/100cm
40"/100cm	48"/120cm

Number of Dice to Roll

Having selected their target, the anti-aircraft guns open fire. The rate of fire (ROF) rating of a weapon reflects how fast the weapon can shoot.

Anti-aircraft weapons roll one dice for each point of ROF they have when firing at Aircraft.

This is not affected by any movement that the firing weapon may have made in its last turn.

However, if the firing team is a Pinned Down unarmoured vehicle, Infantry team, or Gun team it reduces its ROF by half as shown in the ROF when Pinned Down table.

ROF when Pinned Down

ROF	Pinned ROF
1 to 3	1
4 or 5	2
6 or more	3

Heavy Anti-aircraft Guns

While heavy anti-aircraft guns like the famous German '88' are very effective against heavy bombers (and tanks for that matter), they are not as useful against fast-flying fighter-bombers.

Heavy Anti-aircraft weapons only roll one die when firing at Aircraft regardless of their ROF rating.

Self-defence Anti-aircraft Weapons

Some tanks have anti-aircraft machine-guns mounted for protection against air attacks. These weapons are usually fired by the vehicle commander, requiring them to watch the skies for incoming aircraft rather than performing their own job. If the platoon isn't under attack, the commander focuses on their main task rather than worrying about providing anti-aircraft cover for other platoons.

Self-defence Anti-aircraft weapons, such as all AA MG, may only fire Anti-aircraft Fire if one of the platoon's teams would be under the Template (see page 185).

Self-defence Anti-aircraft weapons only roll one die when firing at Aircraft regardless of their ROF rating.

Unlike other Anti-aircraft weapons firing at Aircraft, Self-defence Anti-aircraft weapons can move At the Double, Dig In, Shoot or Assault in their next turn.

Firing Multiple Platoons

As with all shooting in *Flames Of War*, each platoon completes its anti-aircraft fire before the next begins.

You must decide how many teams in a platoon capable of Anti-aircraft Fire will fire before rolling any dice to hit for that platoon.

You may wait until one platoon's Anti-aircraft Fire has been resolved before deciding how many teams to fire from the next platoon.

German Hs 129B3

Conduct Anti-aircraft Fire

Roll to Hit

Unlike ground targets, aircraft have no cover and few stratagems available to make themselves harder to hit. However, a good gun crew will react quicker and estimate the lead and range better than a poor one giving themselves a much better chance of bringing the aircraft down.

Roll a Skill Test with each die using the Score Needed to Hit Table. Any successful roll scores a hit on the Aircraft. There are no modifiers to this roll.

Score Needed to Hit

Firing Team's Skill	Score Needed to Hit
Conscript	5+
Trained	4+
Veteran	3+

Roll to Destroy

Hitting an aircraft isn't always enough to stop it from making its attack. Once the pilot is committed to his dive, little short of blowing the wing off can actually stop him.

Roll a Firepower Test for each hit from Anti-aircraft Fire.

- *If the Firepower Test is successful, reduce the Strength of the Flight by one. If the Strength of the Flight is reduced to zero, remove the Aircraft.*
- *Otherwise, the fire was insufficient to stop the aircraft.*

Flying Tank

Heavily-armoured ground-attack aircraft like the Soviet Il-2 'Shturmovik' and the German Hs129 are known as 'Flying Tanks' because of their comparative invulnerability to anti-aircraft fire. Only large-calibre anti-aircraft guns have much chance of bringing down a flying tank.

Add +1 to the score needed for Firepower Tests against Aircraft rated as Flying Tanks in their Arsenal entry. This makes it impossible for a weapon with Firepower 6 to shoot down a Flying Tank.

Summary

- **Only Anti-aircraft, Heavy Anti-aircraft, and Self-defence Anti-aircraft weapons can fire at aircraft and have 8"/20cm extra range when they do so.**
- **Anti-aircraft weapons must have a Line of Sight and be in Range to fire at Aircraft.**
- **Roll one die to hit per point of ROF needing a Skill Test to hit. Heavy and Self-defence Anti-aircraft weapons only roll one die.**
- **Roll a Firepower Test to reduce the Strength of the Flight for each hit.**
- **Add +1 to the score needed for Firepower Tests if the aircraft are Flying Tanks.**

ROLL TO RANGE IN ON TARGET

Aircraft flying at high speed find it difficult to locate targets. As the enemy are alerted by the first pass, pilots that fail to locate their target simply leave the battlefield.

Once the Aircraft is in position you must Range In on the target team. You only get one attempt to Range In.

Concealment from Aircraft

Crops and foxholes might provide good concealment from troops on the ground, but trails of flattened crops and bare earth thrown up by digging just make troops more obvious to aircraft.

Teams are only Concealed to Aircraft if they are in or within 2"/5cm of tree lines, Bocage Hedgerows, woods or Buildings, or entirely covered by Smoke Markers from a Smoke Bombardment.

Ranging In on the Target

The single biggest factor in determining if a platoon is located is its experience.

Aircraft have no difficulty locating targets that are not Concealed and automatically Range In on them.

The score required for Aircraft to Range In on a target that is Concealed is shown by the Score Needed to Range In on Concealed Targets Table. There are no modifiers to this roll.

If their single Range In attempt fails, the Aircraft could not find the target and leave the battlefield.

Score Needed to Range In on Concealed Targets

Target Team's Skill	Score Needed to Range In
Conscript	2+
Trained	3+
Veteran	4+

Safety Distance

Troops on the ground aren't keen on being bombed by either side. If a friendly aircraft gets too close, they'll warn it off with flags and coloured smoke.

If any friendly teams are within 16"/40cm of the Aircraft model (ignoring the flight stand) when they attempt to Range In, the Aircraft aborts their attack and leave the battlefield.

Original Target Destroyed

If your ground troops' shooting resulted in the destruction of your aircraft's target, they will continue their attack if they see more targets in the area, otherwise they will abort the mission.

If your Aircraft's original target is no longer there for any reason, you may select any other enemy team within 4"/10cm of the aircraft model (ignoring the flight stand) as your target team instead.

If there are no other enemy teams within 4"/10cm of the Aircraft, they abort their attack and leave the battlefield.

SUMMARY

- **Aircraft automatically Range In on targets in the open.**
- **Aircraft need to roll to Range In on a team within 2"/5cm of trees or buildings. The score needed depends on the target's Skill.**
- **Aircraft abort if they are within 16"/40cm of friendly teams.**

Roll to Range In on Target

POSITION THE TEMPLATE

Air attacks differ from normal shooting in that the aircraft are plastering an area with bombs and rockets or strafing everything they can see. As a result everything around the target team is likely to be hit as well.

All air attacks, whether by bombs, rockets, machine-guns or cannon, use the Artillery Template to determine which teams they can hit. Place the Artillery Template (a square measuring 6"/15cm on each side) centred directly over the target team with the sides parallel to the table edges.

Position the Template

ROLL TO HIT TEAMS UNDER THE TEMPLATE

With bomb blasts and bullets saturating the area around the target, it is largely a matter of luck whether any particular soldier is hit or not.

Rather than rolling one die per point of ROF as teams do normally, count up the number of teams at least partly under the Template, and roll that number of dice. Roll hits separately for each platoon under the Template.

As each Aircraft weapon has a To Hit number in place of its ROF characteristic, the score required to hit depends on the weaponry the aircraft are using.

- *A successful to hit roll means that a team was hit by the air attack.*
- *A failed to hit roll means that the team was lucky and escaped harm.*

If the Aircraft have more than one weapon, you must choose which the Aircraft are using before rolling any dice.

One-aircraft Flights

A single aircraft simply cannot deliver enough ordnance to be fully effective.

If the Strength of the Flight is a single aircraft, re-roll all successful rolls to hit targets under the template.

Three-aircraft Flights

Saturating the target with bombs and bullets delivered by three aircraft makes hits more likely.

If the Strength of the Flight is three aircraft, re-roll all failed rolls to hit targets under the template.

Multiple Target Types

Tanks, infantry, and guns, are not interchangeable, so losses to one cannot be made good from another.

Roll to hit each Type of team (Tank, Infantry, Gun and Transport teams) in the platoon separately.

SUMMARY

- **Roll one die for each team at least partly under the template. Roll separately for each platoon and each type of team.**
- **Each type of aircraft has a To Hit number. Single aircraft re-roll hits. Three aircraft re-roll misses.**

ALLOCATE HITS TO TEAMS

Commanders can order soldiers from one team to replace casualties in another to keep important weapons in action.

Your opponent allocates hits to teams of the appropriate type under the Template from the platoon that was hit, subject to the following rules in order of priority.

- *Each team may only be allocated one hit.*
- *Unprotected teams must be allocated hits before teams in Bulletproof Cover.*
- *Unarmoured vehicles must be allocated hits before Armoured vehicles.*
- *Hits must be allocated to operational vehicles and other teams (including Gone to Ground teams) before Bogged Down or Bailed Out vehicles.*
- *Hits must be allocated to Armoured vehicles with lower armour ratings before those with higher armour ratings. Use Top or Side armour depending on the type of weapon being used (see next page).*
- *Hits must be allocated to other teams before teams that are Gone to Ground.*

Riding on Tanks

If an aircraft hits their tank, any troops riding on it are in for a lot of pain.

Do not roll to hit Infantry or Man-packed Gun teams riding on a tank separately from their tank. Instead, if the Tank team is hit, all teams riding on it are also hit.

Hitting Teams in Buildings

When making a bombing run, pilots just plaster an area centred on the target.

Check the teams' positions in the Building to determine which ones are under the Template of an Air Attack in the same way as if they were outside the Building.

SUMMARY

- **Target player allocates hits.**
- **Each team may only be allocated one hit.**
- **Hits must be allocated to unprotected teams before teams in Bulletproof Cover.**
- **Hits must be allocated to Unarmoured vehicles before Armoured vehicles.**
- **Hits must be allocated to other vehicles before Bogged Down or Bailed Out ones.**
- **Hits must be allocated to Armoured vehicles with the lowest Top armour first.**
- **Hits must be allocated to other teams before teams that are Gone to Ground.**
- **If a tank is hit by air attack, any teams riding on it are also hit.**

British Typhoon fighter-bombers rocketing German Panther tanks

PIN DOWN PLATOONS THAT WERE HIT

Air attacks cause considerable confusion amongst their targets as men scatter for cover. Even if little actual damage is done, it can take time to reorganise the unit before it can advance again.

If a platoon takes one or more hits from an air attack, it is automatically Pinned Down.

ROLL SAVES FOR TEAMS THAT WERE HIT

A hit on a team indicates that the bomb landed close enough to be dangerous. The roll to save tells whether or not it actually destroyed the team.

Armoured Vehicle Saves

Armoured vehicles are well protected from most aerial weapons. It takes a lucky hit by a bomb or a heavy cannon to knock out a tank.

Bombs and Rockets

Bombs and rockets are not particularly accurate. Mostly they rely on shock and blast to damage vehicles rather than penetrating their armour directly.

When your Aircraft hits an Armoured vehicle with Bombs or Rockets, the opposing player rolls a die and adds the vehicle's Top armour rating to get their Armour Save score.

Cannon and Machine-guns

Aircraft strafing with guns have to get in close to hit and penetrate their target. This requires a flat approach 'on the deck', rather than diving from above, so shots have to penetrate the side of a tank to hurt it.

When your Aircraft hits an Armoured vehicle with Cannon or Machine-guns, the owning player rolls a die and adds the vehicle's Side armour rating to get their Armour Save score.

Exceeds Anti-tank Rating

If your opponent's Armour Save score is greater than the Aircraft's Anti-tank rating, their Armour Save is successful, and the shot has no effect having bounced harmlessly off the tank's armour.

Equals Anti-tank Rating

If your opponent's Armour Save score exactly equals your Aircraft's Anti tank rating, they failed their Armour Save. Although your shot didn't penetrate the tank's armour, it might still have some effect.

To determine the effect of the hit you must take a Firepower Test. Roll another die.

- *If the roll equals or exceeds your weapon's Firepower rating, the crew panic and Bail Out.*
- *If the roll is lower than your weapon's Firepower rating the shot has no effect and the tank continues in action unharmed.*

Less than Anti-tank Rating

If your opponent's Armour Save score is less than your Aircraft's Anti-tank rating, they failed their Armour Save.

To determine the effect of the hit you must take a Firepower Test. Roll another die.

- *If the roll equals or exceeds your weapon's Firepower rating, the tank is Destroyed.*
- *If the roll is lower than your weapon's Firepower rating the shot failed to do significant damage to the vehicle but the crew still Bails Out of the tank.*

Unarmoured Vehicle Saves

Unarmoured vehicles are totally unprotected from aircraft weapons. Their only hope of survival is that the bullets and shrapnel will only do minor damage.

When your Aircraft hits an Unarmoured vehicle (one with a Top armour rating of '-'), the opposing player rolls a die.

- *If the result is 5+, the vehicle is damaged, but still fully functional.*
- *Otherwise, the vehicle is automatically Destroyed.*

Recce and Warrior Vehicle Saves

Small jeeps and motorcycles are fast-moving targets and hard for aircraft to hit.

Unarmoured vehicles that are Warrior, Independent or Recce teams (including all Motorcycle Reconnaissance teams) save on a roll of 3+ instead of the usual 5+.

US soldier manning a .50 cal AA MG
US Signal Corps, NARA

Sample Ground-attack Aircraft

Just as there are a huge variety of vehicles and ground weapons in World War II, there is an abundance of different aircraft in the skies. This presents some of the more common attack aircraft.

Aircraft	Weapon	To Hit	Anti-tank	Firepower	Notes
BRITISH					
Typhoon	Cannon	3+	8	5+	
	Rockets	3+	6	3+	
GERMAN					
Ju 87D Stuka	Bombs	4+	5	1+	
SOVIET					
Il-2 Shturmovik	Cannon	3+	9	5+	Flying tank.
	Bombs	4+	5	1+	
	Rockets	3+	6	3+	
US					
P47 Thunderbolt	MG	2+	6	5+	
	Bombs	4+	5	1+	

Infantry Saves

Infantry in the open are very vulnerable to strafing aircraft, but once they get into cover, they can be hard to dig out.

When your Aircraft hits an Infantry team, the opposing player rolls a die.

- *If the result is 3+, the team escapes with no serious injury.*
- *Otherwise, unless the team is in Bulletproof Cover, it is Destroyed.*

JU 87 Stuka dive-bomber
IWM GER18

Gun Saves

When attacked by aircraft diving from above, gun shields provide no protection.

When your Aircraft hits a Gun team, the opposing player rolls a die.

- *If the result is 5+, the team escapes with no serious injury.*
- *Otherwise, unless the team is in Bulletproof Cover, it is Destroyed.*

Gone to Ground Gun Saves

When working their gun, gunners are forced to clump together more than infantry. However, if they go to ground, they can spread out and take full advantage of cover, making them much less vulnerable.

Any Gun teams that are Gone to Ground have a 3+ save instead of a 5+ save. This does not apply to teams that are only Gone to Ground because they are behind Smoke.

Bulletproof Cover

To get any real protection from an aerial bombardment you need a deep hole or a good fortified position.

Linear Obstacles like walls or Bocage Hedgerows, and Gun Shields do not provide Bulletproof Cover against Aircraft, although other Bulletproof Cover, (including being Dug In or in Entrenchments) does.

If the target Infantry or Gun teams are in Bulletproof Cover, take a Firepower Test.

- *If the roll equals or exceeds your weapon's Firepower rating, your weapon blew through the cover and the target team is Destroyed.*
- *If the roll is lower than your weapon's Firepower rating, the cover protects the team from harm.*

Passengers in Transports

The best thing to do under air attack is keep driving and pray that you don't get hit. Air attacks are over so fast, and there is little extra safety to the rear, so drivers carry on forward once the attack is over.

Armoured Transports

Armoured vehicles like half-tracks just hope the aircraft doesn't score a direct hit!

Armoured Transport teams roll saves in the same way that Armoured Tank teams do. However, they automatically Remount (see page 102) immediately when Bailed Out by an Air Attack.

If you Destroy an Armoured Transport team, every Passenger carried by the Transport team must pass a 5+ Passenger Save or be Destroyed. Any surviving Passenger teams immediately Dismount Under Fire and the platoon is now Pinned Down (see page 104).

Unarmoured Transports

One of the last places you want to be under air attack is crammed in a vehicle, hoping a bomb doesn't hit you. On the other hand, if you survive, the danger is gone and you may as well carry on as go back.

When you hit an Unarmoured Transport team (whether or not you Destroy it), every Passenger carried by the Transport team must pass a 5+ Passenger Save or be Destroyed. If all of the Passengers in a Transport team are Destroyed but the vehicle is not, the Transport team is Sent to the Rear immediately. The platoon is now Pinned Down (see page 104).

Surviving Unarmoured Transport teams still carrying Passengers remain on table after an air attack, even if other Transport teams in the platoon were Destroyed.

Dismounting Under Fire

If their vehicle is destroyed, the surviving passengers get out and hit the dirt as fast as possible.

If its transport is Destroyed or removed as a result of air attack, any surviving Passenger teams must immediately Dismount, moving no closer to the shooting teams as it does so.

If necessary, Transport teams (other than Wrecks of Armoured Transport teams) can be removed first to create space for the Passengers to Dismount. If there is no room for a Passenger team to Dismount, then the Passenger team is Destroyed.

Passengers on Tanks

If riding in a vehicle is unsafe, clinging to the outside of a tank under fire is even more dangerous.

Infantry or Man-packed Gun teams riding on a tank must take a 5+ Save instead of their usual Infantry or Gun Save when hit. The Passengers are not in Bulletproof Cover, so no Firepower Test is needed to Destroy them. All surviving Passenger teams immediately Dismount Under Fire and the platoon is now Pinned Down (see page 104).

SUMMARY

Roll Saves for Teams that were Hit

Armoured Vehicle Saves

- **Roll a die, add the vehicle's Top armour (for Bombs and Rockets), or Side armour (for MG and Cannon), and compare result to Anti-tank rating:**
  - **If greater, vehicle is unharmed.**
  - **If equal, Firepower Test to Bail Out.**
  - **If less, Firepower test to Destroy, if fail the vehicle is Bailed Out.**

Unarmoured Vehicle Saves

- **Unarmoured vehicles pass a save on a 5+. Unarmoured vehicles that are Warrior, Independent or Recce teams save on a 3+.**

Infantry and Gun Saves

- **Infantry teams save on 3+. Gun teams save on 5+, unless Gone to Ground when they save on 3+. Riders on tanks save on 5+.**

Bulletproof Cover and Passengers

- **A Firepower Test is required to Destroy teams in Bulletproof Cover. Linear Obstacles and Gun Shields do not provide Bulletproof Cover against air attack.**
- **Passengers in Unarmoured transports that were hit or Destroyed Armoured transports must pass a Save of 5+. Survivors immediately Dismount and are Pinned Down.**

Aircraft Return to Base to Rearm

After they have made their attack, all aircraft return to base to rearm for the next strike.

Remove the Aircraft from the table after it has made its attack.

The amount of air support available to you will always be the same. No matter if you lose aircraft or not, the air force will always manage to scrape up more aircraft from somewhere for the next attack.

AIRCRAFT SUMMARY

AIR SUPPORT LEVEL

Your Air Support Level determines Air Support Pool.

- *Priority Air Support gives 7 dice.*
- *Limited Air Support gives 5 dice.*
- *Sporadic Air Support gives 3 dice.*

IN THE STARTING STEP

1 ROLL FOR GROUND ATTACK AIRCRAFT

Roll all of the dice in the Air Support Pool.

- *Ground-attack Aircraft arrive on any roll of 5+.*
- *Each attempt reduces Air Support Pool by one die.*

If successful, roll for Number of Aircraft received:

Score	*Number of Aircraft*
1 or 2	*1 aircraft*
3 to 5	*2 aircraft*
6	*3 aircraft*

2 OPPONENT ROLLS FOR FIGHTER INTERCEPTION

Opponent may roll the dice in their Air Support Pool.

- *Fighter Interception cancels Ground-attack Aircraft on any roll of 6.*
- *Each attempt reduces Air Support Pool by one die.*

3 CHOOSE TARGET AND POSITION AIRCRAFT

Select any enemy team as the target.

Place Aircraft model within 4"/10cm of target team.

IN THE SHOOTING STEP

After all other shooting is completed:

1 CONDUCT ANTI-AIRCRAFT FIRE

Anti-aircraft weapons increase range by 8"/20cm when firing at Aircraft.

Anti-aircraft weapons roll a die to hit for each ROF: Heavy and Self-defence Anti-aircraft weapons only roll one die.

Firing Team's Skill	*Score Needed*
Conscript	*5+*
Trained	*4+*
Veteran	*3+*

Roll Firepower Test to Destroy Aircraft that were hit. Add +1 to the Firepower if the aircraft are Flying Tanks.

2 ROLL TO RANGE IN ON THE TARGET

Range In automatically on a target in the open.

Roll once to Range In on a Concealed target (within 2"/5cm of trees, Bocage, woods, or Buildings, or in smoke).

Target Team's Skill	*Score Needed*
Conscript	*2+*
Trained	*3+*
Veteran	*4+*

Aircraft abort if any friendly teams within 16"/40cm.

3 ROLL TO HIT

Roll against Aircraft's To Hit rating.

Re-roll if appropriate for the number of Aircraft.

Number of Aircraft	*Effect*
1	*Re-roll hits*
2	*No re-rolls*
3	*Re-roll misses*

4 ROLL SAVES FOR TEAMS THAT WERE HIT

Bombs and Rockets hit Top armour. Cannon and Machine-guns hit Side armour. Opponent rolls a die and adds their armour rating and compares the result to the Anti-tank rating:

Roll is	*Result*
Greater	*No effect*
Equal	*Firepower test to Bail Out*
Less	*Firepower test to Destroy otherwise Bail Out*

Roll 5+ save for Unarmoured vehicles, except 3+ save for Warrior, Independent, and Recce teams.

Roll 3+ save for Infantry teams.

Roll 5+ save for Gun teams, unless Gone to Ground, then 3+ save.

Roll Firepower Tests to Destroy Infantry teams, and Gun teams in Bulletproof Cover.

5 MARK OR REMOVE DESTROYED TEAMS

Mark Destroyed Armoured vehicles as Wrecks.

Remove other Destroyed teams.

6 PIN DOWN PLATOONS THAT WERE HIT

Any hit on a platoon by air attack means the platoon is Pinned Down.

7 AIRCRAFT RETURN TO BASE TO REARM

Show's over, the Aircraft leave the table.

SPECIALISTS

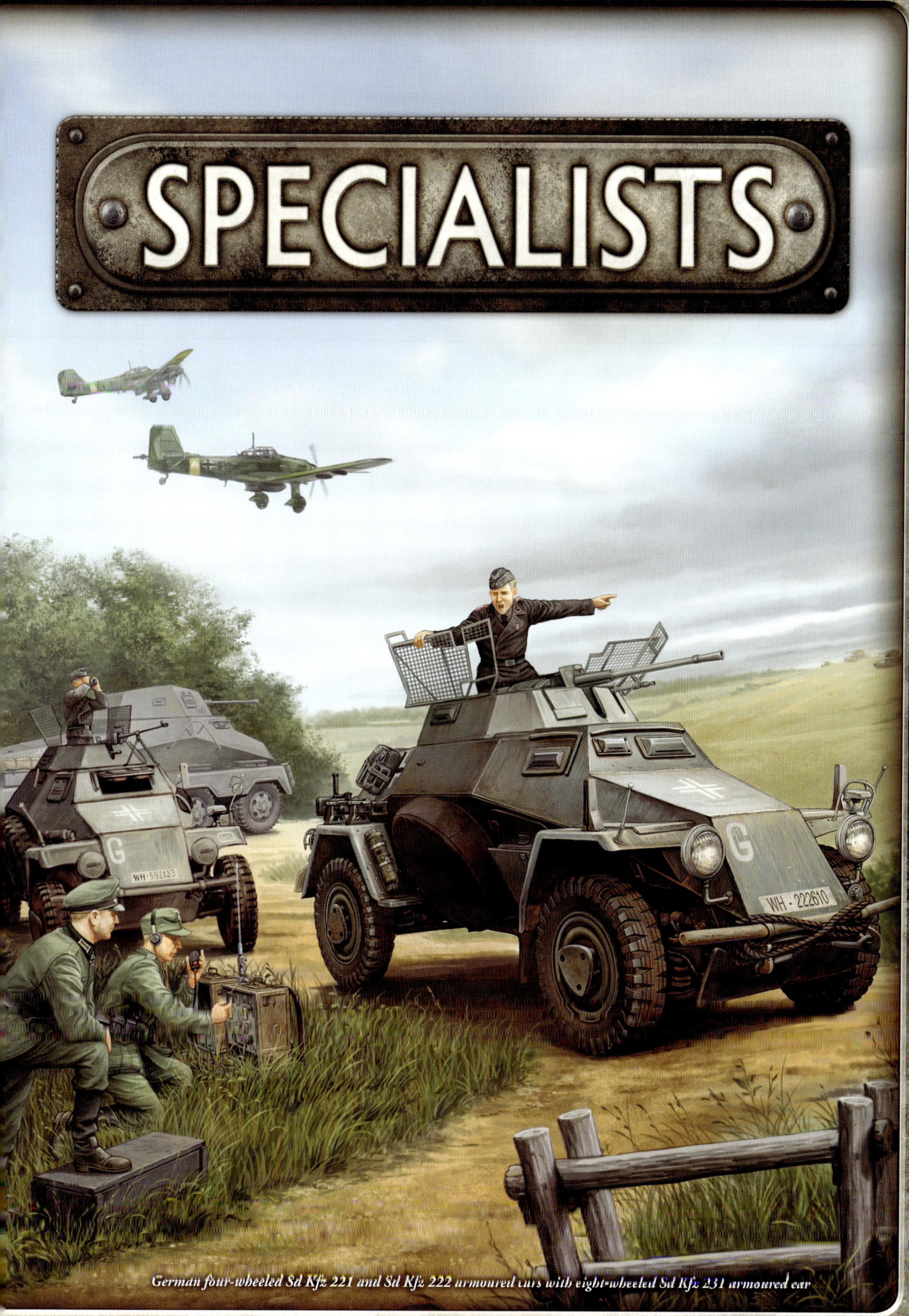

German four-wheeled Sd Kfz 221 and Sd Kfz 222 armoured cars with eight-wheeled Sd Kfz 231 armoured car

An army needs hordes of specialists such as reconnaissance troops, motorcycle scouts, horse-mounted cavalry, man-packed and tank-mounted flame-throwers, tank escort infantry, and even armoured trains. Each of these fills a niche that no other troops can.

CONTENTS

Soviet Cossack cavalry

RECONNAISSANCE

According to an old army saying, 'Time spent on reconnaissance is seldom wasted'. Commanders ignore this hard-learnt lesson at their own peril. With inadequate reconnaissance any force, no matter how powerful, is vulnerable to a surprise attack from a better informed enemy.

Reconnaissance Platoons

The purpose of reconnaissance units is reconnaissance and every soldier in the platoon is trained in the art of stealth and observation.

All teams in a Reconnaissance Platoon are Recce teams.

Recce Vehicle Saves

Reconnaissance jeeps and motorcycles are small and their crews are trained to move stealthily and take cover.

Unarmoured Recce vehicles save on a roll of 3+ instead of the usual 5+.

Cautious Movement

Recce troops are trained to make the best use of any concealment, even when on the move.

Recce and Observer teams are always Gone to Ground, unless they move At the Double, carry Passengers that are not Recce teams, shoot, or assault.

Revealing Ambushes

One of the main roles of reconnaissance troops in an advance is to ensure that the enemy doesn't spring any nasty surprises on the main body of the force.

In addition to the normal restrictions on Ambush placement (see page 266), teams placed from Ambush must be more than 8"/20cm from all enemy Recce teams that are in Line of Sight (apart from Recce teams that are Bogged Down, Bailed Out, or moved At the Double).

Reconnaissance Deployment

Well before the start of any battle the recce troops start working their way forward, searching out the enemy.

After all Deployment, but before the game begins (as specified in the mission), Recce teams Deployed on the table may move as if it was their Movement Step with the following restrictions:

- *If a Recce team is out of Line of Sight of an enemy team, it may not move into Line of Sight while it is within 16"/40cm of the team.*
- *If it is already in Line of Sight of an enemy team within 16"/40cm, it may not move closer to it while still in Line of Sight.*
- *In any case, the Recce team may not move within 8"/20cm of any enemy team, whether in Line of Sight or not.*

Ignore enemy Independent and Warrior teams when making Reconnaissance Deployment Moves. They do not limit a Recce team's movement in any way.

This movement may not be At the Double. If a Recce team is carrying Passengers that are not Recce teams, it may not make a Reconnaissance Deployment Move at all.

If both players have Recce teams, they alternate selecting a platoon with Recce teams and doing their Reconnaissance Deployment Moves with that platoon. The mission or scenario will say which player selects a platoon first.

Reconnaissance Deployment

Disengage!

Recce troops are often lightly armed and armoured, if they are armoured at all! Yet the nature of their job requires that they operate close to the enemy. When attacked, recce troops use their speed and training to evade incoming fire before serious damage is done.

Recce teams may attempt to Disengage when fired on in the enemy Shooting Step as long as they did not move At the Double, shoot, fire an Artillery Bombardment or Anti-aircraft Fire, or assault in their previous turn.

If you wish a Recce team to Disengage, you must declare your intention to do so at the point an enemy platoon fires, but before any dice are rolled To Hit. If you do so, each team shooting at the platoon then fires one shot at the platoon in its current position.

After resolving the effects of these shots, the Recce team has a chance to get away. Make a Skill Test for the platoon to see if they can escape before the full weight of the enemy's fire hits them.

- *If successful, any or all Recce teams in the platoon that are not Bogged Down or Bailed Out may immediately Disengage and move up to their normal movement away from the enemy teams shooting at them. Any movement they make must take them further from the shooting teams. Teams cannot move At the Double when disengaging. Any Recce teams that choose not to Disengage and all non-recce teams remain where they were.*
- *If unsuccessful, the Recce teams do not Disengage and remain in their original position.*

After the Recce teams have Disengaged, all remaining shots are fired at the platoon in its new position. If the whole platoon managed to get out of Range, Line of Sight, or Field of Fire of the enemy, the remaining shots automatically miss.

Disengaging From ROF 1 Weapons

Recce troops are far too fast on their feet to be much bothered by slow-firing riflemen or ponderous big guns.

Weapons that only fire one shot (either because they have ROF 1 or because they moved) do not fire before the Recce teams attempt to Disengage. They must wait and fire at the teams in their final position.

Only Disengage Once

Recce troops might be elusive but they can't avoid every fight, especially if overrun by a concerted enemy advance.

A platoon may only attempt to Disengage once in any Shooting Step. A platoon does not have to attempt to Disengage from the first enemy platoon that shoots at it. Instead it may take fire from one platoon and then Disengage from another later if you want.

Reorganising

Recce troops need a little time to get their bearings, check and report on any damage sustained, regain formation and receive new orders after disengaging.

Recce teams that Disengaged must Reorganise until the end of their next turn. While Reorganising they may not:

- *Move,*
- *Dig In,*
- *Assault,*
- *Conduct Ant-aircraft Fire, or*
- *Take an Objective.*

Reorganising teams are treated as if they moved in their Movement Step, reducing their ROF when shooting.

Other teams in the platoon that did not Disengage continue to operate as normal.

Place a Reorganising marker with teams that Disengaged to remind you of their status in your turn.

Disengage

Eyes and Ears

Eyes and Ears

On the battlefields of World War II, the art of camouflage can render even the largest weapons almost invisible. One of the most vital jobs of recce troops is to seek out enemy hiding places—tanks hidden in haystacks or soldiers lying in long grass. Once these are discovered, the recce trooper lowers his binoculars and reaches for the radio to tell the rest of the force where to look.

A Recce team that did not move, and is not Pinned Down, Bogged Down, or Bailed Out, may attempt to Reveal an enemy platoon within 16"/40cm and Line of Sight that is Gone to Ground.

Immediately before the rest of their platoon shoots, roll a Skill Test for each team attempting to Reveal an enemy platoon.

- *If the Skill Test is passed, all teams from the Revealed enemy platoon in Line of Sight of teams from the Revealing platoon do not count as Gone to Ground for the remainder of the Shooting Step.*
- *Otherwise, the team could not find the enemy and they remain Gone to Ground.*

Each Recce team can attempt to Reveal a different enemy platoon. Declare which enemy platoon each team will attempt to Reveal before rolling to see if it was Revealed.

A team that attempts to Reveal an enemy platoon does not count as having shot, but cannot shoot, assault, or Spot for an Artillery Bombardment this turn.

Smoke and Eyes and Ears

While recce troops are clever and observant, they still can't make a smoke screen go away.

A Recce team using Eyes and Ears on an enemy platoon does not prevent that enemy platoon from being both Concealed and Gone to Ground because it is seen through Smoke Markers (see page 107).

Eyes and Ears at Night

In the dark of night recce troops need to get closer in order to find the enemy.

A Recce team attempting to Reveal an enemy platoon at night cannot do so if the nearest team from the enemy platoon is further away than the distance the platoon can see rolled on the Night Visibility Table (see page 272).

Reconnaissance

SUMMARY

- **All teams in a Reconnaissance platoon are Recce teams. Unarmoured vehicles that are Recce teams have a 3+ save.**
- **Recce teams can remain Gone to Ground while moving (but not At the Double).**
- **Teams cannot be placed from Ambush within 8"/20cm and in sight of Recce teams.**
- **Recce teams can move after Deployment, but must stay more than 16"/40cm away or out of Line of Sight of enemy teams.**
- **Recce teams that did not shoot or assault may Disengage when shot at. After taking one shot from each shooting team, they take a Skill Test to move away. Remaining shots are fired after they move.**
- **Weapons with ROF 1 always shoot after Recce Disengages.**
- **After Disengaging, teams cannot move in their own turn, but count as having moved.**
- **Recce teams that do not move or shoot can take a Skill test to remove Gone to Ground from an enemy platoon within 16"/40cm.**

MOTORCYCLE RECONNAISSANCE

Motorcycle and jeep-mounted infantry are fast-moving troops always in the forefront of the advance. Their speed is their greatest asset as they race forward, dismounting to occupy forward positions or to launch assaults on the enemy.

Motorcycle Reconnaissance

Motorcyclists quickly learn to use their speed and small size to survive.

While still on their vehicles, Motorcycle Reconnaissance teams are Recce Tank teams. While Dismounted, they cease to be Recce teams. If the platoon was Reorganising, it continues to Reorganise after Dismounting.

Dismounting Motorcycles

Motorcycle scouts fight mounted against light opposition, but when things get tough, they dismount and finish the fight on foot, while the drivers take their vehicles to the rear.

A platoon may Dismount all of its Motorcycle Reconnaissance teams and Send their vehicles to the Rear at the start of your Movement Step. If they do so, replace each Motorcycle Reconnaissance team with the equivalent dismounted Infantry or Man-packed Gun team placed anywhere under the area covered by the Motorcycle Reconnaissance team at the start of their movement, e.g. when a Motorcycle Reconnaissance Motorcycle Rifle/MG team Dismounts it is replaced with a normal Rifle/MG team. Even if they do not move further, the Dismounted teams are considered to have moved.

When a Bogged Down (see page 44) Motorcycle Reconnaissance team Dismounts, it immediately ceases being Bogged Down.

Motorcycle Reconnaissance teams may only Dismount if you have appropriate Infantry and Man-packed Gun teams for the dismounted soldiers to replace them with, otherwise, they must stay on their vehicles.

Starting Dismounted

Sometimes motorcyclists are called on to defend their gains, requiring them to start the fight dismounted.

You may start the game with all of the Motorcycle Reconnaissance teams in a platoon Dismounted by replacing each team with the equivalent Infantry team. They may Remount later in the game as if they had sent their vehicles to the rear.

Dismounting Motorcycles

REMOUNTING MOTORCYCLES

Remounting Motorcycles

Once the enemy have been overcome, you may need to bring your motorcycles forward again to continue the advance.

A platoon that has Dismounted its Motorcycle Reconnaissance teams may bring them forward again at the start of your Movement Step provided that no team in the platoon is:

- *within 16"/40cm of any enemy team within Line of Sight, unless Concealed by Terrain from it, or*
- *within 4"/10cm of any enemy team, or*
- *within 8"/20cm of any enemy Recce team that is in Line of Sight (apart from Recce teams that are Bogged Down, Bailed Out, or moved at the Double).*

If they do so, replace each Dismounted Motorcycle Reconnaissance team with the equivalent vehicle placed so that it covers the team it is replacing at the start of their movement.

Once Remounted in this way, the Motorcycle Reconnaissance teams can move as normal. If there is insufficient space for all of the Motorcycle Reconnaissance teams' vehicles, take the normal movement for each team as it is placed, using your movement to make enough space.

The Motorcycle Reconnaissance teams are treated as moving, even if they do not move after Remounting, so if a Motorcycle Reconnaissance team is placed in Rough Terrain, it must take a Bogging Check whether it moves or not.

Motorcycle Reconnaissance teams that Remounted may not shoot in the Shooting Step. They may however move in either the Shooting or the Assault Step if they have a special rule such as Avanti or Stormtroopers (see page 241) that allows them to do so.

Solo Motorcycles

Some armies see motorcycle troops as the logical successors of light horse-mounted infantry. Following this model, they give every soldier his own motorcycle.

Some Motorcycle Reconnaissance teams are Solo Motorcycle teams. They do not have a dedicated driver and simply abandon their motorcycles when they Dismount, so may not Remount after Dismounting.

SUMMARY

- **Motorcycle Reconnaissance teams are Recce Tank teams while mounted. When Dismounted they cease to be Recce teams.**
- **Motorcycle Reconnaissance teams can Dismount and replace their teams with Infantry and Gun teams at the start of their movement.**
- **Motorcycle Reconnaissance teams may start the game Dismounted.**
- **Dismounted Motorcycle Reconnaissance teams can Remount and replace their Infantry and Gun teams with Motorcycle Reconnaissance teams at the start of their movement.**
- **To do this, every team must not be within 8"/20cm of enemy Recce teams or 4"/10cm of other enemy if Concealed or out of sight, or within 16"/40cm if not Concealed.**
- **After Remounting, the Motorcycle Reconnaissance teams move as normal, but cannot shoot after doing so.**
- **Solo Motorcycles cannot Remount.**

FLAME-THROWERS

Flame-throwers work like fire hoses, only instead of water they spray burning fuel. They are terrifying weapons to face, and many men who are willing to risk a bullet will turn tail and run rather than burn.

Flame-throwers saturate the target area in flaming fuel. They don't need to see their targets. They'll hit anyway as long as the operator is competent.

Unlike normal weapons, a Flame-thrower needs an unmodified Skill Test to hit the target.

Only Fully-armoured vehicles have any protection against Flame-throwers. If any other type of vehicle or team is hit, it is automatically Destroyed, even if it is in Bulletproof Cover.

A Fully-armoured vehicle hit by a Flame-thrower does not take an Armour Save. Instead, take a Firepower Test for the Flame-thrower.

- *If it passes, then the vehicle is Bailed Out.*
- *Otherwise, aside from a little coughing fit, the crew are fine but the Tank team and any Tank Escorts it has may not conduct Defensive Fire this turn.*

Any hit by a Flame-thrower automatically Pins Down the whole target platoon.

Flaming on the Move

Flame-throwers drench their target in burning fuel, making them as accurate moving as stationary.

Flame-throwers do not reduce their ROF when moving.

One-use Weapons

Flame-throwers can't carry enough fuel for sustained operations, so they get in, flame and get out again.

Teams with Flame-throwers only carry enough fuel for one turn of shooting with their Flame-throwers.

Slow Down to Flame

A flame-thrower has a very limited range, so a flame-thrower tank has to be very close to its target to start flaming. They can dash up to the target at speed, but must then stop or move very slowly to flame it. Once firing, the smoke and flame of their own flame-thrower hides the target making it impossible to fire other weapons.

A Flame-thrower team cannot fire if the team moved more than 6"/15cm this turn.

A vehicle firing a Flame-thrower may not fire any other type of weapon at the same time.

No Shooting Over Friendly Teams

No sane soldier would fire a flame-thrower over friendly troops, spraying burning fuel all over them.

Flame-throwers can never shoot over friendly teams.

Flame-throwers

Flaming Bunkers

Designed to break the deadlock of World War One trench warfare, flame-throwers are the perfect weapon for suppressing bunkers ,allowing your assault troops to close with and destroy them.

Flame-throwers are particularly effective against all types of Bunkers (see page 217). A hit by a Flame-thrower will automatically pass the Firepower Test to Pin Down a Nest or Pillbox and will Destroy a Nest with a successful Firepower Test, but cannot Destroy a Pillbox.

A Turret Bunker hit by a Flame-thrower does not take an Armour Save. Instead, take a Firepower Test for the Flame-thrower.

- *If it passes, then the Turret Bunker is Bailed Out.*
- *Otherwise, the Bunker may not conduct Defensive Fire this turn.*

Tank Flame-throwers

Mounting flame-throwers in tanks gives them much greater fuel capacity making them more effective, while the armour ensures that the flame-thrower survives long enough to get close and do its terrible work.

Fuel Tanks

Flame-thrower fuel, and the vapour left behind in the tanks, is obviously extremely flammable. Unfortunately, that means that when a flame-thrower tank is hit, it tends to burn very easily.

Re-roll failed Firepower Tests when rolling to Bail Out or Destroy a Flame-thrower tank.

Return to Refuel

Being full of volatile gases, empty fuel tanks are even more explosive than full ones and flame-thrower tanks are too valuable to waste on just one mission. Flame-tanks rarely hang around the battlefield after they fire.

You may remove a Flame-thrower tank from play at the start of your Movement Step once it has fired. They are not counted as Destroyed, but no longer count as part of the platoon.

Flame Tanks Don't Assault

If the thought of an enemy gun penetrating them and setting their fuel alight gives a flame-tank's crew nightmares, the idea of closing with infantry equipped with anti-tank weapons is even worse. Only the red Army's tankers are brave enough to do so, and only because they aren't brave enough to refuse the order to do so!

Flame-thrower tanks may not Charge into Contact and must Break Off rather than Counterattack if assaulted (see page [illegible]).

Soviet Flame-thrower tanks are an exception to this and may Charge into Contact and Counterattack as normal.

Infantry Flame-throwers

Back-pack flame-throwers consist of a heavy fuel tank, a tank of compressed air to propel the fuel, and a hose connecting the tanks to a flame gun carried by the soldier. Infantry flame-throwers only have fuel for a few seconds of flame. Then the operator takes their valuable weapon back to refuel for the next mission.

Infantry Flame-thrower teams are removed from play as soon as they have fired. They are not counted as Destroyed, but no longer count as part of the platoon.

Shooting as a Rifle Team

A flame-thrower operator is escorted by riflemen to keep them alive long enough to get close enough to flame.

An Infantry Flame-thrower team may shoot and fight as a Rifle team until it shoots its Flame-thrower.

Summary

- **Flame-throwers fire on the move with no penalty, but cannot move more than 6"/15cm and shoot.**
- **Flame-throwers can only shoot once. Roll Skill Tests to hit. Any hit automatically Pins Down the target.**
- **A successful Firepower Test against a Fully-armoured vehicle or Turret Bunker Bails it Out, otherwise it cannot Defensive Fire.**
- **Nests and Pillbox Bunkers are automatically Pinned Down by a hit. A successful Firepower Test Destroys a Nest.**
- **Other teams are automatically Destroyed.**
- **Re-roll failed Firepower Tests against Flame-thrower vehicles.**
- **Flame-thrower vehicles cannot assault and must Break Off unless Soviet.**
- **Infantry Flame-thrower teams may shoot and fight as Rifle teams.**
- **You must remove Infantry Flame-thrower teams and may remove vehicle Flame-throwers after they shoot their Flame-throwers.**

TANK ESCORTS

Tanks can be very vulnerable to infantry at close quarters. Some armies attached infantry to tank platoons as close escorts. Their role is to keep enemy infantry off the tanks and assist them in close-quarters fighting.

Tank Escorts are Not Teams

The task of escort infantry is keeping the tanks alive. If some are killed, the others spread out to cover their charges.

Tank Escorts are not teams in their own right. They are an addition to a Tank team that gives it extra capabilities. Tank Escorts cannot be Destroyed while their tank survives and cannot survive the loss of their tank.

A Tank team with Tank Escorts cannot carry teams as Passengers using the Riding on Tanks rule on page 47.

Tank Escorts Shooting

Infantry trained as tank escorts can shoot from their perches on the tank, provided it moves slowly.

A Tank team with Tank Escorts can shoot with its Tank Escorts.

Tank Escorts shoot as if they are separate teams from their Tank teams and may shoot at a different platoon from that which their Tank team is engaging. They shoot as the appropriate type of Infantry team (so Soviet Tankodesantniki SMG Tank Escorts shoot as an SMG team), but always have a ROF of 1 with no penalty for the tank's movement.

If assaulting Infantry teams Sneak Up on a Tank team (see page 153) that has Tank Escorts, the Tank Escorts can conduct Defensive Fire, despite the Tank team being unable to Defensive Fire with any of its own weapons.

Tank Escorts Shooting

German StuG III G with tank riders.

Tank Escorts Assaulting

Tank Escorts Assaulting

Escort infantry don't just protect their tank, they actively hunt out the enemy at close quarters too.

Tank teams with Tank Escorts Roll To Hit with their escorts as well as the Tank team itself giving them two Rolls to Hit in assaults in most circumstances. Even when the Tank team is Bogged Down or Bailed Out, the Tank Escorts can still Roll to Hit on their own.

A hit from a Tank Escort cannot be allocated to a vehicle. If only vehicles are available to allocate the hit to, then ignore the hit.

Tank Escorts in Rough Terrain

One of the roles of escort infantry is to clear enemy out of buildings and other places inaccessible to the tanks.

Assaulting Tank teams with Tank Escorts can elect not to Charge into Contact or to halt its Charge into Contact before entering, crossing, or moving in Rough Terrain. If they do this, they do not need to take a Bogging Check for assaulting a team in Rough Terrain, but they can only Roll to Hit with their Tank Escorts, not with the Tank teams the escorts are on.

Tank Escorts Fall Back

Tank escorts are only flesh and blood. Enough firepower from the defenders will cause them to hang back until the tanks have softened the enemy up.

If the total number of hits from Defensive Fire is five or more, any Tank Escorts on Assaulting Tank teams may not Roll to Hit until the platoon Counterattacks.

Summary

- **If their tank did not move more than 6"/15cm, its Tank Escorts can shoot with ROF 1 with no penalty for moving.**
- **When a Tank team assaults, it rolls To Hit with its Tank Escorts as well.**
- **Tanks may stop outside Rough Terrain and only attack with their Tank Escorts.**
- **If a platoon takes five or more hits from Defensive Fire, its Tank Escorts do not roll To Hit until they Counterattack.**

CAVALRY

Horse-mounted cavalry may seem an anachronism in the age of tanks and blitzkrieg, but they still have a role in less developed areas like the Ardennes and Russia's Pripyat Marshes where their mobility is far greater than road-bound trucks.

ADVANCE AT THE GALLOP

The speed of a cavalry charge means that cavalry may cover more ground in a shorter time.

A platoon with Mounted Cavalry teams may attempt to Advance at the Gallop at the start of the Shooting Step instead of shooting. Roll a Skill Test for the platoon:

- *If the test is successful, the Cavalry teams in the platoon may move another 4"/10cm,*
- *Otherwise the platoon cannot move this step.*

All normal rules apply for this movement. Teams cannot Advance at the Gallop if they moved At the Double.

If a platoon attempts to Advance at the Gallop, Cavalry teams in the platoon may not shoot, or use other special rules that allow movement instead of shooting, even if it fails to make its Advance at the Gallop move. It can still assault or use the Stormtroopers special rule (see page 241) later in the turn.

SHOOTING FROM HORSEBACK

Shooting from horseback is very difficult. Cavalrymen can fire at point-blank range with some effect, but at longer ranges must halt to allow their light machine-guns to dismount temporarily to shoot.

Mounted Cavalry teams always shoot as if they moved but may not shoot at all unless they remain stationary or the range is 4"/10cm or less.

Man-packed Gun teams Mounted as Cavalry cannot shoot until they Dismount.

NO SHOOTING OVER CAVALRY

Cavalrymen on their horses don't have the luxury of hugging the ground when the shooting starts, so it is impossible for supporting troops to attempt to shoot over them.

Cavalry teams shooting at vehicles can shoot over Infantry teams that did not move. Teams cannot shoot over Mounted Cavalry unless the shooting teams are on higher ground and able to see over the cavalry.

ADVANCE AT THE GALLOP

TACTICS

CHARGE!

ADVANCING ACROSS OPEN GROUND CAN BE LETHAL FOR CAVALRY, SO USE ADVANCE AT THE GALLOP TO CHARGE THE ENEMY SOONER. SHOOTING FROM HORSEBACK IS NEVER REALLY EFFECTIVE, SO YOU DON'T REALLY LOOSE MUCH BY NOT DOING SO, BUT YOU WILL NEED SOMEONE ELSE TO PIN DOWN THE ENEMY FOR YOU.

Cavalry Cannot Take Cover

Soldiers mounted on a horses sit tall above the surrounding terrain making it impossible to take cover from enemy fire. If they intend to defend a position, they dismount and send their horses to safety first.

Although Cavalry teams are Infantry teams, they cannot be Concealed in the Open (see page 89).

Mounted Cavalry teams are never in Bulletproof Cover. They cannot Dig In while Mounted. They must Dismount and Send their horses to the Rear first.

Cavalry Charge on Through

Cavalry cannot simply hit the dirt to avoid heavy fire like infantry. Instead their best bet is to ride hard and fast through the fire.

A platoon with all of its Infantry teams Mounted as Cavalry re-rolls failed Motivation Tests to Rally from being Pinned Down.

Cavalry and Buildings

Cavalry don't fare well in towns. Even if you could convince a horse to walk into a building, you couldn't ride it inside! They either have to dismount and fight on foot, or simply avoid the buildings.

Mounted Cavalry teams cannot enter a Building. They must Dismount first and Send their horses to the Rear.

Mounted Cavalry teams cannot Charge into Contact with a team in a Building, and hits from Mounted Cavalry teams cannot be allocated to teams in Buildings. If the only teams available to allocate hits to are in Buildings, then ignore the hits.

Cavalry cannot Assault Tanks

Cavalry have no way of hurting tanks. Sabres, pistols and grenades just won't do anything.

Cavalry cannot use the Sneaking Up on Tanks rule.

A hit from a Cavalry team cannot be allocated to a Fully-armoured Tank team (see page 8) unless it has Passengers. The hit cannot harm the Tank team, but will Destroy all Passengers. If only Fully-armoured Tank teams withour Passengers are available to allocate the hit to, then ignore the hit.

Ride Them Down

Breaking off when fighting cavalry can be a risky business. It's very hard to outrun a horse!

Infantry and Gun teams that Break Off are Destroyed if they end their Break Off movement within 8"/20cm and in Line of Sight of an assaulting Cavalry team, unless they are:

- *in a Building,*
- *in Rough Terrain, or*
- *behind a Linear Obstacle.*

Dismounting Cavalry

While they are modelled as being mounted on their horses, cavalry operates as mounted infantry. They mount and dismount as the tactical situation demands, always keeping their horses handy. This is of vital importance to the individual cavalrymen, but is normal cavalry behaviour and of little concern to you as the company commander. All that matters to you is that your cavalry have their horses with them. For all practical purposes they are still mounted.

Sometimes though, you need to order your cavalry to send their horses to the rear and fight on as infantry.

Cavalry platoons may Dismount and Send their horses to the Rear at the start of your Movement Step. If they do so, replace each Cavalry team with the equivalent dismounted Infantry or Man-packed Gun team placed anywhere under the area covered by the Cavalry team at the start of their movement, e.g. when a Cavalry Rifle/MG team Dismounts it is replaced with a normal Infantry Rifle/MG team. Even if they do not move further, the Dismounted teams are considered to have moved.

A Cavalry platoon may elect either to only Dismount its Man-packed Gun teams, or to Dismount all of its teams. It may not Dismount some of its Infantry teams and leave others mounted.

Cavalry teams may only Dismount if you have appropriate Infantry and Man-packed Gun teams for the dismounted soldiers to replace them with, otherwise, they must stay on their horses.

Starting Dismounted

Cavalry are always ready to dismount if the tactical situation calls for it.

You may start the game with all of the Cavalry teams in a platoon Dismounted by replacing each team with the equivalent Infantry team. They may Remount later in the game as if they had sent their horses to the rear.

Dismounting In Assaults

Having chased off the enemy, cavalry dismount and set up a defensive position to stop any following attacks.

Cavalry teams may Dismount at the start of their Consolidation movement as if this was the Movement Step moving up to 4"/10cm as they do so. Cavalry teams may not Remount while Consolidating.

Remounting Cavalry

Having sent your cavalry's horses to the rear, there are occasions when you need them brought forward again, such as to pursue a defeated foe.

Cavalry platoons that have Dismounted and Sent their horses to the Rear may Bring the horses Forward again at the start of their Movement Step provided that no team in the platoon is:

- *within 16"/40cm of any enemy team within Line of Sight, unless Concealed by Terrain from it, or*
- *within 4"/10cm of any enemy team, or*
- *within 8"/20cm of any enemy Recce team that is in Line of Sight (apart from Recce teams that are Bogged Down, Bailed Out, or moved at the Double).*

If they do so, replace each Dismounted Cavalry team with the equivalent Mounted Cavalry team placed so that it covers the team it is replacing at the start of their movement.

Once Remounted in this way, the Cavalry teams can move as normal. If there is insufficient space for all of the Cavalry teams, take the normal movement for each team as it is replaced, using your movement to make enough space for the horses.

The Cavalry teams are treated as moving, even if they do not move after Remounting.

Cavalry teams that Remounted may not shoot in the Shooting Step nor assault in the Assault Step. They may however move in either step using special rules such as Advance at the Gallop or Stormtroopers.

Summary

Cavalry

- **Cavalry may take a Skill Test to move 4"/10cm instead of shooting.**
- **Cavalry always shoot as if they moved. They are either limited to 4"/10cm range or must remain stationary.**
- **Cavalry cannot be Concealed in the Open, in Bulletproof Cover, or Dig In.**
- **Cavalry re-roll failed Motivation Tests to Rally from being Pinned Down.**
- **Cavalry may not enter Buildings nor assault teams in Buildings.**
- **Teams ending their Break Off movement within 8"/20cm of Cavalry are Destroyed unless they are in or behind Rough Terrain or Buildings, or out of sight.**
- **Cavalry cannot assault Tank teams.**
- **Cavalry can replace its teams with Dismounted Infantry and Gun teams at the start of its movement.**
- **Dismounted Cavalry can replace its Infantry and Gun teams with Cavalry teams at the start of its movement.**

ARMOURED TRAINS

Despite seeming outdated, in a war dominated by tanks, armoured trains performed well in Eastern Europe where roads were few and poor, and distances to be covered were immense.

Armoured trains cost a fortune to build and operate, and they have a set way of doing things to maximise efficiency.

The main parts of any Armoured Train are the Locomotive, Artillery Cars, Infantry Cars (and the Infantry Platoons they carry), and Supporting Tank Platoons.

The Locomotive and each Car or Wagon in an Armoured Train are separate Tank teams, with the whole Armoured Train operating as a single platoon.

An Armoured Train must always operate in the order shown in the Intelligence Briefing. It cannot uncouple cars or change their order, but it may travel in either direction and may enter the table facing either direction.

Artillery Cars

The main function of an armoured train is to provide heavy fire support for other troops using its artillery cars. These can range from cars mounting multiple heavy artillery pieces to tank-hunter cars mounting tank turrets, and even unarmed artillery staff cars to improve the performance of other artillery cars.

The Artillery Cars of an Armoured Train are divided into Artillery Batteries, usually of one Artillery Car per battery, although some have multiple cars in a battery.

Infantry Cars

Like the marines of a battleship, many armoured trains carry an infantry platoon in a specially-equipped assault car for its own protection and to clear obstacles from the track. The infantry platoon travels safe under the thick armour of the infantry car, only dismounting when they are needed.

An Armoured Train with an Infantry Car always Deploys with its Infantry Platoon as Passengers in the Infantry Car. The Infantry Car is a Tank team, but can Mount and Dismount its Infantry Platoon as if it is a Transport team. It is not Sent to the Rear when the infantry Dismount and operates as a Tank team for all other purposes.

The Infantry Platoon operates as a separate platoon with its own Platoon Command team. Treat the Armoured Train and the Infantry Platoon as two separate platoons when calculating the number of platoons held in Ambush or Reserve (see pages 266 and 268), but both arrive together as a single platoon from Reserves.

Supporting Tank Platoons

Many armoured trains have supporting tanks attached to them, mounted either on flat cars or on their own railcars. These tanks can dismount in a matter of a minute or so to deal with attacks on the train.

Supporting Tank Platoons operate as separate platoons with their own Command teams. Treat the Armoured Train and the Supporting Tank Platoons as separate platoons when calculating the number of platoons held in Ambush or Reserves (see pages 266 and 268), but all arrive together as a single platoon from Reserves.

The tanks of Supporting Tank Platoons deploy evenly at each end of the train and move with the Armoured Train as part of it. They may leave the train at the end of any Movement Step, moving up to an additional 4"/10cm in any direction. The tanks may also leave the train to Counterattack if it is assaulted. In this case, simply move the vehicles from their current positions.

Once the tanks of a Supporting Tank Platoon have left the train, they may not rejoin it.

SUMMARY

- **An Armoured Train is a platoon made up of a Locomotive, Artillery Cars, and Infantry Cars which are Tank teams.**
- **An Infantry Platoon Deploys in their Infantry Car, but is a separate platoon.**
- **Supporting Tank Platoons Deploy at the ends of the Armoured Train, but as separate platoons. They Dismount 4"/10cm after the train moves or to Counterattack.**

German armoured train with ex-Polish artillery and tank-hunter cars

Placing Railway Lines

Without railway lines, there can be no armoured trains. Since most gaming tables don't have tracks laid ready for an armoured train to use, we use the following rules to place the tracks before the game begins.

If the table has been set up with Railway Lines, use these for the Armoured Train. Otherwise, at the start of the game before any Objectives or Fortifications are placed on the table, the players place a Railway Line as follows:

1. *The player with the Armoured Train chooses two opposite table edges.*
2. *The opposing player picks a point on one of the chosen table edges.*
3. *The Armoured Train player picks a point on the opposite table edge.*
4. *The Armoured Train player then places a Railway Line running in a straight line between these two points.*

The line cuts through woods, fields, and other flat ground. Rivers or streams are assumed to be crossed with culverts or bridges. Any buildings in the way should be moved aside by the minimum distance necessary. The Railway Line is diverted by the minimum distance necessary to go around hills (even gentle gradients are avoided by Railway Lines.

If both players have Armoured Trains, both place Railway Lines, starting with the attacking player. Each player's Armoured Train must remain on its own track.

Armoured Train Deployment

Armoured trains can only move along railway lines, so their deployment options are usually very limited.

An Armoured Train that would normally be Deployed on the table is held off the table until the start of its first Movement Step, when it moves onto the table. In the turn an Armoured Train moves onto the table, it always moves far enough to bring the entire train and its Supporting Tank Platoons onto the table.

The Armoured Train will move on from the point where the Railway Line crosses the player's Deployment Area, or if it does not do so, at the point the Railway Line crosses a table edge closest to the player's Deployment Area.

Armoured Trains cannot be held in Ambush (see page 266), they are simply too big and obvious, but they may be held in Reserves (see page 268).

Armoured Train Movement

The key to the success of armoured trains is their operational mobility. They can move rapidly to trouble spots and deliver effective support when they arrive. In a country with few modern roads, this is essential.

Armoured Trains can only move on Railway Lines. If the Locomotive is not Bogged Down, Bailed Out, or Destroyed, an Armoured Train can move up to 16"/40cm forward or backward along the Railway Line each turn.

Armoured Train Deployment and Movement

Placing Railway Tracks

Moving Off the Table

Like a battleship at sea, an armoured train is never broken into component parts. Either the whole train is fighting, or it is not.

If any part of an Armoured Train leaves the table, the whole Armoured Train is considered to have left the table and cannot return.

Moving Through Wrecks

A train can push aside the wreck of any tank, no matter how big or heavy.

Move any wreck on the Railway Line by the smallest distance necessary for the Armoured Train to pass.

MOVING THROUGH ENEMY TEAMS AND WRECKS

MOVING THROUGH OTHER TEAMS

Armoured trains push aside any enemy tank that attempts to block their passage. Of course, they are a little more reluctant to ram a friendly tank!

Armoured Trains may not move through friendly teams. Any friendly team on the tracks must move off the tracks before the train can pass.

Armoured Trains are not hindered by enemy teams. Any other enemy team is moved aside by the opposing player by the smallest distance necessary for the train to pass, retaining its current facing.

Staff car and anti-aircraft and artillery car of a German BP42 armoured train.
Bundesarchiv, Bild 101I-639-4252-19A

TRAIN CANNOT MOVE THROUGH FRIENDLY TEAMS

CANNOT MOVE THROUGH A TRAIN

There is nowhere for tanks to drive through an armoured train, and infantry are not foolish enough to move between the wagons, risking getting crushed if the train should move.

Teams cannot move through an Armoured Train unless the Locomotive has been Destroyed. Once the Locomotive is Destroyed, it and other Destroyed cars in the train become Very Difficult Going. Armoured Trains cannot move through other Armoured Trains, even when the other Armoured Train is Destroyed.

SUMMARY

- **Armoured Trains can move 16"/40cm along Railway Lines while the Locomotive is operational.**
- **Armoured Trains push aside enemy teams, but cannot move through friendly teams.**
- **Teams cannot move through a mobile Armoured Train.**

CANNOT MOVE THROUGH TRAIN

Shooting with Armoured Trains

By comparison with a tank moving across country, a train provides a relatively smooth ride.

Armoured Trains do not suffer any penalty for shooting on the move. They retain their full ROF when shooting while moving. Each weapon on an Armoured Train can fire at a different target from the other weapons.

Almost all guns (aside from machine-guns) on an Armoured Train are mounted in Deck Turrets (see page 113). As such, their Field of Fire is restricted by the superstructure and other turrets of the Artillery Car they are mounted on, and possibly by other cars in the train.

Train Machine-guns

A train's machine-guns are usually crewed by separate machine-gun sections, leaving the gun crews free to fire their own guns.

The cars of an Armoured Train fire all of their Train MG's at ROF 2, even when other weapons are firing, including when other weapons are firing an Artillery Bombardment.

The Field of Fire of a Train MG mounted on the side of a car includes everything to the side of a line drawn along the side of the car. The Field of Fire of a Train MG mounted on the end of a car includes everything to the front of a line drawn across the end of the car.

Passenger-fired Machine-guns

Some trains use the infantry platoon to crew the machine-guns. While this saves on manpower, it does mean that the train can't fire its machine-guns once the infantry dismount.

Each Passenger-fired Train MG requires an Infantry or Man-packed Gun team Mounted in an Infantry Car to fire it. The team does not need to be in the same Infantry Car as the Train MG, and each team can fire any Train MG in the train (although only one Train MG per team at any one time).

Artillery Bombardments from Trains

The predictable movement of a train allows it to fire a bombardment on the move. The huge stocks of ready ammunition allow it to do so at a very high rate of fire.

Armoured Trains can fire Artillery Bombardments while moving. When an Armoured Train fires an Artillery Bombardment, count each weapon firing as two weapons firing.

All of the Artillery Batteries in an Armoured Train can combine to fire a single bombardment instead of firing as separate batteries.

Fields of Fire of Armoured Trains

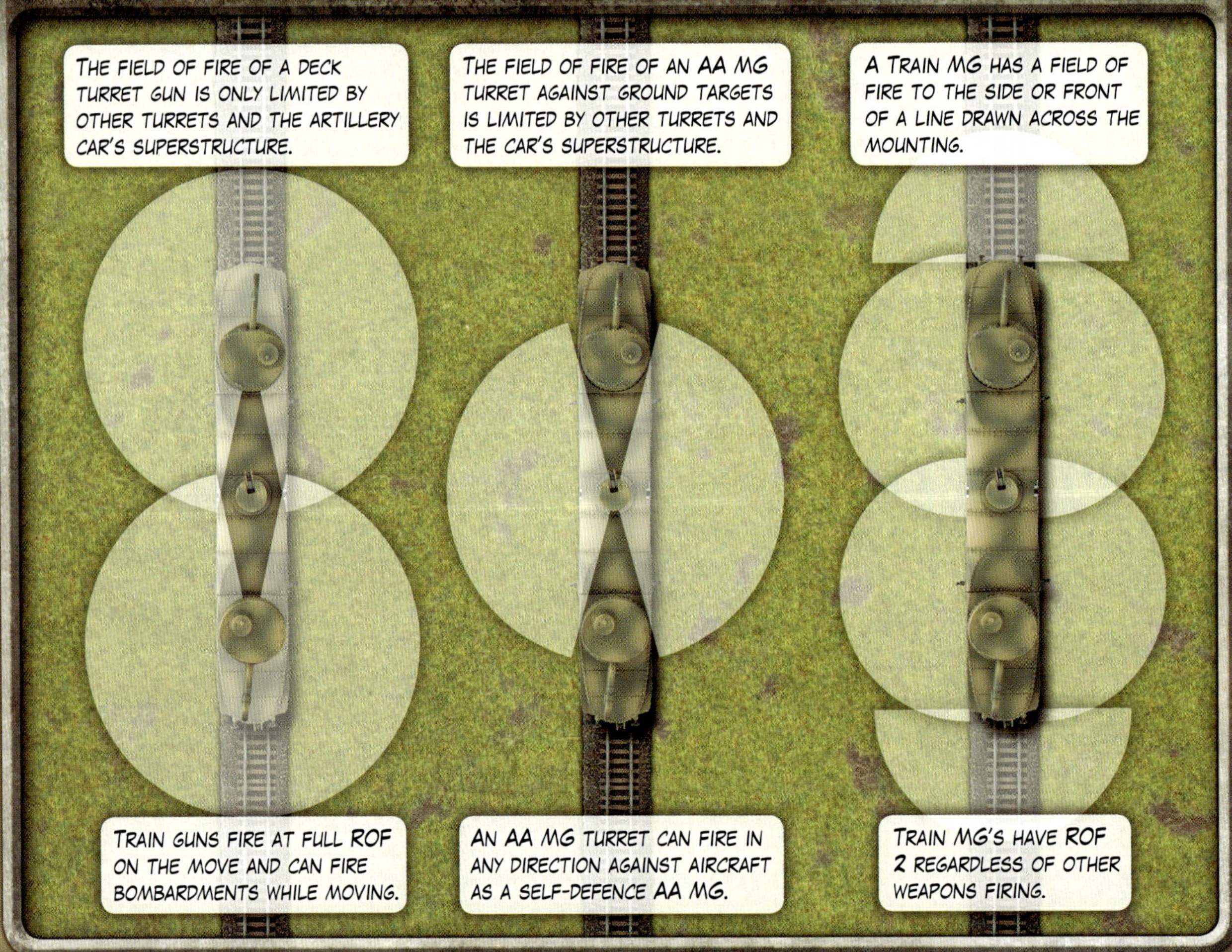

Shooting at Armoured Trains

Armoured trains are remarkably tough unless hit with heavy-calibre guns. Even if the locomotive is disabled and the train halted, the gun cars will still fight on.

Armoured Trains are shot at in the same way as any platoon of tanks. If a car is Destroyed, it ceases to function along with all of its weapons, but does not otherwise hinder the train. The Armoured Train moves with the Destroyed car still in place.

Hit Allocation

While some gunners just shoot at whatever part of the train they are looking at, smart gunners pick out the most dangerous cars and target them first.

The Gun Tank rule (see page 96) can be used to distinguish between different types of car and the Locomotive.

Can the Armoured Train Move

The one part of the train that is truly critical is the locomotive. Without it, nothing moves!

If the Locomotive is Bogged Down, Bailed Out, or Destroyed, the Armoured Train cannot move.

If the Locomotive can still move when the Armoured Train fails a Platoon Morale Check, the whole Armoured Train is removed from the table as it steams off, dragging its wrecked cars with it. If it cannot move, the whole Armoured Train is Destroyed in place if it fails a Platoon Morale Check.

Shooting Across Trains

No one is going to risk taking a shot that might hit their own train, but the enemy doesn't care.

In the same way that teams cannot shoot through any other type of Friendly team, Friendly teams cannot shoot through an Armoured Train.

Enemy teams can shoot through an Armoured Train, but teams at least half obscured by the Armoured Train (including Destroyed cars) are Concealed.

Summary

- **Armoured Trains are shot at like platoons of tanks.**
- **If the Locomotive is operational, Destroyed cars are moved with the rest of the Armoured Train. If the Locomotive is Destroyed, the train cannot move.**
- **Friendly teams cannot shoot through an Armoured Train, but enemy teams can, although their targets are Concealed.**

Shooting Across Armoured Trains

Armoured Trains in Assaults

Armoured trains are difficult to assault with machine-guns bristling from every aperture. These fearsome beasts are not worried by mere infantrymen and can ignore them at will.

Armoured Trains cannot Charge into Contact and do not move when Counterattacking.

If any part of an Armoured Train is assaulted, any part of the train within 16"/40cm of an Assaulting team can Defensive Fire at teams up to 16"/40cm away.

If the Locomotive can still move when an Armoured Train Breaks Off from an assault, the train may move through or past any enemy teams without hindrance, and the train does not need to be more than 4"/10cm from enemy teams for the assault to end. If the Locomotive cannot move when the train Breaks Off, any part of the train within 4"/10cm of the Assaulting Platoon is captured and Destroyed.

Any Infantry Platoon or Supporting Tank Platoon is a separate platoon from the Armoured Train. If the Infantry Platoon is still mounted in the Infantry Car when the Infantry Car is Destroyed in an assault, the whole Infantry Platoon will be Destroyed. Infantry and Supporting Tank Platoons can Dismount to Counterattack if they are assaulted.

SUMMARY

- **Armoured Trains cannot Charge into Contact and do not move to Counterattack.**
- **When assaulted the whole Armoured Train conducts Defensive Fire.**
- **If the Locomotive is operational, the Armoured Train cannot be captured if it Breaks Off.**
- **Infantry and Supporting Tank Platoons can Dismount to Counterattack.**

Armoured Trains in Assaults

Demolishing Railway Lines

Railway lines are remarkably hard to destroy, especially as the train carries spare rails and wooden sleepers or ties to allow its track-repair team to repair minor damage.

The only way to damage a Railway Line during a game is for a Pioneer team to place charges on the tracks. They do this in the same way that they Gap an Obstacle (see page 225). If they succeed, the section of Railway Line adjacent to the team becomes Difficult Going to trains.

Only the Locomotive needs to take a Bog Check when crossing damaged Railway Lines, but it does so whenever the train reaches the damaged section, or if the train starts the turn straddling a damaged section of Railway Line. If a train Bogs Down, only the Locomotive is considered Bogged Down.

BUNKERS
AND FORTIFICATIONS

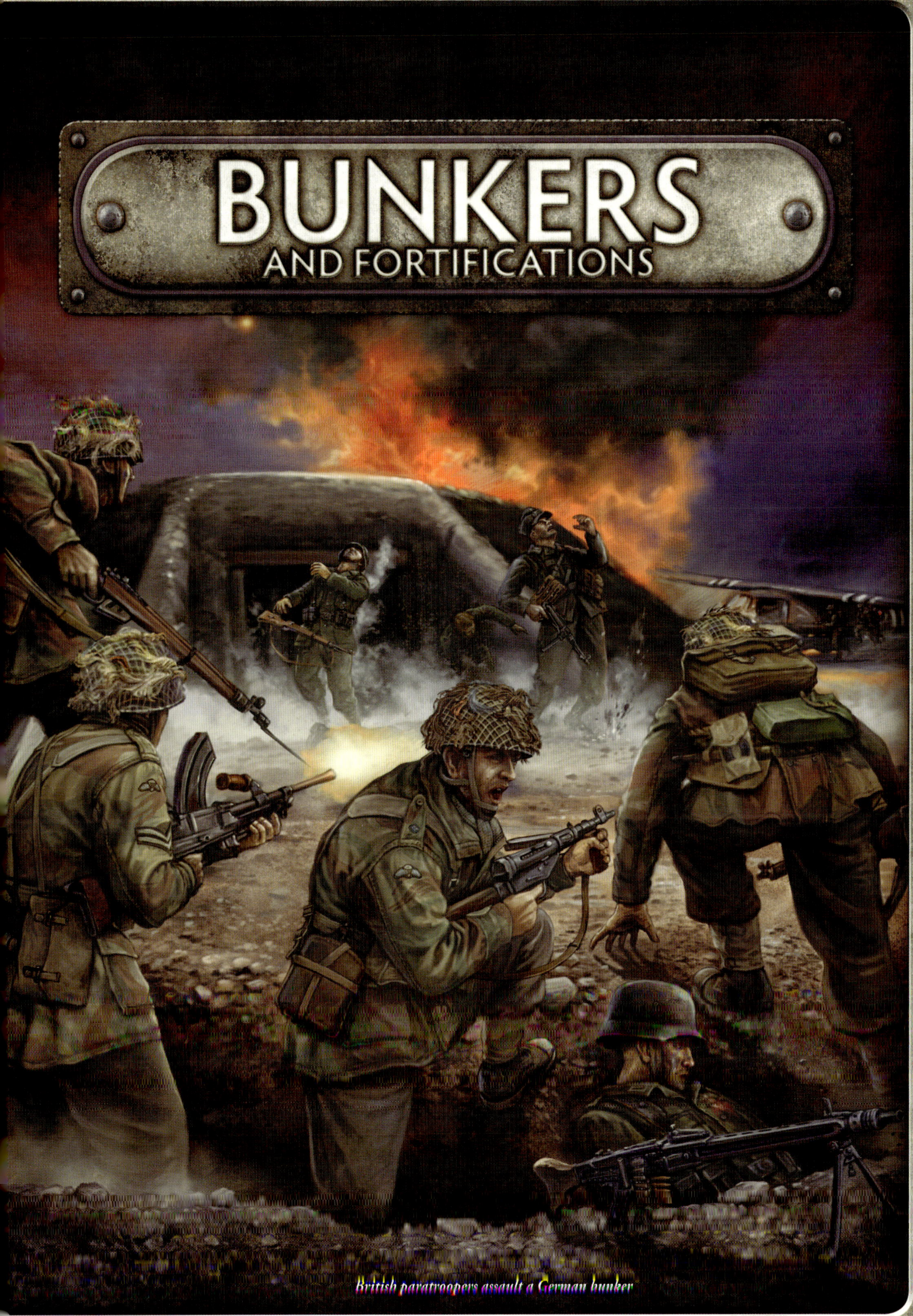

British paratroopers assault a German bunker

The hidden menace of buried land mines, the grim face of weather-worn bunkers, and the hard jut of anti-tank obstacles are often the only thing that can halt the bold strokes of a Blitzkrieg advance. When combined with tangled webs of barbed wire and carefully networked trenches they sway the tides of war in favour of the defender. To defeat such measures pioneers creep forward, under the cover of immense artillery bombardments, determined to open a path for the soldiers behind them. Once the way is clear the troops leading the assault dash through the gaps, seeking to smash a hole in the enemy defences, opening the way once more for sweeping advances.

CONTENTS

FORTIFICATIONS

There are three main types of fortifications: Entrenchments, Bunkers, and Obstacles.

ENTRENCHMENTS

Entrenchments are trench lines and gun pits of the type associated with World War One. They can be Trench Lines, Gun Pits, and Tank Pits.

BUNKERS

Bunkers are heavily protected positions for machine-guns and anti-tank guns. They maximise the effectiveness of the limited number of weapons available to the defence by making them very difficult to knock out, especially at long range. They can be Pillboxes, Nests, or Turrets.

OBSTACLES

Obstacles are barriers to movement. They can be physical barriers like street barricades and anti-tank ditches, or more sophisticated and dangerous obstacles like minefields.

All of them have the effect of limiting the enemy's mobility, and hopefully, channelling them into the killing zones of your weapons. They can be Barbed Wire, Barricades, Minefields, Booby Traps, and Anti-tank Obstacles.

FORTIFIED DEFENCES

Fortifications are deployed as either Area Defences or as part of Fortified Platoons (see page 262).

AREA DEFENCES

Area defences are fortifications (usually obstacles) used to create a continuous barrier across the battlefield, slowing down and channelling the enemy's advance.

FORTIFIED PLATOONS

Fortified platoons occupy strongpoints. These heavily fortified positions are difficult to overrun, and dominate the ground around them with fire.

ENTRENCHMENTS

Given time, troops connect their foxholes into a continuous trench line, allowing them to move about their position safe from enemy fire. Meanwhile the gunners dig pits for their guns to get them below ground along with the crew. Even tankers denied their mobility and ordered to fight as bunkers drive their tanks into pits so only the turrets are visible.

There are three basic types of Entrenchments:

- *Trench Lines,*
- *Gun Pits, and*
- *Tank Pits.*

Trench Lines are World War I-style trenches designed both as firing positions and as protected movement routes. Gun Pits are protected positions for machine-guns, anti-tank guns, and artillery. Tank Pits are protected fighting positions for tanks, making them into improvised bunkers.

Entrenchments are not Terrain Features.

Crossing Entrenchments

Trenches have to be narrow to protect their occupants from artillery fire, so they do not prove much of an obstacle to tanks or troops on foot.

Entrenchments are Slow Going. If they are positioned in Rough Terrain, teams need to take Bogging Checks for the terrain around them as usual.

Infantry and Man-packed Gun teams are not hindered by Entrenchments, but cannot move At the Double into, out of, or across them, but can move At the Double along Trench Lines. Cavalry cannot enter Trench Lines.

Trench Lines are Slow Going for Fully-tracked vehicles, Difficult Going for Half-tracked vehicles and Impassable to all other vehicles and Gun teams.

Assaulting Entrenchments

Infantry assaulting other infantry in a trench will jump into the trench and fight them there. A tank can't get into a trench, but that doesn't stop it from getting at the troops inside. The tank can use its tracks to try and collapse the trench on top of them, or simply park across the trench and machine-gun along it while the commander tosses a few hand grenades in for good measure.

Any team that can cross an Entrenchment can assault troops in the Entrenchment.

Trench Lines

Trenches may seem obsolete in the age of blitzkrieg and mechanised warfare, but they still have their place. Against opposition lacking in tanks, they are as effective as ever, while against mobile forces, they allow infantry to manoeuvre under cover.

Trench Lines come in 8"/20cm long sections. These can be broken up into smaller sections to make it easier to build your trench system around the terrain.

Teams entirely within Trench Lines are Concealed and in Bulletproof Cover. Because Trench Lines are dug in a zigzag pattern, the Concealment and Bulletproof Cover even applies when shot at by troops in the same section of Trench Line. Troops spending their entire turn in a Trench Line without shooting are Gone to Ground in the opponent's next turn, even if they moved.

German fortifications defend Omaha Beach against the Allied landings

ENTRENCHMENTS

TACTICS

COMMUNICATIONS TRENCHES

ONE OF THE IMPORTANT (AND OFTEN OVERLOOKED) FUNCTIONS OF TRENCH LINES IS MOBILITY. TROOPS CAN MOVE QUICKLY AND SAFELY ALONG TRENCH LINES (EVEN WHEN MOVING AT THE DOUBLE), MAKING THEM PERFECT FOR MOVING YOUR RESERVES TO THREATENED AREAS OR SWITCHING TROOPS BETWEEN POSITIONS TO MEET THREATS AS THEY DEVELOP. SCATTERING TRENCHES ABOUT LOSES THIS CAPABILITY, EFFECTIVELY REDUCING THEM TO FOXHOLES.

GUN PITS

While foxholes provide protection for the gun crew, they do nothing to hide the huge mass of their weapon. Digging a gun pit allows them to lower the gun's profile, making it much easier to conceal.

Gun Pits are modelled as a raised parapet around a Gun team. Once placed in a Gun Pit, a Gun team cannot move or rotate, and is not Rotated to face its target when shooting. Gun Pits provide the occupants with Concealment and Bulletproof Cover.

TANK PITS

A tank pit involves digging a big hole and driving a tank into it so that it is 'hull down', deep enough that only the turret is visible.

A Tank team in a Tank Pit cannot move or rotate their hull, but may rotate their turrets as normal. Only the turret matters when determining the tank's facing for deciding whether shots hit the front or side armour, and all shots hit the turret. A Tank team in a Tank Pit is Concealed, so it can benefit from Going to Ground.

Tanks in Tank Pits cannot shoot hull-mounted weapons, so a turretless tank cannot be placed in a Tank Pit.

SUMMARY

ENTRENCHMENTS

- **Entrenchments are Slow Going for Fully-tracked and Half-tracked vehicles and troops on foot, but Impassable to others.**
- **Trench Lines give troops on foot Concealment and Bulletproof Cover. Troops that do not shoot are Gone to Ground, even when they move.**
- **Guns in Gun Pits cannot rotate or move, but are Concealed and have Bulletproof Cover.**
- **Tanks in Tank pits cannot rotate (aside from their turret) or move, but are Concealed. All shots hit the turret.**

BUNKERS

Bunkers maximise the effectiveness of the limited number of weapons available to the defence by making them very difficult to knock out, especially at long range.

There are three basic types of bunker:

- *Nests,*
- *Pillboxes, and*
- *Turrets.*

Nests are roofed foxholes or well-protected fighting pits. They provide good protection, but are vulnerable to accurate close-range fire.

Pillboxes are much more substantial constructions in concrete and steel. Gunfire will not harm them and only close assault or a huge bunker-busting gun can knock them out.

Turrets are made by mounting a redundant tank turret on an underground bunker containing ammunition and accommodation for the crew. They combine the flexibility of a tank with the defensive strength of a bunker.

Where the rules refer to Bunkers, they cover all Nests, Pillboxes and Turrets.

Bunkers are not Terrain Features.

Bunkers are Independent Teams

Bunkers are designed to fight on, even if the enemy surrounds or bypasses them.

Bunkers are Independent teams, but can never Join other platoons or be Joined by Warrior teams.

Skill and Motivation Tests

A bunker's crew are safer inside than running away, so they tend to fight to the end. On the other hand, they are manned by second-line troops lacking in combat experience, making them less proficient in combat.

A Bunker automatically passes all Motivation Tests it is required to take. If a Bunker needs to take a Skill Test, it does so as Trained, succeeding on a 4+.

Pinned Down and Bailed Out Bunkers

Keeping a bunker under fire so that assault teams can get up and knock it out is a good idea. One problem is that the crew are well protected, and they know it. The instant the fire ceases, they are back into action again.

Unlike other Independent teams, Bunkers do not automatically cease to be Pinned Down at the end of a Step. Instead, when Pinned Down, they remain Pinned Down until their next Starting Step, when they automatically Rally.

When Bailed Out, Turret bunkers also automatically Remount in their next Starting Step.

Defilade Walls

Bunkers are often placed in defilade so that the enemy can't engage them until they are in the bunker's killing zone. If the natural terrain doesn't provide a defilade position, concrete walls can be constructed instead.

Some Bunkers are modelled with Defilade Walls. These are not part of the Bunker. They are Impassable and block Line of Sight, preventing the enemy from engaging the Bunker from that direction.

Moving Past Bunkers

A concrete bunker will defeat even tank tracks, and even driving over a machine-gun nest is risky.

Friendly and enemy teams face the same limitations when moving near or past a Bunker as they would if it were a vehicle (see page 38). Teams can never be placed or end their movement on top of a Bunker.

Bunkers (whether intact or Destroyed) are Slow Going. If they are in Rough Terrain, teams need to take any Bogging Check for that terrain when crossing the Bunker.

Bunkers are Impassable to all vehicles other than Fully-tracked and Half-tracked vehicles, and to Gun teams other than Man-packed Gun teams.

Taking Cover Behind a Bunker

A big block of concrete is a good thing to hide behind when someone is shooting at you, and unlike a tank, it won't drive off leaving you stranded.

Bunkers (whether intact or Destroyed) block Line of Sight through them and provide Concealment for teams behind them in the same way as buildings or walls.

SUMMARY

- **Bunkers are Independent teams. They always pass Motivation Tests and pass Skill Tests on 4+.**
- **Pinned Down Bunkers Rally at the start of their own turn.**
- **Bunkers are Slow Going for Fully-tracked and Half-tracked vehicles and troops on foot, but Impassable to others.**
- **Bunkers provide Concealment and block Line of Sight like Buildings.**

Shooting with Bunkers

Aside from being unusually well protected, weapons in bunkers operate the same way as normal guns.

Bunkers use the normal shooting and artillery bombardment rules.

Fields of Fire

In most bunkers the weapons have firing slits that allow them to shoot out. Quite often the side facing the enemy has no firing slits, forcing the enemy to enter a killing zone to deal with them.

Bunkers either have an all-round Field of Fire or a 180-degree Field of Fire from each Firing Slit.

Most Nests have a single Firing Slit with a 180-degree Field of Fire. Others like Tobruk Pits, Normandy 5cm KwK Nests, and Flak Nests have an all-round Firing Slit giving them an all-round Field of Fire (where not limited by a Defilade Wall). This is noted in the Nest's characteristics where applicable.

Pillboxes have one or more Firing Slits as shown on the model, giving them a 180-degree Field of Fire from each Firing Slit.

Turrets have an all-round Field of Fire.

Measuring To and From Bunkers

The walls of bunkers are so thick that only fire at the firing slits can have an effect.

Draw Line of Sight and measure Range to and from any part of a Nest with an all-round Field of Fire. Draw Line of Sight and measure Range to and from the Firing Slit of other Nests.

Draw Line of Sight and measure Range to and from any Firing Slit of a Pillbox.

Draw Line of Sight and measure Range to and from any part of the turret of a Turret Bunker, ignoring the base and concrete mounting.

In no case can Line of Sight be drawn or range measured from protruding gun barrels, Defilade Walls or the like.

Bombardments with Bunkers

Some bunkers are built to house coastal-defence artillery or rocket-launcher batteries, and are designed to allow the weapons in them to fire bombardments.

Bunkers able to fire an Artillery Bombardment have a Skill rating of Trained when firing Artillery Bombardments.

Fields of Fire

Shooting at Bunkers

Bunkers are almost invulnerable to the fire of most weapons. The best that most troops can do is to suppress one allowing their assault groups to get close enough to knock it out. Even this is difficult as bunkers are well camouflaged and hard to hit. Even then, only hits near the firing slit have any effect.

A team must be able to draw a Line of Sight to and be within 16"/40 cm of the Firing Slit of a Nest or Pillbox, or any part of a Turret to be able to shoot at it.

How Many Dice

A bunker's firing slit is a small target requiring precise shooting. Firing from the halt is usually much more effective than firing on the move for such a difficult shot.

Teams shooting at Bunkers roll the same number of dice as they would in shooting at any other target (see page 91).

Score to Hit

Shooting at a bunker is quite different from shooting at a tank. The target is small and precise, but isn't moving about or trying to hide. What's needed is skilful and accurate shooting.

Unlike normal shooting, teams roll a Skill Test to hit a Bunker. The Skill Test is not modified in any way.

No Special Rules

Shooting at bunkers is quite different from engaging other types of targets. It requires precision shooting, making tricks like stabilisers and volley firing unhelpful.

Teams cannot use special rules like Stabilisers or Volley Fire when shooting at Bunkers, unless specifically stated in their rules.

Knocking Out Nests

Hits close to a nest will force the crew to duck, reducing their rate of fire. A good square hit will kill the crew, destroying the bunker.

If a weapon hits a Nest, roll a Firepower Test.

- *A successful Firepower Test will Pin Down the Nest.*
- *Otherwise the Nest is unharmed.*

If a weapon Pins Down a Nest, immediately roll a second Firepower Test.

- *If the second Firepower Test is successful, the Nest is Destroyed.*
- *A failed second Firepower Test leaves the Nest Pinned Down, but otherwise unharmed.*

Pinning Down Pillboxes

Better built and designed than nests, pillboxes are invulnerable to normal weapons, but the crew can still be forced to take cover by accurate fire at the firing slits.

If a weapon hits a Pillbox, roll a Firepower Test.

- *A successful Firepower Test will Pin Down the Pillbox.*
- *A failed Firepower Test leaves the Pillbox unharmed.*

Knocking Out Turrets

Tank turrets do not have firing slits. The only way to put them out of action is to penetrate their armour.

If a weapon hits a Turret, the owning player must take an Armoured Vehicle Save (see page 97) and the shooting player a Firepower Test as if it was an Armoured vehicle. As a Turret has no hull, whether shots hit the Front or Side Armour is determined solely by the turret facing.

Shooting at a Bunker

Shooting at a Pillbox

Bunker Busters

Some guns are so big that they can smash through the walls of a bunker or rip a turret from its mounting. One hit from these bunker busters and it's all over.

Any hit by a weapon rated as a Bunker Buster automatically Destroys any type of Bunker without any Firepower Test being needed.

Artillery and Aircraft

Bunkers are immune to artillery and air attacks because the chances of a direct hit are so small, and nothing less will hurt them.

Artillery Bombardments and Air Support cannot harm a Bunker at all. Bunkers cannot be used as the Aiming Point for an Artillery Bombardment or the target team for Air Support.

Summary

Shooting at Bunkers

- Bunkers can only be shot at by teams within 16"/40cm, needing Skill Tests to hit.
- A Successful Firepower Test Pins Down a Nest or Pillbox. A second Successful Firepower Test Destroys a Nest.
- Turrets take an Armoured Vehicle Save like a Tank team. All shots hit the turret.
- A Bunker is automatically Destroyed by any hit from a Bunker Buster.
- Artillery and Aircraft cannot target or harm a Bunker.

Shooting at Turrets

Assaulting Bunkers

Because bunkers are almost immune to shooting, the best way to destroy a bunker is to assault it with demolition charges. Once the assault team reaches the bunker, its destruction is almost certain.

Bunkers fight in an assault in the same way as Gun teams with the following changes.

Defensive Fire

Bunkers are usually laid out in a mutually supporting network. With each bunker covering the others, they are difficult to assault unless all are pinned down at the same time.

Bunkers conduct Defensive Fire as normal when within 8"/20cm of an Assaulting team (see page 152). In addition, when one Bunker is assaulted, every other Bunker within 16"/40cm can conduct Defensive Fire against any Assaulting teams within 16"/40cm of it.

Assaulting Bunkers

Once your troops reach the bunker they place an explosive charge on the gun slit to finish it off.

All teams in contact with a Nest with an all-round Field of Fire or a Turret can Roll to Hit, but only teams in contact with a Firing Slit of Pillboxes or other Nests, and only one per Firing Slit, can Roll to Hit. Any hits from teams attempting to hit a Bunker must be allocated to the Bunker. Pioneer teams can re-roll failed Skill Tests to hit a Bunker in an assault.

Bunker Saves in Assaults

Bunkers have open firing slits for their weapons, allowing a skilful soldier to post a demolition charge, finishing off the bunker. Turret bunkers are trickier since the weapons and view slits are protected by armoured mantlets.

When a Nest or Pillbox is hit in an assault it is automatically Destroyed.

When a Turret is hit in an Assault, the owning player rolls an Armoured Vehicle Save (see page 97) treating the Bunker as having a Top Armour rating of 1. If they fail the save, the Turret will be Bailed Out or Destroyed as if it was an Armoured vehicle.

Tanks Assaulting Bunkers

Bunkers are simply too strongly built for a tank to have any impact on them in an assault.

Hits from Tank teams cannot be allocated to Bunkers in assaults.

Bunkers Always Counterattack

There is nowhere safer than behind the concrete walls of a bunker, so the crew tend to fight on rather than running away.

A Bunker will always pass the Motivation Test to Counterattack (see page 162), even if the rest of the Defending platoons Break Off.

Assaulting a Bunker

Counterattacking with a Bunker

The troops in a bunker will not sit passively by while the enemy attempts to blow them up.

When Counterattacking, a Bunker rolls one die.

- *On a score of 4+, it hits an enemy team within 2"/5cm of and in the Field of Fire of its Firing Slit or Turret.*
- *On any other roll, the enemy is unharmed, but must still take a Motivation Test to Counterattack as if it had been hit.*

Infantry teams hit by a Counterattacking Bunker are Destroyed as usual. Tank teams hit by a Counterattacking Bunker use their Side armour rating in the same way that Tank teams hit by Gun teams do (see page 157).

Consolidating around Bunkers

Mopping up a disabled bunker is relatively simple once the protective infantry have been chased off, but getting too close to a bunker still in operation is not wise.

When the enemy Consolidates, they cannot move within 2"/5cm of any surviving enemy Bunkers.

SUMMARY

Assaulting Bunkers

- **When a Bunker is assaulted, all Bunkers within 16"/40cm can Defensive Fire.**
- **Only one team can assault each Firing Slit. All teams in contact can assault a Nest with all-round fields of fire or a Turret.**
- **Nests and Pillboxes are automatically Destroyed when hit. Turrets make an Armour Save with Top Armour 1.**
- **Tanks cannot Assault Bunkers.**
- **Bunkers always pass Motivation Tests to Counterattack, and hit on a score of 4+.**
- **Victorious teams cannot Consolidate within 2"/5cm of a Bunker.**

German coastal defence bunker in Normandy
US Signal Corps, NARA

Firing Smoke at Bunkers

Bunkers have their entire field of fire measured out and ranges calculated, making them exceptionally dangerous. Even amidst a swirling smoke screen, they can deliver accurate fire against a partially glimpsed target.

As normal, a Bunker cannot see another team at over 16"/40cm if all Lines of Sight between them pass through Smoke Markers. However, unlike other teams, Bunkers shooting through Smoke Markers do not automatically treat the target team as Concealed and Gone to Ground. Instead, the score to hit the target team ignores the effect of the smoke.

Firing Smoke at Bunkers

If you get close enough, you can fire smoke at a bunker, although with their extensive ammunition supplies and zeroed-in weapons, it might not have much effect.

Before shooting at a Bunker, you may state that you are firing Smoke. If you do this, use the usual rules for shooting at a Bunker, rolling Skill Tests to hit the Bunker as usual, but instead of Pinning Down, Bailing Out, or Destroying the Bunker, place two Smoke Markers (see page 107) directly in front of a Firing Slit on the Bunker for each hit scored.

Smoke Bombardments

Bunkers are not particularly mobile, making them easy targets for artillery wanting to screen distant movement from them.

A Bunker can be the Aiming Point for a Smoke Bombardment. If it is, treat it as a Concealed (but not Gone to Ground) Trained team when calculating the score required to Range In.

SUMMARY

Firing Smoke at Bunkers

- **Bunkers do not treat targets seen through Smoke as Concealed and Gone to Ground.**
- **Smoke Bombardments can use a Bunker as an Aiming Point, treating it as a Concealed Trained team.**

OBSTACLES

Obstacles are barriers to movement. They can be physical barriers like street barricades or anti-tank ditches, or more dangerous obstacles like minefields. All have the effect of limiting the enemy's mobility, and channelling them into the killing zones of your weapons.

There are five basic types of Obstacles:

- *Barbed Wire Entanglements,*
- *Street Barricades,*
- *Minefields,*
- *Booby Traps, and*
- *Anti-tank Obstacles.*

Barbed Wire Entanglements are the classic World War I-style barbed wire obstacles designed to halt infantry in front of machine-guns. Street Barricades are improvised obstacles piled up by the defenders whenever the inhabitants of a city find themselves fighting for their homes. Minefields are areas strewn with carefully buried mines designed to blow a track off a tank or a foot off an unwary infantryman. Booby traps are explosives and mines hidden in unexpected places to trap unwary invaders. Anti-tank obstacles can either be wide ditches, solid barriers, or concrete obstacles like 'dragons teeth'.

Obstacles are not Terrain Features.

Obstacle Sections

To make things simpler, all obstacles come in standard sections of the same length and width.

Obstacles come in 8"/20cm long by 2"/5cm deep sections. You reduce the length to fit between terrain features, for example to block a road between two buildings.

Crossing Obstacles

Obstacles are designed to hinder movement. Troops spend as little time hung up on them as they can.

All Obstacles are Slow Going. Most Obstacles require a Skill Test to cross safely. The specifics of this test and the consequences for failure are covered in each Obstacle's rules.

Teams moving across an Obstacle must do so by the shortest route, leaving the Obstacle as soon as possible after crossing it.

Mined Obstacles

Minefields and booby traps are not just a hindrance to movement, they are deliberately designed to kill or maim the troops crossing them. It takes considerable guts to enter an obstacle like that.

A platoon attempting to cross one or more Mined Obstacles must make a Motivation Test before moving.

- *If they pass the Motivation Test, they move as normal attempting to cross the Obstacles.*
- *If they fail the test, the platoon's teams stop at the edge of the first Mined Obstacle facing towards the Obstacle (or stop immediately if already in a Mined Obstacle), and cannot move further or assault this turn.*

If a Soviet platoon containing a Komissar fails its Motivation Test to cross a Mined Obstacle, the owning player may use the Komissar special rule (see page 249) to re-roll the test.

Crossing Obstacles

Across is Across

Sometimes it is impractical or impossible to entirely cross an obstacle and a team is left sitting on the obstacle.

Teams starting their movement on an Obstacle, but square up against its edge, or partly off the Obstacle, are effectively across the Obstacle. They do not suffer any further penalties if they move directly off the Obstacle across the adjacent edge.

Other teams starting their movement on an Obstacle, that then move along or across the Obstacle are treated as crossing the Obstacle again, and need to take all relevant tests, including another Motivation Test for attempting to cross a Mined Obstacle if relevant.

Gaps Between Obstacles

If obstacles are placed too far apart, their value is nullified as the enemy simply moves through the gaps.

Teams can only move through gaps between Obstacles (without crossing the Obstacle itself) if the gap is at least as wide as they are (see page 42).

Moving Near the Enemy

Obstacles are two-way things. They limit the enemy's movement, but they can also prevent you from interfering with the enemy's activities in other ways.

Obstacles are 2"/5cm deep, so teams can move right up to them, even if there are enemy teams on the far side.

Assaulting across Obstacles

Many obstacles work best if they are defended, making assaults across obstacles quite common.

Assaulting across a Mined Obstacle

When an officer orders an assault across a minefield, they hope that their soldiers are brave and committed enough to get up and follow them.

If the Assaulting platoon will Charge into Contact into or across an Obstacle that requires a Motivation Test to enter, the platoon must take any Motivation Test it needs to take to enter the Obstacle before Charging into Contact. If it fails the test, the Assaulting platoon refuses to assault and the assault is over.

German soldier gapping barbed wire
IWM HU27741

Teams Must Cross an Obstacle to Fight

Obstacles are designed to make it difficult for the enemy to assault troops on the far side. Teams must cross the obstacle to get at the enemy.

Obstacles are 2"/5cm deep, so teams need to enter or cross an Obstacle to Roll to Hit a team on the other side in an assault.

Counterattacking Across Obstacles

Once a platoon has its blood up in an assault, the dangers of a minefield seem less than the risk of not dealing with the enemy at hand.

Platoons do not need to take a Motivation Test to Counterattack across a Mined Obstacle, but they still need to take any relevant Skill Tests to cross the Obstacle if they need to, and suffer the usual consequences of failure.

Teams Counterattacking enemy teams in an Obstacle need to take any relevant Skill Tests as if they were attempting to cross the Obstacle themselves in the same way as if they were assaulting into Rough Terrain (see page 149).

Breaking Off across Obstacles

When not crossing a minefield means capture or death, the risk seems much less than otherwise.

Platoons do not need to take a Motivation Test to Break Off across a Mined Obstacle, but they still need to take any relevant Skill Tests to cross the Obstacle if they need to, and suffer the usual consequences of failure.

If a team that is Breaking Off is unable to cross the Obstacle, leaving it too close to the victors, it will be captured as usual (see page 165).

Consolidating across Obstacles

Once the excitement of the assault subsides, the victors' caution returns as they survey the cost and establish positions for the next phase of the battle.

When making Consolidation moves, the victorious platoon follows all the normal rules for crossing Obstacles, including the Motivation Test for crossing Mined Obstacles.

SUMMARY

Obstacles

- **Obstacles are Slow Going.**
- **Mined Obstacles require a Motivation Test to enter.**
- **Platoons charging across a Mined Obstacle do not assault if they fail their Motivation Test.**
- **Platoons Counterattacking or Breaking Off across a Mined Obstacle do not need to take a Motivation Test.**

GAPPING OBSTACLES

Infantry and Pioneers

While it is usually best for the leading waves to simply push on through an obstacle and take the resulting casualties, it is important to clear gaps behind them for following troops and valuable equipment. This hazardous task can be performed by infantry if necessary, but is best left to trained pioneers.

To attempt to gap an Obstacle an Infantry team must have started the turn square up against the Obstacle, and not be Pinned Down.

A team attempting to gap an Obstacle cannot have moved in the Movement Step nor be Gone to Ground. They will not be Concealed in the Open, being treated as if they had moved.

In the Shooting Step, each team attempting to gap an Obstacle rolls a Skill Test instead of shooting.

- *If any team passes the test, remove the whole section of the Obstacle.*
- *If they all fail, more work is needed and they will have to try again next turn.*

If several teams in a platoon are adjacent to multiple Obstacles, the owning player must declare which Obstacle each team will attempt to gap before rolling any of the platoon's Skill Tests.

Infantry Must Re-roll Successes

Pioneers are equipped with all kinds of special obstacle-breaching equipment and are trained in their use. Regular infantry can do the same job with whatever is to hand, but take longer to do it.

Due to their lack of training, Infantry teams that are not Pioneer teams must re-roll successful Skill Tests to gap Obstacles.

Pioneer Supply Vehicles Allow Re-rolls

A lot of pioneer equipment is heavy or power operated making it impossible to carry on foot. If the pioneer's supplies are brought up by a vehicle, work proceeds much faster.

A team that has a Pioneer Supply vehicle within Command Distance (see page 65) may re-roll failed Skill Tests to gap Obstacles.

Gapping Anti-tank Obstacles

Anti-tank obstacles are the brute-force school of obstacles. It takes a lot of work to make them, and a lot of work to breach them.

Unlike other Obstacles, an Anti-tank Obstacle is not removed after a single successful Skill Test. Instead, place a die beside the Anti-tank Obstacle showing the total number of successful Skill Tests. If at the end of the Shooting Step the total number of successful tests from all Infantry teams working on an Obstacle in this and previous turns is six or more, remove the Obstacle.

Gapping Obstacles

BULLDOZERS

Bulldozers are useful for filling in craters and anti-tank ditches, or burying anti-tank obstacles blocking the armour's advance.

BURYING BUNKERS

Tanks fitted with dozer blades sometimes simply buried bunkers rather than trying to knock them out.

Tank teams fitted with Bulldozer blades can assault a Bunker in the same way as an Infantry team. If the Bunker is a Turret, it is automatically Destroyed if hit.

GAPPING ANTI-TANK OBSTACLES

Bulldozers are particularly useful for cutting tracks down into and out of anti-tank ditches and burying other types of anti-tank obstacles.

A Bulldozer can gap Barbed Wire Entanglements, Street Barricades, and Anti-tank Obstacle in the same way that a Pioneer team gaps an Obstacle. It removes the Anti-tank Obstacle after one success, rather than requiring six successes. Pioneer Supply vehicles do not give Bulldozers a re-roll of their Skill Test.

GAPPING ROUGH TERRAIN

Especially when armoured or fitted to tanks, dozers can also be invaluable in offensives across harsh terrain.

Bulldozers can create a Slow Going gap in Difficult or Very Difficult Going (such as a Bocage Hedgerow), other than Obstacles in the same way. A successful Skill Test creates a 2"/5cm wide gap in a Linear Obstacle or a gap 2"/5cm wide by 4"/10cm long in Area Terrain that no longer requires a Bogging Check to cross.

MINE FLAILS AND ROLLERS

A mine flail uses a rapidly rotating spindle mounted on arms in front of the tank to whip the ground with long lengths of chains. The chains either slap the mine hard enough to disable it or to strike the pressure plate and detonate it well clear of the crew hunkered behind the tank's armour. Rollers function very similarly to mine flails, but instead of striking the mine with chains they simply roll a heavy steel drum over the top of them.

Tanks fitted with Mine Flails or Mine Rollers do not need to make a Motivation Test to enter a Minefield. However, they do need to take a Skill Test to cross safely and risk being Destroyed in the same way as other vehicles if they fail it.

British Sherman Crab mine flail
IWM B011918

If a Mine Flail or Mine Roller passes safely through a Minefield without being Bailed Out or Destroyed, remove the section of Minefield they crossed.

ASSAULT BRIDGES

Ditches and streams delay the advance of motorised troops and bridging them normally takes hours. Mechanised assault bridges reduce this to minutes. The simplest are light vehicle-mounted bridges lifted into place by the pioneer crew, while others use hydraulic rams to lift tank-mounted bridges into place without the crew ever exposing themselves to the enemy.

A vehicle with an Assault Bridge can place it over an adjacent Anti-tank Ditch in the Shooting Step instead of shooting. The team cannot be Gone to Ground while doing so.

Once placed, the Assault Bridge is Slow Going. Once laid, it cannot be retrieved. Bridges laid by Half-tracked vehicles cannot be crossed by Fully-tracked vehicles.

BRIDGING STREAMS AND DITCHES

Assault bridges are ideal for keeping motorised advances going by bridging creeks, streams and small ditches.

A vehicle with an Assault Bridge can also use the same method to place its Assault Bridge across a crater, stream, ditch or to provide a ramp up a bank up to 1"/2.5cm high.

SUMMARY

GAPPING OBSTACLES

- **Infantry teams that did not move and are not Pinned Down must pass a Skill Test to gap an Obstacle instead of shooting.**
- **Teams that are not Pioneer teams re-roll successful Skill Tests. Teams within Command Distance of a Pioneer Supply vehicle re-roll failed Skill Tests.**
- **Anti-tank Obstacles require six successful Skill Tests to gap.**
- **Bulldozers can assault Bunkers.**
- **Bulldozers require a single passed Skill Test to gap an Anti-tank Obstacle or clear a path through Rough Terrain.**
- **Mine Flails and Rollers do not need a Motivation Test to enter a Minefield, and gap the Minefield if they cross successfully.**
- **Assault Bridges are placed instead of shooting. The Assault Bridge is Slow Going.**

BARBED WIRE ENTANGLEMENTS

Composed of masses of densely coiled wire interwoven with sharp barbs, entanglements are capable of holding up the advance of anything short of a tank.

Infantry and Man-packed Guns Crossing

Although intact barbed wire entanglements are virtually impassable to infantry, the preliminary bombardment that usually precedes an assault tends to blow gaps in the wire, if the infantry can find them. If not, experienced troops use improvised measures such as the lead soldiers hurling themselves flat over the wire and the rest running across their backs.

Each Infantry team (excluding Cavalry) and Man-packed Gun team must make a Skill Test to cross a Barbed Wire Entanglement.

- *If they pass the test, they cross the Barbed Wire Entanglement unhindered.*
- *If they fail, the team must halt on reaching the Barbed Wire Entanglement.*

Pioneer teams may re-roll failed Skill Tests when attempting to cross Barbed Wire Entanglements.

Tracked Vehicles Crossing

Tanks were originally designed to drive through barbed wire and clear out enemy machine-guns ahead of the infantry. They have evolved into much more, but still fulfil this role extremely well.

Fully-tracked vehicles treat Barbed Wire Entanglements as Slow Going. Half-tracked vehicles treat Barbed Wire Entanglements as Very Difficult Going.

Trains Ignore Barbed Wire

It takes more than a little barbed wire to stop an armoured train with a full head of steam!

Trains ignore Barbed Wire Entanglements.

Other Teams Cannot Cross

While infantry can sneak through small gaps and tanks simply crush it, barbed wire entanglements are an insurmountable barrier to trucks and horses.

Barbed Wire Entanglements are Impassable to all other types of teams.

SUMMARY

- **Infantry and Man-packed Gun teams must pass a Skill Test to cross a Barbed Wire Entanglement. Pioneer teams may re-roll.**
- **Barbed Wire Entanglements are Slow Going to Fully-tracked vehicles and Very Difficult Going to Half-tracked vehicles.**
- **Trains ignore Barbed Wire Entanglements.**
- **Other teams cannot cross Barbed Wire Entanglements.**

Barbed Wire Entanglements

STREET BARRICADES

When defending their city, the inhabitants pile up building rubble, wrecked cars, trucks and street trams, and pretty much anything else they can find to make barricades. Street barricades are built high and wide, making them difficult to cross. And, unlike barbed wire, they don't tend to have gaps blown in them by artillery fire.

Street Barricades are Linear Obstacles and are Very Difficult Going. They are Impassable to Cavalry and Trains.

Teams must stop their movement on reaching a Street Barricade. They must start their movement square up against a Street Barricade to cross it.

Teams cannot end a Step sitting on a Street Barricade. Like a Linear Obstacle, teams must be on one side or the other and clearly either up against the Street Barricade or back from it.

TAKING COVER BEHIND A BARRICADE

The height and solidity of a street barricade gives the defenders a distinct advantage since the enemy can't see them moving about behind it.

Street Barricades provide Concealment and Bulletproof Cover against shooting from the other side for teams square up against them, and block Line of Sight to teams beyond them in the same way as other Linear Obstacles. Being Linear Obstacles, they provide no protection against Artillery Bombardments or Ground-attack Aircraft.

ASSAULTING A STREET BARRICADE

Like a fortress wall of old, a street barricade is difficult to assault. Even throwing grenades across it requires care, as a grenade that fell short would be lethal to the thrower and their comrades.

As with any Linear Obstacle, Assaulting teams that contact a Street Barricade can Roll to Hit and be hit by enemy teams on the other side of the Street Barricade.

However, unlike other Linear Obstacles, teams may only Roll to Hit against teams on the other side of the Street Barricade if they started their Charge into Contact square up against the Street Barricade.

GAPPING STREET BARRICADES

Street barricades are quite massive and difficult to demolish completely.

Do not remove a Street Barricade when it is gapped (see page 225). Instead, remove the middle piece, creating a gap in the Street Barricade rated as Difficult Going. The remainder of the Street Barricade continues to function as normal.

BUNKER BUSTERS AGAINST STREET BARRICADES

Assault tanks like the German *Brummbär* or the Soviet SU-152 have little to worry about from a street barricade. They simply settle down and pound it until they blow a gap right through it.

Weapons rated as Bunker Buster can attempt to gap a Street Barricade. A Bunker Buster must not move in the Movement Step, and must be able to draw a Line of Sight to a Street Barricade and be within 16"/40cm of it to attempt to gap it.

Roll a Skill Test for the Bunker Buster in the Shooting Step instead of shooting.

- *If the test is successful, the Street Barricade is gapped,*
- *Otherwise, it remains intact.*

SUMMARY

- **Teams must stop when they reach a Street Barricade. Street Barricades are Very Difficult Going, but Impassable to Cavalry and Trains.**
- **Street Barricades provide Concealment and Bulletproof Cover.**
- **Assaulting teams must start their Charge into Contact adjacent to the Street Barricade.**
- **Bunker Busters can gap an Street Barricade within 16"/40cm with shooting by passing a Skill Test.**

Street Barricade

MINEFIELDS

Minefields make no-man's land a real devil's garden, springing up around every defensive position and littering the battlefield wherever trench warfare sets in.

Minefields are Mined Obstacles (see page 223). As such, platoons need to pass a Motivation Test before they can cross them.

SKILL TESTS TO CROSS A MINEFIELD

Once the troops have worked up the courage to enter a minefield, they must muster all of their skill to avoid triggering a mine. Experienced infantry can make their way across looking for telltale signs, avoiding mines, while raw conscripts must trust to dumb luck.

Roll a Skill Test for each team that crosses a Minefield.

- *If the team passes the Skill Test, they are unharmed.*
- *If they fail, they take a hit from a mine and must stop moving when they reach the far side of the Minefield.*

If any team in a platoon is hit by a mine, whether the hit causes a casualty or not, the entire platoon is Pinned Down at the end of their movement.

ARMOURED VEHICLES HIT BY MINES

Tanks are remarkably tough, and with luck, a heavy tank can even survive driving over a mine. Armoured cars are not usually so fortunate, however.

Treat hits from mines on Armoured vehicles as a hit on the Top armour by a weapon with an Anti-tank rating of 5 and a Firepower rating of 1+.

UNARMOURED VEHICLES HIT BY MINES

Driving over a mine in a truck is bad news. Aside from ripping off a wheel, the blast usually makes a serious mess of the bodywork!

Unarmoured vehicles that are hit by mines are Destroyed.

INFANTRY AND GUNS HIT BY MINES

Though they do their best to pick their steps carefully and creep their way through at a snail's pace, it is only a matter of time before someone hits a mine.

Roll a save for each Infantry or Gun team hit by mines. An Infantry team survives on a roll of 3+, but is Destroyed otherwise. Gun teams survive on a roll of 5+.

PASSENGERS HIT BY MINES

With a little luck, the passengers in a vehicle or tank riders on a tank that hits a mine might survive unharmed as the vehicle takes the worst of the blast.

Passengers carried in or on a vehicle Destroyed by mines must roll a 5+ save. If they pass the save, they have survived crossing the minefield and are placed adjacent to their Destroyed vehicle on the far side of the minefield. Otherwise they are Destroyed with their vehicle.

GAPPING MINEFIELDS

Trying to clear a minefield is a dangerous task. Even a careful sweep for mines might miss one, blowing up the clearing party. To make matters worse, mines are often booby trapped to go off if lifted as well.

If a team fails its Skill Test to gap a Minefield (see page 225), it is hit by mines as if it failed its Skill Test to cross the Minefield.

SUMMARY

- **Minefields are Mined Obstacles requiring a Motivation Test to enter.**
- **Teams that fail a Skill Test when crossing a Minefield are hit by a mine with Anti-tank 5 and Firepower 1+. Unarmoured vehicles are Destroyed automatically.**
- **Teams that fail their Skill Test to gap a Minefield are hit by a mine.**

US combat engineers [illegible]
US Signal Corps, NARA

BOOBY TRAPS

Retreating troops often booby-trapped areas before withdrawing. The pursuing troops usually had little warning of booby traps and relied on their skill to detect and neutralise any they encountered. Those unwary enough not to notice them suffered accordingly.

Booby Traps are Mined Obstacles (see page 223). As such platoons need to pass a Motivation Test before they can cross or move off them.

Unlike other Obstacles, a Booby Trap occupies the area of a small base (1¼"/32mm x 1"/25mm).

A Booby Trap only affects the first team to move across or off the Booby Trap base. After that the Booby Trap is expended and removed.

PLACING BOOBY TRAPS

Booby traps are always carefully hidden and come as a surprise to the enemy.

Booby Traps do not need to be deployed before the game begins. Instead, they may be placed at the same time as Ambushing platoons during each Starting Step.

Booby Traps may be placed anywhere in your own Deployment Area or No Man's Land, including under enemy troops. However, you may not place Booby Traps under teams already on Booby Traps, nor under Dug In teams or those that deployed in Prepared Positions and have not yet moved.

TRIPPING BOOBY TRAPS

Because booby traps are carefully hidden, soldiers can find themselves in a dangerous situation without having realised it.

If a Booby Trap is placed under a team, the team's platoon will test as if crossing the Booby Trap when it first moves off it. Otherwise the Booby Trap goes off when a team first crosses it.

Roll a Skill Test for a team that crosses a Booby Trap.

- *If the team passes the Skill Test, they are unharmed.*
- *If they fail, they take a hit from the Booby Trap and must stop moving immediately.*

In either case, the Booby Trap is removed.

If any team in a platoon is hit by a Booby Trap, whether the hit causes a casualty or not, the entire platoon is Pinned Down at the end of their movement.

BOOBY TRAP MARKER

Booby Traps are not usually spotted until a team stumbles across them. Booby Trap markers show their location once revealed.

ARMOURED VEHICLES HIT BY BOOBY TRAPS

Booby traps are normally small and intended for infantry on foot rather than tanks, but some of them are much larger and can knock out an unlucky tank.

Treat hits from Booby Traps on Armoured vehicles as a hit on the Top armour by a weapon with an Anti-tank rating of 3 and a Firepower rating of 5+.

UNARMOURED VEHICLES HIT BY BOOBY TRAPS

Booby traps are usually powerful enough to wreck a truck, but a lucky driver might find themselves shocked but unharmed.

Unarmoured vehicles that are hit by a Booby Trap save on a roll of 5+.

INFANTRY AND GUNS HIT BY BOOBY TRAPS

Infantry are generally cautious in booby-trapped areas, but occasionally they make a serious miscalculation and pay the price.

Roll a save for each Infantry or Gun team hit by a Booby Trap. An Infantry team survives on a roll of 3+, but is Destroyed otherwise. Gun teams survive on a roll of 5+.

PASSENGERS HIT BY BOOBY TRAPS

With a little luck, the passengers in a vehicle or tank riders on a tank that hits a booby trap survive unharmed.

Passengers carried in or on a vehicle Destroyed by a Booby Trap must roll a 5+ save. If they pass the save, they Dismount Under Fire (see page 101).

GAPPING BOOBY TRAPS

Booby traps are designed to be tricky to locate and hard to disarm. One mistake and the clearing team is in serious trouble.

If a team fails its Skill Test to gap a Booby Trap (see page 225), it is hit by mines as if it failed its Skill Test to cross the Booby Trap.

SUMMARY

- **Booby Traps are Mined Obstacles requiring a Motivation Test to enter.**
- **Booby Traps are placed in your Deployment Area or No Man's Land when placing Ambushing platoons.**
- **Teams that fail a Skill Test when crossing a Booby Trap are hit by a mine with Anti-tank 3 and Firepower 5+.**
- **Teams that fail their Skill Test to gap a Booby Trap are hit by a mine.**

ANTI-TANK OBSTACLES

Anti-tank obstacles have been around almost as long as the tanks they are designed to stop. The most primitive form is an anti-tank ditch deep and wide enough to stop a tank. With more time, armies emplace rows of steel or concrete 'dragons teeth' or erect high, thick concrete anti-tank walls.

Crossing Anti-tank Obstacles

Anti-tank obstacles tend to do their job well and are serious impediments to vehicles of all types, but do not slow down infantry on foot.

Anti-tank Obstacles are Impassable to all vehicles (including Trains), Cavalry teams, and non-Man-packed Gun teams. Infantry and Man-packed Gun teams are not slowed by Anti-tank Obstacles, but cannot move At the Double in or across them.

US riflemen advancing through anti-tank obstacles
US Signal Corps, NARA

Taking Cover in Anti-tank Obstacles

While anti-tank obstacles stop tanks cold, they have an unintended benefit for attacking infantry. Once they get up to them they can shelter from enemy fire in and behind the obstacles.

Anti-tank Obstacles provide Concealment and Bulletproof Cover for Infantry and Man-packed Gun teams in or immediately behind them against shooting from the other side. As with Linear Obstacles, they provide no protection against Artillery Bombardments, or Aircraft.

Gapping Anti-tank Obstacles

Filling in an anti-tank ditch or blowing up enough dragons teeth to get vehicles through the gap is extremely hard work.

Anti-tank Obstacles require six successful gapping attempts to create a gap in them (see page 225).

SUMMARY

- **Only Infantry and Man-packed Gun teams can cross an Anti-tank Obstacle.**
- **Anti-tank Obstacles provide Concealment and Bulletproof Cover for Infantry and Man-packed Guns immediately behind.**
- **Anti-tank obstacles require six successful gapping attempts to gap.**

Anti-tank Obstacles

DEMOLITION CARRIERS

Germany developed remote-controlled demolition carriers as a way of destroying fortifications without risking pioneers' lives. There were two types of demolition carriers, the Goliath and the Borgward BIV.

CONTROLLING TEAMS

While the demolition carrier is the more obvious part of the weapon system, even more important is the control system. The control equipment and the demolition carrier must be calibrated to each other before the battle begins, a time-consuming process, without which the carrier is just one big unexploded bomb.

Every Demolition Carrier must have a Controlling team, and each Controlling team can only control their own Demolition Carrier.

If the controlling team is Destroyed, the Demolition Carrier is Destroyed as well. Since they are expendable machines, Demolition Carriers are ignored for Platoon Morale Checks.

BORGWARD BIV

The Borgward BIV is controlled by a tank and carries 1100lb/500kg (that's half a tonne!) of explosives on the front, making it vulnerable to shooting.

A Borgward BIV Demolition Carrier is a Half-tracked Transport team with Front, Side, and Top armour ratings of 0. It operates separately from its Controlling tank until Switched to Remote Control.

Re-roll failed Firepower Tests to Destroy a Borgward BIV when hit by shooting.

A Borgward BIV Demolition Carrier has Firepower 2+.

BORGWARD BIV				
Mobility	Front	Side	Top	Firepower
Half-tracked	0	0	0	2+

GOLIATH

The Goliath is a 5'/1.5m-long mini-tank carrying 132lb/60kg of explosives. They are pulled by pioneers on a wheeled trolley until they are in position to go.

Place the Goliath miniature with the Controlling Pioneer team to indicate its presence until it is Switched to Remote Control. It counts as part of the Controlling team and cannot be hit by shooting or assaults separately from its Controlling team. The Controlling team cannot cross Very Difficult Going while they have the Demolition Carrier.

A Goliath Demolition Carrier has Firepower 4+.

DEMOLITION CARRIERS

Switch to Remote Control

When it's time to use the carrier it is switched on and sent forward by remote control to explode at its target.

A Controlling team that is not Pinned Down and did not move can switch their Demolition Carrier to remote control and move the carrier up to 16"/40cm instead. The Demolition Carrier must be within Line of Sight of the controller for the entire movement. This movement may pass through friendly or enemy teams without restriction.

In the Shooting Step, the Demolition Carrier attacks an adjacent team, Building, Bunker, or Obstacle, Destroying itself in the process.

Moving across Obstacles

Driving a demolition carrier by remote control is tricky, especially if the ground is anything but flat and open.

The Demolition Carrier only moves 4"/10cm (instead of 16"/40cm) if it enters, crosses, or moves through Rough Terrain, and is Destroyed if it fails a Bogging Check. Demolition Carriers cannot cross Barbed Wire Entanglements or Anti-tank Obstacles. They do not need to take a Motivation Test to cross a Minefield, but the controlling team must pass a Skill Test. If they fail, the Demolition Carrier is Destroyed by a mine.

Attacking a Team

When a demolition carrier comes for you, your only option is to get out of the way, or be very lucky.

To attack a team, the controlling player chooses one team that is in contact with the Demolition Carrier, or directly across a Linear Obstacle from the Demolition Carrier, at the end of its movement.

If it is a Dug In Infantry or Man-packed Gun team, any other type of Gun team (whether Dug In or not), or a Bogged Down or Bailed Out vehicle, it is hit automatically. Otherwise the controlling team must pass a Skill Test to hit it.

An Infantry team takes a 3+ Infantry Save if hit. If it fails, it or another Infantry team within Command Distance of it chosen by the Targeted player is Destroyed.

If it is a Gun team, it is automatically Destroyed with no save at all.

If an Unarmoured vehicle is hit, it is Destroyed.

If an Armoured vehicle is hit, take a Firepower Test for the Demolition Carrier.

- *If it passes, the vehicle is Bogged Down. If it was already Bogged Down or Bailed Out, it is Destroyed.*
- *If it fails, the vehicle is unharmed.*

Attacking a Building

A demolition carrier makes a mess of a building and anything inside.

To attack a Building, the controlling player chooses one of the Buildings in contact with the Demolition Carrier.

The Demolition Carrier automatically hits all teams in the selected Building. The teams are affected as above.

Attacking a Bunker

Demolition carriers were originally designed to knock out bunkers, and do a good job of it.

To attack a Bunker, the controlling player picks a Bunker in contact with the Demolition Carrier and takes a Firepower Test.

- *A successful test Destroys the Bunker.*
- *A failed test Pins Down the Bunker.*

Attacking an Obstacle

Demolition carriers are great at clearing fortifications. The sheer blast of the explosion detonates mines and flattens other types of obstacle.

To attack an Obstacle, the controlling player picks an Obstacle in contact with the Demolition Carrier and takes a Firepower Test.

- *A successful test removes the Obstacle, unless it was an Anti-tank Obstacle in which case it counts as if a Pioneer team passed a Skill Test to gap it, adding to the total of successful Skill Tests.*
- *A failed test leaves the Obstacle intact.*

A Demolition Carrier can attempt to blow a gap in an adjacent Bocage Hedgerow in the same way as it gaps an Obstacle. If it succeeds, it creates a 2"/5cm wide Gate in the hedgerow.

SUMMARY

- **A Demolition Carrier is Destroyed if its Controlling team is Destroyed.**
- **If the Controlling team did not move and is not Pinned Down, instead of shooting it switches on the Demolition Carrier and moves it 16"/40cm to contact the target.**
- **A Dug In Infantry or Man-packed Gun team, any other type of Gun team (whether Dug In or not), or a Bogged Down or Bailed Out vehicle is automatically hit. Otherwise a Skill Test is needed to hit.**
- **If it hits a vehicle, it is Bogged Down on a successful Firepower Test. If it was already Bogged Down, it is Destroyed instead.**
- **It hits every team inside a Building.**
- **A successful Firepower Test Destroys a Bunker or gaps an Obstacle.**

BUNKERS AND FORTIFICATIONS SUMMARY

ENTRENCHMENTS

Entrenchments are Slow Going for Fully- and Half-tracked vehicles and troops on foot, otherwise Impassable.

Trench Lines give Concealment and Bulletproof Cover. If they do not shoot, teams are Gone to Ground (even if moving).

Guns in Gun Pits cannot rotate or move, but are Concealed and have Bulletproof Cover.

Tanks in Tank Pits cannot rotate (aside from their turret) or move, but are Concealed. All shots hit the turret.

BUNKERS

- *Pinned Down Bunkers Rally at start of their own turn.*
- *Bunkers are Slow Going for Fully- and Half-tracked vehicles and troops on foot, otherwise Impassable.*
- *Bunkers Conceal and block Line of Sight like Buildings.*

SHOOTING WITH BUNKERS

Bunkers either have an all-round Field of Fire or a 180-degree Field of Fire from each Firing Slit.

Draw Line of Sight and measure Range to and from the Firing Slit of a Pillbox or Nest, to any part of a Nest with an all-round Field of Fire, or any part of a Turret.

Bunkers are Trained when firing Artillery Bombardments.

SHOOTING AT BUNKERS

Bunkers can only be shot at by teams within 16"/40cm needing Skill Tests to hit.

A Successful Firepower Test Pins Down a Nest or Pillbox. A second Successful Firepower Test Destroys a Nest.

Turrets take an Armoured Vehicle Save like a Tank team.

Bunker Busters Destroy Bunkers with any hit.

Artillery and Aircraft cannot target or harm a Bunker.

ASSAULTING BUNKERS

When a Bunker is assaulted, all Bunkers within 16"/40cm can Defensive Fire.

One team can assault each Firing Slit. All teams in contact can assault a Nest with all-round fields of fire or a Turret.

Nests and Pillboxes are automatically Destroyed when hit. Turrets make an Armour Save with Top Armour 1.

Bunkers Counterattack and hit on a score of 4+.

Teams cannot Consolidate within 2"/5cm of a Bunker.

FIRING SMOKE AT BUNKERS

Bunkers do not treat targets seen through Smoke as Concealed and Gone to Ground.

Smoke Bombardments can use a Bunker as an Aiming Point, treating it as a Concealed Trained team.

OBSTACLES

Obstacles are Slow Going.

Mined Obstacles require a Motivation Test to enter.

Platoons charging across a Mined Obstacle do not assault if they fail their Motivation Test.

Platoons Counterattacking or Breaking Off across a Mined Obstacle do not need to take a Motivation Test.

GAPPING OBSTACLES

Infantry teams that did not move and are not Pinned Down take a Skill Test to gap Obstacles instead of shooting. Non-Pioneer teams re-roll successes. Teams within Command Distance of a Pioneer Supply vehicle re-roll failures.

Bulldozers can assault Bunkers and require a single Skill Test to gap an Anti-tank Obstacle or Rough Terrain.

Mine Flails and Rollers do not need a Motivation Test to enter a Minefield, and gap it if they cross successfully.

Place Assault Bridge as Slow Going instead of shooting.

BARBED WIRE ENTANGLEMENTS

Infantry and Man-packed Gun teams need a Skill Test to cross Barbed Wire. Pioneer teams may re-roll.

Barbed Wire Entanglements are Slow Going to Fully-tracked vehicles and Very Difficult Going to Half-tracks. Other teams cannot cross Barbed Wire Entanglements.

STREET BARRICADES

Teams stop when they reach a Street Barricade. They are Very Difficult Going, but Impassable to Cavalry.

Street Barricades are Concealment and Bulletproof Cover.

Bunker Busters can gap a Street Barricade within 16"/40cm with shooting by passing a Skill Test.

MINEFIELDS AND BOOBY TRAPS

Take a Motivation Test to enter a Minefield or Booby Trap.

Teams that fail a Skill Test when crossing are hit by a mine with Anti-tank 5 and Firepower 1+. Unarmoured vehicles are Destroyed automatically.

Teams that fail their Skill Test to gap Minefields or Booby Traps are hit.

ANTI-TANK OBSTACLES

Only Infantry and Man-packed Gun teams can cross an Anti-tank Obstacle. They provide Concealment and Bulletproof Cover for Infantry and Man-packed Guns.

Anti-tank Obstacles require six successful gapping attempts.

NATIONAL
SPECIAL RULES

German infantry hold their trenches against Soviet infantry supported by an IS-2 heavy tank

US SPECIAL RULES

The United States of America utilise their superior technology and mass production to equip their troops with the best weapons available. Their doctrines emphasise heavy artillery support for infantry breakthroughs, then fast-moving operations to defeat the enemy.

TANKS

STABILISERS

A stabiliser is a device fitted to the tank's gun that keeps it level when the tank is moving. US tanks are the first in the world to be equipped with gyrostabilisers as standard. With the assistance of the gyrostabiliser, the gunner can stay on target while the tank is moving.

A moving tank fitted with a Stabiliser can fire its main gun at its full ROF, but adds a penalty of +1 to the score needed to hit.

Before shooting, a tank can choose not to use its Stabiliser and fire at the normal rate if that would give it a better chance.

HEDGEROW CUTTERS

Many American tanks were fitted with the 'Culin Device' for the breakout from Normandy. This allowed them to punch through the *Bocage*.

When a tank fitted with a Hedgerow Cutter attempts to cross a Bocage Hedgerow, it successfully crosses on a roll of 2+ rather than a Skill Test. If it fails, the tank Bogs Down on the Hedgerow as normal, but ignores the Belly Up rule (see page 58).

If it crosses successfully, then any other Fully-tracked Tank teams that started their movement adjacent to the Hedgerow can follow it through on a roll of 2+ instead of a Skill Test as well.

US M4A1 (76mm) Sherman tank

TRANSPORTS

Dismounting Machine-guns

Lots of transport vehicles carry anti-aircraft machine-guns. Normally they're left on the vehicle, but when the platoon needs more firepower, they can be taken off the vehicles and fired from a tripod mount.

Any Infantry team carried as a Passenger in a Transport team may Dismount in the Movement Step with the vehicle's Passenger-fired .50 cal AA MG, becoming an M2 .50 cal team, or with its Passenger-fired AA MG becoming a LMG team. If the Infantry team was a Command team, it remains a Command team.

An Infantry team normally mounted in a vehicle can start the game Dismounted with their vehicle's Passenger-fired machine-gun.

Once the machine-gun has been Dismounted from a vehicle, all of the platoon's vehicles must be Sent to the Rear (see page 48) and cannot be Brought Forward again.

You may not Dismount a Passenger-fired .50 cal AA MG or AA MG unless you have the appropriate model to replace the Infantry team that Dismounted it.

Dismounting Machine-guns

Mounting HMG's and LMG's

Machine-gunners don't just laze around watching the scenery from their armoured half-tracks. Instead, they mount their machine-guns on the sides and blaze away at the enemy as they ride into battle.

Up to two HMG or LMG teams carried as Passengers in a half-track can fit their machine-guns to the sides of the vehicle, converting them to side-mounted AA MG's. When the team Dismounts or is Destroyed, its machine-gun goes with it.

Mounting HMG's and LMG's

TANK DESTROYERS

Tank Destroyer Command was tasked with stopping armoured breakthroughs and developed a doctrine based on operating en masse to ambush fast moving tank attacks. The following rules reflect their unique doctrine set out in their motto 'Seek, Strike, and Destroy'.

A Self-propelled Anti-tank Platoon, Tank Destroyer Platoon, or Towed Tank Destroyer Platoon is a Reconnaissance platoon.

Each platoon has two components:

- *a Security Section consisting of its Jeep, Recon Jeep, and M20 scout car teams and any Carbine teams apart from the Command team of the Tank Destroyer Section, and*
- *a Tank Destroyer Section of the rest of the platoon.*

SEEK, STRIKE, AND DESTROY

Each tank destroyer platoon has its own reconnaissance and security element to translate doctrine into reality.

At the start of the game before deployment you may choose to either:

- *deploy your Tank Destroyer Section as normal at the start of the game, leaving the Security Section off table for the whole game, or*
- *deploy only the Security Section, holding the Tank Destroyer Section off the table ready to be placed later using the Tank Destroyer Section rule.*

SECURITY SECTION

The security section keeps track of the enemy while the tank destroyers work their way into position.

If the Platoon Command team of the Security Section is Destroyed, nominate any of the Carbine, Recon Jeep, or M20 scout car teams as the Platoon Command team.

If all of the Carbine, Recon Jeep, and M20 scout car teams of the Security Section are Destroyed, mark the location of the Platoon Command team when it was Destroyed. The Tank Destroyer Section must be placed in the player's next turn as if the Platoon Command team were still where it was when it was Destroyed.

TANK DESTROYER SECTION

Once they have reached the ideal ambush positions, the tank destroyers reveal themselves with a volley of shots.

Place the Tank Destroyer Section on the table at the start of any of your turns when Ambushes are revealed so that every team in the Tank Destroyer Section is:

- *within Command Distance of a team from the Security Section, and*
- *In Command when the Security Section is removed.*

In addition, each team must not be:

- *within 16"/40cm of any enemy team within Line of Sight, unless Concealed by Terrain from it, or*
- *within 4"/10cm of any enemy team, or*
- *within 8"/20cm of any enemy Recce team that is in Line of Sight (apart from Recce teams that are Bogged Down, Bailed Out, or moved at the Double).*

Once the Tank Destroyer Section is placed, the Security Section is permanently removed from the table. The Tank Destroyer Section can move and fight as normal during the turn it appears.

When it takes Platoon Morale Checks, the Tank Destroyer Section ignores any teams from the Security Section that were Destroyed.

TANK DESTROYER SECTION COMMAND TEAM

Some tank destroyer platoons are not shown with a Command team for the Tank Destroyer Section. In this case add a Command Carbine team to a Towed Tank Destroyer Platoon, or appoint one of the tank destroyers as the Command team for self-propelled platoons.

TANK DESTROYERS

INFANTRY

Automatic Rifles

The US Army is equipped with the M1 Garand self-loading rifle, M1 Carbine, and the Browning Automatic Rifle (BAR), giving their infantry intense short-range firepower and allowing them to maintain their rate of fire while moving.

Rifle and Carbine teams do not suffer the usual +1 to hit penalty for firing a ROF 1 weapon while moving or Pinned Down.

When not Pinned Down, Rifle and Carbine teams re-roll all failed rolls to hit in Defensive Fire during assaults.

The Truscott Trot

Long-distance speed marches were a major feature of an infantryman's training. Some officers, like General Truscott of the 3rd Infantry Division, trained their troops so hard that they dubbed speed marching the 'Truscott Trot'.

All this practice paid off during Patton's drive to Palermo in the Sicily campaign. The men of the 3rd Infantry Division marching on foot were able to keep pace with the neighbouring 2nd Armored Division!

Infantry and Man-packed Gun teams move 16"/40cm instead of the normal 12"/30cm when moving At the Double.

The US Army was the only army in the world to fully equip its soldiers with semi-automatic weapons. The M1 Garand rifle reloaded itself after each shot, firing as fast as the soldier could pull the trigger, while other armies relied on bolt-action rifles that required the soldier to work the bolt after each shot. Combined with the Browning Automatic Rifle (B A R , but never 'bar' to a GI), the Garand gave each American soldier more firepower than any other.

Other armies lacking the same individual firepower relied on smaller squads armed with a light machine-gun to supplement their firepower. This provided them with greater firepower when defending, but was of less benefit when advancing.

Flames Of War reflects this in the squad-level firepower of the different platoons. US rifle squads have three Automatic Rifle teams, while most other armies have squads of just two Rifle/MG teams. This gives the American squad three shots whether advancing or defending, and when assaulted it re-rolls any misses, effectively adding another one or two shots. By comparison any other squad only has two shots when advancing, but manages four shots when defending.

This makes the Americans much more effective in attacks, and nearly as effective at long range and potentially more effective at short range when defending—a triumph of American industrial might and manpower.

AIR OBSERVATION POSTS

Column Security

In the breakout from Normandy the American forces started to use their air observation posts (AOP) for column security as well as for artillery spotting. They would fly along the intended route of advance looking for enemy ambushes, then warn the advancing ground troops.

If a US AOP (see page 139) did not act as an Observer team in its own turn, then in the opponent's turn, their teams may not be placed from Ambush (see page 266) within 12"/30cm of the AOP while in Line of Sight of it.

ARTILLERY

EXCELLENT COMMUNICATIONS

No other army has the communications resources of a US force. Plentiful radios give every officer the opportunity to request and range in artillery fire quickly and accurately.

Platoon and 2iC Command teams can act as Spotting teams and request artillery fire in the same manner as a Company Command team, suffering the same +1 penalty to Range In.

UNDER COMMAND

The mortar and assault gun platoons cooperate closely with the combat companies. Constant practice and excellent radio communications allow them to bring down quick and effective fire to support their combat platoons.

Company, 2iC, and any Platoon Command teams do not suffer their normal +1 penalty to Range In when calling for Artillery Bombardments from platoons taken as a Combat or Weapons platoon choice (including Weapons Platoons, Mortar Platoons, and Assault Gun platoons), as well as Cannon Platoons and Chemical Mortar Platoons taken as Support platoon choices.

HIT 'EM WITH EVERYTHING YOU'VE GOT

When a US observer team places a request for fire, the artillery battalion fire direction centre assesses its priority and assigns all available artillery batteries to the fire mission. This ensures that the battalion's artillery resources are used in the most efficient manner.

When a US artillery platoon that has a Staff team fires a bombardment, you may choose to group other artillery platoons into the same Artillery Bombardment before rolling to Range In. Treat all of the weapons as if they were from the same platoon when determining the effect of the Bombardment. Use the Mixed Bombardment rule on page 131 for the combined bombardment.

TIME ON TARGET

US artillery staffs have sophisticated fire-control computers. After checking the wind, temperature, and range, the battery staff officer selects the corresponding book and looks up the settings for every gun. This scientific marvel allows the officer to compute the flight time for each shell.

By working backwards, they can have every shell land at the same time without warning. With no time to react, troop concentrations caught in such a 'time on target' (TOT) bombardment are smashed before they have time to find cover.

Of course, once the first rounds have landed, the enemy has already taken cover, so a prolonged bombardment is no more effective than usual.

If an Artillery Battery with a Staff team Ranges In on their first attempt, they can fire a TOT Bombardment.

Every team hit by a TOT Bombardment must re-roll successful Saves in the first turn of the Bombardment as they scramble for cover and batten down the hatches.

This is for the first turn of the Bombardment only and does not apply to artillery firing an All Guns Repeat! Bombardment.

SUCCESSFUL AND FAILED SAVES

A successful Save is one where the Saving team is completely safe from harm without any Firepower Tests needing to be rolled. A team may fail their Save, and thereby not need to re-roll the Save, but still turn out to be unharmed. An example of this would be the target player rolling an Armour Save and exactly equalling the artillery's Anti-tank rating—a failed save, but then the US player fails their Firepower Test resulting in no harm to the target.

US M12 155mm GMC heavy self-propelled gun

German Special Rules

For over a century, the German Army has trained hard to a standardised doctrine while emphasising initiative in its junior officers. This combination created an army with unique tactical flexibility.

DOCTRINE

STORMTROOPERS

German soldiers have inherited the Stormtrooper ethos from their fathers in the First World War. While other armies wait for orders, the Stormtroopers are racing ahead to take their objective.

Any German platoon with a Platoon Command team may attempt a Stormtroopers move in its Assault Step.

Roll a Skill Test for each platoon.

- *If the test is passed, the platoon treats the Assault Step as a Movement Step in which it can move up to another 4"/10cm, regardless of its normal movement distance.*
- *If the test is failed, the platoon cannot move any further this turn.*

Either way, a platoon that attempts to make a Stormtroopers move cannot take any part in an assault in the same turn.

Although it is not the Movement Step, teams making a Stormtroopers move may Mount and Dismount as if it was the Movement Step.

Platoons cannot make Stormtroopers moves if they moved At the Double. Bogged Down or Bailed Out vehicles cannot make Stormtroopers moves.

Only Armoured vehicles can make Stormtroopers moves if they are Pinned Down. Other types of teams cannot make Stormtroopers moves if they are Pinned Down.

A team that used Eyes and Ears to reveal Gone to Ground enemy troops cannot make a Stormtroopers move.

Immobile Gun teams and Gun teams that shot earlier in the turn cannot make a Stormtroopers move. Teams of any type that have fired an Artillery Bombardment cannot make a Stormtroopers move. Trains cannot make a Stormtroopers move.

STORMTROOPERS

Kampfgruppe

The *Kampfgruppe*, or battle group, is an important part of German military operations. Leaders at every level form mission-specific task forces from any troops available.

At the start of the game before any platoons are Deployed and before any Combat Attachments are made, any company with a 2iC Command team may take up to half of the teams (counting the Platoon Command team) from any Combat or Weapons platoons in the company and place them in a special Kampfgruppe Platoon. The 2iC Command team is the Command team for this platoon.

You must leave at least two Tank teams or three other teams in each of the Combat or Weapons platoons you take teams from. Teams placed in the Kampfgruppe Platoon are no longer part of their original platoons.

If a platoon attaching troops to the Kampfgruppe has Transport teams, you must take the Transport team that normally carries a team into the Kampfgruppe with it. If that Transport team normally carries other teams as well, they must join the Kampfgruppe as well.

The Kampfgruppe Platoon may include any HQ Support Weapons (including Infantry teams). Any remaining HQ Support Weapons must be attached out as normal.

A Kampfgruppe made from the teams of a Fortified Platoon is not a Fortified Platoon and may not contain any of its component platoon's Fortifications.

The Kampfgruppe Platoon has the lowest Motivation rating and the lowest Skill rating of any of the teams in it.

Mission Tactics

Before battle, every soldier in the company is briefed on their mission and how it relates to the overall battle plan. Far from compromising security, this trust allows any soldier to take over when their superior is killed.

If a Platoon Command Infantry team is Destroyed, another team takes over immediately. Remove any other Infantry team in the platoon that is within Command Distance of the Command team and replace it with the original Platoon Command team. If the Platoon Command team was a Warrior team, it is now just a standard Platoon Command team.

If a Platoon Command Tank team is Destroyed, another team takes over immediately. Nominate any other Tank team in the platoon that is within Command Distance of the Destroyed Command team to be the new Platoon Command team.

If there is no team of an appropriate type within Command Distance, then the Platoon Command team is Destroyed and the platoon is left leaderless.

The original Platoon Command team can still use this rule while a Warrior team is leading the platoon and acting as its Command team, but the rule does not apply to the Warrior team.

Reich Divided

The Nazi leadership of the German Third Reich may have shared common goals, but they all wanted to be top dog. *Reichsmarschall* Hermann Göring attempted to expand the control and influence of his *Luftwaffe* (Air Force) as much as possible, even going to the extent of forming 'parachute' armoured divisions and dozens of infantry divisions. *Reichsführer* Heinrich Himmler meanwhile was expanding his *SS* (*Schutzstaffel* or Protection Squad) to include not only the infamous *Gestapo* and concentration camps, but also full armoured corps and dozens of infantry divisions as well. Both the *Luftwaffe* and the *SS* were considered 'politically reliable', distinguishing them from the 'reactionary' *Heer* (Army) with its long-standing traditions.

All of these fell under the command of the *Heer* (Army) in the field, but jealously guarded their prerogatives in every other respect, having separate recruiting and training and even their own generals. All three competed for the latest equipment and replacements. This competition often limited their cooperation in the field.

Heer, Luftwaffe, and SS are all treated as Allies (see page 70). Fallschirmjäger are part of the Luftwaffe, so are not Allies to them, but are Allies to the Heer and SS.

German Panther tank

ARMOURED INFANTRY

Mounted Assault

German armoured half-tracks are unique in having a dedicated vehicle commander (who crews the machine-gun) as well as a driver. This gives them a greater degree of independence than similar vehicles in other armies. They have learned to fight from their half-tracks in contrast to others who just use their half-tracks as battle taxis.

Armoured Transport teams in a platoon with the Mounted Assault special rule are Mounted Assault Transports.

A Mounted Assault Transport has a dual nature. While empty, it is just an ordinary Transport team, except that they do not have to be Sent to the Rear when empty—they can remain on the table and continue to fight.

When carrying Passengers, a Mounted Assault Transport is treated as a Tank team for everything except Platoon Morale Checks. If it is carrying two or more Passenger teams, it also has Tank Escorts.

As a Tank team, a Mounted Assault Transport team carrying Passengers may Charge into Contact and fight in assault combat. As Open-topped Tank teams, the platoon will be forced to Fall Back by five hits or two Destroyed or Bailed Out vehicles in Defensive Fire (see page 154).

If a Mounted Assault Transport team is Destroyed by Defensive Fire, all surviving Passengers Fall Back 2"/5cm away from the teams they were charging. If the Passengers cannot do this, they are Destroyed. The platoon is not automatically Pinned Down when the Passengers Dismount, and will only Fall Back if it takes five hits as usual. If a Mounted Assault Transport team is Destroyed during the assault, any Passengers are Destroyed with it.

The Passengers do not need to Dismount to Counterattack. They can stay Mounted or Dismount as they wish. If they Dismount to Counterattack, their Transport team will be Sent to the Rear.

If the platoon voluntarily Breaks Off instead of Counter-attacking, and the entire platoon is mounted in Mounted Assault Transport teams, they may use the Break Off Through the Enemy rule (see page 166) as if they were Tank teams.

At the end of the Assault Step, Mounted Assault Transport teams that are Bailed Out are Sent to the Rear if they have no Passengers, or automatically Remount (see page 102) and are no longer Bailed Out if they have Passengers.

Mounted Assault

TIGER ACES

Tiger tanks are considered vital to Germany's war effort and only the best candidates are selected to crew them. Once in battle, the tough hides of their mounts gives the crews unprecedented survivability, letting them learn the nuances of the battlefield while racking up impressive scores of destroyed enemy tanks and guns.

These men were highly skilled and led by some of the best tank commanders that have ever been. Officers like Michael Wittmann and Otto Carius learned their trade on lesser Panzer tanks or StuG assault guns.

Once in command of the fearsome Tiger tank, they showed what they could do with the best equipment available.

To reflect the abilities and experience of these exceptional soldiers, *Flames Of War* gives each platoon of Tiger tanks its own Tiger Ace Skill. This skill gives them the ability to perform the incredible feats of the real tankers that manned these formidable machines.

At the start of the game before deployment, roll a die for each Warrior or platoon with the Tiger Aces special rule (including any Kampfgruppe made entirely teams from platoons with the Tiger Aces special rule), then look up their Tiger Ace Skill on the table below.

If the Tiger Ace Skill is specifically rolled for the Platoon Command team or a Warrior team, it only applies to that team unless it is Schnell, Clever Hans, or For the Fatherland, in which case any platoon it is part of also receives the benefit.

TIGER ACE SKILLS

SCHNELL!

This platoon believes in the importance of speed and most of their kills have been racked up through being at the right place at the right time!

The platoon may make Stormtroopers moves on a roll of 2+.

CLEVER HANS!

The drivers of this platoon are masters of their vehicles. No matter how difficult the terrain or how firmly stuck they appear to be, they'll have their tank through the obstacle in no time.

Tanks in this platoon re-roll failed Bogging Checks to cross Rough Terrain and Skill Tests to free a Bogged Down tank. If they have Wide Tracks (see page 61), they roll to Free themselves (see page 44) after re-rolling the Bogging Check.

FOR THE FATHERLAND!

The soldiers of this platoon love their country. They know how important their part in Germany's final victory is and will fight to their utmost to secure it.

The platoon passes Motivation Tests on a roll of 2+.

EVERY SHOT COUNTS!

The outstanding teamwork and excellent gunners of this platoon ensure that almost every shot hits its target.

Tiger tanks in this platoon re-roll any failed roll to hit when they shoot.

RAPID FIRE!

Superb teamwork between the commander, the gunner, and the loader means that this platoon maintains a high rate of fire in combat.

The 8.8cm tank guns of the Tiger tanks in this platoon have ROF 3.

TOP ACE!

The commander of this platoon is a top gun, a real *Kanone*!

Roll again to determine the platoon's Tiger Ace Skill. If you roll 6 again, you may choose the platoon's skill.

In addition, Roll a third time to generate an extra skill specifically for the Platoon Command tank. This gives the platoon commander two Tiger Ace Skills (the one for the platoon as a whole, and their own one specific to them). If you roll a 6 or the same number as the platoon's Tiger Ace Skill, you may choose the platoon commander's extra skill.

TANKS

Schürzen

Schürzen are the thin armoured plates hung on the sides of some German tanks to protect them from infantry anti-tank weapons, like anti-tank rifles and bazookas.

When a tank that is protected by Schürzen is hit by a weapon with a Firepower of 5+ or 6 on the Side armour by shooting and fails its Armour Save, roll a special 4+ Schürzen save:

- *If the save is successful the Schürzen protects the tank from the side shot.*
- *If the save is not successful the shot penetrated the side armour as normal.*

Begleit Escorts

The Germans copied the Soviet practice of providing their assault guns with *Begleit,* or escort, infantry to protect them against infantry assaults. While aboard, the *Begleit* troops fire the assault gun's machine gun across the roof, freeing the gun's crew to concentrate on providing cannon support.

Assault guns with Tank Escorts use all the normal Tank Escort rules. In addition, an assault gun with Tank Escorts may fire its Hull MG at the same time as its hull-mounted main gun. This does not prevent the Tank Escorts from shooting as well.

ARTILLERY

Armoured Rocket Launchers

Armoured rocket launchers can fire all of the rockets quickly before scooting off to a new location.

An Artillery platoon equipped with Armoured Rocket Launcher teams that fired may take a Skill Test in the Assault Step instead of making a Stormtroopers move or taking part in an Assault:

- *If they pass the Skill Test, remove the Smoke Trail markers from all Rocket Launcher teams (see page 138).*
- *Otherwise, they are too slow in getting away, leaving them vulnerable to counterbattery artillery fire.*

Stuka zu Fuss

Sd Kfz 251 half-tracks in the third platoon of the *Panzerpionierkompanie* are fitted with *Wurfrahmen,* frames for six huge 28cm rockets. These were so devastating that they were called *Stuka zu Fuss*—Stuka on foot.

Each Stuka zu Fuss rocket launcher can only fire one Artillery Bombardment in a game, but counts as six weapons firing when it does so.

You may take up to six attempts to Range In with each Stuka zu Fuss rocket launcher. Each failed attempt reduces the number of weapons firing by one. If you fail all six attempts to Range In, the rockets have all been fired, but missed, and no Bombardment is possible.

If multiple Stuka zu Fuss rocket launchers from the same platoon fire, place a separate Template and roll to Range In separately with each as if they were separate artillery batteries. Complete each Stuka zu Fuss rocket launcher's Bombardment before beginning the next

The half-track is still available to transport its passengers after the Stuka zu Fuss fires.

German armoured infantry fighting alongside their Sd Kfz 251 half-tracks

BRITISH SPECIAL RULES

It has been said of the British Army that they always start a war by losing battles. However, they are nothing if not stubborn and persistent, and in the end they always come out winning the critical campaigns.

DOCTRINE

BRITISH BULLDOG

Some 200 years ago, a French general remarked that the British troops his infantry attacked appeared to have taken root and be stuck to the ground. They refused to run away when other troops would have. Nothing has changed and British soldiers still have a reputation for tenacity and stubbornly refusing to give up ground that they have taken.

When British platoons test their Motivation to Counterattack in assaults, you may re-roll the die and apply the re-rolled result to all British platoons that failed on the original roll.

CARRY ON, SERGEANT

The backbone of the British Army is its Sergeants. Many a new subaltern has been advised to let the Sergeant run the platoon and to follow his advice. If the officer is killed, the Sergeant is more than able to keep the platoon fighting.

A British platoon may Charge into Combat and Consolidate without having a Platoon Command team, and if it does so, the Assaulting teams do not need to be or remain In Command.

NIGHT ATTACK

British infantry often timed major attacks to start in the middle of the night. In theory this provided the infantry with a cloak of darkness to conceal them from enemy fire until they had taken their objectives and dug in to hold them.

In practice, delays often meant that the attack found itself still embroiled with the enemy at dawn and subjected to vicious counterattacks as the day began.

A player commanding a British Infantry Company may elect to make a Night Attack in missions that do not use the Meeting Engagement special rule (see page 264). If they do so, the game starts at night and uses the Dawn rules on page 273.

When making a Night Attack, the company has the Always Attack special rule (see page 257), and all British platoons containing only Infantry teams can use the Spearhead special rule (see page 261).

ANTI-TANK GUNS

TIP AND RUN

Portee-mounted anti-tank guns were originally meant to dismount to fight. Adventurous crews soon devised tactics for hiding behind a ridge, scoring a quick, short-range volley, then running before the enemy can catch them out.

A British Platoon with the Tip and Run special rule may attempt to Tip and Run immediately after shooting.

Roll a Skill Test for the platoon.

- *If the test is passed, the platoon treats the remainder of the Shooting Step as a Movement Step in which it can move up to another 4"/10cm away from all enemy platoons that it shot at.*
- *If the test is failed, the platoon remains where it is.*

Either way, a platoon that attempts to Tip and Run cannot take any part in an assault in the same turn.

TOW HOOKS

The infantry often had difficulty getting their anti-tank guns forward after attacks, so an armoured brigade in Tunisia devised a very clever solution. They fitted their tanks with tow hooks allowing them to tow the 6 pdr guns. It worked so well that soon almost every British tank was fitted with a tow hook.

Any tank fitted with a tow hook may tow a 6 pdr or 17 pdr gun, carrying the crew as Passengers riding on the Tanks (see page 47).

TANKS

Semi-indirect Fire

British heavy tanks often open fire at very long ranges, where their prolific use of ammunition can compensate for the difficulty of hitting the target. It means that their ammo racks empty fast, but there's plenty more available for resupply.

Weapons capable of Semi-indirect Fire that didn't move in the Movement Step may re-roll failed rolls to hit when shooting their main guns at platoons with all teams more than 16"/40cm away.

Tally Ho!

British doctrine requires cruiser tanks to either remain concealed or be moving when under fire. Under no circumstances should they halt in the open. For this to work, the tanks have to be capable of firing accurately on the move.

To facilitate accurate shooting on the move, cruiser tanks have high-speed power traverse systems capable of spinning the turret through a full circle in 10 seconds and freely-mounted guns. The 2 pdr guns have no elevating controls. Instead the gunner aims the gun using his shoulder, making them very accurate on the move at short ranges.

Tally Ho! means that the listed weapon does not suffer any penalty to its ROF for shooting on the move at ranges up to 16"/40cm. In effect, it is assumed to be firing on the move at all times!

Teams with Tally Ho! still cannot shoot when moving At the Double.

Broadside

The British view tank battles as land-based naval battles with the 'cruiser' squadrons steaming out to battle enemy tanks while the other arms watch and wait for their fate to be decided. As a result, cruiser tanks 'steam' in naval formations such as 'line abreast' and charge through the enemy lines firing 'broadsides'.

Only the turret facing is used in determining whether a shot hits the front or the side armour of a tank with a weapon that uses the Tally Ho! rule. The facing of the hull is irrelevant.

The Broadside rule does not apply when the tanks move At the Double, as they always march with their turrets pointing forwards.

Looking Good on the Move

Britain was one of the few armies to put a full turret crew of commander, gunner, and loader in their tanks right from the beginning. This efficient arrangement would normally give a better rate of fire, but the Tally Ho! rule trades this for the ability to fire on the move instead.

With Tally Ho! allowing British Cruisers to race around the table, the Broadside rule makes them look good while they are doing it. With Broadside, players can have their tanks racing past the enemy firing as they go.

British OQF 25 pdr field guns

ARTILLERY

Eight-gun or Twelve-Gun Batteries

British artillery batteries have two or three mostly independent troops of four guns apiece. By comparison, most countries have only four guns in the whole battery!

British Artillery Batteries with Staff teams use the Independent Command, Combined Bombardment, and Mixed Battery special rules. In the Mid and Late-war periods, they also use the Mike Target special rule. British Artillery Batteries in the Early-war period never use the Mike Target special rule.

Independent Command

British artillery used a flexible battery structure with two or three semi-independent troops. These troops could operate separately, but fire together allowing more guns to be brought to bear on the target without creating a clumped target for enemy artillery or aircraft.

The battery's Staff team must be attached to a Gun Troop from its battery at the start of the game before deployment. However, any Gun Troop within Command Distance of the battery's Staff team, counts as having a Staff team (allowing it to use the All Guns Repeat! rule).

If the battery has an HQ Troop Command team, it must also be attached to a Gun Troop from its battery at the start of the game before deployment, becoming the Platoon Command team for the Gun Troop. If the HQ Troop Command team is Destroyed, the original Platoon Command team resumes that role.

Combined Bombardment

In the First World War, British gunners quickly learned that it took an immense amount of heavy artillery to destroy dug-in infantry, more than they could muster. What they found worked better was smothering the target with lighter shells to pin the defenders down before the infantry assaulted them.

The Gun Troop with the battery's Staff team, or any other Gun Troop within Command Distance of the battery's Staff team, may act as the base of a Combined Bombardment using the Mixed Bombardment rule on page 131. Any other Gun Troops from the battery (whether or not they are near the Staff team) may join the base troop before rolling to Range In and fire as a single combined Artillery Battery.

If a Gun Troop from another battery that has the Combined Bombardment special rule has a Staff team or is within Command Distance of its Staff team, it may also be combined into the Bombardment, along with any other Gun Troops from its battery.

Mike Target

Prewar British artillery doctrine called for precision fire aimed at destroying individual positions. While this was useful for small colonial wars, in the fast-moving battles in the desert, the gunners soon learned that getting rounds on the ground as fast as possible was more important. Now British artillery has the fastest response times in the world.

Within minutes of a target being identified British artillery can arrange a 'stonk' on any target. If necessary, the observer used the code 'Mike Target' when ordering a bombardment. A Mike Target required every gun in the regiment that wasn't otherwise occupied to join in!

Within a relatively short space of time 24 guns would be pounding the target as fast as the loaders could shove the rounds in the breach. The effect was dramatic, leading German prisoners to ask to see the 'belt-fed' artillery on their way to the rear!

A battery may re-roll their first failed attempt to Range In. If they fail on the re-roll, they still have two more ranging attempts left as normal. They do not get a re-roll on their second and third attempts.

When a battery repeats a Bombardment using the All Guns Repeat! rule, the entire regiment joins in. As a result any teams caught under the Bombardment must re-roll successful Saves.

Some rules refer to Bombardments using the Mike Target special rule as Stonks or Murders.

Successful Saves

A successful Save is one where the Saving team is completely safe from harm without any Firepower Tests needing to be rolled.

HMG Bombardments

The British concentrated most of their Vickers medium machine-guns (rated as heavy machine-guns by most nations!) in specialist machine-gun battalions. These used the full range of machine-gun tactics, including long range area bombardments.

Some units, such as the machine-gun platoon of a motor battalion, did not receive such specialised training and used their weapons in a more conventional fashion.

British Vickers HMG teams, and HMG Carriers firing as HMG teams, can fire bombardments (unless their platoon entry specifically says otherwise). These are conducted in the same way as any other Artillery Bombardment. However, since they have Anti-tank and Firepower ratings of '-', they cannot harm Armoured vehicles or Destroy teams in Bulletproof Cover, although they can still Pin them Down.

Soviet Special Rules

The Red Army entered the war in a state of chaos. Stalin's purges had eliminated the professional officers before the war, then German victories wiped out the entire prewar army within months. The Red Army desperately rebuilt its strength with barely-trained conscripts. Years of hard fighting forged the survivors into a war-winning force capable of taking on and beating the best the enemy could offer.

DOCTRINE

Komissar

A Komissar is a Communist Party official who supervises the soldiers to make sure they display the proper level of enthusiasm in battle. A lack of heroism in driving the Hitlerites from Mother Russia is not acceptable and the Komissar will not hesitate to shoot soldiers who show fear during battle. As Comrade Stalin said, 'It takes a brave man not to be a hero in the Red Army.'

A Komissar team may attempt to force their troops to obey orders after failing a Motivation Test to Rally from being Pinned Down, to Counterattack in an assault (provided the Komissar is an Assaulting team), or to pass a Platoon Morale Check (but not for Tank Terror or any other Motivation Tests).

A Komissar attempting to force their troops to obey orders must be In Command, and must immediately Destroy one Infantry or Gun team from their own platoon (Soviet company) that is within the Command Distance of the Komissar team. The Komissar team cannot Destroy an Warrior team, Independent team, or itself in this way.

If you roll a 1 for a Motivation Test re-rolled using this rule, the soldiers are pushed past the point of breaking and revolt against the Komissar! In this case the Komissar team is Destroyed as well.

If the Company Command team of the company (Soviet battalion) or a Higher Command team has joined the company, re-roll the Motivation Test for the commander's influence first. If the unit fails the re-roll, the Komissar can then attempt to force the platoon (Soviet Company) to obey orders. This is an exception to the rule preventing a test from being re-rolled more than once (see page 20).

Battalion Komissar

As well as the Komissar assigned to each company, your battalion has a senior Komissar responsible for the entire battalion. Their role is to assist their deputies in removing particularly dangerous traitors and restoring discipline should it break down.

The Battalion Komissar team in the company (Soviet battalion) HQ is a Warrior team. If the Battalion Komissar team Joins a platoon (Soviet company), it takes over the duties of the normal Komissar team. The Komissar team has no effect as long as the Battalion Komissar team remains joined to the platoon (Soviet company).

Komissar

Centralised Control

The Soviet economy and social system emphasises centralised planning and control by the government, and this applies to the army as well. Soviet generals prefer their troops to strictly obey orders, rather than think for themselves. To reflect this, Soviet forces are organised differently from other armies. For game purposes, a Soviet company is treated as a single platoon and a whole battalion operates like most armies' companies.

Wherever the rules talk about a platoon, you can also read that as a Soviet company. Where the rules talk about a company, you can also read that as a Soviet battalion.

Thus a Soviet company is led by a Platoon Command team and operates like a large platoon. A Soviet battalion is led by a Company Command team and operates as a large company. This means that while a German platoon must remain in command to move freely, an entire Soviet company must be in command to do the same. Similarly, while the enemy shoots at a US platoon, they shoot at a Soviet company.

Infiltration

Soviet soldiers have a reputation for being long-suffering and tough-minded. They swim freezing rivers and wade through trackless swamps in the pitch darkness to reach positions close to, or even behind, the enemy before the battle begins. Of course, one careless slip, a too loud curse, and the enemy are alerted too soon!

A platoon that has the Infiltration special rule lists the types of platoon (Soviet company) that they can Infiltrate with. The platoon may Infiltrate with one platoon (Soviet company) of the listed type, and any Warrior teams that Join them, when they are attacking in a mission with Prepared Positions and have the first turn.

Instead of making a Recce Deployment Move, the Infiltration platoon and the platoon and Warriors Infiltrating with it move up to 16"/40cm (regardless of their Movement Distance), remaining within Command Distance of each other, and taking any rolls needed to cross Rough Terrain and Obstacles. Their movement may not take them within 8"/20cm of any enemy team.

Any Infiltrating team that ends this movement within 16"/40cm and in of Line of Sight of an enemy team is automatically detected if they are either not Concealed from the enemy team, or the enemy team is a Recce team.

If the Infiltrating troops are not automatically detected, the opposing player rolls a die:

- *On a roll of 6, they are detected.*
- *Otherwise, they have infiltrated undetected.*

If the Infiltrators are detected, the Infiltrating player gives the first turn to their opponent.

Ignore enemy Warrior and Independent teams when Infiltrating. They do not limit an Infiltrating team's movement in any way and cannot detect them.

ARTILLERY

Steel Wall

The Soviet Union combined 122mm howitzers with 76mm guns in their divisional artillery battalions. The lighter guns are deadly rolled forward to shoot over open sights while the howitzers bombard from behind. Combined, their bombardments are highly effective.

Artillery batteries (Soviet artillery battalions) combining 76mm guns (such as the 76mm ZIS-3), 122mm howitzers (such as the 122mm obr 1938), and 120mm mortars (such as the 120-PM-38) may fire their 122mm howitzers and 120mm mortars as a separate battery apart from their 76mm guns.

If any 122mm howitzer or 120mm mortar fires an Artillery Bombardment, you must elect to either:

- *include any or all of the 76mm guns in the Bombardment (using the Mixed Bombardment rule on page 131), but not shoot with the remaining 76mm guns, or*
- *exclude all of the 76mm guns from the Artillery Bombardment, shooting normally with the 76mm guns instead.*

This rule overrides the No Splitting of Artillery Fire rule on page 123.

Roll Up the Guns

The Red Army has a doctrine of keeping its guns right up in the front line where they can fire over open sights. To make this possible, they design their guns to be light enough for the crews to push.

Soviet Medium and Heavy Gun teams and Staff teams move as if they were Light Gun teams.

Volley Fire

When the advancing Soviet army came across a German strongpoint, assault guns and artillery batteries stopped to blast it using a massive centralised volley.

If they did not move in the Movement Step, Gun teams and Turretless Tank teams (such as the SU-76, SU-122, and ISU series) may re-roll failed rolls To Hit when shooting, provided the easiest team to hit in the target platoon is within 16"/40cm.

It takes time to build up the volume of fire that Soviet gunners prefer, making it impossible to use volley fire tactics effectively in a hastily-organised ambush.

The Volley Fire rule does not apply to vehicle machine-guns, HMG teams or any Anti-aircraft weapon, nor when firing Artillery Bombardments, in Defensive Fire, or conducting an Ambush or Ambuscade.

INFANTRY

Quality of Quantity

The Russians have a saying that 'quantity has a quality all of its own.' The big formations used by the Red Army take a lot of shooting to stop.

A platoon (Soviet company) with at least fifteen Infantry or Gun teams In Command has Quality of Quantity. Include the Komissar team, any attached teams, and any Warrior and Independent teams that have Joined it when determining if a platoon (Soviet company) has Quality of Quantity.

A platoon (Soviet company) starting the Shooting Step with Quality of Quantity must take at least ten hits (instead of the usual five) in a single Shooting Step before they become Pinned Down, although a single hit from an Artillery Bombardment still Pins them Down.

Teams from a platoon (Soviet company) starting the Assault Step with Quality of Quantity may Charge into Contact and Counterattack from 12"/30cm away from the enemy rather than 8"/20cm as usual. Teams further than 12"/30cm are still Non-assaulting teams.

A platoon (Soviet company) with at least fifteen Assaulting Infantry teams must take at least ten hits in Defensive Fire before they are Pinned Down and forced to Fall Back.

Shtraf Companies

Stalin's infamous Order 227—Not One Step Back—formed *Shtrafniye Roti* or Penal Companies in each Army. These were used as assault troops on risky operations where they could redeem themselves with their blood.

Since the soldiers of the Shtraf Company can only gain pardon for their crimes (such as spreading defeatist propaganda, failing to report defeatist talk, failing to shoot traitors attempting to desert or surrender, etc.) with their blood, they tend to be hard to stop.

Any battalion fielding a Shtraf Company must Always Attack in any mission. As an assault unit, a Shtraf Company can never attempt to Dig In and never benefits from the Prepared Positions special rule.

Soldiers were sent to serve in a Shtraf Company because of failure on the battlefield. As such, a Shtraf Company always passes a Motivation Test on a roll of 2+.

Because it is expected to die, a Shtraf Company is totally ignored when taking a Company Morale Check. It does not add to the number of operational platoons, nor does it count as Destroyed if it suffers that fate.

Soviet ISU-152 assault-gun

TANKS

Hen and Chicks

Soviet tank losses were incredible. In 1942, they built 10,000 light tanks, 12,000 medium tanks, and 2,000 heavy tanks, and received 4,500 more from Britain, Canada, and America. In that year they lost 16,000 of them, far more tanks than any other army even possessed! The only way the Red Army could keep up with such losses was to rush tank crews into battle with minimal training. Combined with a lack of radios and a preference for going into battle with all hatches closed, this resulted in Soviet tanks blindly following their company commander, as the Germans described it 'like chicks following the mother hen'.

If a Platoon Command team moves in the Movement Step, all of the Tank and Transport teams in its platoon (Soviet company) must move as well.

If the Platoon Command team does not move, only Tank and Transport teams that started the Movement Step Out of Command may move.

Any vehicle that moves adds +1 to the score required to hit when shooting with its main gun or guns. This gives a cumulative penalty of +2 for ROF 1 weapons. Machine-guns and Flame-throwers do not suffer this penalty.

Cupolas

From the middle of 1943 new T-34 tanks were fitted with a commander's cupola to improve their vision.

Tanks fitted with a commander's cupola do not suffer the effects of Limited Vision (see page 118).

Tankodesantniki

The tanks of the Red Army suffered heavy losses to infantry tank-hunter teams. The solution was to protect the tanks with *tankodesantniki*, submachine-gun armed troops who ride to battle on the back of their tanks.

Tanks with Tankodesantniki have Tank Escorts (see pages 200 and 201).

Tank-rider Companies

The Red Army backed up the *tankodesantniki* tank escorts with tank rider companies trained to ride tanks into battle, then dismount and clear terrain ahead of the tanks.

Teams from Tank-rider Companies have a 3+ Save while Mounted on a Tank team as Passengers. They do not need to Dismount Under Fire when hit. They can remain on the tanks instead.

Hen and Chicks

MISSIONS

German StuG assault guns and SS infantry assault American paratroopers

CONTENTS

German infantry run past a burnt out Soviet T-34 obr 1942 tank
IWM HU28381

PLAYING MISSIONS

While you can just stick your forces on the table and fight until one side is completely destroyed, missions and scenarios can add a whole new level to the game as players struggle to take or defend specific objectives or achieve other goals vital to their side's war effort.

What's in a Mission

All missions in *Flames Of War* are organised to give you the critical information you need to play the mission in the order you need it.

Description and Special Rules

Each mission starts with a general briefing explaining the mission and a list of the special rules to be used. You can find the special rules on pages 264 to 271).

Your Orders

The second section defines the goals of both the attacking and defending players in general terms. This gives the battle some context and guides the players towards victory.

Table Map

Each mission has a table map that provides a visual reference for the deployment areas, objective areas, and the location of No man's Land, as well as indicating where any reserves and reinforcements will come from.

Preparing for Battle

The next section explains how the battle is set up. Most missions have objectives that the players have to capture, and this section tells where the objectives are placed. It also defines the deployment areas of both players and tells them how to deploy their forces.

Beginning the Battle

This section tells the players the state of their forces at the beginning of the battle and tells them who gets the first turn. It also walks them through last-minute pre-battle activity such as advanced reconnaissance and sneaky infiltration by one or both sides.

Ending the Battle

The next section defines the ending conditions of the game, usually either the capture of an objective or clear evidence of its successful defence.

Deciding Who Won

The last section tells which of the players has won the game and how well they did. This is a more game-based definition of the players goals than those given in the Your Orders section and is usually based on who holds certain objectives at the end of the battle.

Standard Missions

There are twelve standard missions included in the rule book. Similar missions are grouped together so that you can select new variations on a mission you've tried before rather than playing the same mission again.

Fair Fight Missions

In Fair fight missions the attackers and defenders face identical challenges.

- **Free-for-all:** A typical meeting engagement where players face off across the table, trying to take objectives in the opponent's area.
- **Encounter:** Similar to Free-for-all, but with half of each force coming on as scattered reserves.
- **Dust Up:** Similar to Encounter, but fought diagonally across the table with aggressive reserves arriving near the objectives.

Defensive Battle Missions

In defensive missions, the attacker seeks to capture objectives held by the defender.

- **No Retreat:** A basic attack/defence mission where the defender has a platoon in ambush, but half of their force in reserve.
- **Hold the Line:** Similar to No Retreat, but with two defending ambushes and the reserves arriving later.
- **Pincer:** Similar to No Retreat, but with the reserves arriving later and on the attacker's flanks.
- **Surrounded:** The defender starts with their entire force in play, but under attack from two directions.
- **Fighting Withdrawal:** The defender starts with their entire force in play, but must withdraw platoons as the game goes on, holding out for eight turns.

Mobile Battle Missions

In mobile warfare missions the defender is forced to fight a mobile battle to hold their objectives.

- **Hasty Attack:** Both sides start with half their forces in reserve, although the attacker's reserves are closer.
- **Cauldron:** The defender is cut off and must be relieved by their reserves.
- **Breakthrough:** The defender's mobile troops rush to stop an outflanking attack by the attacker.
- **Counterattack:** The attacker must stop the defender from linking up with a trapped pocket.

Trench Warfare Mission

No Man's Land is a special mission for battles taking place in No Man's Land between two fortified forces.

WHICH MISSION TO PLAY

A common question when two players arrange a game is 'which mission shall we play?'. There are a number of ways of answering this question.

Some players just elect to play Free-for-all since it is the simplest mission. The downside of playing endless games of Free-for-all is that games get rather same-ish— always the same tactical challenges and objectives.

Another way of deciding which mission to play is to roll on the Random Mission Table. This is quick and simple and provides a wide variety of tactical challenges and differing objectives for both sides.

A third method is to look at the forces and the table set up and pick a mission that looks challenging and interesting (or perhaps just one you haven't played in a while). This method takes a bit more thinking, but can result in really interesting and challenging games. A fun variant on this is to get a mutual friend to pick a mission for you. This can result in some really intriguing games as forces struggle to overcome their own limitations and the terrain to best an opponent facing equally challenging, but different problems.

Finally, if you are feeling like something really different, you could take one of the missions as a basic idea and modify it. Reading about historical battles can provide inspiration for scenarios like this. As you are reading, you might think, 'that sounds like Dust Up, but different'. In that case, take the Dust Up mission and play around with the rules, perhaps giving one side more troops on table, but making the other side's reserves come on faster to better match the actual battle.

You can take this a step further by specifying the forces that both sides will use for your scenario. Adding this last step can lead to some truly fiendish situations where you or your friends have to hold against desperate odds, only saved by the river with just two bridges that the enemy has to cross, or perhaps it really is a doomed last stand and the goal isn't to win, just to see how long you can hold out and how much you can make the enemy pay for your eventual defeat!

In the end, it's up to your combined imaginations how far you take it. You might even want to model some specific terrain features or paint up some new units (or even a whole company) to recreate the battles you read about in history.

German SS soldier

RANDOM MISSIONS

Roll a die to determine which group of missions you'll play, then another to pick the specific mission.

FAIR FIGHT MISSIONS	
1. Free-for-all	page 276
2. Encounter	page 277
3. Dust Up	page 278
DEFENSIVE MISSIONS	
4. No Retreat	page 279
5. Hold the Line	page 280
6. Pincer	page 281

DEFENSIVE MISSIONS (CONTINUED)	
1. Surrounded	page 282
2. Fighting Withdrawal	page 283
MOBILE WARFARE MISSIONS	
3. Hasty Attack	page 284
4. Cauldron	page 285
5. Breakthrough	page 286
6. Counterattack	page 287

DECIDING WHO ATTACKS

The forces fighting a battle are rarely perfectly matched. One side or the other will be better equipped to launch an attack having masses of tanks or specialised engineering equipment like armoured flame-throwers. By the same token, a force may be heavily fortified with lots of infantry and guns, more ready to conduct a stout defence than an attack. The nature of the two sides determines which side attacks in any battle.

Every force is described in its Intelligence briefing as a Tank, Mechanised, Infantry or Fortified Company.

Tank Companies Attack

Tanks are expensive to build and maintain. They are held in reserve until the time is right for a big attack.

A Tank Company will always be the attacker against a Mechanised, Infantry, or Fortified Company.

Mechanised Companies Attack

Armoured infantry follow the tanks, expanding the breakthrough and holding the gains against enemy counterattacks.

A Mechanised Company will always be the defender against a Tank Company and the attacker against an Infantry or Fortified Company.

Infantry Companies Defend

Infantry are the workhorse of any army. They hold the line during quiet periods, and launch attacks against opposing infantry.

An Infantry Company will always be the defender against a Tank or Mechanised Company and the attacker against a Fortified Company.

Fortified Companies Defend

Soldiers manning fortifications hunkered down behind barbed wire and minefields, sheltering in bunkers, waiting for the enemy to attack. In static warfare, neither side will launch an all-out attack. Instead they aggressively patrol No Man's Land, particularly at night.

A Fortified Company will always be the defender against a Tank, Mechanised, or Infantry Company.

Always Attacks

Forces like breakthrough tank units and *Shtraf* penal units, are only sent to the front for major attacks.

Some companies have a special rule requiring them to Always Attack. These forces will always attack any other force that does not have the Always Attack special rule.

Always Defends

Some forces are focused on defence, holding the line until other formations can launch a decisive counterattack.

Some companies have a special rule requiring them to Always Defend. These forces will always defend against any other force that is not a Fortified Company and does not have the Always Defend special rule.

Roll for Ties

While there is a natural tendency for tanks to attack and infantry to defend, when two forces of the same type face each other, it is up to the vagaries of the battlefield as to which will attack and which defend.

When two companies of the same type face off, both players roll a die and the player with the higher score attacks. In the event of a tie roll again.

When two Fortified Companies face off, we recommend that they play the No Man's Land mission (see page 288) rather than normal missions.

SUMMARY

- **Tank Companies attack Mechanised Companies who attack Infantry Companies who attack Fortified Companies.**
- **Always Attacks and Always Defends override the normal rules.**
- **In a tie, roll off with higher score attacking.**
- **Two Fortified Companies should play the No Man's Land mission.**

British soldier

MISSION OBJECTIVES

Though skirmishes where enemies randomly encounter each other happen, most battles are fought over specific objectives that are pivotal to the plans of both armies.

Modelling Objectives

While you can use a spare large base as an objective marker, it is a lot more fun to do a little modelling and stick a broken-down tank or stack of supplies on the base and create a mini diorama.

Objectives are modelled on a standard large base (2½"/63mm wide by 2"/50mm deep).

Objectives are not Terrain, regardless of what is modelled on the base. They do not hinder movement or provide Concealment or Bulletproof Cover, nor do they block Line of Sight. They are simply markers to indicate the importance of this point to the combatants.

> If combat takes place on and around an Objective, it can be easier to replace the Objective with a plain large base until the fighting moves away again.

Placing Objectives

Commanders set a wide variety of objectives ranging from woods, towns, isolated buildings, and hilltops to lines drawn across open ground on a map.

You may not place an Objective where it will not sit flat (or relatively flat) on the table or a piece of terrain, such as leaning up against a hedge or a cliff for instance.

You may place an Objective in a building. If the building is too small to fit the Objective Marker inside it, treat the whole building as the Objective. If the building is smaller than an Objective Marker, it is too unimportant to be an Objective.

You also may not place an Objective in Impassable Terrain, or in a place that could only be reached from the enemy Deployment Area by crossing Impassable Terrain.

Taking Objectives

In most missions your company can only claim victory by occupying the objective after driving the enemy off.

You have Taken an Objective if you start your turn with a team within 4"/10cm of the Objective and the enemy has no teams within 4"/10cm of the Objective.

Objectives cannot be Taken by Tank teams that are Bailed Out or Bogged Down, Transport teams, or Independent teams (but can be taken by Warrior Teams). Nor can these teams prevent the enemy from Taking an Objective. On the other hand, Pinned Down teams can both Take and prevent the enemy from Taking an objective.

Teams that moved At the Double or Disengaged in their previous turn cannot take an Objective nor prevent the enemy from taking it.

Failed Company Morale

It's not much of a victory to take an objective only to abandon it moments later.

If you fail a Company Morale Check (see page 175), your force flees the battlefield leaving all Objectives to be automatically Taken by the enemy.

SUMMARY

- **Objectives are modelled on a large base and must be placed flat on the table.**
- **Take Objectives by having the only active teams within 4"/10cm of it.**
- **If the enemy fails their Company Morale Check, you take all of the Objectives.**

Taking Objectives

DEPLOYING YOUR FORCE

Each mission has its own variations on where and when the players deploy their forces, but they all have a number of things in common.

Deployment Area

Armies move and fight as a single entity, so when they clash with the enemy, there is usually a clearly defined area that is 'ours' and one that is 'theirs', separated by a No Man's Land belonging to neither.

Each mission describes the Deployment Area of each player and shows it on the map. Unless otherwise stated, a player's teams must be placed in their Deployment Area. Many missions have a space between the players' Deployment Areas called No Man's Land.

In some missions a player will not have a Deployment Area, but will have specific instructions on how to deploy their force instead. In this case there is not a No Man's Land either.

Deploying Companies

A company is made up of its headquarters and its platoons. The commander's role is to assign tasks to each of these assets.

A company is Deployed by assigning its HQ Support Weapons and making Combat Attachments, Deploying its platoons and then Deploying its Warrior teams and Independent teams.

Deploying Platoons

Unit cohesion is vital to an army as it deploys for battle. If units are allowed to drift out of command there is no way to adjust orders and ensure that they are in proper position for the start of the battle.

When you Deploy a platoon, place all of its teams in your Deployment Area (or wherever the mission or scenario instructs) so that all of the teams are In Command.

Some forces (such as the Italians with their Eight Million Bayonets special rule) do not know their Skill rating until after they deploy. In this case Deploy the unit so that it would be In Command no matter what they roll for their Skill rating.

Multi-part Platoons

Some platoons operate as a number of detached patrols rather than as a single large entity.

A Multi-part Platoon is made up of several platoons, each with their own Platoon Command team. Each platoon is separate for all purposes, including deployment.

In missions with Ambushes or Reserves (see pages 266 and 268), each platoon is counted separately when working out how many platoons may be held in Ambush or Reserve.

Deploying Transports

Transport vehicles are a significant advantage to an army on the move, but they can quickly become a liability when the battle begins.

You may Deploy Transport teams with their platoons, or leave them off the table and bring them on later using the Bringing Transports Forward rule (see page 48). Transport teams that are Deployed must have at least one Passenger team Mounted, aside from German platoons with the Mounted Assault rule (see page 243).

Transport Platoons

Although every army would have liked to field fully-mechanized forces, the vehicles to do so simply weren't available. As a compromise, platoons of supply trucks were sent forward to carry troops on long marches.

You may either keep a Transport Platoon off table at the beginning of the game and bring it on later using the Bringing Transports Forward rule (see page 48) or Deploy it with another platoon.

A Transport Platoon that will be Deployed at the start of the game must be assigned to another non-Transport platoon before any platoons are Deployed. It is Deployed at the same time as the other platoon and every Transport team in the Transport Platoon must have teams from the other platoon Mounted as Passengers. Once they are Deployed, the Transport Platoon and its passengers revert to being totally separate platoons.

Platoons Deployed after the Transport Platoon may be Deployed Mounted in the Transport Platoon's vehicles if there is space for them.

In missions with Reserves (see page 268), Transport Platoons and the platoon they are assigned to are counted as one platoon when working out how many platoons may be Deployed on the table. When the platoon arrives from Reserves, it may do so Mounted in the Transports, or it may Send the Transports to the Rear, ready to be Brought Forward when they are needed.

Warriors and Independent Teams

While the positioning of platoons is dictated by the battle plan and is difficult to change, commanders and artillery observers can react to the changing situation.

Unless otherwise stated, Warrior teams that are not a permanent part of a platoon and Independent teams Deploy after all platoons have been deployed. They can be Deployed with a platoon or on their own anywhere in their Deployment Area.

If the mission has Reserves (see page 268), you may elect to hold them in Reserve and bring them on with a platoon arriving from Reserves later in the game.

HQ Support Weapons

Company commanders often kept a few heavier weapons with their headquarters and allocated them out to their platoons as and when they were needed.

The 2iC and Company Command and other Warrior teams (and their transports) form the core of any Company HQ. All remaining teams (and their transports) are HQ Support Weapons.

HQ Support Platoon

When the company HQ retained support weapons under its own command, it was the second-in-command's responsibility to manage them.

Any HQ Support Weapons that are not attached to other platoons form an additional platoon with the 2iC Command team as the Platoon Command team. If the force has no 2iC Command team, appoint one of the teams as the Platoon Command team at the start of the game.

Attaching Out HQ Support Teams

When the 'Old Man' gives a weapon to a platoon, it becomes the platoon commander's responsibility.

At the start of the game before any platoons are Deployed or assigned to Reserves, you may attach some of your HQ Support Weapons to your Combat and Weapons platoons as described below.

Any attachments from the HQ Support Platoon must be to Combat and Weapons platoons within the same company. All attached teams become part of the platoon they are attached to for all purposes.

Cannot Attach Tank Teams

Additional tanks in the HQ are there to provide a reserve or a fire-support base for the manoeuvre platoons.

Tank teams that are HQ Support Weapons must remain in the HQ Support Platoon.

Must Attach Infantry Teams

Bazookas and other light weapons are often held in the HQ for assignment to platoons as needed.

You must attach all of the Infantry teams that are HQ Support Weapons to Combat or Weapons platoons.

May Attach Gun Teams

Company commanders usually retain small mortar sections and the like in the HQ as a base of fire, while anti-tank weapons are assigned to platoons in vulnerable positions needing a little extra protection against tanks.

You have two choices with Gun teams in the HQ Support Platoon:

- *You can attach them all out.*
- *You can attach out up to half of the Gun teams and retain the rest in the HQ Support Platoon. If you do this, you must keep at least two Gun teams in the HQ Support Platoon, and no more than half of the Gun teams in the HQ Support Platoon (but always at least one gun) may be attached to any one platoon.*

HQ Support Platoon Transport

Transport is either assigned to carry a weapon and allocated out with it, or part of a central pool.

If the HQ Support Weapons teams being attached out have Transport teams, you must attach the Transport team that normally carries a team with it. If that Transport team normally carries other teams as well, they must all be attached to the same platoon together.

Transport teams that do not have passengers in their section must be attached to Combat or Weapons platoons in the same company.

Combat Attachments

Many armies in World War II chose to centralise their heavier infantry-support weapons, keeping them together in some form of heavy weapons platoon. This gave a commander the flexibility to allocate the heavier weapons as combat attachments to specific infantry platoons as and when they were needed.

An Intelligence Briefing will specify which platoons in it are eligible to make Combat Attachments, and the platoons that they can attach weapons to.

If you want to make Combat Attachments, you must do so before Deploying any of your platoons. You may either Combat Attach up to half of the teams (excluding the Platoon Command team and Transport teams) or Combat Attach all of the teams except the Platoon Command team. If you choose to attach out all of the teams, the Platoon Command team is removed from the game and the platoon itself ceases to exist for the duration of the game.

A platoon may Combat Attach teams to any or all eligible platoons, but may not Combat Attach more than half its teams (again excluding the Platoon Command team and Transport teams) to any one platoon.

If the platoon making Combat Attachments has Transport teams, you must Combat Attach the Transport team that normally carries a team with it. If that Transport team normally carries other teams as well, they must all be Combat Attached to the same platoon together.

Once all Combat Attachments have been made, the Combat-attached teams become part of the platoon they are attached to for all purposes for the whole game.

Spearhead Deployment

Some commanders and units drove hard, pushing forward at every opportunity. These troops did not wait for orders and careful plans. Instead, they advanced when and wherever possible, seeking to throw the enemy off balance before the battle even begins.

Teams that are capable of Spearhead Deployment, whether because of their platoon's abilities, the nature of their force, or the special rules of a Warrior, may make Recce Deployment Moves (see page 193) at the start of the game as if they were Recce teams. This movement must take every team in a platoon with Spearhead Deployment out of its own Deployment Area.

Teams using this rule can only make their Reconnaissance Deployment Moves after all Recce teams in the force that are going to make Reconnaissance Deployment Moves have done so.

Random Deployment

While most battles have clearly delineated front lines, some battles are marked by the confused intermingling of both sides. It was not unusual for troops to take shelter for the night or from a blizzard or sand storm, only to find the enemy in their midst when visibility cleared.

Mark the table's centre point, divide it into quarters, and number them from 1 to 4.

When a player Deploys a platoon under the Random Deployment special rule, they roll a die to determine where it is Deployed.

- *On a roll of 1 to 4, Deploy the platoon in the table quarter corresponding to the die roll.*
- *On a roll of 5 or 6, the player may Deploy the platoon in a table quarter of their choice.*

All teams must Deploy more than 16"/40cm from enemy teams within Line of Sight, or more than 8"/20cm from teams that are entirely out of Line of Sight.

Roll for, and Deploy, each platoon in turn. Do not roll for the next platoon until the current one is Deployed.

Warrior teams that are not a permanent part of a platoon and Independent teams may choose to Deploy in any table quarter. They do not need to roll to determine their location.

Summary: Deploying your Force

- **Unless otherwise stated, teams must be placed in your Deployment Area with platoons placed In Command.**
- **HQ Support Weapons form a platoon under the 2iC, except that Infantry teams must be, and Gun teams may be, attached to Combat and Weapons platoons.**
- **Some platoons can Combat Attach half or all of their teams to other platoons.**
- **Spearhead Deployment allows teams to make Recce Deployment Moves that take them out of their Deployment Area.**
- **For Random Deployment, roll a die for each platoon you place. On a 1 to 4, place it in the numbered quarter. On a 5 or 6, choose the quarter. Place teams 16"/40cm from the enemy, or 8"/20cm if out of sight.**

US armoured rifle squad with their M3 half-track

DEPLOYING FORTIFICATIONS

Bunkers and fortifications take a lot of time and effort to build and rarely come as a surprise to the enemy.

You must place all Fortifications before the opposing player places any Objectives (see page 258) unless the mission specifies otherwise.

Entrenchments and Bunkers must be placed in your Deployment Area (see page 259). Obstacles may be placed in either your Deployment Area or in No Man's Land.

Entrenchments and Bunkers cannot be placed in a stream, river, swamp, lake or other water feature.

BUNKER DEPLOYMENT

Bunkers are usually built with mutual support in mind and are usually not placed right next to each other.

Bunkers may not be placed:

- *within 2"/5cm of another Bunker, nor*
- *on a road, track, bridge, railway line, blocking a ford, or in any other way obstructing a constructed route.*

Bunkers can be placed in the ground floor of Buildings. If the Building is large enough, place the Bunker in the Building, otherwise, declare the whole Building to be a Bunker. Use Openings in the Building as the Bunker's Firing Slits.

Objectives may not be placed in, on or under Bunkers.

REMOVE EMPTY GUN PITS

Sometimes additional gun pits are dug as decoy positions to confuse the enemy as to where the artillery is actually positioned. The truth of the matter quickly becomes clear once the fighting begins.

Remove any unoccupied Gun Pits and Tank Pits from the table at the end of deployment before the game begins.

NOT PLACING YOUR FORTIFICATIONS

Sometimes Fortified Platoons may be operating away from their fortifications.

You may choose to not place any or all of your Fortifications in a game. If you do this the Fortifications are not used during the game.

AREA DEFENCES

Area defences are dispersed across the frontage being defended to strengthen weak areas.

Fortifications for Area Defence are deployed as described above. A force with two or more Bunkers in its Area Defences is a Fortified Company and will Always Defend (see page 257).

FORTIFIED PLATOONS

Fortified platoons occupy strongpoints to defend an area, using firepower to deny the surroundings to the enemy.

Fortified Platoons place their fortifications at the same time as other Fortifications before objectives are placed.

Mark a spot on the table (use a die or counter) as the centre of each Fortified Platoon's position. All of the platoon's Fortifications must be placed entirely within 12"/30cm of the marked point, but may not be placed within 6"/15cm of any Fortification from another Fortified Platoon or of either side table edge.

DEPLOYING THE COMPANY HQ

The company commander usually chooses to place themselves in a central position within easy reach of all of the other fortified platoons or safely within the crucial position.

The Company HQ of a Fortified Company may deploy as part of another Fortified Platoon, amalgamating their Fortifications as a single position. If it does not do this, it deploys in its own fortifications which are placed as if it were a Fortified Platoon on its own.

DEPLOYING FORTIFIED PLATOONS

Strongpoints are assigned to a particular unit to defend, and woe betide any commander who abandons his position before a battle.

When the teams of a Fortified Platoon are Deployed, they must be placed in the Trench Lines, Gun Pits, and Tank Pits that come with their platoon. Only teams from the Fortified Platoon may be deployed in its Entrenchments. If there are insufficient Entrenchments for the platoon, any teams that do not fit in the Entrenchments may not be used in the game.

If a Fortified Platoon elects not to place any of its Fortifications, it is no longer a Fortified Platoon. However, such a platoon never benefits from the Prepared Positions special rule (see page 264) as they have not had time to dig alternative positions.

Fortified Platoons cannot be deployed in Ambush or Reserves of any sort unless it elects not to deploy any of its Fortifications.

Area Defences

Fortified Platoons

Pioneer Supply Vehicles

Pioneers need their supply vehicle for the heavy duty tasks like constructing fortifications.

In missions that use the Prepared Positions special rule, you may place:

- *one Minefield, or*
- *three Barbed Wire Entanglements*

in No Man's Land or your Deployment Area for each of your Pioneer Supply vehicles that begins the game on the table. Place these Obstacles when you place the Pioneer Supply vehicle.

SUMMARY

- **Place Fortifications before the opposing player places any Objectives. Obstacles may be placed in No Man's Land, others must be placed in your Deployment Area.**
- **Fortified Platoons must place their Fortifications within 12"/30cm of a point and 6"/15cm from other Fortified Platoons. Their Infantry and Gun teams must be placed in their Entrenchments.**
- **A Pioneer Supply vehicle can place a Minefield or three Barbed Wire Entanglements.**

MISSION SPECIAL RULES

To reflect their unique circumstances most missions use a number of special rules that make them more realistic and add exciting tactical twists to each engagement. Each mission tells you which special rules apply.

Meeting Engagement

Not all engagements in war have the benefit of careful planning. Many battles start when two mobile columns collide, with neither side fully prepared for battle. While one side may be quicker with their triggers, most of the opening shots will be fairly wild. In a meeting engagement both sides are manoeuvring for position when they encounter the enemy. They can either launch an immediate attack or desperately attempt to dig in before the onslaught begins.

In a Meeting Engagement, the following rules apply in the first Shooting Step of the player who has the first turn. They do not apply in the second player's turn, nor in subsequent turns.

- *Treat all teams belonging to the player who has the first turn as having moved for calculating their ROF and Score Needed to Hit when Shooting in their first Shooting Step, whether they actually moved or not.*
- *Teams belonging to the player who has the first turn cannot fire Artillery Bombardments in their first Shooting Step.*
- *The player who has the first turn cannot use Ground-attack Aircraft in that turn.*

These rules only apply in the Shooting Step of the player taking the first turn. Their teams can still move, Dig In, or Go to Ground as normal in their Movement Step, and launch assaults in the Assault Step. As usual, all teams start the game Gone to Ground (see page 90).

Prepared Positions

It doesn't take long for soldiers to learn to dig in every time they halt. It gives them protection from random fire, security against a surprise attack, and cover against an incoming assault.

Most attack-defend missions start with both sides dug in reflecting the time taken by the attacker to organise a major attack.

In a mission with Prepared Positions, both players may have all of their Infantry and Gun teams Dug In (see page 51) and Gone to Ground (see page 90) at the start of the game.

SUMMARY

Meeting Engagement

- **In a Meeting Engagement the first player must shoot as if they moved, and cannot fire Artillery Bombardments or use Ground-attack aircraft in their first turn.**

Prepared Positions

- **Prepared Positions allows both players to start Dug In.**

Meeting Engagement

A Soviet strongpoint under attack from Finnish and German forces

Ambush

One of the defender's biggest advantages in a battle is the ability to wait concealed in ambush for the enemy before opening fire once the enemy is in the perfect position.

In missions with the Ambush special rule, the ambushing player holds one or more platoons (as specified in the mission) in Ambush when they Deploy. Platoons held in Ambush are treated as being on the table, but their location isn't specified until they reveal themselves. They are held off the table at the start of the game.

Ambushing from Prepared Positions

While the location of an ambush may be a surprise to the attacker, it is no surprise to the defender. When the rest of the force dug their foxholes, the ambushing force dug theirs, and alternate positions, at the same time.

In missions with Prepared Positions, the troops in Ambush will be Dug In in the same way as they would be if they had Deployed on table at the start of the game.

Already There

Ambushing troops take their time and do not open fire until they are good and ready.

Ambushing teams do not have to move. They can remain where they are placed and shoot at their full ROF.

Placing Ambushes

It is far easier to select the ideal place for an ambush in real life, where the minor details of the terrain and small pieces of intelligence on the enemy's activities give you clues, than in a game. To reflect this, the ambushing player does not need to decide where their ambush will take place until it is revealed.

At the start of your turn, in the Starting Step, you may place any or all platoons that you have been holding in Ambush. You must place an entire platoon at a time and the platoon must be placed so as to be In Command.

You may place a team from Ambush anywhere in your Deployment Area, provided that it is not:

- *within 16"/40cm of any enemy team within Line of Sight, unless Concealed by Terrain from it, or*
- *within 4"/10cm of any enemy team, or*
- *within 8"/20cm of any enemy Recce team that is in Line of Sight (apart from Recce teams that are Bogged Down, Bailed Out, or moved at the Double).*

You do not have to decide where your platoon will be placed until you place it.

Heavy and Immobile Gun teams and vehicles equipped with a weapon rated as a Bunker Buster cannot be placed in Ambush closer than 16"/40cm to any enemy team within Line of Sight.

Revealing Ambushes

Recce Reveal Ambushes

Tactics

Recce, Recce, Recce!

When advancing into enemy territory, it pays to check out likely ambush points. The enemy can't deploy from ambush close to your troops, so if you move a small unit up to a likely ambush position the enemy has to either spring the ambush early or lose the opportunity of ambushing you from there (at least until you vacate the area again).

Surprise Ambushes

With the proper cover and concealment, troops can remain completely secure even when the enemy is right on top of them. Thus it doesn't matter if a team is deployed using the ambush rule right where artillery fell or an enemy platoon passed through in a previous turn. It suffers no casualties since it was safe in deep trenches, well sheltered, or moved into that position just before being revealed. Historically it was not uncommon for ambushes to catch a force in the flank, or appear long after an area was considered secure, so a good commander must maintain awareness of exposure on more than just their front line. For example:

- **Russia, 1942:** German anti-tank guns in the Soviet Union routinely waited until tanks had driven through their positions before engaging them from the rear.
- **Italy, 1943:** A New Zealand force cleared a village and prepared to move on to the next objective, only to come under fire from the supposedly cleared village. They cleared it again, only to have the same thing happen. Clearing it a third time solved the problem.
- **France, 1944:** Canadians attacking south of Caen in Normandy repeatedly came under fire from villages behind them. Although they had cleared the villages of German troops, they later learned that there were caves and tunnels honeycombing the area that the Germans were using to move around undetected.

Warrior and Independent Teams

Commanders, artillery observers, and similar individuals have specific jobs that prevent them from sneaking off to hide with ambushing troops.

Warrior teams that are not a permanent part of a platoon and Independent teams cannot be held in Ambush.

Immediate Ambush

Ambushing forces can't always afford to wait for an ideal opportunity to attack. Sometimes they must spring their ambush at the first target that presents itself.

Immediate Ambush is the same as Ambush, except that a player must place platoons they are holding in Immediate Ambush on the table at the start of the game after all other Deployment, but before the game begins.

Summary

Ambush

- Do not place platoons held in Ambush on the table until you reveal them.
- Place Ambushing platoons at the start of any turn. Teams cannot be placed within 8"/20cm of enemy Recce teams or 4"/10cm of other enemy if Concealed or out of sight, or within 16"/40cm if not Concealed.
- Heavy and Immobile Gun teams and Bunker Busters cannot be placed within 16"/40cm of the enemy unless out of sight.
- Immediate Ambush is the same as Ambush, but is placed before the first turn.

Reserves

Reserves are troops held behind the front line used to reinforce critical sectors in the defence or to turn a successful attack into a major victory.

In missions that use the Reserves special rule, players with reserves hold one or more platoons (as specified in the mission) in reserve when they Deploy. Place these platoons to one side at the start of the game.

At the start of your first turn roll a die. On a roll of 5+ your first Reserve platoon arrives. It may be any platoon of your choice, but must arrive now.

At the start of your second turn roll two dice. Each roll of 5+ results in another platoon arriving from your Reserves. So, if you're lucky, you could have up to two platoons arriving from Reserve during your second turn.

Keep rolling at the start of each of your following turns adding one more die than the previous turn, so at the start of turn three you roll three dice, at the start of turn four you roll four dice, and so on. Each roll of 5+ brings another platoon on from your Reserves.

At Least One Platoon Arrives

Even when things are looking grimmest, a trickle of reserves always makes its way through.

If you rolled three or more dice to get Reserves in this turn, but failed to score any rolls of 5+, you automatically receive a single platoon from Reserve anyway.

Arriving from Reserve

Dispatch riders, radio messages, and the rumble of engines signal the imminent arrival of reserves.

When a Reserve platoon arrives, place its Platoon Command team at your edge of the table to remind you of its arrival. During your Movement Step move the newly-arrived platoon on from the table edge indicated in the mission briefing.

Infantry and Gun teams may arrive Mounted in or Limbered to their Transport teams if they have them, or on foot. Cavalry and Motorcycle Reconnaissance teams may arrive Mounted on their horses or vehicles, or Dismounted on foot. Immobile Gun teams can move up to 4"/10cm on the turn they arrive if they arrive Dismounted rather than Limbered to a Transport team.

Nowhere to Arrive

Sometimes the battlefield can get very crowded and reserves may have to fight their way onto the battlefield.

It is not appropriate to attempt to prevent the enemy's reserves from arriving by blocking the edge of the table with your own troops. In reality this would simply move the fight a few hundred metres with no other effect.

Sometimes you will find you have blocked the enemy reserves from arriving by accident. If this happens, place the Reserve platoon on the edge of the table, pushing the enemy back the minimum necessary so that they are 2"/5cm from the newly arriving platoon.

British 'Desert Rats' Cromwell tank

Armoured Reserves

When a force is placed on the defensive, most of its tanks are withdrawn to a central reserve.

In a mission with both the Reserves and Prepared Positions special rules where it is defending:

- *a Mechanised Company may only Deploy up to two Fully-armoured Platoons,*
- *a Infantry Company may only deploy a single Fully-armoured Platoon, and*
- *a Fortified Company may not Deploy any Fully-armoured Platoons on table.*

These companies must hold all other Fully-armoured Platoons in Reserves. Fully-armoured Platoons are those entirely equipped with Fully-armoured Tank teams (see page 8), none of which are also Recce teams.

Type of Company	*Maximum Armoured Platoons on Table*
Tank	*Any number*
Mechanised	*2*
Infantry	*1*
Fortified	*None*

Delayed Reserves

It is often unsafe to hold reserves too close to the front line. Unfortunately, this means that reserves frequently take longer to arrive.

The Delayed Reserves special rule works the same as the normal Reserves special rule except that the player does not start rolling for their Reserves until turn three, and then they get one die.

This increases by one die per turn as normal, so that on turn four they roll two dice, on turn five they roll three dice, and so on.

Scattered Reserves

Sometimes a battle will take a force by surprise. Its reserves will be scattered over a wide area and could arrive at the front from just about any direction.

The Scattered Reserves special rule operates in the same way as the Reserves special rule with the following exception.

When each platoon arrives from reserve, the owning player rolls a die to determine from which table edge or corner it will arrive. The mission map shows the edge or corner for each roll.

If a platoon arrives from Scattered Reserves on a table edge, it may enter the table anywhere along that table edge. If the platoon arrives from Reserves on a corner, they must enter the table within 16"/40cm of the corner

Mobile Reserves

If a commander doesn't have enough troops to cover the entire front they will often have to maintain everything they can in a mobile reserve—ready to move quickly and concentrate at the point they are needed most.

In a mission employing the Mobile Reserves special rule, the defender may deploy any or all platoons that do not have vehicles on table, but only one platoon with vehicles. Any other platoons, including those that wish to use their tanks and transport, must be held in Reserves or Delayed Reserves as specified by the mission.

Platoons with Armoured Transport teams may either deploy on table without their vehicles (they cannot Bring them Forward later in the game), or be deployed in Reserves.

If this would result in a single platoon being deployed on table, the defender may deploy a second platoon with vehicles, as long as this leaves at least two platoons in Reserves.

Warrior teams, Independent teams, and Supply, Ammo, and Recovery Transport vehicles (including Pioneer Supply vehicles) may be deployed on table in addition to the otherwise allowed vehicles.

SUMMARY

Reserves

- **Roll a die at the start of your first turn. On a 5+ one of your platoons held in Reserves arrives. Increase the number of dice rolled each turn by one, with any roll of 5+ bringing another platoon from Reserves.**
- **If rolling three or more dice, a platoon always arrives, even if you fail all die rolls.**
- **Mechanised Companies can only have two Fully-armoured platoons on table in missions with Reserves. Infantry Companies can have one such platoon, while Fortified Companies must hold all Fully-armoured platoons in Reserves.**
- **With Delayed Reserves you do not start rolling until your third turn.**
- **With Scattered Reserves you roll a die to see where your Reserves arrive.**
- **With Mobile Reserves you may only Deploy one platoon with vehicles. All other platoons with vehicles are held in Reserves.**

Strategic Withdrawal

It is a universal truth that only a fool stays in a losing position, so after a crushing defeat you have elected to exercise the more discretionary part of valour and pull what is left of your main forces off the line. It now falls on your rearguard to not only give your main forces time to regroup, but to also conduct their own withdrawal to the new defensive line.

Timing a Platoon Withdrawal

Your force must not only hold its current position, but must also disengage from the enemy and get back to the next defence line. To do this you must filter platoons back in an orderly fashion.

Starting with turn three, in the Starting Step when they would roll for Reserves if they had any, the defending player counts the number of platoons and Delay Counters that they have on table.

- *If the number is 5 or more, the defender must Withdraw one platoon.*
- *If they have less than 5 platoons, they gain a Delay Counter instead.*

Delay Counters

Delay Counters represent the rearguard's growing desperation and the pressure mounting for their own withdrawal. Delay counters count as platoons when working out the number of platoons still on the table.

The defender starts the game with no Delay Counters, but gains one each time they do not Withdraw a platoon.

Add the number of Delay Counters to the number of platoons that you have on table when working out whether to Withdraw a platoon this turn.

When you Withdraw a platoon, remove all Delay Counters as well.

How to Withdraw Platoons

Once the window of opportunity occurs a commander has no choice but to withdraw their forces. Often this is a simple matter of ordering the platoon to fall back, but if they are embroiled in close-quarters battles it can be quite risky to try and disengage.

When the defending player is required to Withdraw a platoon they may Withdraw any platoon on the table. All of the teams of that platoon are removed from the table and it is considered to have Withdrawn.

If a Withdrawing platoon has More Teams Destroyed than Still Fighting (see page 173) and has teams within 8"/20cm of enemy teams, there is a chance of their Withdrawal breaking into a rout. Make a Skill Test before removing the teams.

- *If the platoon passes, they successfully Withdraw.*
- *If they fail, they Withdraw, but the whole platoon is Destroyed.*

Company Morale

The company gets steadily weaker as platoons withdraw, so heavy losses can make the morale of the rearguard decidedly shaky as they wait for their turn to withdraw.

Platoons that Withdraw without being Destroyed are ignored and do not count as either present on table or Destroyed for Company Morale Checks.

Platoons that were Destroyed during their Withdrawal are Destroyed for Company Morale Checks.

Phased Objective Withdrawal

As your main battle force withdraws, your rearguard must hold the line and protect your vital assets and positions. You must give your forces time to remove sensitive documents, gather essential supplies, and destroy everything that can't be carried. Then they can fall back to focus on defending other critical sites.

At the start of their turns six and seven the defender removes one of the Objectives placed by the attacker.

Since this happens in the defender's turn, the Objectives won't be there in the attacker's turn when it comes time to check whether they have won. This makes it possible to steal victory out from the enemy's grasp, so the attacker needs to be aware of the timing of the Objective removal.

SUMMARY

Strategic Withdrawal

- **The defender has to remove a platoon from the table each turn starting on turn three. If the defender has less than five platoons, they gain a delay counter instead.**
- **If a withdrawing platoon has More Teams Destroyed than Still Fighting and has teams within 8"/20cm of the enemy, it must pass a Skill Test or be Destroyed.**
- **On turns six and seven the defender removes an Objective that they placed.**

Turn	Event
3	Withdraw a platoon if 5+ platoons, otherwise gain a delay counter.
4	Withdraw a platoon and remove all counters if 5+ platoons or counters, otherwise gain delay counter.
5	Repeat withdrawal.
6	Remove Objective. Repeat withdrawal.
7	Remove Objective. Repeat withdrawal.
8	Check Company Morale if necessary. Game over.

Over the Wire

While your fortifications normally serve to keep the enemy out of your own positions, they can be a hindrance to patrols conducting a trench raid.

In a mission with the Over the Wire special rule both players place all their Obstacles (see page 223) in their opponent's side of the table at least 8"/20cm back from the centre line. The Obstacles may be in No Man's Land or the opponent's Deployment Area. This overrides the normal Fortification Placement rules on page 262.

All other types of Fortifications are placed in their Deployment Area using the standard Fortification Placement rules.

Normally players place their obstacles to hinder their opponent's attempts to cross No Man's Land and reach their positions. However, in the No Man's Land mission, the player is trying to get out of their own defences and into No Man's Land, so their own obstacles would get in their way. The Over the Wire special rule has players place their obstacles as if they were the enemy's defences to cause the enemy difficulties in getting out of their defences and into No Man's Land.

No Man's Land Patrol

When two forces face each other from fortified lines they engage in aggressive patrolling to gain information on the enemy's positions.

In a mission with the No Man's Land Patrol special rule each player nominates one platoon deployed on table to be their Patrol. The nominated platoon must have at least five Infantry teams.

Only the Infantry teams of a platoon become the Patrol. Any vehicles, Gun teams and Fortifications in the Patrol platoon remain where they were deployed.

Any vehicles and Gun teams in the platoon are treated as a leaderless platoon for the duration of the battle. Warrior teams can never appoint a new Platoon Command team for this platoon. It does not count as a platoon for Company Morale Checks.

SUMMARY

Over the Wire

- **Place Obstacles in the enemy table half at least 8"/20cm back from the centre line. Place all other Fortifications as usual.**

No Man's Land Patrol

- **Remove the Infantry teams from a Fortified Platoon as a Patrol.**

Soviet assault sappers defend their trenches against German Panther tanks

NIGHT FIGHTING

While most battles take place in daylight, some were fought at night. Some armies even specialised in launching their attacks at night. These rules allow you to fight battles in the dark or in conditions of limited visibility.

Moving at Night

Moving at night, without lights, is slow and painstaking. In the darkness shapes blend and blur turning tanks into houses, and rocks and trees into tanks.

Teams may not move further than 8"/20cm or move At the Double at night.

Teams must re-roll successful Bogging Checks when moving through Rough Terrain at night.

Shooting at Night

Few things are as difficult as finding targets at night. Everything looks dangerous. Tanks look like houses and trees like tanks making it tricky to pick your target, unless they shoot, then their muzzle flash gives them away.

Your artillery and mortars fire illuminating flares and officers use their flare pistols when they think they see a target, but often these don't help as the sudden light dazzles the eyes and the enemy freezes into immobility until the flare burns out.

Each time you select a platoon, or a Warrior or Independent team that has not Joined a platoon, to shoot with at night, roll a die and consult the Night Visibility Table. The result is the maximum distance that Line of Sight can extend for the platoon's teams against targets that did not shoot. This only applies to that platoon for this turn.

The platoon can only shoot at teams within that distance unless the target team fired its weapons. Anything further away is invisible in the darkness.

The maximum distance does not affect Line of Sight when shooting at enemy teams that fired in their previous Shooting Step.

Roll to determine the visibility distance before you select your targets. If there isn't anything in sight due to poor visibility, your platoon can elect not to shoot at all.

Night Visibility

Dice Roll	Distance
1	4"/10cm
2	8"/20cm
3	12"/30cm
4	16"/40cm
5	20"/50cm
6	24"/60cm

Artillery Bombardments at Night

Artillery gunners don't need to see their target to be able to hit it. As long as their spotter can see the target, they just need to fire their shells wherever they are told to.

When you fire an Artillery Bombardment at night, you must roll to see how far the Spotting team's Line of Sight extends. If the Spotting team is part of a platoon, this will be the same roll as used for the rest of the platoon's shooting. If the Spotting team is a Warrior or Independent team operating on its own, it will make its own roll.

The Spotting team must choose a team that is within the rolled Line of Sight distance, or one that shot in their previous Shooting Step, as their Aiming Point. The teams actually firing the Artillery Bombardment do not need Line of Sight to the target, so are unaffected by darkness.

Concealment

Even on a clear night it is tricky to accurately pinpoint the enemy. Even when shooting at muzzle flashes, you are firing mostly by guesswork.

All teams count as Concealed at night. This only benefits teams that are not already Concealed.

Any team that is Gone to Ground (see page 90) is harder to hit in their opponent's Shooting Step as it is automatically Concealed.

Night is not Concealing Terrain, however, so Ambushing troops must deploy at least 16"/40cm from the enemy when in the open (see page 266).

The Concealment of night does not allow reconnaissance troops to use Cautious Movement. They must still be Concealed by Terrain.

Line Of Sight at Night

You do not need to roll to see how far line of sight extends for every action you take, so we restrict the limit on Line of Sight at night to shooting.

Line of Sight at night is the same as it is during daylight, aside from when shooting (as shown above). This means that rules like the one preventing teams from being placed from Ambush within 8"/20cm and in Line of Sight of a Recce team (see page 193) operate exactly as they do in daylight.

No Air Support at Night

With nothing but their eyes to guide them, there is no way for aircraft to accurately identify targets to attack.

Air Support may not be requested on turns where the night-fighting rules are in effect.

AOP's and other similar aircraft cannot be used at night. They will arrive on the first friendly turn of daylight.

TIME OF DAY

Battles occur at any time. Most battles happen in daylight, but many fights stretch into the night or start under the cover of darkness.

There are four times of day: Daylight, Darkness, Dawn, and Dusk.

DAYLIGHT

Most battles take place by day where the soldiers and their officers can see what they are doing and face less risk of running into unexpected enemy fire.

In a mission being played in Daylight, the night fighting rules are not used.

DARKNESS

Some smaller battles take place entirely at night. These are mostly raids and accidental meetings of small forces manoeuvring in the dark.

In a mission played in Darkness, the night fighting rules are used for the entire game.

DAWN

Dawn is a popular time for attacks. The attackers can move into position for the assault under cover of darkness, but have the benefit of daylight once the fighting starts in earnest.

In a mission being played at Dawn, the game starts in Darkness, with the night fighting rules in effect.

At the start of the defender's turn three immediately before revealing Ambushes, roll a die:

- *On a score of 5+, morning has broken. The rest of the battle is fought in Daylight.*
- *If the roll is unsuccessful, at the start of the attacker's turn four, they roll two dice with morning breaking on any roll of 5+.*
- *If it is still dark at the start of the defender's next turn, they roll three dice, and so on until morning breaks on any roll of 5+.*

Once morning breaks, the night fighting rules are no longer used, and it is Daylight for the rest of the game.

DUSK

Dusk is a useful time to launch surprise attacks. If the initial attack succeeds quickly, the enemy's counterattack will be hampered by darkness.

In a mission being played at Dusk, the game starts in Daylight.

At the start of the defender's turn three immediately before revealing Ambushes, roll a die:

- *On a score of 5+, night has fallen. The rest of the battle is fought in Darkness.*
- *If the roll is unsuccessful, at the start of the attacker's turn four, they roll two dice with night falling on any roll of 5+.*
- *If it is still light at the start of the defender's next turn, they roll three dice, and so on until night falls on any roll of 5+.*

Once night falls, the night fighting rules come into effect and it is Darkness for the rest of the game.

SUMMARY

- **Teams cannot move more than 8"/20cm at night, and cannot move At the Double. Re-roll successful Bogging Checks at night.**
- **Roll on the Night Visibility Table to see how far each platoon can see before shooting.**
- **All teams are Concealed at night, but Ambushes and Cautious Movement still need Concealing Terrain.**
- **Aircraft cannot operate at night.**
- **Roll a die on the defender's turn three in Dawn missions. On a 5+ it is now Daylight. If not, each player rolls, increasing the number of dice rolled each player's turn by one, with any roll of 5+ bringing Daylight.**
- **Roll a die on the defender's turn three in Dusk missions. On a 5+ it is now Night. If not, each player rolls, increasing the number of dice rolled each player's turn by one, with any roll of 5+ bringing Night.**

Heavy artillery firing at night
US Signal Corps, NARA

ENDING THE BATTLE

At some point it becomes obvious to a commander that they have lost the battle. Either the enemy have taken their objective, or their own forces have failed under the stress of battle. At this point there is no practical option but to fall back and organise a new line of defence.

The Ending the Battle section of the mission briefing tells you when the game is over. It is important to note that the Ending the Battle section does not tell you who won, it simply tells you the conditions under which the battle ends. Go to the Deciding Who Won section to see who actually won once the game is over.

FAILING COMPANY MORALE

There's no victory as decisive as one where the enemy runs from the field of battle. With all opposition gone, you can occupy your objectives and prepare for a pursuit or dig in ready for a counterattack undisturbed.

As well as the mission specific conditions for ending the battle, a battle can end when one side or the other fails a Company Morale Check and is Destroyed. In this case, the game ends and the opposing player automatically captures all of the Objectives.

RUNNING OUT OF TIME

At the other end of the spectrum are battles that drag out into a stalemate. Either both sides fight each other to a standstill, unable to mount a decisive attack, or bloody fighting is halted by nightfall or other external events before a result is achieved.

Whether or not a set finish time was set for the game (always a good idea in a tournament), it's always possible that you simply run out of time to finish a game.

In this case, check the Deciding Who Won section to see who (if anybody) actually won the game. Often that will be the defending player representing the fact that they, despite fighting at a disadvantage, managed to hold the attacker at bay—the whole purpose of defence in the first place. This puts the onus on the attacker to achieve a decisive victory, rather than the defender somehow having to turn the tables and chase the attacker off.

HOW LONG IS A GAME?

There are two approaches to how long a game should run. You can either play on until one player wins or the other gracefully concedes defeat, or you can play to a time limit such as an hour and a half or two hours. This later option works well if a player has a deadline by which they have to leave.

SPORTING PLAY

One of the important aspects of any game is sporting play—playing in a friendly way rather than trying to stretch the rules. Some dastardly spoilsports have been known to deliberately play slowly when defending in an effort to win by running out of time. Not only is this silly and no fun at all, it is definitely not at all sporting.

SUMMARY

- **The Ending the Battle section of a mission tells when the game is over.**
- **The game also ends if any player fails a Company Morale Check, or the players run out of time.**

American soldiers mill around a captured German Panther tank
US Signal Corps, NARA

DECIDING THE WINNER

Victory points measure the extent of your victory. The more victory points you win, the greater the glory!

Use the Deciding Who Won section of the mission briefing to figure out who won, then refer to the rules below to determine the extent of the victory.

Winning with No Losses

The goal of most military operations is to achieve the objective with the least losses possible. Obtaining victory without losing a single platoon is as good as it gets!

If the winner did not lose any platoons at all, they win 6 Victory Points and the loser gains 1 Victory Point.

Losing a Single Platoon

Winning while limiting your losses to a single platoon is still a major achievement.

If the winner only lost one platoon, they win 5 Victory Points and the loser gains 2 Victory Points.

Losing Two Platoons

Even at the cost of high casualties, a victory is still a victory—far better than a defeat.

If the winner lost two or more platoons, they win 4 Victory Points and the loser gains 3 Victory Points.

Large Forces

While losing troops is never a good thing, some forces have to rely on numbers over individual strength to succeed. Here even small losses can wipe out platoons, but the overall effect on the force is minimal.

If the winner started their first turn with nine or more platoons (including those held in Reserves, but not any Transport platoons), they may ignore the first platoon that is Destroyed when working out their Victory Points.

There are No Draws

With two equally-matched forces slogging away at each other, it can be difficult to win a clear-cut victory. Sometimes the two forces simply grind each other down into a stalemate where both sides lose.

In Fair Fight missions both players lose a game that runs out of time—there is no such thing as a draw in Flames Of War.

If neither player wins, both players look up the number of Surviving Platoons the enemy force has as though their opponent was the winner and use the Loser's Points column to determine their own Victory Points.

Go Down Fighting!

In a Fair Fight mission you only get victory points by winning outright, or by weakening the enemy. So if you don't think you can win, you may as well attack to do as much damage to the enemy as you can and go down fighting! You never know, you might actually win, but at least you'll score more points than you will by hanging back.

SUMMARY

- **The Deciding Who Won section of a mission tells who won.**
- **Only the winning player's losses matter for Victory Points.**
- **Forces with nine or more platoons ignore their first loss.**
- **If neither player wins a Fair Fight mission, both treat the opponent as having won for Victory Points.**

Victory Points Table

Winner's Losses	Result	Winner's Victory Points	Loser's Victory Points
0 platoons	Stunning Victory	6	1
1 platoon	Major Victory	5	2
2 or more platoons	Minor Victory	4	3

Large Forces

Forces with 9 or more platoons ignore first platoon Destroyed.

FREE-FOR-ALL (FAIR FIGHT)

In highly-mobile engagements it is not uncommon for forces to suddenly find themselves in contact with the enemy. The freewheeling battles that result are little more than all-in brawls.

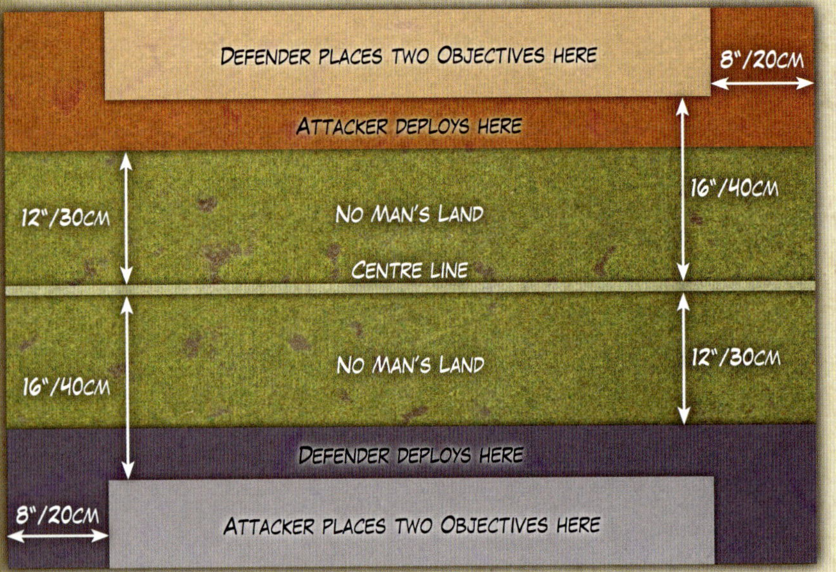

YOUR ORDERS

ATTACKER

Your forces have broken through the enemy front line. The enemy must be ruthlessly crushed before they can occupy proper defences! You must seize one of your objectives before the enemy seizes one of theirs.

DEFENDER

The enemy has broken through. Your company must occupy and defend critical objectives before the enemy secures them. Capture one of your objectives before the enemy takes one of theirs.

MISSION SPECIAL RULES

Free-for-All uses the **Meeting Engagement** (page 264) special rule.

PREPARING FOR BATTLE

1. Both players roll a die. The player with the higher score chooses one of the long table edges to attack from. The other player defends from the opposite table edge.
2. Starting with the attacking player, both players place two Objectives on the opponent's side of the table. The Objectives must be at least 16"/40cm from the centre line of the table and may not be placed within 8"/20cm of the side table edges. Both of a player's Objectives must be within 48"/120cm of each other.
3. Each player's Deployment Area is their own half of the table, excluding the area within 12"/30cm of the centre line. Both players, starting with the attacking player, alternate Deploying their platoons.
4. Both players, starting with the attacking player, now Deploy any Warrior teams that are not part of a platoon and all Independent teams.

BEGINNING THE BATTLE

1. Starting with the attacker, both players make Reconnaissance Deployment moves for any Recce teams they have on table.
2. Both players now roll a die. The player who finished Deploying their platoons first adds +1 to their roll. The player with the higher result has the first turn. In the event of a tie roll again.

ENDING THE BATTLE

The battle ends when:

- a player starts their turn having Taken either of the Objectives that they placed in the enemy Deployment Area.

DECIDING WHO WON

The player that took their Objective has secured a key piece of terrain on the field, forcing the enemy onto the defensive and winning the day.

Calculate your Victory Points using the Victory Points Table on page 275.

If neither side won use the Fair Fight special rule to determine their Victory Points.

ENCOUNTER (FAIR FIGHT)

On the open flanks of the main battle, a small force can encounter a lot of trouble very easily. Having found it, they call for support and the action escalates.

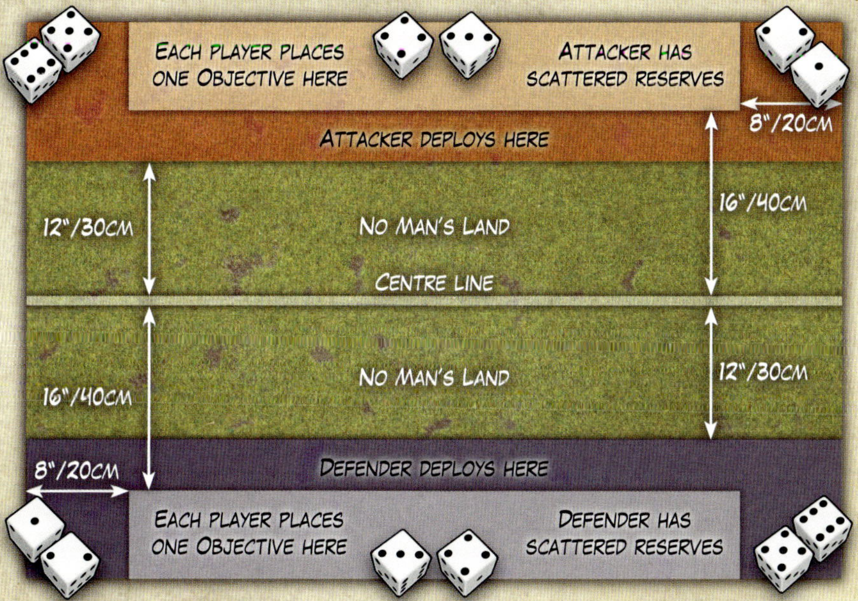

YOUR ORDERS

ATTACKER

You have encountered strong opposition and called for assistance, but so has the enemy. You must attack now while they are still weak and seize one of your objectives before the enemy captures one of theirs.

DEFENDER

A section of the line has crumbled and it's fallen upon your shoulders to repel the enemy advance. Act aggressively until assistance arrives, then capture one of your objectives before the enemy captures one of theirs.

MISSION SPECIAL RULES

Encounter uses the **Delayed Reserves** (page 269), **Meeting Engagement** (page 264), and **Scattered Reserves** (page 269) special rules.

PREPARING FOR BATTLE

1. Both players roll a die. The player with the higher score chooses one of the long table edges to attack from. The other player defends from the opposite table edge.
2. Starting with the attacker, both players place an Objective in their own half of the table.
3. Both players, having placed an Objective in their own half of the table, now place a second Objective, this time in their opponent's half of the table, again starting with the attacking player. All Objectives must be at least 16"/40cm from the centre line of the table and may not be placed within 8"/20cm of the side table edges.
4. Starting with the attacker, both players now nominate at least half of their platoons to be held off the table in Delayed and Scattered Reserves.
5. Each player's Deployment Area is their own half of the table, excluding the area within 12"/30cm of the centre line. Both players, starting with the attacking player, now alternate Deploying their remaining platoons.
6. Again starting with the attacker, both players now Deploy any Warrior teams that are not part of a platoon and all Independent teams.

BEGINNING THE BATTLE

1. Starting with the attacker, both players make Reconnaissance Deployment moves for any Recce teams they have on table.
2. Both players now roll a die. The player who finished Deploying their platoons first adds +1 to their roll. The player with the higher result has the first turn. In the event of a tie roll again.

ENDING THE BATTLE

The battle ends when:

- a player starts their turn having Taken either of the Objectives that were placed in the enemy Deployment Area.

DECIDING WHO WON

The player that took an Objective in the opponent's Deployment Area wins the battle. They have secured key terrain, forcing the enemy onto the defensive, and opening the way for the final, decisive blow.

Calculate your Victory Points using the Victory Points Table on page 275.

If neither side won use the Fair Fight special rule to determine their Victory Points.

DUST UP (FAIR FIGHT)

Two advancing forces clash, each determined to get through to their objectives. Soon a whirling battle develops as reserves arrive on the flanks and are thrown into the fray.

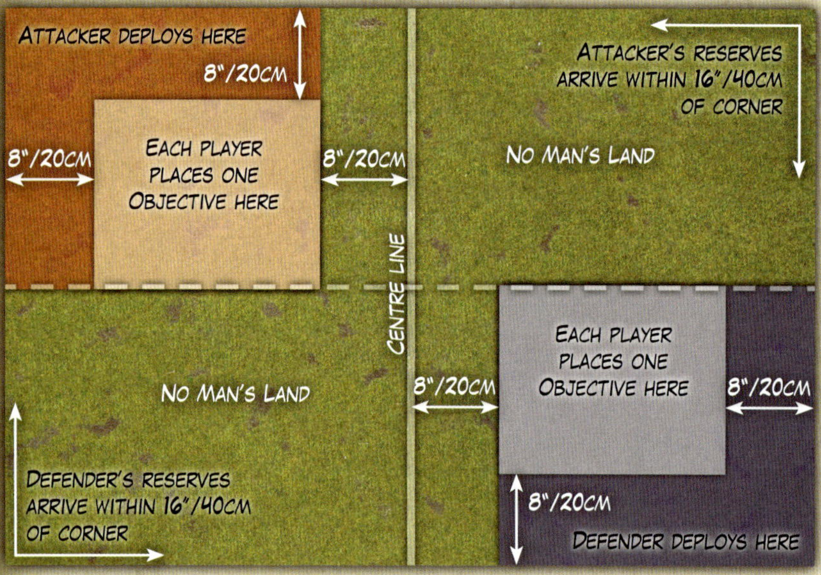

YOUR ORDERS

ATTACKER

Seize the initiative and thrust your forces into the enemy's defences and secure a key objective. He who hesitates is lost. You must capture one of your objectives before the enemy captures one of theirs.

DEFENDER

Parry your opponents thrust and manoeuvre your forces to take and hold a key position behind their lines. Be ready to attack when the time is right. Strike hard and fast to take an objective before the enemy does so.

MISSION SPECIAL RULES

Dust Up uses the **Delayed Reserves** (page 269) and **Meeting Engagement** (page 264) special rules.

PREPARING FOR BATTLE

1. Mark the centre of the table so that the table quarters are obvious to both players.
2. Both players roll a die. The player with the higher score chooses a table quarter to attack from, leaving the other table quarter in their own end empty.
3. The other player deploys in the opposite table quarter, likewise leaving the other table quarter in their own end empty. Each player's Deployment Area is their assigned quarter, excluding the area within 8"/20cm of the centre line.
4. Starting with the attacker each player places an objective in their own Deployment Area at least 8"/20cm from all table edges.
5. Next starting with the attacker each player places an objective in the enemy Deployment Area at least 8"/20cm from all table edges.
6. Starting with the attacker, both players nominate at least half of their platoons to be held off the table in Delayed Reserves.
7. Each player's Reserves arrive up to 16"/40cm from the corner in the empty table quarter at the enemy's end of the table.
8. Both players, starting with the attacker, alternate Deploying platoons.
9. Again starting with the attacker, both players now Deploy any Warrior teams that are not part of a platoon and all Independent teams.

BEGINNING THE BATTLE

1. Starting with the defender, both players make Reconnaissance Deployment moves for any Recce teams they have on table.
2. Both players now roll a die. The player who finished Deploying their platoons first adds +1 to their roll. The player with the higher result has the first turn. In the event of a tie roll again.

ENDING THE BATTLE

The battle ends when:

- a player starts their turn having Taken either of the Objectives that were placed in the enemy Deployment Area.

DECIDING WHO WON

The player that took an Objective in the opponent's Deployment Area wins the battle. They have secured key terrain, opening the way for the decisive blow.

Calculate your Victory Points using the Victory Points Table on page 275

NO RETREAT (DEFENSIVE BATTLE)

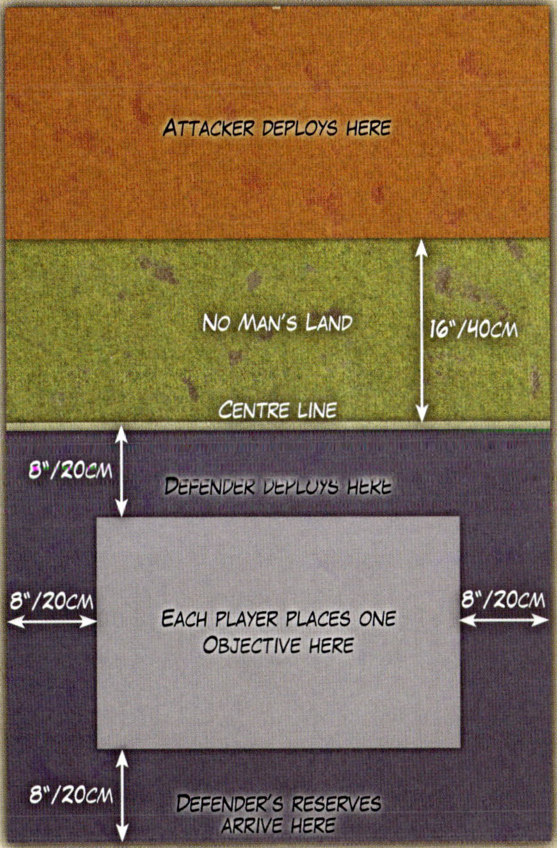

There comes a time in every conflict when a force must dig in and prepare to repel a massive assault from the enemy. Often the deciding battles of their campaigns, these desperate defences can turn the tides and determine the momentum of entire wars.

YOUR ORDERS

ATTACKER

The enemy has fallen back to defend a single choke point of your advance. Their lines disorganized, their reserves in tatters, you must crush their resistance and open a path to victory! You must assault and capture one of your objectives.

DEFENDER

The situation is desperate and your path is grim, but if you can mount a heroic defence against their coming advance you could turn the tide of this war. Reinforcements are coming, and your superiors have promised you support, until they arrive, you are on your own. There can be no retreat. You must hold the objectives and push the enemy back.

MISSION SPECIAL RULES

No Retreat uses the **Ambush** (page 266), **Reserves** (page 268), and **Prepared Positions** (page 264) special rules.

PREPARING FOR BATTLE

1. The defending player chooses which short table end they will defend. This half of the table is their Deployment Area. The attacking player will deploy in the other table half.
2. Starting with the defender, both players now place one Objective each in the defender's end of the table. The Objectives must be at least 8"/20cm from the centre line of the table, and may not be placed within 8"/20cm of any table edge.
3. Next the defending player nominates at least half of their platoons to be held off the table in Reserve at the start of the game. The troops held in Reserves will arrive along the short table edge in the defending player's table half.
4. The defender may then nominate one of the remaining platoons to be held in Ambush.
5. Finally, they Deploy the remaining platoons.
6. The attacking player's Deployment Area is their half of the table, excluding the area within 16"/40cm of the centre line. The attacker now Deploys all of their platoons.
7. Both players now Deploy any Warrior teams that are not part of a platoon and all Independent teams, starting with the defending player.

BEGINNING THE BATTLE

1. Starting with the defender, both players make Reconnaissance Deployment moves for any Recce teams they have on table.
2. The attacking player has the first turn.
3. As both sides are in Prepared Positions, all platoons may begin the game Dug In.

ENDING THE BATTLE

The battle ends when either:

- the attacker has Taken any of the Objectives at the start of their turn, or
- the defender starts any of their turns from turn six with no attacking teams in the defender's half of the table.

DECIDING WHO WON

The attacker wins if the game ended because they started one of their turns holding an Objective. They have broken the defence and forced the enemy to fall back.

Otherwise the defender wins. The attack has been beaten off. Now they must prepare their counterstroke.

Calculate your Victory Points using the Victory Points Table on page 275.

HOLD THE LINE (DEFENSIVE BATTLE)

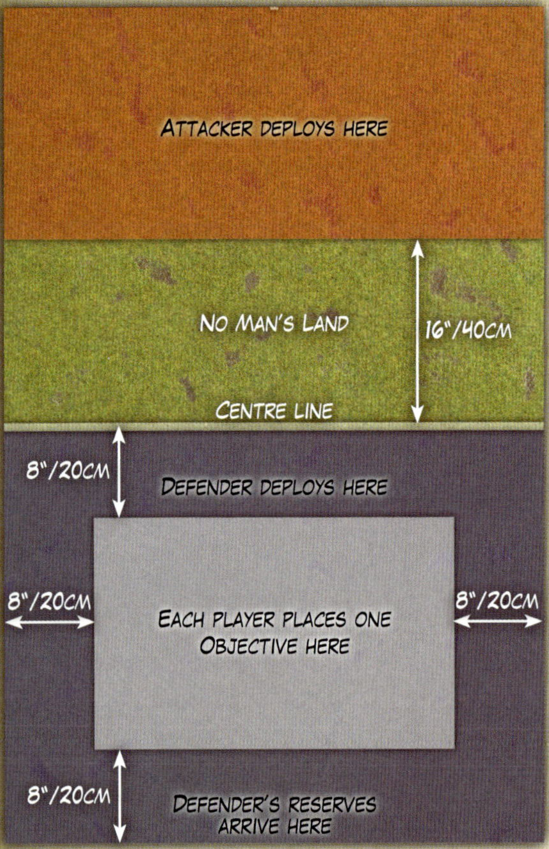

Surprise is paramount in any military operation, and never more so than in defence. When significantly outnumbered with no hope of immediate reinforcement, a defender has to rely even more on intangibles like surprise to even the odds.

YOUR ORDERS

ATTACKER

Your opponent is weak and isolated, ripe for destruction. Attack immediately, smash them quickly and seize your objectives.

DEFENDER

You have been assigned a near impossible task. Only your ability to misdirect the enemy into thinking that you are weaker than you are can save you. Use surprise well. Ambush the enemy and prevent them from taking their objectives, then push them back when help arrives.

MISSION SPECIAL RULES

Hold the Line uses the **Ambush** (page 266), **Delayed Reserves** (page 269), and **Prepared Positions** (page 264) special rules.

PREPARING FOR BATTLE

1. The defending player chooses which short table end they will defend. This half of the table is their Deployment Area. The attacking player will deploy in the other table half.
2. Starting with the defender, both players now place one Objective each in the defender's end of the table. The Objectives must be at least 8"/20cm from the centre line of the table, and may not be placed within 8"/20cm of any table edge.
3. Next the defending player nominates at least half of their platoons to be held off the table in Delayed Reserve. These Reserves will arrive along the short table edge in the defending player's table half.
4. The defender may then nominate up to two of the remaining platoons to be held in Ambush.
5. Finally, they Deploy the remaining platoons. It is entirely possible that all of the defending platoons on the table will be in Ambush with none visible to the enemy at the start of the game.
6. The attacker's Deployment Area is their half of the table, excluding the area within 16"/40cm of the centre line. They now Deploy all of their platoons.
7. Both players now Deploy any Warrior teams that are not part of a platoon and all Independent teams, starting with the defending player.

BEGINNING THE BATTLE

1. Starting with the defender, both players make Reconnaissance Deployment moves for any Recce teams they have on table.
2. The attacking player has the first turn.
3. As both sides are in Prepared Positions, all platoons may begin the game Dug In.

ENDING THE BATTLE

The battle ends when either:

- the attacker has Taken any of the Objectives at the start of their turn, or
- the defender starts any of their turns from turn six with no attacking teams in the defender's half of the table.

DECIDING WHO WON

The attacker wins if the game ended because they started one of their turns holding an Objective. They have overcome the element of surprise and triumphed.

Otherwise the defender wins. Their ambushes stunned the enemy, allowing time to counterattack in strength.

Calculate your Victory Points using the Victory Points Table on page 275.

PINCER (DEFENSIVE BATTLE)

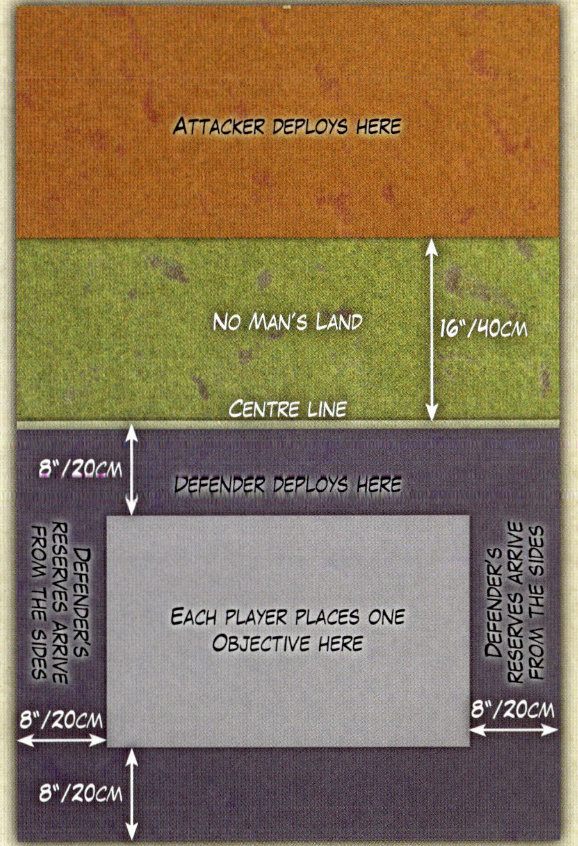

The Germans developed a clever technique for pinching off Soviet penetrations. The front-line troops did their best to limit the penetration, then the reserves struck the flanks of the penetration to cut it off and destroy it.

YOUR ORDERS

ATTACKER

You have found a weak point in the enemy defences. Punch through the front line to create a jumping off point for the exploitation force following behind. You must break into the enemy position to capture one of your objectives.

DEFENDER

You do not have the strength to prevent the enemy from breaking into your lines somewhere, so you must rely on a well-planned counterattack to regain your defences. You must hold the objectives and push the enemy back.

MISSION SPECIAL RULES

Pincer uses the **Ambush** (page 266), **Delayed Reserves** (page 269), and **Prepared Positions** (page 264) special rules.

PREPARING FOR BATTLE

1. The defending player chooses which short table end they will defend. This half of the table is their Deployment Area. The attacking player will deploy in the other table half.
2. Starting with the defender, both players now place one Objective each in the defender's end of the table. The Objectives must be at least 8"/20cm from the centre line of the table, and may not be placed within 8"/20cm of any table edge.
3. Next the defending player nominates at least half of their platoons to be held off the table in Delayed Reserve. These troops will arrive along either of the long table edges in the defending player's table half. The defending player may choose the edge that each platoon arrives from when it arrives from Reserves.
4. The defender may then nominate one of the remaining platoons to be held in Ambush.
5. The defender Deploys their remaining platoons.
6. The attacking player's Deployment Area is their half of the table, excluding the area within 16"/40cm of the centre line. The attacker now Deploys all of their platoons.
7. Both players now Deploy any Warrior teams that are not part of a platoon and all Independent teams, starting with the defending player.

BEGINNING THE BATTLE

1. Starting with the defender, both players make Reconnaissance Deployment moves for any Recce teams they have on table.
2. The attacking player has the first turn.
3. As both sides are in Prepared Positions, all platoons may begin the game Dug In.

ENDING THE BATTLE

The battle ends when either:

- the attacker has Taken any of the Objectives at the start of their turn, or
- the defender starts any of their turns from turn six with no attacking teams in the defender's half of the table.

DECIDING WHO WON

The attacker wins if the game ended because they started one of their turns holding an Objective. Their penetration has secured a jump-off for the following troops.

Otherwise the defender wins. They have eliminated the penetration and restored their defensive positions.

Calculate your Victory Points using the Victory Points Table on page 275.

SURROUNDED (DEFENSIVE BATTLE)

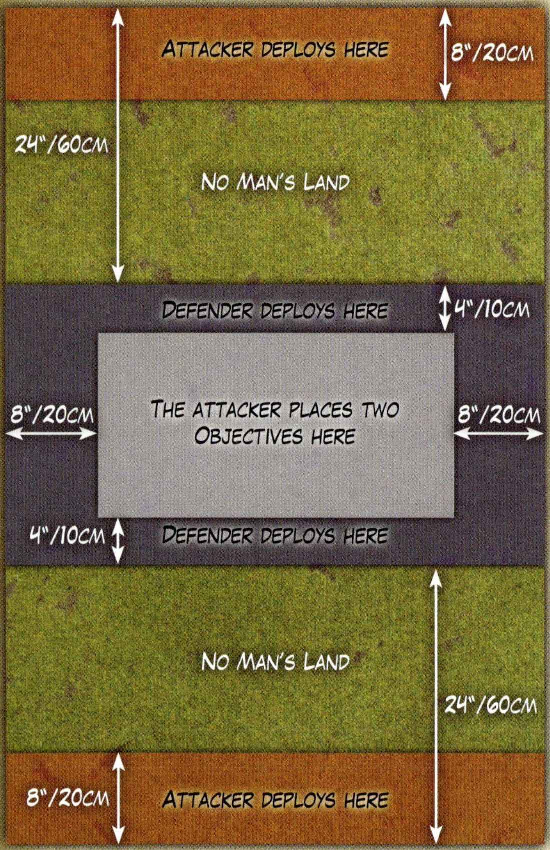

After a successful attack trapped the defenders in a pocket, only one slender corridor remains linking them to the outside world. Recognising the importance of this lifeline, both sides throw everything they have into the battle.

YOUR ORDERS

ATTACKER

You have the enemy on the ropes. One more strong blow will crush them. Cut the corridor and the surrounded enemy pocket will fall. You must seize one of the objectives, breaking the enemy's lifeline.

DEFENDER

You are the only thing standing between your army and disaster. While you hold the corridor open, the pocket will hold out, and a counterattack can be launched to relieve it. If you fail, the whole pocket will be captured. You must prevent the enemy from attaining their objectives.

MISSION SPECIAL RULES

Surrounded uses the **Immediate Ambush** (page 265) and **Prepared Positions** (page 264) special rules.

PREPARING FOR BATTLE

1. The attacker's Deployment Area extends 8"/20cm onto the table from both short ends. The defender's Deployment area is the centre of the table more than 24"/60cm from both short table ends.
2. The attacker now places two Objectives in the defender's Deployment Area at least 4"/10cm from the edges of the Deployment Area and at least 8"/20cm from the table edges.
3. Next the defender nominates one platoon to be held in Immediate Ambush, then Deploys the remaining platoons.
4. The attacking player now Deploys their entire force. They may Deploy their platoons in either part of their Deployment Area, but must Deploy at least one platoon in each half of their Deployment Area.
5. Both players now Deploy any Warrior teams that are not part of a platoon and all Independent teams, starting with the defending player.

BEGINNING THE BATTLE

1. The defender places the platoon they held in Immediate Ambush.
2. Starting with the defender, both players make Reconnaissance Deployment moves for any Recce teams they have on table.
3. The attacking player has the first turn.
4. As both sides are in Prepared Positions, all platoons may begin the game Dug In.

ENDING THE BATTLE

The battle ends when either:

- the attacker has Taken any of the Objectives at the start of their turn, or
- the defender starts any of their turns from turn six with no attacking teams within 16"/40cm of either Objective.

DECIDING WHO WON

The attacker wins if the game ended because they started one of their turns holding an Objective. They have cut the corridor and sealed the fate of the pocket.

Otherwise the defender wins. The corridor has held and supplies will continue to flow into the pocket.

Calculate your Victory Points using the Victory Points Table on page 275.

FIGHTING WITHDRAWAL (DEFENSIVE BATTLE)

A fighting withdrawal allows defeated commanders to preserve the bulk of their forces while falling back to a more defensible location.

YOUR ORDERS

ATTACKER

To exploit an earlier victory you must smash the enemy rearguard and turn their retreat into a rout. Break through the enemy line and capture one of the objectives before it is too late.

DEFENDER

You must cover your withdrawal as the army falls back to the next defensible position. The enemy is moving around your flanks so you cannot stay too long. Hold the objectives until the rest of the army gets clear.

MISSION SPECIAL RULES

Fighting Withdrawal uses the **Ambush** (page 266), **Prepared Positions** (page 264), and **Strategic Withdrawal** (page 270) special rules.

PREPARING FOR BATTLE

1. The defender chooses a long table end to defend. This half of the table is their Deployment Area. The attacking player will deploy in the other table half.
2. The defender places an Objective on their side of the table at least 8"/20cm away from all table edges and at least 8"/20cm back from the centre line.
3. The attacker now places two Objectives in the same area so that no two Objectives are more than 48"/120cm apart and all are more than 8"/20cm from any other Objective.
4. The defender Deploys their entire force. They may hold one platoon in Ambush. The attacker's Deployment Area is their half of the table, excluding the area within 16"/40cm of the centre line. The attacker now Deploys their force.
5. Both players, starting with the defending player Deploy any Warrior teams that are not part of a platoon and all Independent teams.

BEGINNING THE BATTLE

1. Starting with the defender, both players make Reconnaissance Deployment moves.
2. The attacking player has the first turn.
3. As both sides are in Prepared Positions, all platoons may begin the game Dug In.

ENDING THE BATTLE

The battle ends when either:

- the attacker has Taken any of the Objectives at the start of their turn, or
- at the start of the defender's eighth turn (remember to check Company Morale if necessary before determining who won).

DECIDING WHO WON

The attacker wins if the game ended because they started one of their turns holding an objective. The attacker has smashed the rearguard and seized their objectives.

Otherwise the defender wins. The rearguard has held out long enough for the army to get safely away and now withdraws its last elements.

Calculate your Victory Points using the Victory Points Table on page 275.

TURN	EVENT
3	Withdraw a platoon if 5+ platoons, otherwise gain a delay counter.
4	Withdraw a platoon and remove all counters if 5+ platoons or counters, otherwise gain delay counter.
5	Repeat withdrawal.
6	Remove Objective. Repeat withdrawal.
7	Remove Objective. Repeat withdrawal.
8	Check Company Morale if necessary. Game over.

HASTY ATTACK (MOBILE BATTLE)

While most commanders faced with a prepared defence seek to build up the maximum forces for the attack, sometimes they do not have the time and must attack immediately with whatever is on hand.

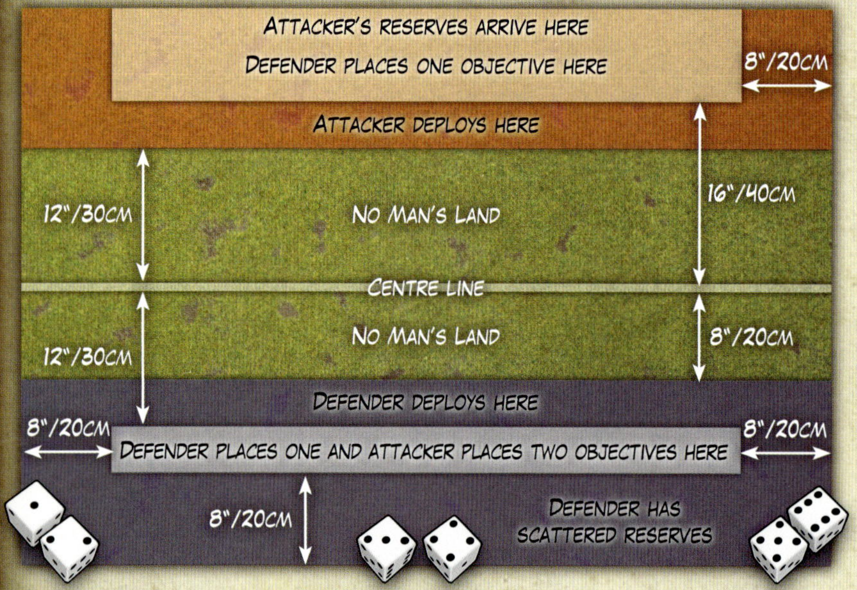

YOUR ORDERS

ATTACKER

Find a weak point in the enemy line and punch through. You must seize one of your objectives before the enemy rallies and pushes you back.

DEFENDER

Hold the initial assault, then force the enemy back when your reserves arrive. You must prevent the enemy from taking their objectives, then counterattack and take your own.

MISSION SPECIAL RULES

Hasty Attack uses the **Delayed Reserves** (page 269), **Immediate Ambush** (page 267), **Reserves** (page 268), **Scattered Reserves** (page 269), and **Prepared Positions** (page 264) special rules.

PREPARING FOR BATTLE

1. The defending player chooses the long table edge that they will defend. Their Deployment Area is their half of the table, excluding the area within 8"/20cm of the centre line. The attacking player's Deployment Area is the other half of the table, excluding the area within 12"/30cm of the centre line.
2. The defending player places one Objective in the attacker's Deployment Area at least 16"/40 cm from the centre line and not within 8"/20cm of either side table edge.
3. The defender then places one Objective and then the attacker places two Objectives in the defender's Deployment Area at least 12"/30cm from the centre line and not within 8"/20cm of any table edge.
4. The attacker nominates at least half of their platoons to be held off the table in Reserves. These arrive from the long table edge in their Deployment Area.
5. The defender then nominates at least half of their platoons to be held off the table in Delayed and Scattered Reserves. They may then nominate one of the remaining platoons to be held in Immediate Ambush. The defender Deploys their remaining platoons.
6. The attacker now removes one of the Objectives that they placed on the table.
7. The attacker Deploys their remaining platoons.
8. Both players now Deploy any Warrior teams that are not part of a platoon and all Independent teams, starting with the defending player.

BEGINNING THE BATTLE

1. The defender places the platoon they held in Immediate Ambush.
2. Starting with the defender, both players make Reconnaissance Deployment moves for any Recce teams they have on table.
3. The attacking player has the first turn.
4. As both sides are in Prepared Positions, all platoons may begin the game Dug In.

ENDING THE BATTLE

The battle ends when:

- a player starts their turn having Taken any of the Objectives that were placed in the enemy Deployment Area, or
- the defender starts any of their turns from turn six with no attacking teams in the defender's table half.

DECIDING WHO WON

A player wins if the game ended because they started one of their turns holding an Objective in the opponent's Deployment Area.

Otherwise the defender wins. The defender has held their front line and halted the attacker's offensive.

Calculate your Victory Points using the Victory Points Table on page 275.

CAULDRON (MOBILE BATTLE)

When night falls on the battlefield both sides traditionally exercise a tacit truce and rebuild their forces, resupply, and tend to the wounded.

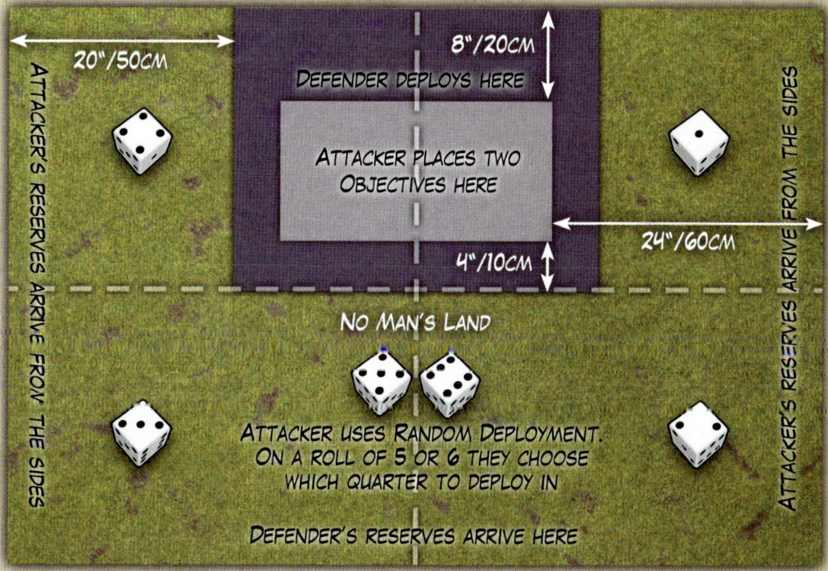

YOUR ORDERS

ATTACKER

A massive enemy offensive has punched through the front line, taking up positions amongst yours during the night. You must attack immediately to restore the situation.

DEFENDER

You have pushed through the front lines during the night and taken vital ground from the enemy. Now, with dawn breaking, you must form a solid defence against the inevitable counterattack and hold your gains.

MISSION SPECIAL RULES

Cauldron uses the **Immediate Ambush** (page 267), **Prepared Positions** (page 264), **Reserves** (page 268), **Delayed Reserves** (page 269), **and Random Deployment** (page 261) special rules.

PREPARING FOR BATTLE

1. The defending player chooses the long table side where they will defend. Their Deployment Area is this half of the table excluding the area within 20"/50cm of the side table edges.
2. The attacking player places *two* Objectives in the defender's Deployment Area at least 4"/10cm from the centre line of the table, at least 8"/20cm from long table edge and at least 24"/60cm from the short table edges.
3. The defender nominates at least half of their platoons to be held in Delayed Reserve. These will arrive on the opposite table edge.
4. The defender may hold one platoon in Immediate Ambush.
5. The defender deploys the remaining platoons.
6. The attacker must nominate at least half of their platoons to be held in Reserve. These will arrive from either short table edge. The attacking player may choose which edge each platoon will arrive from when it arrives from Reserves.
7. Any remaining platoons are deployed using the Random Deployment special rules.
8. Both players now Deploy any Warrior teams that are not part of a platoon and all Independent teams, starting with the defending player.

BEGINNING THE BATTLE

1. The defender places the platoon they held in Immediate Ambush.
2. Starting with the attacker, both players make Reconnaissance Deployment moves for any Recce teams they have on table.
3. The defending player has the first turn.
4. As both sides are in Prepared Positions, all platoons may begin the game Dug In.

ENDING THE BATTLE

The battle ends on or after turn six when either:

- the attacker has Taken any of the Objectives at the start of their turn, or
- the defending player starts their turn with no attacking teams within 16"/40cm of either Objective.

DECIDING WHO WON

The attacker wins if the game ended because they started one of their turns holding an objective. The enemy penetration has been neutralized and the defensive line held.

Otherwise the defender wins. All enemy counterattacks have been held off and the enemy force 'written down,' bringing a major breakthrough that much closer.

Calculate your Victory Points using the Victory Points Table on page 175.

BREAKTHROUGH (MOBILE BATTLE)

A widely-stretched front has forced the defenders into a hedgehog defence. The attacker has sent a flanking force through the gaps between the defended positions while launching a frontal assault to pin the enemy.

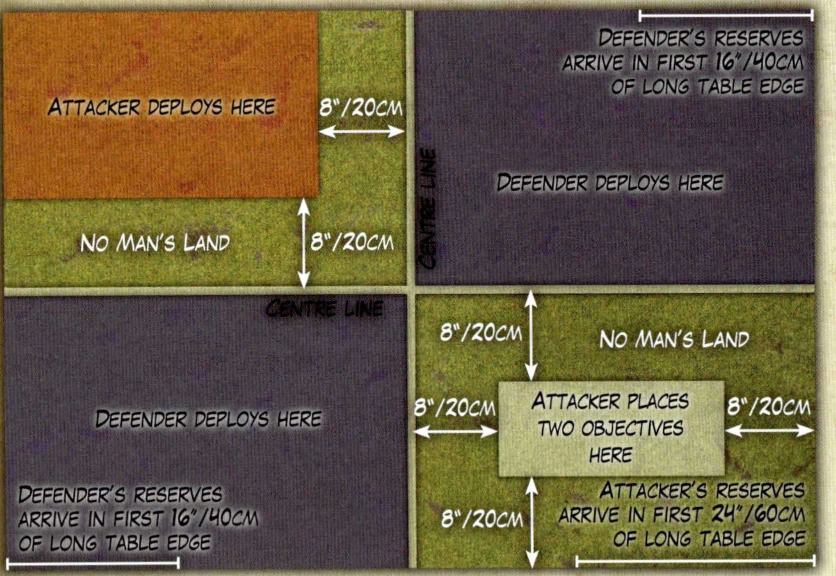

YOUR ORDERS

ATTACKER

The enemy does not have sufficient strength to cover the entire front. You must seize one of the objectives, either by direct assault, or with a cunning flank attack.

DEFENDER

Your reconnaissance troops report a strong attack force moving around your flank while another strong force is massing for a frontal attack. You must secure the objectives and drive the enemy back.

MISSION SPECIAL RULES

Breakthrough uses the **Delayed Reserves** (page 269), **Mobile Reserves** (page 269), and **Prepared Positions** (page 264) special rules.

PREPARING FOR BATTLE

1. Mark the centre of the table so that the table quarters are obvious to both players.
2. The defending player chooses two diagonally-opposite table quarters as their Deployment Areas.
3. The attacker then chooses one of the remaining table quarters. Their Deployment Area is all of this table quarter that is more than 8"/20cm from both table centre lines.
4. The attacker places two Objectives in the final table quarter. They must be at least 8"/20cm from the table centre lines and edges.
5. The defender Deploys any or all of their platoons using the Mobile Reserves special rule.
6. All remaining platoons are held off the table in Reserve. The troops held in Reserves will arrive along the long table edges in their Deployment Areas within 16"/40cm of the table corner.
7. The attacker must hold at least one platoon, and may hold up to half of their platoons, off table to make a flank attack as Delayed Reserves. The troops held in Delayed Reserves will arrive along the long table edge within 24"/60cm of the corner in the quarter containing the Objectives.
8. The attacker now Deploys the rest of their force.
9. Both players now Deploy any Warrior teams that are not part of a platoon and all Independent teams, starting with the defending player.

BEGINNING THE BATTLE

1. Starting with the defender, both players make Reconnaissance Deployment moves for any Recce teams they have on table.
2. The attacking player has the first turn.
3. As both sides are in Prepared Positions, all platoons may begin the game Dug In.

ENDING THE BATTLE

The battle ends on or after turn six when either:

- the attacking player has Taken any of the Objectives at the start of their turn, or
- the defending player starts their turn with no attacking teams within 16"/40cm of either Objective.

DECIDING WHO WON

The attacker wins if the game ended because they started one of their turns holding an Objective. They have broken through, deep behind the enemy line.

Otherwise the defender wins. The breakthrough has been cut off and the front lines held.

Calculate your Victory Points using the Victory Points Table on page 275.

COUNTERATTACK (MOBILE BATTLE)

The enemy is making a counterattack to relieve their cut off comrades. Complete the encirclement and ensure the destruction of the trapped enemy troops.

YOUR ORDERS

ATTACKER

The enemy have found a weak point in your encirclement. They are launching a counterattack to link up with their surrounded comrades. You must close the gap before they can make the link up.

DEFENDER

You are expecting a relieving force at any moment. You must exploit the weakness in the enemy encirclement and link up with them. Prevent the enemy from taking their objectives and completing the encirclement.

MISSION SPECIAL RULES

Counterattack uses the **Ambush** (page 266), **Mobile Reserves** (page 269), **Prepared Positions** (page 264), and **Reserves** (page 268) special rules.

PREPARING FOR BATTLE

1. Mark the centre point of the table so that the table quarters are obvious to both players.
2. The defender chooses a table quarter as their Deployment Area. Their reserves will arrive from the diagonally opposite quarter.
3. The attacker chooses one of the table quarters on the other diagonal to deploy in. Their Deployment Area is all of this table quarter that is more than 8"/20cm from both table centre lines.
4. The defender places one Objective in their Deployment Area at least 8"/20cm from both centre lines and at least 8"/20cm from any table edge.
5. The attacker then places one Objective in the table quarter opposite their Deployment Area at least 8"/20cm from both table centre lines and 8"/20cm from any table edge.
6. The defender Deploys any or all of their platoons using the Mobile Reserves special rule. One of the platoons to be Deployed may be held in Ambush.
7. All remaining platoons are held off the table in Reserve. The troops held in Reserves will arrive within 16"/40cm of the table corner opposite their Deployment Area.
8. The attacker then Deploys their entire force.
9. Both players now place any Warrior teams that are not part of a platoon and all Independent teams starting with the defender.

BEGINNING THE BATTLE

1. Starting with the defender, both players make Reconnaissance Deployment moves for any Recce teams they have on table.
2. The attacking player has the first turn.
3. As both sides are in Prepared Positions, all platoons may begin the game Dug In.

ENDING THE BATTLE

The battle ends on or after turn six when either:

- the attacking player has Taken any of the Objectives at the start of their turn, or
- the defending player starts their turn with no attacking teams within 16"/40cm of either Objective.

DECIDING WHO WON

The attacker wins if the game ended because they started one of their turns holding an Objective. The attacker has prevented the defender from linking up with the encircled force.

Otherwise the defender wins. The defender has broken the encirclement, freeing the trapped troops.

Calculate your Victory Points using the Victory Points Table on page 275.

NO MAN'S LAND (TRENCH WARFARE)

All is quiet in your fortified sector of the line. It seems like a good time to send out a patrol and see what the enemy is up to.

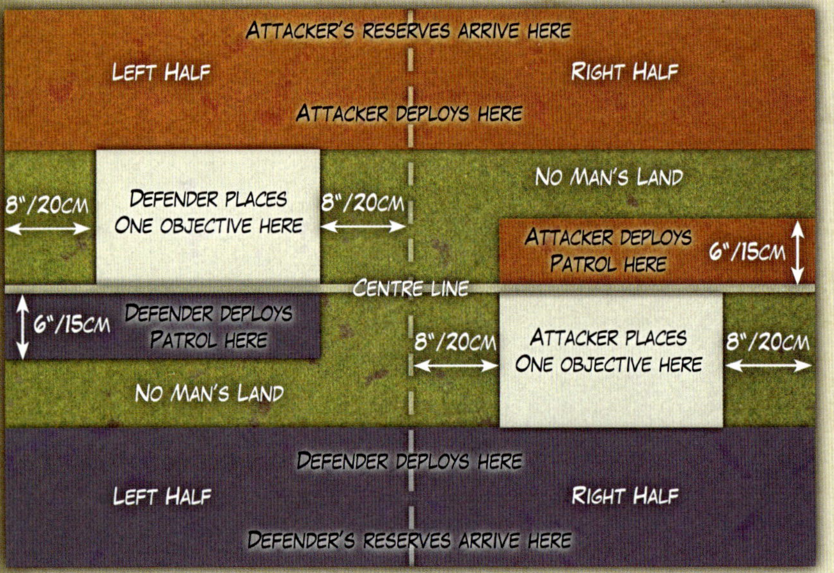

YOUR ORDERS

ATTACKER

Tonight's patrol ran into a strong enemy patrol. Reinforce them and secure the objective.

DEFENDER

Push the enemy out of No Man's Land and hold your objective.

MISSION SPECIAL RULES

No Man's Land uses the **Darkness** (page 273), **Delayed Reserves** (page 269), **No Man's Land Patrol** (page 271), and **Over the Wire** (page 271) special rules.

PREPARING FOR BATTLE

1. Both players must field a Fortified Company.
2. Both players roll a die with the higher score choosing a long table edge to attack from. The defender has the opposite table half. The players' Deployment Areas are their halves of the table excluding the area within 12"/30cm of the centre line.
3. Starting with the defender, both players place all of their Fortifications (but not their Obstacles).
4. Again starting with the defender, both players place all of their Obstacles in the opponent's table half using the Over The Wire mission special rule.
5. Starting with the defender, both players Deploy their Fortified Platoons. All remaining platoons are held in Delayed Reserve, arriving anywhere along the long table edge in their own Deployment Area.
6. Starting with the attacker, both players nominate one platoon to be their Patrol using the No Man's Land Patrol special rule, and remove it from the table.
7. Divide the table into left and right halves across both Deployment Areas at right angles to the centre line.
8. Both players roll another die. The player with the higher score chooses the left or right half to place their Objective and Patrol. They place an Objective on the opposing side of the table at least 8"/20cm from the dividing line between the left and right halves, and at least 8"/20cm from the table edges.
9. The other player then places an Objective in the same manner in the opposite half.
10. The first player then places their Patrol on their side of the table in the same half as they placed the Objective, within 6"/15cm of the centre line and at least 8"/20cm from the dividing line between the left and right halves.
11. The other player then places their Patrol in the same manner in the opposite half.
12. Again starting with the defender, both players Deploy any Warrior teams that are not part of a platoon and all Independent teams in any Trench Lines in their Deployment Area.

BEGINNING THE BATTLE

1. The entire battle is fought in Darkness.
2. Both players roll a die. The defender adds +1 to their roll. The player with the higher result has the first turn.

ENDING THE BATTLE

The battle ends when:

- a player starts their turn having Taken the Objective placed by the opposing player.

DECIDING WHO WON

The player that took an Objective wins the battle. They have established their dominance over No Man's Land.

Calculate your Victory Points using the Victory Points Table on page 275.

No Man's Land is a Fair Fight, so if neither win the battle, use the There are No Draws rule on page 275 to determine each player's Victory Points.

INDEX

• INDEX •

• INDEX •

QUICK REFERENCE

Turn Sequence

1 Starting Step
2 Move Step
3 Shooting Step
4 Assault Step

Skill Test

Skill	Score Needed
Conscript	5+
Trained	4+
Veteran	3+

Motivation Test

Motivation	Score Needed
Reluctant	5+
Confident	4+
Fearless	3+

Company Command Team

Re-roll failed Motivation Tests if Company or Higher Command team Joins platoon.

STARTING

Starting Step

1 Check Sole Surviving Teams
2 Check Company Morale
3 Check Victory Conditions
4 Reveal Ambushes
5 Roll for Air Support
6 Roll for Reserves
7 Rally Pinned Down Platoons
8 Re-mount Bailed Out Vehicles
9 Free Bogged Down Vehicles
10 Remove Smoke Markers

Bogged Down or Bailed Out

May not move, shoot, or assault.

Remount Bailed Out Vehicles

Pass a Motivation Test to Remount a Bailed Out vehicle.

Free Bogged Down Vehicles

Pass a Skill Test to free a Bogged Down vehicle.

Rally Pinned Down Platoons

Pass a Motivation Test to Rally a Pinned Down platoon.

Pinned Down Platoons

Unless armoured, reduce ROF and no moving closer to enemy.

MOVEMENT

Movement Step

1 Select a Platoon to Move
2 Bring Forward Transports
3 Move Teams in the Platoon
- a Dismount Passengers before moving Transports
- b Move Transports before or after Mounting Passengers
- c Take Bogging Checks in Rough Terrain
- d Take Skill Tests to Enter Contested Buildings

4 Send Empty Transports to Rear
5 Select Next Platoon to Move

Rough Terrain

No Bogging Checks in Slow Going.

Roll 2+ to avoid Bogging Down in Difficult Going.

Roll a Skill test to avoid Bogging Down in Very Difficult Going.

Wrecked armoured vehicles are Slow Going and Concealment.

Movement Distances

Type	Cross Country	Road	Rough Terrain
Fully-tracked Tanks and Transports			
Standard Tank	12"/30cm	12"/30cm	8"/20cm
Light Tank	16"/40cm	16"/40cm	8"/20cm
Slow Tank	8"/20cm	8"/20cm	8"/20cm
Very Slow Tank	6"/15cm	6"/15cm	6"/15cm
Other Tanks and Transports			
Jeep, Motorcycle	16"/40cm	24"/60cm	4"/10cm *
Half-tracked	12"/30cm	18"/45cm	4"/10cm
Wheeled	12"/30cm	18"/45cm	4"/10cm *
Slow Wheeled, Wagon	8"/20cm	12"/30cm	4"/10cm *
Infantry			
Cavalry	10"/25cm	10"/25cm	10"/25cm **
Infantry	6"/15cm	6"/15cm	6"/15cm **
Guns			
Man-packed Guns	6"/15cm	6"/15cm	6"/15cm **
Light Guns	6"/15cm	6"/15cm	4"/10cm *
Medium and Heavy Guns	4"/10cm	4"/10cm	4"/10cm *
Immobile Guns		Cannot Move	

* Cannot move in Very Difficult Going ** No Bogging Checks required

Move twice as far At the Double. Take direct route 8"/20cm from enemy.

Command Distance

Experience	Tanks	Others
Conscript	4"/10cm	2"/5cm
Trained	6"/15cm	4"/10cm
Veteran	8"/20cm	6"/15cm

Moving teams must attempt to end any movement In Command.

Passengers

Dismount at the start of their movement or mount at the end of their movement.

Bring Transports Forward

Must be placed within 4"/10cm of own platoon, and 8"/20cm from enemy Recce or 4"/10cm from others if Concealed, or 16"/40cm from any if not.

Entering Buildings

Need Skill Test to enter if no friendly team inside or at opening.

SHOOTING

Shooting Step

1 Select the Shooting Platoon
2 Select the Target Platoons
3 Who Shoots at What
4 Check that the Target is Valid
- a Check Line of Sight
- b Check Range
- c Check Field of Fire

5 Rotate to Face the Target
6 Check if Target is Concealed
7 Roll to Hit
8 Allocate Hits to Target Teams
9 Roll Saves
10 Roll Firepower Tests
11 Remove Destroyed Teams
12 Return to 1
13 Pin Down Platoons Hit 5 Times

Moving or Pinned Down ROF

ROF	ROF when Moving
1 to 3	1
4 or 5	2
6 or more	3

Roll 2x dice against At the Double.

Smoke Ammunition

Fire Smoke first. Place two 2"/5cm markers for each hit.

Smoke Markers

Line of Sight limited to 16"/40cm, all targets seen through smoke are Concealed and Gone to Ground.

Score to Hit

Target	Score Needed
Conscript	2+
Trained	3+
Veteran	4+

Add +1 to score needed if:
- Range is over 16"/40cm
- Concealed
- Gone to Ground while Concealed
- ROF 1 weapon moving

Concealment

Teams are Concealed if at least half hidden by terrain. Stationary Infantry and Man-packed Guns are Concealed.

Gone to Ground

Teams that don't move, shoot, or assault are Gone to Ground.

Hit Front or Side

Hit Front if Line of Sight in front of line across front of hull or turret. Hit Side otherwise.

Roll if front and side both visible:
- 1 to 3—hit hull
- 4 to 6—hit turret

Bunker Busters

Moving Bunker Busters can't hit vehicles unless they are Bogged Down or Bailed Out.

Allocate Hits

Allocate hits as follows:
- Only valid targets
- Roll 5+ to pick out Gun Tanks
- Allocate hits evenly
- Priority targets first
  - Best Firepower to Priority
- Others before Gone to Ground
- Operational before Bogged Down or Bailed Out
- Within 16"/40cm first
- Unarmoured before Armoured
- Lowest Armour first
  - Best Anti-tank to Armoured
  - Lower Armour get lower Anti-tank
- Bunker Busters to Buildings
- Unprotected before in Bulletproof Cover
  - Best Firepower to Bulletproof Cover

Pinned Down

Pinned Down if take a total of 5 hits. Armoured teams ignore being Pinned Down.

Platoon Morale

If more teams Destroyed than still fighting and had teams Destroyed or Bailed Out, pass a Motivation test or be Destroyed.

Roll Armour Save

Target player rolls and adds:
- Armour rating
- +1 if range is over 16"/40cm

Outcome:
- If less than Anti-tank, roll Firepower Test to Destroy tank, otherwise Bail Out tank.
- If equal to Anti-tank, roll Firepower Test to Bail Out tank.
- Otherwise, no effect.

Roll Other Saves

Target	Score Needed
Infantry	3+
Guns	5+
Gone to Ground Guns	3+
Unarmoured Vehicles	5+
Passengers	5+
Recce Vehicles	3+
Warrior Vehicles	3+

No save against Breakthrough Gun or Bunker Buster.

Vehicles with Gun Shields

No Save if hit across Gun Shield, but Firepower Test needed to Destroy vehicle.

Bulletproof Cover

If team is in Bulletproof Cover attacker must make a successful Firepower Test to Destroy it.